MORMON POLYGAMY
A HISTORY

SECOND

MORMON
POLYGAMY
A HISTORY

RICHARD S. VAN WAGONER

SIGNATURE BOOKS
SALT LAKE CITY
1989

To Mary, Lisa Jane, Amanda,
Michelle, Soshanna, and Jennifer Leigh

© 1989 by Signature Books, Inc. All rights reserved
Signature Books is a registered trademark of Signature Books, Inc.
First edition 1986
Printed in the United States of America
96 95 94 93 92 91 90 89   6 5 4 3 2 1

Book and cover design: LaPine/O'Very

Cover photo: Joseph F. Smith family, courtesy LDS Archives

Library of Congress Cataloging-in-Publication Data

Van Wagoner, Richard S.
  Mormon polygamy.

  Bibliography: p.
  Includes index.
  1. Polygamy—United States—History. 2. Mormon Church
—History. 3. Church of Jesus Christ of Latter-Day
Saints—History. I. Title.
BX8641.V36 1989   289.3   89–6222
ISBN 0-941214-79-6 pbk.
ISBN 0-941214-35-4 cloth

Table of Contents

Preface to the Second Edition

Mormon polygamy is anything but passé. Latter-day Fundamentalists, excommunicated Mormons who practice plural marriage despite the LDS church's ban, continue to make headlines. Since late 1985, when the first edition of *Mormon Polygamy: A History* went to press, one of the leaders of the largest Fundamentalist group, the fatherly LeRoy Johnson, died of natural causes and was quietly replaced by equally nondescript Rulon T. Jeffs. Less inconspicuously, Ervil LeBaron's fanatical followers murdered at least six more people, disaffected members of their own group and potential rivals. And members of the Singer/Swapp families bombed a Mormon chapel, then killed a police officer during a highly publicized seige on the family compound.

In addition to Fundamentalists in the news, important new studies and published works on nineteenth-century polygamy have appeared recently. When the first printing of *Mormon Polygamy: A History* sold out it seemed appropriate to revise and update the work with a second edition. This also gave me the chance to correct a few minor errors in the first edition which were pointed out by readers.

INTRODUCTION

Polygamy—or, more precisely, polygyny, the marriage of two or more women to one man—has been a controversial subject in the history of the Church of Jesus Christ of Latter-day Saints (LDS or Mormon). The church's founder, Joseph Smith, Jr., privately advocated such plural marriages during the early 1840s and perhaps earlier, calling them part of "the most holy and important doctrine ever revealed to man on earth" and insisting that without them no one could attain the "fullness of exaltation" in the hereafter.

The small group of friends and church leaders Smith entrusted with his secret teachings continued the practice after his violent martyrdom in 1844. Under the leadership of Brigham Young, they formed the 1847 nucleus of the colonization of the Rocky Mountain Great Basin, then Mexican territory, where they hoped to practice their religion without interference from the United States. As barren and distant as the region seemed, it was not far enough away to avoid four decades of public outcry after the Mormon church officially announced in 1852 its advocacy of polygamy. This lengthy protest, and the accompanying government pressures, influenced church president Wilford Woodruff to issue a public announcement in 1890 which advised members against contracting new plural marriages. Church-sanctioned polygamy continued on a covert basis until 1904, however, when President Joseph F. Smith, under congressional pressure, authorized the excommunication of all who continued to perpetrate the practice.

Today polygamy has fallen into disrepute among the majority of mainstream Mormons. Indeed, no group seems more anti-polygamous than Utah Mormons. Church leaders avoid the topic and until recently even worked with law enforcement officials to have polygamists arrested. Church instruction manuals often treat plural marriage, when broached at all, as an embarrassing relic of the past; scholars at church institutions have sometimes been discouraged from publishing articles on the subject; and practicing polygamists are quickly excommunicated from church fellowship.

Despite the social and economic difficulties for those who continue to practice polygamy, surveys indicate there are approximately 30,000 or more Fundamentalists, as they prefer to be called, in the western United States, particularly in Utah, Arizona, and Montana. Customized draperies manufactured in a polygamist industry enhance the windows of many of Salt Lake City's finest homes. One of Utah's most successful coal mines is a Fundamentalist co-op. And perhaps one of the best Spanish omelets in the Salt Lake Valley is served at a polygamist-owned restaurant.

Though most Fundamentalists shun the public spotlight, preferring instead a life of anonymity, they often become the inadvertant, even unwilling, object of media attention. John Singer, a Fundamentalist who refused to send his children to Utah public schools, was shot to death in 1979 by law enforcement officials. Nine years later four members of his family were sentenced to prison for their role in the early 1988 bombing of an LDS church building and the subsequent killing of a law enforcement official during a lengthy standoff.

Members of a small sect in Ogden, Utah, known as "The Company," also received wide press coverage for reportedly advocating divinely mandated lesbian practices as well as polygamy. Southern Utah polygamist Leland Freeborn announced on 2 October 1983 that in forty days the United States would suffer nuclear attack from the Soviet Union. Quizzed by the 12 October 1983 *Central Utah Journal* as to why God would send such a critical warning through him, Freeborn replied, "I don't know, but if the Lord could speak through Balaam's ass [see Num. 22:22-30], I suppose he could speak through the mouth of a poor farmer from Parowan." Other self-proclaimed Fundamentalistic prophets emerged the following year when two Utah County brothers were charged and found guilty of the ritualistic 24 July 1984 slaying of their sister-in-law and her infant daughter, apparently because the woman had opposed, among other things, their teachings on polygamy.

The interest in modern polygamy transcends the boundaries of the Intermountain West. The *San Francisco Examiner* on 7 April 1985 noted a power struggle in Colorado City (formerly Short Creek), Arizona, brought about by the deteriorating health of the community's ninety-six-year-old Fundamental patriarch, LeRoy Johnson. The *Examiner*, citing testimony of dissidents, reported activities in the polygamous community where women wear ankle-length dresses, shun makeup, wear their hair in buns, and "do little else but breed." Charges that "obedient disciples are rewarded with teen-age brides" and that sect leaders "squabble over desirable young girls" were dismissed by Johnson's loyal followers as "exaggerated and motivated by revenge."

Johnson's disciples then numbered more than three thousand. But many polygamists remain independent of formal groups. Two of Utah's most married men, independent Fundamentalists Alex Joseph and Royston Potter, were 1983 guests on the nationally televised Phil Donahue Show. Joseph, mayor of Big Water, a small community in the desert region of Southern Utah, is a one-time Marine, police officer, school teacher, freighter, used car salesman, bookkeeper, fire fighter, and ginseng root enterpriser. Current wives include a lawyer, a school teacher, a nurse, a professional calligrapher, and a skilled plumber and electrician. One of his wives is even a former beauty contest winner. Joseph joined the Mormon church in 1969 because, as he put it, "an angel told me to." Excommunicated in 1973 for his outspoken views on polygamy, the charismatic Joseph began collecting wives and formed his own polygamous church, the Church of Jesus Christ in Solemn Assembly.

Less flamboyant and more typical of Mormon Fundamentalists is ex-policeman Royston Potter. Named Murray, Utah's, Employee of the Month in April 1982, Potter was fired the following December. A whistle-blowing citizen raised "questions about [Potter's] ability to comply with his oath of office," since he was in violation of Utah Code 76-7-101(1)—the anti-polygamy statute. Like most polygamists with Mormon roots, Potter viewed the Utah law as unconstitutional, an interference with his First Amendment rights. In early October 1985, however, the United States Supreme Court declined to review Potter's appeal, leaving intact, at least for the present, the ruling of lower courts that polygamy is not a constitutional right.

Despite Potter's public profile and release from the police force for violation of the law, criminal charges were never brought against him. Since the 1960s prosecution of polygamists has come to a standstill in Utah and surrounding states. Citizens are more tolerant of variant lifestyles today, and polygamists are viewed more as religious fanatics than as criminals. Experience has convinced law enforcement officials that strict enforcement of anti-polygamy laws is both nonproductive and unacceptably expensive. Utah's Salt Lake County Attorney said in 1983 that although polygamous cases are not considered insignificant, his office was "busy with cases involving property loss or personal harm."

Many Utahns—especially those whose polygamous ancestors suffered harsh treatment and humiliation at the hands of the federal government in the late nineteenth century—sympathize to some degree with today's polygamists. Though earthly laws prohibit the temporal practice of polygamy, plural marriage is believed by many Saints to be the law of the highest degree of heaven, further complicating the ambivalence modern Mormons feel towards polygamy.

Despite the historical significance of plural marriage in Mormonism, and the fact that many Mormons are descendants of nineteenth-century polygamists, most church members today are often no better informed on their polygamous past than non-Mormons. Rich collections of archival materials and specialized scholarly works are available on the subject, but there has been no comprehensive study of polygamy from its earliest stirrings in the 1830s to its current practice among Mormon Fundamentalists. This revised and expanded edition of my 1986 general history of Mormon polygamy is intended to be a reliable introduction to a complex subject for both Mormons and non-Mormons alike.

Although descended from Mormon polygamists, I have written *Mormon Polygamy: A History* neither to promote nor to assail plural marriage. During my research and writing I tried to weigh carefully the bias of each documentary source. To prevent digression from the basic chronological sequence, however, I have tried to confine the academic discussion of controversial sources within the notes that follow each chapter. Furthermore, in efforts to preserve the original flavor and accuracy of direct quotations, I have retained original punctuation, spelling, grammar, and emphasis.

While I accept full responsibility for my interpretation, I am grateful to the following friends and colleagues who shared materials and offered criticism for the first edition, and pointed out corrections and additional suggested revisions for the second: Thomas G. Alexander, J. Max Anderson, Ian G. Barber, Lowell "Ben" Bennion, Gary J. Bergera, Mary L. Bradford, Lyndon W. Cook, Everett Cooley, Jessie L. Embry, Lawrence G. Foster, Scott G. Kenney, H. Michael Marquardt, Brent Lee Metcalfe, Linda King Newell, Charles S. Peterson, Steven Pratt, Ronald L. Priddis, George D. Smith, Susan Staker, Mary C. Van Wagoner, and Steven C. Walker. I also deeply appreciate the assistance of the staffs of the Historical Department, Church of Jesus Christ of Latter-day Saints, Salt Lake City, Utah; the Utah State Historical Society; Archives and Manuscripts, Special Collections, Harold B. Lee Library, Brigham Young University, Provo, Utah; and Special Collections, Western Americana, J. Willard Marriott Library, University of Utah, Salt Lake City.

One

THE "RESTORATION OF ALL THINGS"

Joseph Smith, Jr., the charismatic founder of Mormonism, emerged from the ferment of Jacksonian America during a time when religion was regaining its hold over American life, when abolitionist groups, temperance movements, and benevolent societies were thriving. Utopian experiments testified to the exuberance of a nation advancing from infancy to childhood. Innocent vitality, limitless resources, a booming economy, and westward expansion nurtured a profound belief in America as a land of new hope, a light to the world.

Into this light came Joseph Smith, the twenty-four-year-old New York farmer who founded a religion based on his translation of a set of gold plates delivered by an angel. The Book of Mormon, a record of God's dealings with the pre-Columbian ancestors of the American Indian, not only explained the Hebrew origins of the Indian but established America as a chosen land destined to receive the fullness of the everlasting gospel. Written in King James English, Smith's translation sounded biblical, but its location and conceptual framework were American. The Book of Mormon gave America a sacred past and a millennial future. It became the keystone of a new American religion.

God could not have chosen a better place, a better time, or a better people than early nineteenth-century Americans for the "restoration of all things." After a decade of religious revivalism, the blossoming economy of the 1830s had ripened millennial expectations. Word of angelic visitations was greeted enthusiastically. The heavens were being rolled back. Old men were dreaming dreams and young men prophesying. Women were speaking in tongues and children conversing with angels. New faiths mushroomed.

Western New York, where Joseph Smith grew up, was so frequently swept by the fires of religious enthusiasm that it came to be known as the "burned-over district." It was in this milieu that Smith organized the Church of Christ on 6 April 1830, later renamed the Church of Jesus Christ of Latter-day Saints. Like other dynamic movements of the day, the foundling church was influenced not only by restoration Protestant sectarianism but by flourishing contemporary social experiments. Smith's ability to blend current ideas with his own visionary experiences is evident in the growth of his communal

1

vision. His earliest exposure to utopian thought and practices may have stemmed from a religious sect called the Believers in Christ's Second Appearing. Popularly known as Shakers, the group established a community a few miles from Smith's birthplace in Vermont (Arrington, Fox, and May 1976, 20). Mother Ann Lee's celibate society was one of the first communitarian organizations of this kind in the United States.

Joseph Smith was probably also familiar with the Harmonists, who claimed that George Rapp, a Lutheran minister and social reformer, was responding to a vision from the angel Gabriel when in 1804 he brought his followers from Germany to Harmony, Pennsylvania, twenty-five miles north of Pittsburg. The Harmonists, who migrated to Indiana to found New Harmony in 1815 before returning to Ambridge, Pennsylvania, in 1825, experimented, like the Shakers, with shared property and celibacy.[1]

Robert Owen, a wealthy Scottish reformer and industrialist, may have also indirectly shaped Joseph Smith's utopian ideas through one of his most influential American followers. Arriving in the United States in the mid-1820s, Owen promised a "new Eden in the far west" and began establishing communities based on common ownership and equality of work and profit. After purchasing New Harmony from the Harmonists in 1825, he established several other communitarian societies in Ohio, at Kendal and Yellow Springs. Sidney Rigdon, a prominent Protestant minister in the Western Reserve area of Ohio and a follower of Alexander Campbell's Disciples of Christ, attended a debate between Owen and Campbell in 1829. Taken with Owen's system of "family commonwealths," he tried to implement such a communal order within the Disciples of Christ (Ericksen 1922, 17). Campbell's objections caused Rigdon to leave the Disciples and, with other dissenters, to set up "common-stock" societies at Mentor and Kirtland, Ohio. By the fall of 1830 Rigdon and more than one hundred members of "the family," as they were known, had converted to Mormonism, which, by then, numbered nearly one thousand.

After arriving in Ohio from New York in February 1831, Joseph Smith convinced Rigdon's communal group to abandon the common-stock principle in favor of the "more perfect law of the Lord." On 9 February 1831 Smith announced God's "Law of Consecration and Stewardship." Members were advised that "all things belong to the Lord" and were directed to deed all personal property to the bishop of the church. The bishop then returned a "stewardship" to each head of a household, who was expected to turn over any accrued surplus to the church. Known as the "Order of Enoch," "the Lord's Law," and the "United Order," the Mormon principle of stewardship was intended as a pattern of social and economic reorganization for all mankind. The dream was to unify "a people fragmented by their individualistic search for economic well-being." The Saints, as a group, divested of personal selfishness and greed, were to be prepared by this communal discipline to usher in the millennial reign of Jesus Christ (Arrington, Fox, and May 1976, 2-3).

Smith's ideas derived much from the New Testament Christian Primitivism of the day. But the deeper roots of his theology lay in his interpretation of the Old Testament. His concept of the Kingdom of God paralleled Israelite theocracy. The idea of a temple, as well as accompanying ordinances of washings, anointings, and covenants, was central to Hebrew worship. Smith's theology of marriage and family too may have drawn on ancient Israelite traditions. Like the biblical patriarchs of old, Mormon males empowered with priesthood were entitled to receive divine guidance in family matters. Women, on the other hand, were denied both priesthood and hierarchic position. This Old Testament focus evidently also drew Smith to the idea of biblical polygamy as part of the "restitution of all things." According to a close friend, Joseph B. Noble, Smith became convinced of the theological necessity of polygamy "while he was engaged in the work of translation of the Scriptures" ("Plural Marriage," 454), evidently a reference to Smith's and Rigdon's early 1830 revision of the Bible published later as *The Inspired Version*.

Though polygamy is strongly denounced in several Book of Mormon passages (Jac. 1:15; 2:23-27; 3:5; Mos. 11:2-4, 14; Eth. 10:5), a reading of the Old Testament provides ample evidence that it was acceptable in ancient Israel. Abraham was not the only husband of multiple wives. Jacob had two wives and two concubines (Gen. 29-30); Elkanah had two wives (1 Sam. 1:2); Rehoboam had eighteen wives and sixty concubines (2 Chron. 11:21); Abijah married fourteen women (2 Chron. 13:21); David had a large harem (1 Chron. 14:3); and Solomon managed seven hundred wives and more than three hundred concubines (1 Kings 11:3).

It is difficult to determine exactly when Joseph Smith first felt compelled to practice polygamy. W. W. Phelps recollected three decades after the fact in an 1861 letter to Brigham Young that on 17 July 1831, when he and five others had gathered in Jackson County, Missouri, Smith stated: "It is my will, that in time, ye should take unto you wives of the Lamanites and Nephites [Indians], that their posterity may become white, delightsome and just." Phelps added in a postscript that "about three years after this was given, I asked brother Joseph, privately, how 'we,' that were mentioned in the revelation could take wives of the 'natives' as we were all married men?" He claimed that Smith replied, "In the same manner that Abraham took Hagar and Keturah; and Jacob took Rachel, Bilhah and Zilpha, by *Revelation*."[2]

In 1869 Mormon apostle Orson Pratt added another perspective, remembering that in early 1832 "Joseph told individuals, then in the Church, that he had inquired of the Lord concerning the principle of plurality of wives, and he received for answer that the principle of taking more wives than one is a true principle, but the time had not yet come for it to be practiced"

3

(JD 13 [7 Oct. 1869]: 192).[3] Polygamy would not be a public practice of Mormonism until 1852, eight years after Smith's death. Smith never publicly advocated polygamy. New Testament monogamy, the official church position throughout his lifetime, was clearly outlined in Smith's 1831 revelations: "Thou shalt love thy wife with all thy heart, and shall cleave unto her and none else" (D&C 42:22); "It is lawful that [a man] should have one wife, and they twain shall be one flesh" (49:16).

But from the early days of the church rumors hinted that Smith maintained a private position different from his public posture. His abrupt 1830 departure with his wife, Emma, from Harmony, Pennsylvania, may have been precipitated in part by Levi and Hiel Lewis's accusations that Smith had acted improperly towards a local girl. Five years later Levi Lewis, Emma's cousin, repeated stories that Smith attempted to "seduce Eliza Winters &c.," and that both Smith and his friend Martin Harris had claimed "adultery was no crime" (*Susquehanna Register*, 1 May 1834, reprinted in Howe 1834, 268; see also Newell and Avery 1984, 64). Similar allegations in Hiram, Ohio, reportedly caused problems for Smith in 1832. One account related that on 24 March a mob of men pulled Smith from his bed, beat him, and then covered him with a coat of tar and feathers. Eli Johnson, who allegedly participated in the attack "because he suspected Joseph of being intimate with his sister, Nancy Marinda Johnson, . . . was screaming for Joseph's castration" (Brodie 1975, 119).[4]

Rumors about Smith multiplied. Benjamin F. Winchester, Smith's close friend and leader of Philadelphia Mormons in the early 1840s, later recalled Kirtland accusations of scandal and "licentious conduct" hurled against Smith, "this more especially among the women. Joseph's name was connected with scandalous relations with two or three families" (Winchester 1889).[5]

One of the women whose name was linked to Smith in Kirtland was Vienna Jacques. A second-hand story remembered many years after the event by a "Mrs. Alexander" contended that Polly Beswick, a colorful two-hundred-pound Smith domestic, told her friends that "Jo Smith said he had a revelation to lie with Vienna Jacques, who lived in his family" and that Emma Smith told her "Joseph would get up in the night and go to Vienna's bed." Furthermore, she added, "Emma would get out of humor, fret and scold and flounce in the harness," then Smith would "shut himself up in a room and pray for a revalation . . . state it to her, and bring her around all right."[6]

During an 1873 interview Martin Harris, Book of Mormon benefactor and close friend of Smith, recalled another such incident from the early Kirtland period. "In or about the year 1833," Harris remembered, Joseph Smith's "servant girl" claimed that the prophet had made "improper proposals to her, which created quite a talk amongst the people." When Smith came

4

to him for advice, Harris, supposing that there was nothing to the story, told him to "take no notice of the girl, that she was full of the devil, and wanted to destroy the prophet of god." But according to Harris, Smith "acknowledged that there was more truth than poetry in what the girl said." Harris then said he would have nothing to do with the matter; Smith could get out of the trouble "the best way he knew how" (Metcalf n.d., 72).

William E. McLellin, a Mormon apostle who was excommunicated in 1838, further detailed this situation with the unnamed "servant girl" in an 1872 letter to the Smith's eldest son, Joseph III: "I visited your Mother and family in 1847, and held a lengthy conversation with her, retired in the Mansion house in Nauvoo. I did not ask her to tell, but I told her some stories I had heard. And she told me whether I was properly informed. Dr. F[rederick] G. Williams practiced with me in Clay Co. Mo. during the latter part of 1838. And he told me that at your birth [6 November 1832] your father committed an act with a Miss Hill—a hired girl. Emma saw him, and spoke to him. He desisted, but Mrs. Smith refused to be satisfied. He called in Dr. Williams, O. Cowdery, and S. Rigdon to reconcile Emma. But she told them just as the circumstances took place. He found he was caught. He confessed humbly, and begged forgiveness. Emma and all forgave him. She told me this story was true!!"

Accounts such as these have led some historians to conclude that Joseph Smith was licentious. But others have countered that these stories merely indicate his involvement in a heaven-sanctioned system of polygamy, influenced by Old Testament models (Bachman 1975; Hill 1968; Foster 1981).

If Smith did take a plural wife in Kirtland during the early 1830s under such a system, the woman was likely Fanny Alger. McLellin's 1872 letter described Alger's relationship with Smith. "Again I told [your mother]," the former apostle wrote, that "I heard that one night she missed Joseph and Fanny Alger. She went to the barn and saw him and Fanny in the barn together alone. She looked through a crack and saw the transaction!!! She told me this story too was verily true." McLellin also detailed the Alger incident to a newspaper reporter for the 6 October 1875 *Salt Lake Tribune*. The reporter stated that McLellin informed him of the exact place "where the first well authenticated case of polygamy took place." According to the article, the marriage occurred "in a barn on the hay mow, and was witnessed by Mrs. Smith through a crack in the door!"[7]

Fanny Ward Alger, one of ten children born to Mormons Samuel Alger and Clarissa Hancock, was nineteen years old when she became a maidservant in the Smith home in 1835. Benjamin F. Johnson, a long-time friend of Smith, described Fanny as "a varry nice & Comly young woman . . . it was whispered eaven then that Joseph *Loved her*." Warren Parrish, Smith's personal secretary, told Johnson that he and Oliver Cowdery both knew that

"Joseph had Fanny Alger as a wife for They were Spied upon & found together" (Zimmerman 1976, 38).

Rumors of Smith's relationship with Alger, whispered about Kirtland during the summer of 1835, may have been the catalyst for the church's announcement of its official position on marriage as well as motivation for Smith's frequent addresses on marital relationships that fall. While Smith was in Michigan his secretary, W. W. Phelps, presented to the church's 17 August 1835 General Assembly a "Chapter of Rules for Marriage among the Saints." This declaration stipulated in part: "Inasmuch as this church of Christ has been reproached with the crime of fornication, and polygamy; we declare that we believe, that one man should have one wife; and one woman, but one husband, except in the case of death, when either is at liberty to marry again." The assembled Saints voted to accept the statement as part of "the faith and principle of this society as a body" by canonizing it in the official Doctrine and Covenants of the church.[8]

This important document, probably introduced by Phelps at Joseph Smith's own request,[9] includes a marriage ceremony and what may be the first scriptural reference to the concept of eternal marriage. Evidently alluding to this, Phelps wrote to his wife Sally on 9 September 1835: "I have it in my heart to give you a little instruction, so that you may know your place, and stand in it, believed, admired, and rewarded, in time and in eternity." One week later he noted that "Br[other] Joseph has preached some of the greatest sermons on the duty of wives to their husbands and the role of all Women, I ever heard." Phelps then expounded on his newly gained understanding of eternal marriage, "Sally . . . you closed your 4th letter to me . . . after the manner of the Gentiles: says Sally 'I remain your till death.' " But, Phelps explained, "you will be mine, in this world and in the world to come . . . you may as well use the word 'forever,' as 'till death.' " Phelps's letters make clear that "eternal marriage" was distinct from polygamy, at least in his mind: "I have no right to any other woman in this world nor in the world to come according to the law of the celestial Kingdom."

Despite these 1835 indications of an understanding of the principle of eternal marriage, which would subsequently become synonymous with plural marriage, a distinctly polygamous marriage ceremony was apparently not performed until Joseph Smith was "sealed" to plural wife Louisa Beaman on 5 or 6 April 1841.[10] Smith evidently viewed all marriages prior to this time, including his own to Emma, as valid for "time" only. As late as 1840 he occasionally signed letters to Emma with the benediction "your husband till death."[11] It was not until a 28 May 1843 meeting of the Endowment Council[12] in Nauvoo, Illinois, that the Joseph and Emma Smith were finally sealed for time and eternity in the "new and everlasting covenant of marriage" (Ehat 1982, 2).

But as early as 1835 Smith wanted Mormon couples married by Mormon elders rather than by civil authorities or leaders of other religions. Ohio law refused to recognize Mormon elders as ministers. In a bold display of civil disobedience on 14 November 1835, Smith married Lydia Goldthwait Bailey to Newel Knight. Initially Seymour Brunson, who held a valid minister's license, was to perform the marriage. But as Hyrum Smith began the introductory comments, Joseph Smith stepped forward, stopped his brother, and declared his intent to officiate. The bride later recalled his saying, "Our Elders have been wronged and prosecuted for marrying without a license. The Lord God of Israel has given me authority to unite the people in the holy bonds of matrimony. And from this time forth I shall use that privilege and marry whomsoever I see fit" (Homespun 1893, 31).

Smith's performance of this marriage was one of his earliest efforts to apply heavenly guidelines on earth despite legal technicalities. Not only was Smith not a lawfully recognized minister, but Lydia Bailey, whose non-Mormon husband had deserted her, was never formally divorced. Obviously, Smith saw marriage not as a secular contract but as a sacramental covenant to be sealed by priesthood rather than by civil authority. He commented at the conclusion of the Knight ceremony "that marriage was an institution of heaven, instituted in the garden of Eden; that it was necessary it should be solemnized by the authority of the everlasting Priesthood" (HC 2:320).

During the next few weeks Smith officiated at numerous other weddings. At the January 1836 wedding of Mormon apostle John F. Boynton and Susan Lowell, he read aloud a license granting any "Minister of the gospel the privilege of solemnizing the rights of matrimony." He then alluded to an "ancient order of marriage" and pronounced upon the bride and groom "the blessings of Abraham, Isaac and Jacob." The next day he signed a certificate of marriage for William F. Calhoon and Nancy M. Gibbs affirming that the ceremony had been performed "agreeable to the rules and regulations of the Church of Jesus Christ of Latter-day Saints on Matrimony" (ibid., 377).

Smith's plans for Mormon utopia in Ohio and Missouri failed. A national recession devastated his economic plans in Kirtland. And non-Mormons in both places became increasingly nervous about the growing political clout of Mormons. Ohio and Missouri natives were suspicious of the close-knit Mormon lifestyle so contrary to mainstream American life. Disaffected Mormons vied with non-Mormons in hurling accusations against the church. Speculations that the Saints were practicing polygamy compounded such problems.

Within such an environment of suspicion, detractors suspected that the Mormon "Law of Consecration" included a "community of wives." If churchmen could share their property, why not their wives, too? Similar communitarian groups advocating a "community of wives" and other marital variations may have become confused with Smith's followers in the public mind. Parallels were compelling. In the early 1830s another group of "Saints" emerged from the social upheaval in New York. Disciples of revivalist preachers Erasmus Stone, Hiram Sheldon, and Jarvis Rider claimed they were perfect and could no longer sin. They became known as "Perfectionists." As a part of their doctrine, adherents advocated "spiritual wifery," a concept nearly identical to Mormon eternal marriage, wherein "all arrangements for a life in heaven may be made on earth . . . spiritual friendships may be formed, and spiritual bonds contracted, valid for eternity" (Ellis 1870). In 1832 Mormon missionary Orson Hyde, a former member of Sidney Rigdon's "family," visited a group he called "Cochranites" and disdainfully described in his 11 October 1832 journal the group's "Wonderful lustful spirit, because they believe in a 'plurality of wives' which they call spiritual wives, knowing them not after the flesh but after the spirit, but by the *appearance they know one another after the flesh.*"

Another practitioner of spiritual wifery was Robert Matthews, alias "Matthias the Prophet." Matthews announced that "all marriages not made by himself, and according to his doctrine, were of the devil, and that he had come to establish a community of property, and of wives" ("Memoirs"). In 1833 Matthews convinced two of his followers that, as sinners, they were not properly united in wedlock. He claimed power to dissolve the marriage, married the woman himself, prophesied that she was to "become the mother of a spiritual generation," and promised to father her first "spiritual child" himself. After a brief prison sentence, Matthews turned up on Joseph Smith's doorstep in Kirtland as "Joshua, the Jewish Minister" (Ms History, 8 Nov. 1835). Smith's account of the two-day meeting is sketchy, but apparently Matthews was sent on his way after a disagreement on the "transmigration of the soul."

Linked in the public mind with such colorful religionists as Matthias, Shakers, Harmonists, Perfectionists, Rappites, and Cochranites, Joseph Smith was viewed skeptically by many outsiders. But the real problems in Ohio were caused by insiders. The instability created by disastrous financial decisions involving Smith's Kirtland Safety Anti-Banking Society was compounded by stories about Smith's 1835 relationship with Fanny Alger. Benjamin Johnson years later noted that the Alger incident was "one of the Causes of Apostacy & disruption at Kirtland altho at the time there was little Said publickly upon the subject" (Zimmerman 1976, 39). At least one account indicated that Fanny became pregnant. Chauncy G. Webb, Smith's grammar teacher, later reported that when the pregnancy became evident, Emma Smith drove Fanny from her home (Wyl 1886, 57). Webb's daughter, Ann Eliza Webb Young, a divorced wife of Brigham Young, remembered that Fanny was taken into the Webb home on a temporary basis (Young 1876, 66-67). In fact Joseph Smith's journal entry for 17 October 1835 may contain a cryptic reference to this event:

"Called my family together arranged my domestick concerns and dismissed my boarders."[13]

Fanny left Kirtland in September 1836 with her family. Though she married non-Mormon Solomon Custer on 16 November 1836[14] and was living in Dublin City, Indiana, far from Kirtland, her name still raised eyebrows. Fanny Brewer, a Mormon visitor to Kirtland in 1837, observed "much excitement against the Prophet . . . [involving] an unlawful intercourse between himself and a young orphan girl residing in his family and under his protection" (Parkin 1966, 174).

Much of the excitement was evidently caused by the strong reaction of Smith's close counselor and friend Oliver Cowdery to Smith's presumed liaison with Alger. Apostle David W. Patten, visiting from Missouri in the summer of 1837, went to Cowdery in Kirtland to "enquire of him if a certain story was true respecting J[oseph] Smith's committing adultery with a certain girl." Patten later said that Cowdery "turned on his heel and insinuated as though [Smith] was guilty, he then went on and gave a history of some circumstances respecting the adultery scrape stating that no doubt it was true. Also said that Joseph had told him, he had confessed to Emma" (Cannon and Cook 1983, 167).

Church leaders in Missouri questioned Cowdery regarding the Alger incident when he arrived in Far West in the fall of 1837. Thomas B. Marsh, president of the Quorum of Twelve Apostles, stated that when Cowdery was asked "if Joseph Smith jr had confessed to his wife that he was guilty of adultery with a certain girl," Cowdery "cocked up his eye very knowingly and hesitated to answer the question saying he did not know as he was bound to answer the question, yet conveyed the idea that it was true."[15]

Later that fall, during a discussion at the Far West home of George W. Harris, Marsh reported a conversation "between Joseph Smith and Oliver Cowdery when J. Smith asked him if he had ever confessed to him that he was guilty of adultery, when after a considerable winking &c, he said *No*." Smith then gave an apologetic history of the "girl business," adding that "Oliver Cowdery had been his bosom friend, therefore he intrusted him with many things" (ibid., 167-68).

After Smith returned to Ohio from Missouri in late 1837 rumors circulated that Cowdery had spread scandalous lies about the prophet and had been chastened by him. The "Second Elder" was furious. He dashed off a 21 January 1838 letter to Smith complaining, "I hear from Kirtland, by the last letters, that you have publickly said, that when you were here I confessed to you that I had willfully lied about you—this compels me to ask you to correct that statement, and give me an explanation—until then you and myself are two" (in Cowdery to Cowdery). Apparently the word from Kirtland had come from Warren Cowdery, Oliver's brother, because Oliver included a copy of the letter to Smith in a separate letter to Warren. "I can assure you and bro.

Lyman [Cowdery]," Oliver angrily wrote to his brother, "I never confessed insinuated or admitted that I ever willfully lied about him. When he was there we had some conversation in which in every instance, I did not fail to affirm that what I had said was strictly true" in the matter of "a dirty, nasty, filthy affair of his and Fanny Algers."

Smith did not respond to Cowdery's letter. He was embroiled in trying to hold the church together in Kirtland. Prominent church leaders Luke Johnson, John Boynton, Warren Parrish, and others had united to denounce Smith as a heretic and "fallen prophet." They urged church members to rally around them in re-establishing the "old standards." After a clamor of accusations from both sides, leaders of the Johnson faction were excommunicated. But then one of the dissidents obtained a warrant for Smith's arrest on a charge of fraud. Under cover of darkness on 12 January 1838 he and first counselor Sidney Rigdon decided to "escape mob violence, which was about to burst upon us under the color of legal process" (HC 3:1). They fled to Far West, Missouri.

While Smith was en route to Missouri, charges against Oliver Cowdery's church membership were initiated in Far West. Prominent on the list of nine charges was "seeking to destroy the character of President Joseph Smith jr by falsely insinuating that he was guilty of adultry &c."[16] Though Smith arrived at Far West on 14 March 1838, he evidently would not grant Cowdery a requested interview. The Second Elder was excommunicated 12 April 1838, effectively disarming his accusations against the prophet.

Confusion over the exact nature and extent of Joseph Smith's involvement with Fanny Alger has remained to this day. That there was a sexual relationship seems probable. But was Smith's association with his house servant adulterous, as Cowdery charged? Or was she Smith's first plural wife? Apostle Heber C Kimball, many years later, introduced Fanny's brother John Alger in the Saint George Temple as "brother of the Prophet Josephs first Plural Wife" (Zimmerman 1976, 45). And in 1899 church leaders performed a proxy marriage for the couple. "The sealings of those named," a temple recorder noted of Alger and the ten other women listed, "were performed during the life of the Prophet Joseph but there is no record thereof. President Lorenzo Snow decided that they be repeated in order that a record might exist; and that this explanation be made" (Tinney 1973, 41).

If Smith and Alger were sealed in a plural marriage as 1899 church leaders were persuaded, who stood as witness for the ordinance? Who performed the ceremony? In the absence of an officiator or witness, did God himself seal the couple, or did Smith, as God's only legitimate earthly agent, marry himself to Alger? Smith did not claim publicly the power to "bind on earth and seal eternally in the heavens" until 3 April 1836, perhaps one year after the Alger incident (D&C 110:13-16). Could he have viewed her as his common-law wife, married by connubial relationship rather than by wedding ceremony?[17]

Unfortunately, Smith himself provided no help in clarifying his relationship with Alger. His public denouncements of polygamy during this period compounded the confusion. Only three weeks after Cowdery's excommunication, Smith published a statement in the July 1838 *Elder's Journal* answering several questions about Mormonism. To the question, "Do the Mormons believe in having more wives than one?" he responded emphatically, "No, not at the same time." Several months later, in mid-December, while incarcerated in Liberty, Missouri, he wrote a "Letter to the Church" which reflected his personal difficulties. Perhaps alluding to the Alger rumors, he asked, "Was it for committing adultery that we were assailed?" He then denied the charge as the "false slander" of "renegade 'Mormon dissenters' . . . running through the world and spreading various foul and libelous reports against us." He dismissed the persistent allegation that the Mormons had "not only dedicated our property, but our families also to the Lord; and Satan, taking advantage of this, has perverted it into licentiousness, such as a community of wives, which is an abomination in the sight of God" (HC 3:230).

The difficulties between Smith and Cowdery could probably have been resolved if Smith had admitted, at least to Cowdery, that he was introducing plural marriage into the church. But Cowdery, who left viewing Smith's behavior as adulterous, never became reconciled to Mormon polygamy. Church leaders much later unfairly accused Cowdery of taking a plural wife himself. Brigham Young is recorded in 1872 as having said that "while Joseph and Oliver were translating the Book of Mormon, they had a revelation that the order of Patriarchal Marriag and the Sealing was right." Cowdery, according to Young, proposed to Smith, "Why dont we go into the Order of Polygamy, and practice it as the ancients did? We know it is true, then why delay?" Smith warned that "the time has not yet come." Ignoring the prophet's counsel, "Oliver Cowdery took to wife Miss Annie Lyman, cousin to Geo A. Smith. From that time he went into darknes and lost the spirit. Annie Lyman is still alive, a witnes to these things" (Larson and Larson 1980, 1:349).[18]

This second-hand statement of Young, who may not have even been a Mormon at the time of the purported incident, lacks credibility. The Book of Mormon not only consistently denounces polygamy, but it would have been impossible for Cowdery to have been living polygamously during the period charged by Young (1827-30). Cowdery's marriage to his only wife, Elizabeth Ann Whitmer, occurred in 1832, three years after the translation of the Book of Mormon.[19] Furthermore no charges of sexual misconduct were made against Cowdery during his 1838 excommunication trial when there would have been ample opportunity and strong incentive for such retaliation.

Cowdery returned to Mormonism for a short time before his death in 1850 and was shocked when his sister and her husband, Daniel and Phebe Jackson, wrote to him from Illinois in 1846 confirming that polygamy was being practiced by church leaders. "I can hardly think it possible," he wrote, "that though there may be individuals who are guilty of the iniquities spoken of—yet no such practice can be preached or adhered to as a public doctrine." Cowdery viewed polygamy as morally and culturally unthinkable: "Such may do for the followers of Mohamet, it may have done some thousands of years ago, but no people professing to be governed by the pure and holy principles of the Lord Jesus, can hold up their heads before the world at this distance of time, and be guilty of such folly—such wrong—such abomination."[20]

Neither Oliver Cowdery's dim view of polygamy nor the difficulties the Fanny Alger situation caused seriously hampered Joseph Smith's apparent enthusiasm for plural marriage. But shortly after Cowdery's excommunication, events in Far West reached such crisis proportions that the church was again forced to uproot and move.

NOTES

1. Rapp's Harmony is not the community where Joseph Smith lived intermittently from 1825 to 1827. Smith's Harmony, now Oakland, was located three hundred miles to the east in the northeastern section of the state.

2. Though the Phelps letter has been widely touted as the earliest source documenting the advocacy of Mormon polygamy, it is not without its problems. For example, Phelps himself, in a 16 September 1835 letter to his wife, Sally, demonstrated no knowledge of church-sanctioned polygamy: "I have no right to any other woman in this world nor in the world to come according to the law of the celestial kingdom." Other contemporary evidence suggests, however, that Smith's revelation was not intended to foreshadow polygamy but rather to remove obstacles to missionary work which Indian agents in Kansas-Missouri had created. Ezra Booth, a prominent ex-Protestant minister turned Mormon apostate, was also in Missouri in 1831 and published an account of the revelation in the 8 December 1831 *Ohio Star*. According to Booth, "it has been made known by revelation," that it would be "pleasing to the Lord if the elders formed a matrimonial alliance with the natives," whereby Mormons might "gain a residence" in Indian territory, despite the opposition of government agents. (See also Whittaker 1985, 35.)

Oliver Cowdery and Parley P. Pratt had led a team of missionaries to Kansas-Missouri in the spring of 1831. Though the group had high hopes of success among the Indian tribes in the area, Cowdery wrote that the Indian agent was a "difficult man and we think some what strenuous respecting our having liberty to visit our brethren the Lamanites" (*Messenger and Advocate*, Oct. 1835). Pratt added that the men "were soon ordered out of the Indian country as disturbers of the peace" (Pratt 1874, 57).

Phelps could also have mistaken the "we" in his recollection. Smith may have intended miscegenation as a general Mormon rule rather than a specific directive to the seven men on the trip. Though intermarriage between Mormon males and Indian women became an accepted Mormon custom, none of the seven men married an Indian woman. Mormons of Brigham Young's day, however, commonly taught that the Indians would become a "white and delightsome people" through intermarriage. As early as 1852 William Hall noted that Young taught "the curse of their color shall be removed" through intermarriage (p. 59). And Elder James S. Brown, an 1853 missionary to the Shoshone, recalled instructions from church leaders "to identify our interests with theirs, even to marrying among them, if we would be permitted to take young daughters of the chief and leading men. . . . It was thought that by forming that kind of an alliance we could have more power to do them good and keep the peace among the adjacent tribes" (Brown 1900, 320).

The concept of Indians becoming a "white and delightsome people" is based on such Book of Mormon passages as 2 Nephi 30:6: "The scales of darkness shall begin to fall from their eyes; and many generations shall not pass away among them, save they shall be a white and delightsome people." Though the printer's copy and the 1830 and 1837 editions of the Book of Mormon all read "white and delightsome," Mormon church leaders in 1981 changed the verse to read "pure and delightsome," paralleling the 1840 edition.

3. Pratt made essentially the same comments before an 1878 audience of RLDS Mormons in Plano, Illinois. He recalled that his 1832 missionary companion, Lyman Johnson, told him that "Joseph had made known to him as early as 1831, that plural marriage was a correct principle. Joseph declared to Lyman that God had revealed it to him, but that the time had not come to teach or practice it in the Church, but that the time would come" (MS 40 [16 Dec. 1878]: 788).

4. That an incident between Smith and Nancy Johnson precipitated the mobbing is unlikely. Sidney Rigdon was attacked just as viciously by the group as was Smith. And the leader of the mob, Simonds Ryder, later said that the attack occurred because members of the mob had found some documents that led them to believe "the horrid fact that a plot was laid to take their property from them and place it under the control of Smith" (Hill 1977, 146). Besides, John Johnson had no son Eli. His only sons were John, Jr., Luke, Olmstead, and Lyman (Newell and Avery 1984, 41).

Nancy Johnson, who married Orson Hyde in 1834, became one of Smith's plural wives in February 1842 while Hyde was on a mission to Palestine (Quinn, "Prayer Circles," 88). Mrs. Hyde evidently first became linked with Smith's secretary, Apostle Willard Richards, whose wife was in Massachusetts. Ebenezer Robinson, who lost his job as editor of the *Times and Seasons* because of his wife Angeline's support of Emma Smith's anti-polygamy stance, noted in *The Return* 2 (Oct. 1890): 346-47 that in late January 1842, after his family vacated the printing office, "Willard Richards nailed down the windows, and fired off his revolver in the street after dark, and commenced living with Mrs. Nancy Marinda Hyde." John C. Bennett made the same accusations in his book (1842, 241-43). Sidney Rigdon's *Latter Day Saint's Messenger and Advocate* in a 15 March 1845 letter "TO THE SISTERS OF THE CHURCH OF JESUS CHRIST OF LATTER DAY SAINTS" commented: "If R[ichards] should take a notion to H[yde]'s wife in his absence, all that is necessary to be done is to be sealed. No harm done, no adultery committed; only taking a little advantage of rights of priesthood. And after R[ichards] has gone the round of dissipation with H[yde]'s wife, she is afterwards turned over to S[mith] and thus the poor silly woman becomes the actual dupe to two designing men, under the sanctimonious garb of rights of the royal priesthood. H[yde] by and by finds out the trick which was played off upon him in his absence, by his two faithless friends. His dignity becomes offended, (and well it might) refuses to live with his wife, but to be even with his companions in iniquity, takes to himself three more wives."

Orson and Nancy Hyde continued to live together for a short time after arriving in the Salt Lake Valley. But their relationship was unsteady, ending in divorce in 1870 (Quinn, "Prayer Circles," 98). Ann Eliza Young commented in her 1876 book that when Hyde returned from his mission "it was hinted to him that Smith had had his first wife sealed to himself in his absence, as a wife for eternity." She added that years later Brigham Young "informed his apostle that [Nancy] was his wife only for time, but Joseph's for eternity" (1876, 324-26).

5. When Winchester was excommunicated after Smith's death for "disobeying counsel," he alleged that the real reason for church action was because he was a "deadly enemy of the spiritual wife system and for this opposition he had received all manner of abuse from all who believe in that hellish system" (Grant to Young, 7 Sept. 1844).

6. Vienna Jacques was eighteen years older than Joseph Smith. She lived to be more than ninety, and was sealed to Smith by proxy on 28 March 1858 (Jessee 1984, 293-94).

7. Newell and Avery have surmised that McLellin in his "old age" perhaps confused Fanny Alger with the Fanny Hill of John Cleland's 1749 novel and "came up with the hired girl, Miss Hill" (1984, 66). But McLellin's wording implies two separate situations. After telling young Joseph the Miss Hill story he then wrote, "*Again* I told [your mother]. . . . She told me this story *too* was verily true" (italics mine). Also Martin Harris's account of the servant girl noted "In or about the year 1833," while McLellin's account says at the time of Joseph III's birth—6 November 1832. Alger did not live in Smith's home until 1835.

8. Mormons have not given the 1835 marriage statement the attention deserved by its pivotal historical significance. The neglect is understandable: the section is no longer in Mormon scripture. When the church officially announced its polygamy in 1852, the 1835 statement seemed obsolete. It was removed in 1876, replaced with a revelation on "celestial marriage" (D&C 132) which had been revealed to Smith on 12 July 1843 but not accepted by the Saints until 1852.

An additional reason the 1835 marriage statement receives little attention despite its status as the present law of the church is that Smith was not present during the 17 August general assembly which voted on the measure. He had planned a brief missionary venture to Michigan to coincide with the 17 August meeting. Cowdery remained behind not only to conduct the conference but to be with his wife, Elizabeth, who gave birth to a daughter, Maria, on 21 August.

Rumors circulated years later that Cowdery authored the marriage statement against Joseph Smith's wishes (see Brigham Young, in Joseph F. Smith Journal, 9 Oct. 1869). If true, Smith would have had ample opportunity to modify or delete the statement before publication. A "Notes To The Reader" addendum in the 1835 edition, detailed changes in the statement after it had been canonized but prior to publication. No changes were made to the section detailing the opposition to fornication and polygamy. Moreover Smith later authorized the second printing of the edition after proofreading the text.

Statements that Smith and other church leaders subsequently made, as well as the fact that Smith performed marriages using the ceremony canonized in the 1835 declaration, argue for his approval of the statement. In 1842 Smith declared the 1835 marriage statement the only "rule of marriage . . . practiced in this Church" (TS 3 [1 Oct. 1842]: 939). President Wilford Woodruff added in court testimony in 1893 that before the revelation on plural marriage was given in 1843, "there could not have been any rule of marriage or any order of marriage in existence at that time except that prescribed by the Book of Doctrine and Covenants" (*Complainants*, 304). Woodruff further testified at the same hearing that this was "all the law on the question" of marriage that was given "to the body of the people" (p. 309). Lorenzo Snow, president of the Quorum of the Twelve Apostles, added that the section on marriage was the "doctrine and law of the church upon marriage at that time [early Nauvoo]" (p. 317).

In addition, the ceremony outlined in the marriage statement was evidently used by Smith in performing marriages—even plural marriages. Mercy Fielding testified in 1893 that on 4 June 1837 Smith married her to Robert Blashel Thompson using the "ceremony prescribed by the Church and set forth in the Book of Doctrine and Covenants." She added that the ceremony was also used when she became the plural wife of Hyrum Smith in 1843 (*Complainants*, 344-45).

9. An examination of the W. W. Phelps papers at LDS Archives reveals that Phelps was Smith's ghostwriter on several occasions. In 1844, for example, after Phelps had written Smith's U.S. presidential platform position entitled "Views of the Powers and Policy of the General Government," Smith directed Phelps to read the paper at many private and public settings (HC 6:210, 214, 221).

10. Louisa Beaman (also spelled Beeman or Beman), daughter of Alva and Betsy Beaman, was born in Livonia, New York, 7 February 1815. She was sealed to Smith for eternity and to Brigham Young for time on 14 January 1846. She died in Salt Lake City four years later on 15 May 1850.

11. Joseph Smith to Emma Smith, 20 Jan. 1840 (Jessee 1984, 454). See also Joseph Smith to Emma Smith, 9 Nov. 1839 (Smith and Smith 1952, 2:376-77). Jessee (1984, 448-49) cites the latter letter but explains that the closing benediction and Smith's signature have been cut away. Interestingly, in a 16 August 1842 letter to Emma, Smith closes "your affectionate husband until death, through all eternity for evermore" (Jessee 1984, 527). This letter precedes by more than nine months the Smith's eternal sealing on 28 May 1843.

12. This secret organization was also called the "Endowment Quorum," the "Holy Order," the "Quorum of the Anointed," "Joseph Smith's Prayer Circle," or simply the "Quorum." Its primary function was to introduce a select group of men and women to instructions that would help them obtain full salvation with God. A secondary function was to "test" initiates' ability to keep a secret prior to their introduction to plural marriage. The introduction of Masonry to Mormonism in 1842 also apparently served this purpose. See Quinn, "Prayer Circles."

13. If Alger did become pregnant in 1835, the baby either died or was raised by someone else. Her first known child, listed on the 1850 census of Dublin City, Indiana, was a daughter born in 1840.

14. Wayne County, Indiana, marriage license, copy in author's possession. Fanny and Solomon, the parents of nine children, lived in Dublin City their entire married life and were members of the Universalist church (*Richmond Telegraph*, 1 April 1885). For additional background information on Fanny Alger Custer, see Samuel Alger/Clarissa Hancock Alger Family Group Sheet, LDS Genealogical Archives; Samuel Alger Obituary, *Deseret News*, 6 Oct. 1874; Wayne Co., Indiana, census records 1850, 1860, 1880 (Dublin City). The 1850 and the 1860 census list the Custer's children: Mary A. (b. 1840), Lewis A. (b. 1844), Benjamin Franklin (b. 1850), and Lafayette (b. 1854).

15. See further details in Thomas B. Marsh's letter in *Elder's Journal*, July 1838, 45-46. Marsh worried "that such foul and false reports" were being circulated, but he assured Smith that "none but those who wish your overthrow, will believe them, and we presume that the above testimonies will be sufficient to stay the tongue of the slanderer."

16. The following list of charges is from the "Far West Record": "1st, For stirring up the enemy to persecute the brethren by urging on vexatious Lawsuits and thus distressing the innocent. 2nd, For seeking to destroy the character of President Joseph Smith Jr by falsely insinuating that he was guilty of adultry &c. 3rd, For treating the Church with contempt by not attending meetings. 4th, For virtually denying the faith by declaring that he would not be governed by any ecclesiastical authority nor Revelation whatever in his temporal affairs. 5th, For selling his lands in Jackson county contrary to the Revelations. 6th, For writing and sending an insulting letter to President T. B. Marsh while on the High Council, attending to the duties of his office, as President of the council and by insulting the whole Council with the contents of said letter. 7th, For leaving the calling, in which God had appointed him, by Revelation, for the sake of filthy lucre, and turning to the practice of the Law. 8th, For disgracing the Church by being connected in the "Bogus business" as common report says. 9th, For dishonestly retaining notes after they had been paid and finally for leaving or forsaking the cause of God, and betaking himself to the beggerly elements of the world and neglecting his high and Holy Calling contrary to his profession."

17. Apostle Willard Richards in December 1845 entered into such a plural marriage with Alice Longstroth. His 23 December diary entry reads: "At 10.P.M. took Alice L[ongstrot]h by the [hand] of our own free will and avow mutually acknowledge each other husband & wife, in a covenant not to be broken in time or Eternity for time & for all Eternity, to all intents & purposes as though the seal of the covenant had been placed upon us. for time & all Eternity & called upon God. & all the Holy angels-& Sarah Long[stro]th. to witness the same."

Apostle Abraham H. Cannon noted in his 5 April 1894 diary that both George Q. Cannon and Wilford Woodruff approved of such arrangements. "I believe in concubinage," George Q. is recorded as saying, "or some plan whereby men and women can live together under sacred ordinances and vows until they can be married." Woodruff responded to Cannon's suggestion, "If men enter into some practice of this character to raise a righteous posterity, they will be justified in it."

18. See also George Q. Cannon's second-hand account in the *Juvenile Instructor* 16 (15 Sept. 1881): 206; and Joseph F. Smith's account in JD 20 (7 July 1878): 29.

19. In addition, Cowdery was ordained an "Associate President" of the church on 5 December 1834—a position superior to counselors in the First Presidency. He also helped to supervise the selection of the original Quorum of Twelve Apostles in 1835, administered the first endowments in the Kirtland Temple in 1836, and on 3 April 1836 shared with Smith a temple vision of Jesus, Moses, Elias, and Elijah. It is unlikely that Cowdery would have been allowed to participate in any of these events had the "Associate President" been involved in an unsanctioned polygamous relationship.

20. Another example of Cowdery's opposition to polygamy is found in his 25 January 1836 "sketchbook" entry: "Settled with James M. Carrel who left the office. I gave him a reproof for urging himself into the society of a young female while he yet had a wife living, but he disliked my admonition: he however confessed his impropriety." A third example is in an 1884 reminiscence of Cowdery's former law partner, W. Lang, who said, "Cowdery never gave me a full history of the troubles of the Mormons in Missouri and Illinois but I am sure that the doctrine of polygamy was advocated by Smith and opposed by Cowdery" (Ivins Collection, Notebook 2:33-34).

Two

STIRRINGS IN NAUVOO

Far West was chosen as a site for Mormon resettlement in the summer of 1836 by Missouri church leaders W. W. Phelps and John Whitmer. By the fall of 1838 the city had mushroomed to nearly five thousand inhabitants. As in Ohio earlier, original settlers resented the Mormon presence. Disputes between the Saints and Missourians soon escalated to the point of bloodshed. On 30 October 1838 an undisciplined unit of the Missouri state militia attacked a small Mormon colony at Haun's Mill, killing seventeen men and boys. The next day militia leaders arrived at Far West demanding that Mormons surrender their leaders, weapons, and property and leave the state. Joseph Smith, Sidney Rigdon, and other prominent Mormons were jailed during the fall and winter of 1838-39 on a long list of trumped-up charges ranging from arson to murder. By the end of April nearly all Missouri Mormons had resettled in the area surrounding Quincy, Illinois.

Difficult as it was, the exodus proved to be the unifying and strengthening force the Saints needed. As soon as Smith reached Illinois after escaping from jail in the spring of 1839,[1] he began building a Mormon city on the banks of the Mississippi at Commerce. Renamed Nauvoo, Smith's city rapidly developed into one of the largest in the state. A special mission "to go over the great waters" to Great Britain sent the twelve apostles on a quest that brought the first of thousands of European Mormon emigrants to America. By the summer of 1841 Nauvoo was home to nearly seven thousand citizens. The thriving metropolis boasted paved streets, schools, dozens of shops, two sawmills, a steam-powered flour mill, a foundry, a tool factory, numerous gardens and orchards, and a cooperative farm on the outskirts of the city. A Nauvoo Agricultural and Manufacturing Association had been incorporated, and a large hotel, the Nauvoo House, was planned. The most ambitious project was a limestone temple that would eventually rise sixty feet above a prominent hill overlooking the Mississippi River.

Much of the city's progress was due to a colorful newcomer on the Mormon scene: John Cook Bennett. Bennett, a Campbellite minister in Ohio, was acquainted with Sidney Rigdon and other Campbellites-turned-Mormon. The self-trained lawyer, doctor, thirty-third-degree Mason, brigadier general in the Illinois Invincible Light Dragoons, and quartermaster general of Illinois arrived in Nauvoo in August 1840. The absence of the missionary-apostles and the periodic illness of Rigdon may have contributed to a power vacuum in the church. Glib, bombastic, and seemingly aristocratic Bennett filled this void by ingratiating himself into the inner circles of the church; his rapid rise to the hierarchical pinnacles of Mormonism remains virtually unprecedented.

Some long-time church members were uncomfortable with Bennett's influence on Smith. But Smith, not always a shrewd judge of people, was so impressed by his new convert that he adopted many of Bennett's personal mannerisms, including his oratorical style, his military dress and bearing, and his habit, no doubt enhanced by Smith's sometime-secretary W. W. Phelps's own penchant for aliteration and Latinisms, of using a wide variety of foreign phrases for emphasis in written communication.[2] In a 5 January 1841 address, Smith went so far in his enthusiasm for Bennett as to rank the doctor above the ancient apostle Paul. "[Paul] was a good orator," Smith explained, "but Doctor Bennett is a superior orator, and like Paul is active and diligent always employing himself in doing good to his fellow men" (Ehat and Cook 1980, 59).

When the apostles returned in the summer of 1841 they discovered that, in their absence, Bennett had engineered passage of the liberal Nauvoo charter through the Illinois legislature to create a virtually autonomous city-state and had been "unanimously" elected mayor. In addition, Bennett had either been named or appointed major general of the Nauvoo Legion,[3] master in chancery for Hancock County, chancellor of the newly established University of Nauvoo, chief justice of the Nauvoo Municipal Court, and a director of the Nauvoo Agricultural and Manufacturing Association. A January 1841 revelation had declared: "I have seen the work which he hath done, which I accept if he continue, and will crown him with blessings and great glory" (D&C 124:17). Perhaps even more impressive was his 8 April 1841 calling by Smith as "Assistant President" of the church, an apointment that, in the eyes of many Saints, placed him between the prophet and the Quorum of the Twelve.

Despite his "heavenly accolade" and lofty church position, Bennett's relationship with Smith began to crack in early 1842. Details of the falling out have become muddled by accusations, denials, and countercharges, but a power struggle fueled by disagreements about polygamy seems to have been the major cause. Polygamy, a criminal act under the 1833 Illinois Antibigamy Laws,[4] was so unacceptable to monogamous nineteenth-century American society that Smith could introduce it only in absolute secrecy. Despite Smith's explicit denials of plural marriage, stories of "spiritual wifery" had continued to spread.[5] Oliver Olney, a Nauvoo Mormon, wrote in his 1842 journal of rumors that "an introduction of principles that would soon be, that the ancient order of God that was formerly, would again have its rounds, as it was in the days of old Solomon and David. They had wives and concubines in abundance, as many as they could support. The secret whispering was, that the same will eventually be again" (p. 5).

Reactions to the rumors varied. Most Saints, many with rigid New England Puritan backgrounds, found polygamy as distasteful as adultery. Joseph Smith's younger brother, Don Carlos, for example, was reported to have said in June 1841: "Any man who will teach and practice 'spiritual wifery' will go to hell, no matter if it is my brother Joseph" (Robinson, *The Return* 3 [Feb. 1891]: 28). But others apparently accepted polygamy without reservation. The Quorum of Twelve Apostles, though not without exception, proved to be the main source of support from 1843 on. Accustomed to Smith's revelations which introduced gospel principles "line upon line, precept upon precept," the majority of the Twelve was prepared by Smith to live polygamy as part of the "restitution of all things."[6]

Considerable difficulty for the church was caused by a small group of Mormons who enthusiastically equated Smith's teachings with "free love." John C. Bennett evidently subscribed to this notion. Smith, according to his 1 July 1842 account in the *Times and Season*, received a letter shortly after Bennett arrived in Nauvoo warning him that the doctor was a "very mean man, and had a wife, and two or three children in McConnelsville, Morgan county, Ohio." Though Bennett had been known in Ohio as early as 1833 by some church leaders, his marriage was apparently a well-kept secret in Nauvoo (TS 2 [1 June 1841]: 431-32). Smith sent Bishop George Miller to Ohio to investigate. Shortly after the January 1841 revelation praising Bennett's "work," Miller wrote that Bennett appeared to be an adventurous malcontent who had lived in at least twenty different places and believed himself the "smartest man in the nation . . . always ready to fall in with whatever is popular." Miller added that the doctor's wife, Mary, had "left him under satisfactory evidence of his adulterous connections," and "it has been Dr. Bennett's wish that his wife should get a bill of divorcement, but as yet she has not" (TS 3 [1 July 1842]: 842).

This report did not prevent Smith from appointing Bennett assistant president to the church in early April 1841. But three months later Smith received another communication pointing out that "Bennett had a wife and children living" (ibid., 840). This letter, from Smith's brother Hyrum and William Law soon became public knowledge. Bennett, who had been courting Nauvoo women as a bachelor, found his position among the Saints declining when his marital status became known. Smith alleged that Bennett was so distraught over the exposure that he attempted suicide by poison, and declared that the "public impression" was that Bennett was so "ashamed of his base and wicked conduct, that he had recourse to the above deed to escape the censures of an indignant community" (ibid.). Smith and Bennett remained on relatively good terms for several months after the "suicide attempt," and in mid-January 1842 they engaged in a friendly series of debates on the issue of "Lamanites and Negroes."

In a retrospective newspaper account months later, Martha Brotherton, a young Nauvoo woman, reported that during the same week the debates were held she was privately approached by Brigham Young and asked "were it lawful and right . . . could [you] accept of me for your husband and companion?" Young stated that "Brother Joseph has had a revelation from God that it is lawful and right for a man to have two wives; for as it was in the days of Abraham, so it shall be in these last days . . . if you will accept of me, I will take you straight to the celestial kingdom." Brotherton reported that when she hesitated, Young left the room and returned ten minutes later with Smith. "Well, Martha," she reported the prophet as saying, "just go ahead, and do as Brigham wants you to. . . . I know that this is lawful and right before God. . . . I have the keys of the kingdom, and whatever I bind on earth is bound in heaven, and whatever I loose on earth is loosed in heaven." Martha begged for time to consider the offer, then left for St. Louis, where she published her story in the 15 July 1842 *St. Louis Bulletin*.

Even before Martha left Nauvoo, rumors of the incident began to circulate. Hyrum Smith, believing the prophet's public posture that polygamy was not being practiced, publicly addressed the Saints on 7 April 1842 "in contradiction of a report in circulation about Elders Heber C. Kimball, Brigham Young, himself, and others of the Twelve, alleging that a sister had been shut in a room for several days, and that they had endeavored to induce her to believe in having two wives." Joseph, who addressed the group after Hyrum, added, "There is no person that is acquainted with our principles who would believe such lies" (HC 4:585-86).[7]

Joseph and Hyrum were not the only Smiths denying the polygamy accusations being thrown against the church. Emma Smith was using her powerful position as president of the church's all-female Relief Society to protect the prophet from scandal and to suppress the polygamy rumors. "A Record of the Organization and Proceedings of the Female Relief Society of Nauvoo," in the handwriting of secretary Eliza R. Snow, provides substantial evidence of Emma's opposition to polygamy. In the organizational minutes of 17 March 1842, Emma remarked that members should "deal frankly with each other to watch over the morals and be very careful of the character and reputation of the members of the Institution." The meaning of her comments became clear during the 24 March meeting when she reported "Clarissa Marvel was accus'd of scandalous falsehoods on the character of Pres[iden]t. Joseph Smith without the least provocation."

Clarissa, who had lived with Don Carlos Smith's widow, Agnes Coolbrith Smith, for a year had thought she detected a relationship between Joseph Smith and his widowed sister-in-law—a relationship Bennett also accused Smith of pursuing (Bennett 1842, 256). After considerable pressure from Emma and others, Clarissa marked an X by the statement: "This is to certify that I never have at any time or place, seen or heard any thing improper or unvirtuous in the conduct or conversation of either President Smith or Mrs. Agnes Smith. I also certify that I never have reported any thing derogatory to the characters of either of them."

During the society's 30 March meeting Emma read a secret epistle to the group from Joseph and others warning against "iniquitous characters . . . [who] say they have authority from Joseph or the First Presidency" and advising them not to "believe any thing as coming from us, contrary to the old established morals & virtues & scriptural laws, regulating the habits, customs & conduct of society." The sisters were urged to denounce any who made polygamous proposals and to "shun them as the flying fiery serpent, whether they are prophets, Seers, or revelators: Patriarchs, Twelve Apostles, Elders, Priests, Majors, Generals, City Councillors, Aldermen, Marshals, Police, Lord Mayors or the Devil, [they] are alike culpable & shall be damned for such evil practices: and if you yourselves adhere to anything of the kind, you also shall be damned."[8]

The prophet repeated his warning in a 10 April public address, pronouncing a "curse upon all adulterers, and fornicators, and unvirtuous persons, and those who have made use of my name to carry on their iniquitous designs" (HC 4:587). Though not mentioned by name, "spiritual wifery," or polygamy, was obviously intended. This was made clear during the Relief Society meeting of 16 March 1844. Emma spoke of "J. C. Bennets spiritual wife system. That some taught it as the doctrine of B[rother] Joseph—she advised that all abide the book of Mormon and D[octrine] and Covenants &c then read that Epistle of President J. Smith written in this Book of Record"— the 30 March 1842 epistle on "the old established morals." Emma "exhorted [the sisters] to follow the teachings of Pres. J[oseph] Smith from the stand— said their could not be stronger language used than that just read and that these are the words of B[rother] Joseph her husband."

Despite the prophet's anti-polygamous teachings "from the stand," a small group of Smith's inner circle, including Bennett, were aware that polygamy was being practiced. Bennett's liberal interpretation of Smith's teachings and his personal thirst for power resulted in his disaffection from Smith and eventual downfall from the Mormon hierarchy. During a 7 May parade and sham battle of the Nauvoo Legion attended by Bennett's close friend, Judge Stephen A. Douglas, and other dignitaries from Carthage, Smith refused Major General Bennett's request to "take command of the first cohort." He also declined Bennett's second request to take a position at the rear of the calvary, instead choosing his "own position" at the head of the ranks. Smith's young son, Joseph III, later recalled that in the sham battle Bennett "lost control of colonel Brower's horse which he was riding, and it ran away with him. There followed quite a commotion, and some thought a conspiracy to injure Father had been sprur.g, with confusion as a cloak" (Anderson and Hulmes 1952, 47). The official church account of the incident also saw Bennett's actions of the day as a plot to have Smith killed (HC 5:4).

Though the conspiracy theory is accepted by some, it is possible that Bennett was merely trying to enhance his own position with the dignitaries by embarrassing Smith. Bennett had earlier announced in the 30 April Nauvoo *Wasp* that "a sham battle will be fought between the mounted Riflemen under the immediate command of Lieutenant General Smith, and the Invincibles under the immediate command of Major General Bennett." Smith, a military novice, unfamiliar with the command of troops, would have been no match for Bennett's military expertise in the maneuvers. One of Smith's closest Nauvoo friends suggested that Joseph's likely response to such an attempt would have been to belittle Bennett. Though he was "social and eaven conviv[i]al at times," Benjamin F. Johnson said of Smith, "He would alow no arogance or undue liberties[,] and criticism Even by his associates was Rarely Acceptble & Contradiction would Rouse in him the Lion at once For by no one of his Fellows would he be Superseded or disputed" (Zimmerman 1976, 19-20).

If church leaders did conspire to unseat Bennett from his positions of power as he later charged, the sham battle was the turning point. Four days later the first public move to align Bennett with the "spiritual wifery" rumors was undertaken. Church leaders on 11 May drew up a document which announced that the hand of fellowship would be withdrawn from Bennett because "having been labored with from time to time, to persuade him to amend his conduct," he would not toe the mark of chastity (TS 3 [1 July 1842]: 842).

Six days later on 17 May, Smith sent a letter to church recorder James Sloan instructing him to "be so good as to permit Bennett to withdraw his name from the Church record, if he desires to do so, and this with the best of feelings towards you and General Bennett" (Bennett 1842, 40-41). Two days later at a Nauvoo City Council meeting, Bennett turned over the mayorship to Smith "on account of the reports in circulation in this city this day, concerning the ex-Mayor, and to quiet the public mind." Asked if he had anything against Smith, the former counselor responded that he had "no difficulty with the heads of the Church." He further avowed that "any one who has said that I have stated that General Joseph Smith has given me authority to hold illicit intercourse with women is a liar in the face of God." Smith, not satisfied with Bennett's answer, requested a more detailed response: "Will you please state definitely whether you know anything against my character, either in public or private?" "I do not," replied Bennett. "In all my intercourse with General Smith in public and in private, he has been strictly virtuous" (HC 5:38-39.)[9]

Had Bennett been willing to leave Nauvoo at this point, things would have been much easier for Smith and the church. But the former mayor evidently thought his difficulties with the church would be resolved. "I intend to continue with you," he informed the city council on 19 May, hoping that "the time may come when I may be restored to full confidence, fellowship, and my former standing in the church" (ibid.). On 25 May, Bennett was told that the document withdrawing his fellowship was to be made public. Alleging that his non-Mormon mother would be devastated by the details of his disfellowshipment, Bennett pleaded for her sake that the document not be published. Smith relented on condition that Bennett make a confession of his involvement in "spiritual wifery" before his Masonic brethren. The next evening, reportedly weeping like a child, Bennett asked forgiveness before one hundred men in the Masonic Hall. To the astonishment of many, Smith pleaded mercy for his former counselor.

Earlier that afternoon of 26 May, while addressing the Relief Society, Smith made a similar request, though not specifically naming Bennett: "Hold your tongues about things of no moment—a little tale will set the world on fire. At this time the truth on the guilty should not be told openly—we must use precaution in bringing sinners to justice [for] in exposing their heinous sins, we draw the indignation of a gentile world upon us." As soon as Smith had finished, Emma, perhaps feeling that Joseph's comments had been directed towards her, addressed the group in strong anti-polygamy tones: "Sin must not be covered, especially, those sins which are against the law of God and the Laws of the country—all who walk disorderly must reform, and any knowing of heinous sins against the law of God, and refuse to expose them, becomes the offender."

Though Bennett's accounts of his two years in Nauvoo whitewash his own behavior, he was clearly in a privileged position to witness Smith's involvement in polygamy. William Law, a member of the First Presidency (1841-44), wrote in 1871 that although he did not know in 1842 of Smith's involvement in polygamy, he believed "now that John C. Bennett did know it, for he at that time was more in the secret confidence of Joseph than perhaps any other man in the city" (Stenhouse 1873, 198). Bennett's 1842 book, *The History of the Saints: Or an Expose of Joe Smith and the Mormons*, offers considerable evidence that he knew of several of Smith's earliest polygamous relationships. He referred in code to seven women who can be identified as plural wives of the prophet. For example, "Miss L***** B*****" (Louisa Beaman), the first of Smith's plural wives sealed to him through a marriage ceremony, was noted in Bennett's book. In addition, he correctly reported that the couple had been married by Joseph Bates Noble—a fact that only a handful of people knew at the time (Bennett 1842, 256).[10]

Noble, brother-in-law to Louisa Beaman, indicated in 1880 that Smith first approached him about Louisa in the fall of 1840. "To convince [me] of the truth of [this]," he said, "was no small matter. Joseph bore testimony that he had received a revelation on this principle [plural marriage] in Kirtland, but the Lord told him not yet. The Angel of the Lord came to him in Nauvoo and told him the time had come" (St. George Minutes). The prophet then requested Noble "to step forward and assist him in carrying out the said principle" by sealing him to Beaman (Roberts 1930, 2:201).[11] Apostle Erastus Snow spoke in 1883 of "his first wife's sister: Louisa Beeman, being the first Morman that entered Plural Marraige in this last dispensation, Br[other] Nobles officiating in a grove Near Main Street in the City of Nauvoo. The Prophet Joseph dictating the ceremony and Br[other] Nobles repeating it after him" (Larson and Larson 2:610).[12]

Bennett's first-hand awareness of Smith's polygamy evidently led him to think an assistant president of the church had the same right to take "spiritual wives" and encourage others to do so as did the church president. This presumption not only strained his relationship with Smith but threatened to expose Smith's own polygamous behavior, bringing reproach upon the church. Oliver Olney confirmed in his 16 June 1842 diary that Smith and Bennett had "moved together in all their windings. If Bennett had not moved ahead so fast all would have been well now, as I look at things with them." And Smith may have been commenting on this very point when Erastus Snow heard him say at the time, "many of the Elders were doing things because they saw him [Joseph] do them, but many by this means would fall" (St. George Minutes).

The first public hint of the difficulties caused by the introduction of polygamy to Nauvoo are detailed in the "Minutes of The High Council of The Church of Jesus Christ of Latter-day Saints, Nauvoo Illinois." Several 1842 entries describe individuals charged with "unchaste and unvirtuous conduct" under the pretense that church leaders had sanctioned such behavior. On 20 May 1842, for example, Chauncy Higbee's case was considered. The minutes note that "three witnesses testified that he had seduced them and at different times been guilty of unchaste and unvirtuous conduct with them and taught the doctrine that it was right to have free intercourse with women if it was kept secret &c and also taught that Joseph Smith authorized him to practise these things &c."

The women testifying against Higbee were Margaret and Matilda Nyman and Catherine Fuller Warren. The report of the Nymans was later printed in the 29 May 1844 *Nauvoo Neighbor*. The sisters said that Higbee had advised them that Smith approved of "spiritual wifery" but gave instructions to keep the matter a secret because "there was no sin when there is no accuser." Catherine Fuller Warren in her 20 May 1842 testimony responded to charges of "unchaste and unvirtuous conduct with John C. Bennett and others" by admitting to having intercourse not only with him but with Chauncy Higbee and the prophet's younger brother, Apostle William Smith. Speaking in her defense, however, she insisted that the men had "taught the doctrine that it was right to have free intercourse with women and that the heads of the Church also taught and practised it which things caused her to be led away thinking it to be right."

Another Nauvoo woman, Mary Clift, testified in high council affidavits of 29 August and 4 September 1842 that she was pregnant with Gustavius Hills's child. She said he told her that "the heads of the Church practiced such conduct & that the time would come when men would have more wives than one." Hills was excommunicated, as was Higbee. Despite Catherine Warren's testimony implicating William Smith along with Bennett and Higbee, instead of being excommunicated, he was sent on a mission to Tennessee. Retained in his apostleship, he became presiding church patriarch on 24 May 1845.[13]

Bennett continued to reside in Nauvoo at the Robert Foster home until mid-June. Though Joseph Smith had opposed exposing Bennett, pressures from his wife and others, combined with testimony before the high council, apparently caused him to change his mind. On 18 June he spoke "his mind concerning the iniquity & wickedness of Gen. John Cook Bennet, & exposed him before the public" (Kenney 1983-85, 2 [18 June 1842]: 179). Bennett, who may have thought his difficulties with Smith were on the mend, was incensed at the sudden turn of events.[14] He left Nauvoo a few days later, insisting that his life was in danger, and wrote a 27 June letter to a Springfield, Illinois, newspaper, the *Sangamo Journal*, promising to expose Mormonism. The 8 July edition of the *Journal*, after receiving the letter, called publicly upon Bennett to "come out NOW. . . . To produce 'documentary evidence,' that the public may form opinions that cannot be gainsaid."

NOTES

1. Smith and several others spent six months in jail at Liberty, Missouri. On 6 April 1839 they were taken to Daviess County for trial. After several days of testimony a change of venue was granted for Boone County. On 15 April the prisoners and guard set out for their destination. But before they had traveled far, the sheriff, according to Hyrum Smith, said, "I'll take a good drink of grog and go to bed. And you may do as you have a mind to." As soon as the guards were comfortably drunk, the prisoners escaped to Illinois (HC 3:321).

2. TS 2 (1 June 1841): 431-32 reflects church leaders' view of Bennett: "General Bennett's character as a gentleman, an officer, a scholar, and physician, stands too high to need defending by us; suffice it to say, that he is in the confidence of the Executive, holds the office of Quarter-Master-General of this State, and is well known to a large number of persons of the first respectability throughout the state. He has, likewise, been favorably known for upwards of eight years by some of the authorities of the Church."

3. The city charter granted the power to "organize the inhabitants of said city, subject to military duty, into a body of independent military men, to be called the

'Nauvoo Legion.' " The legion was subject to the call of the mayor in executing the laws and ordinances of the city and responsible to the governor for public defense.

4. The law, enacted 12 February 1833, read: "Bigamy consists in the having of two wives or two husbands at one and the same time, knowing that the former husband or wife is still alive. If any person or persons within this State, being married, or who shall hereafter marry, do at any time marry any person or persons, the former husband or wife being alive, the person so offending shall, on conviction thereof, be punished by a fine, not exceeding one thousand dollars, and imprisoned in the penitentiary, not exceeding two years" (*Revised Laws*, 198-99).

5. Though "spiritual wifery" in Mormon usage much later came to be equated with promiscuous intercourse or "free love," this was evidently not the contemporary Nauvoo meaning. "Polygamy," "spiritual wifery," "spiritual marriage," and "plural marriage" were all apparently interchangeable in Mormon and non-Mormon contexts during the early 1840s. Emily Dow Partridge, a plural wife to Smith and later to Brigham Young, for example, uses "spiritual wife" as a reference to herself and others: "Spiritual wives, as we were then termed, were not very numerous in those days and a spiritual baby was a rarity indeed" ("Autobiographical Sketch," 72). Helen Mar Kimball Whitney, another plural wife to Smith, added that in Nauvoo "spiritual wife was the title by which every woman who entered into this order [plural marriage] was called" (Whitney 1882, 15).

Bathsheba Smith, wife of Apostle George A. Smith, explained in court testimony that during the Bennett fracas the church "preached against him from the stand, and against plural marriage, the secret wife system, secret marriages. The spiritual wife system was the system by which a man had two wives at the same time" (*Complainants*, 362). And Ebenezer Robinson, who was introduced to polygamy by Hyrum Smith, when asked, "did you understand from Hyrum Smith in 1843 that polygamy & spiritual wifery was identical?", responded, "I did" (Robinson to Briggs). Heber C. Kimball in 1855 chided the Saints for opposing the "spiritual wife doctrine the Patriarchal Order, which is of God" (JD 3 [6 Oct. 1855]: 125).

6. Smith was obviously anxious when the apostles returned from Europe that they be introduced to polygamy by him, rather than by Bennett or someone else. Helen Mar Kimball, daughter of Heber C. Kimball, wrote that when her father, Brigham Young, and John Taylor docked in Nauvoo, 1 July 1841, Smith was waiting at the landing. She noted that Smith "seemed unwilling to part with my father and from that time kept the Twelve in Council early and late." She added that her mother "never dreamed that [Smith] was during those times revealing to them the principles of Celestial Marriage" (Whitney, "Retrospection"). George A. Smith, the prophet's cousin, arriving in Nauvoo 13 July, detailed in a 9 October 1868 letter to Joseph Smith III, that "at one of the first interviews" after he arrived from England, Smith surprised him by teaching him the new doctrine of "Patriarchal Marriage."

7. To discredit Martha Brotherton, the 27 August 1842 *Wasp*, a Nauvoo newspaper, denounced Bennett as "the pimp and file leader of such mean harlots as Martha H. Brotherton and her predecessors from old Jezebel." After Brotherton's death, however, according to Salt Lake Endowment House Records, Brigham Young was sealed to her by proxy on 1 August 1870.

8. Though the epistle was read to the Relief Society on 30 March, it was not included in the minutes until 25 September. Vienna Jacques, a member of the Relief Society in Nauvoo, related similar rhetoric in an 1876 interview with Joseph Smith III. She recalled going to Emma Smith in Nauvoo to ask her about the "subject of spiritual wifery": "She told me she had asked her husband, the prophet, about the stories which were being circulated among the women concerning such a doctrine being taught,

and that he had told her to tell the sisters of the society that if any man, no matter who he was, undertook to talk such stuff to them in their houses, just to order him out at once, and if he did not go immediately, to take the tongs or the broom and drive him out, for the whole idea was absolutely false and the doctrine an evil and unlawful thing" (Anderson and Hulmes 1952, 263-64).

9. Hyrum Smith added that during this time he witnessed a private confrontation between his brother and Bennett in which the prophet charged: "Doctor! Why are you using my name to carry on your hellish wickedness? Have I ever taught you that fornication and adultery were right, or polygamy or any such practice? [Bennett] said You never did. Did I ever teach you anything that was not virtuous—that was iniquitous, either in public or private? He said You never did" (*Wasp*, 27 July 1842). Bennett, however, claimed in his 2 July *Sangamo Journal* letter that Smith, with loaded pistol, coerced him into making the favorable statements. "The peace of my family requires that you should sign an affidavit," Bennett reported Smith as saying, and "make a statement before the next city council, exonerating me from all participation whatever, whether directly or indirectly, in word or deed, in the spiritual wife doctrine, or private intercourse with females in general, and if you do not do it with apparent cheerfulness, I will make catfish bait of you." Francis M. Higbee, a close friend of Bennett and son of one of Smith's close friends, swore in a 30 June 1842 affidavit that "Joseph Smith told [me] that John C. Bennett could easily be put aside or drowned, and no person would be the wiser for it, and that it ought to be attended to . . . fearing as he said, that Bennett would make some disclosures prejudicial to said Smith" (*Sangamo Journal*, 15 July 1842).

10. The exact number of women sealed to Joseph Smith during his lifetime is difficult to assess. Assistant church historian Andrew Jenson documented twenty-seven from statements of the women themselves or witnesses to the ceremonies (*Historical Record* 6:233-34). D. Michael Quinn (1973, 278) identifies thirty-four, Fawn Brodie (1975, 435-65) and Danel Bachman (1975, 333-36) both name forty-eight, while Stanley S. Ivins, after extensive research in Nauvoo Temple records, Salt Lake Endowment House records, and other genealogical records, put forth eighty-four women as possible wives of the prophet. None of these studies undertakes the near-impossible task of determining if these women were connubial wives, eternal or "celestial" wives, or merely linked by name to Smith. In addition, the numbers do not reflect the hundreds of women—such as Josephine Bonaparte, Madam Victor Hugo, St. Therese, St. Helene (mother of Constantine), and Matilda (empress of Germany)—who were sealed to him by proxy after his death (Tinney 1973).

11. Noble was likely rewarded for his part in marrying the prophet to Beaman by being allowed to take a plural wife himself. William Clayton recorded in his 17 May 1843 journal that "J. B. Noble when he was first taught this doctrine set his heart on one & pressed [Smith] to seal the contract but [he] never could get opportunity. It seemed that the Lord was unwilling. Finally another came along & he then engaged that one and is a happy man" (Ehat 1982, 69).

12. Apostle Erastus Snow also identified Louisa Beaman as "the First wife that Joseph had sealed to him in the holy order of Plural Marriage" in a discourse on 17 December 1876 (Larson and Larson 1:438). Erastus's wife, Artimesia Beman Snow, added elsewhere: "My sister, Louisa Beman, next older than myself, was the first woman given in plural marriage. She lived and died a good, faithful Latter-day Saint, true to the principles she embraced and is now rejoicing with her husband, our beloved Prophet, in the eternal worlds" (Larson 1971, 747).

13. Catherine Fuller Warren's testimony consists of five documents. The one dated 25 May 1842 names William Smith twice (Hutchins 1977, 33). Quorum of the

Twelve president Lorenzo Snow later referred to William Smith's guilt: "Brigham Young was once tried to the very utmost by the Prophet, and for a moment his standing in the Church seemed to tremble in the balance. Wm Smith, one of the first quorum of apostles in this age had been guilty of adultery and many other sins. The Prophet Joseph instructed Brigham (then the Pres. of the Twelve) to prefer a charge against the sinner, which was done. Before the time set for the trial, however, Emma Smith talked to Joseph and said the charge preferred against William was with a view to injuring the Smith family. After the trial had begun, Joseph entered the room and was given a seat. The testimony of witnesses concerning the culprit's sins was then continued. After a short time Joseph arose filled with wrath and said, 'Bro. Brigham, I will not listen to this abuse of my family a minute longer. I will wade in blood up to my knees before I will do it.' This was a supreme moment. A rupture between the two greatest men on earth seemed imminent. But Brigham Young was equal to the danger, and he instantly said, 'Bro. Joseph, I withdraw the charge' " (Abraham H. Cannon Journal, 9 April 1890).

14. It is possible that Bennett's public admissions of "spiritual wifery" were a pre-arranged plan to protect his friend William Smith and others from exposure. Similar circumstances are seen, for example, in the case of Joseph Smith's secretary William Clayton. Writing in his 19 October 1843 journal, Clayton noted that when Emma Smith found out that his plural wife (sealed to him by Joseph Smith) was pregnant, she was very upset. Joseph told him to "keep her at home and brook it and if they raise trouble about it and bring you before me I will give you a awful scouraging & probably cut you off from the church and then I will baptise you & set you ahead as good as ever" (Tanner and Tanner 1982).

"PROTECTING THE LORD'S ANOINTED"

Four days after John C. Bennett penned his 27 June 1842 letter, Joseph Smith published in the 1 July issue of the *Times and Seasons* a letter "To the Church of Jesus Christ of Latter Day Saints, and to All the Honorable Part of the Community." Smith's explanation of his former counselor's behavior was that Bennett had approached "some Nauvoo women" who "knew nothing of him but as an honorable man, & began to teach them that promiscuous intercourse between the sexes, was a doctrine believed in by the Latter-Day Saints, and not only sanctioned, but practiced" by Smith and others. When "the women" asked Bennett why the prophet "preached so much against it," Bennett reportedly replied that such action was necessary because "of the prejudice of the public, and that it would cause trouble in [Smith's] own house."

Bennett's promised expose, an open letter dated 15 July, detailed Smith's polygamous proposals to several Nauvoo women, including Sarah Pratt, wife of Apostle Orson Pratt, and Nancy Rigdon, daughter of Sidney Rigdon of the First Presidency. Bennett claimed that while Pratt was a missionary in Europe, Smith had confided to him that he was smitten by the "amiable and accomplished" Sarah Pratt. According to Bennett's account, Smith told him that he wanted Sarah for "one of his *spiritual wives*, for the Lord had given her to him."

The Bennett story further related that shortly after Smith's admission of affection toward Sarah Pratt, Smith and Bennett allegedly went to Sarah's house with some of the doctor's sewing. In the course of the visit, Smith reportedly said, "Sister Pratt, the Lord has given you to me as one of my spiritual wives. I have the blessings of Jacob granted me, as he granted holy men of old, and I have long looked upon you with favor, and hope you will not deny me." "I care not for the blessings of Jacob," the feisty Sarah was said to have replied; "I have one good husband, and that is enough for me." After another attempt by Smith to convince her of the correctness of polygamy, she reportedly told him, "Joseph, if you ever attempt any thing of the kind with me again, I will make a full disclosure to Mr. Pratt on his return home." "Sister Pratt," Smith is said to have replied, "I hope you will not expose me; if I am to suffer, all suffer; so do not expose me. Will you agree *not* to do so?" "If you will never *insult* me again," Sarah countered, "I will not expose you unless strong circumstances require it." "If you should tell," Bennett quoted Smith, "I will ruin your reputation; remember that."

According to Bennett, Sarah kept her word, though ensuing circumstances made it difficult. Sarah later recalled the details herself: "Shortly after Joseph made his propositions to me . . . they enraged me so that I refused to accept any help from the tithing house or the bishop." She added that "Bennett, who was of a sarcastic turn of mind, used to come and tell me about Joseph to tease and irritate me" (Wyl 1886, 61). Even after Orson Pratt returned from his mission, Sarah kept the incident to herself. Public difficulties between Joseph and Orson did not surface until a year later. Bennett claimed the problems at this point resulted from Smith's approaching Sarah and kissing her.

When Sarah told Orson of Smith's behavior, Bennett reported in his 15 July account, Pratt became enraged and told Smith "never to offer an insult of the like again." Though full details of the confrontation between the two men are unknown, subsequent events indicate that Smith not only denied Sarah's account but accused her of being Bennett's paramour. A veiled reference to this accusation against Bennett may be evident in a harsh 22 July *Times and Season* article. The paper charged that though Bennett "professed to be virtuous and chaste, yet he did pierce the heart of the innocent, introduce misery and infamy into families, reveled in voluptuousness and crime, and led the youth that he had influence over to tread in his unhallowed steps; he professed to fear God, yet did he desecrate His name, and prostitute his authority to the most unhallowed and diabolic purposes; even to the defiling of his neighbor's bed."

Though he did not initially expose Smith, Orson Pratt refused to become part of the 11 May 1842 move to withdraw church fellowship from Bennett. Pratt insisted "he knew nothing against the man." Sarah's brother-in-law, William Allred,[1] in a 5 July letter to Bennett wrote: "Mr. Pratt would write, but he is *Afraid* to. He wishes to be *perfectly still*, until your second letter comes out – then you may hear."[2] Chauncy Higbee reported in another letter to Bennett that the Pratts were privately saying "if Smith ever renews the attack on them, they will come out against him, and stand it no longer" (Bennett 1842, 45). The day before Bennett's piece appeared in the *Sangamo Journal*, visitors to Nauvoo heard Smith renew the public attack on Sarah Pratt by calling her a "***** from her mother's breast."[3] To complicate matters further for the Pratts, Bennett's 15 July letter urged Sarah to come forth and confirm the details of Smith's polyandrous proposals to her.

As may have been his custom during personal turmoil, Orson Pratt sought solitude. When a note he left behind was interpreted as suicidal, Smith "caused the Temple hands and the principle men of the city to make search for him" (Ms History, 15 July 1842). Ebenezer Robinson later remembered the excitement: "Apostle Pratt had been told Joseph wanted Orson's wife as his own plural wife and John C. Bennnett was accused of having committed adultery with his wife. Both men denied these charges. Under these circumstances his mind temporarily gave way, and he wandered away, no one knew where" (Robinson, *Return* 2 [Nov. 1890]:287).

The missing apostle was found five miles below Nauvoo and immediately brought back. Smith called a public meeting to explain the unusual events. The official account of the meeting states that Smith "gave the public a general outline of John C. Bennett's conduct" (Ms History, 15 July 1842). Brigham Young, who was probably at the meeting, was more expansive two days later in a letter to Orson's brother Parley, who was still a missionary in England: "Br Orson Pratt is in trubble in consequence of his wife, hir feelings are so rought up that he dos not know whether his wife is wrong, or whether Josephs testimony and others are wrong and due L[ie] and he [has been] decived for 12 years or not." Brigham told Parley that Orson "is all but crazy about matters, you may aske what the matter is concirning Sister P. – it is enoph, and doct. J. C. Bennett could tell all about [crossed out in original: "it if he"] himself & hir – enoph of that – we will not let Br. Orson goe away from us he is to good a man to have a woman destroy him."

Nauvoo and the surrounding area were buzzing with rumors about the Pratts. The 29 July *Sangamo Journal* editorialized that if Orson were to capitulate to "the denunciations and schemes of Joe Smith – if he fails to defend the reputation of himself and of the woman he has vowed to protect before high heaven – he will fix a stain upon his character which he can never wash out." Pratt stood by his wife. Brigham Young said that during this period he and other members of the quorum labored constantly with "Elder Orson Pratt, whose mind became so darkened by the influence and statements of his wife, that he came out in rebellion against Joseph, refusing to believe his testimony or obey his counsel." When Pratt insisted "he would believe his wife in preference to the Prophet," according to Young, "Joseph told him if he did believe his wife and follow her suggestions he would go to hell."[4] Even the threat of losing his quorum membership did not deter Pratt; he responded fearlessly to quorum president Brigham Young's hints that his position might be in jeopardy, advising Young to ordain Amasa Lyman "in my stead" (Watson 1968, 120-21).

Joseph Smith was not directly involved in the "excommunication" of the rebellious Pratts on 20 August 1842. He was walking a tightrope, secretly courting both thirty-eight-year-old Eliza R. Snow and seventeen-year-old Sarah Ann Whitney, while fighting extradition to Missouri as "an accessory to an assault with intent to kill" former governor Lilburn W. Boggs.[5] Smith was also at odds with his long-time friend and counselor Sidney Rigdon over a reputed polygamous proposal on 9 April 1842 to Rigdon's unmarried daughter Nancy.[6] George W. Robinson, a prominent Nauvoo citizen married to another of Rigdon's daughters, wrote to James A. Bennett, a New York friend to the church, on 22 July that "Smith sent for Miss Rigdon to come to the house of Mrs. [Orson] Hyde, who lived in the under rooms of the printing-office" (Bennett 1842, 245-47). According to Robinson, Nancy "inquired of the messenger . . . what was wanting, and the only reply was, that Smith wanted to see her." Robinson claimed that Smith took her into a room, "locked the door, and then stated to her that he had had an affection for her for several years,[7] and wished that she should be his; that the Lord was well pleased with this matter, for he had got a revelation on the subject, and God had given him all the blessings of Jacob, &c., &c. and that there was no sin in it whatever." Robinson reported that Nancy "repulsed him and was about to raise the neighbors if he did not unlock the door and let her out" (ibid.).

Nancy's brother, John, recounting the incident years later in an affidavit, remembered that "Nancy refused him, saying if she ever got married she would marry a single man or none at all, and took her bonnet and went home, leaving Joseph." Nancy withheld details of the situation from her family until a day or two later, when a letter from Smith was delivered by Smith's personal secretary, Willard Richards. "Happiness is the object and design of our existence," the letter began. "That which is wrong under one circumstance, may be, and often is, right under another." The letter went on to teach that "whatever God requires is right, no matter what it is, although we may not see the reason thereof till long after the events transpire. . . . Our Heavenly Father is more liberal in his views, and boundless in his mercies and blessings, than we are ready to believe or receive."[8]

Nancy showed Smith's letter to her father and told him of the incident at the Hyde residence. Rigdon demanded an audience with Smith. George W. Robinson reported that when Smith came to Rigdon's home, the enraged father asked for an explanation. Smith "attempted to deny it at first," Robinson said, "and face her down with the lie; but she told the facts with so much earnestness, and the fact of a letter being present, which he had caused to be written to her, on the same subject, the day after the attempt made on her virtue," that ultimately "he could not withstand the testimony; he then and there acknowledged that every word of Miss Rigdon's testimony was true" (ibid., 246). Much later, John Rigdon elaborated that "Nancy was one of those excitable women and she went into the room and said Joseph Smith you are telling that which is not true you did make such a proposition to me and you know it [crossed out in original: "the woman who was there said to Nancy are you not afraid to call the Lords anointed a cursed liar no she replied I am not for he does lie and he knows it"]" ("Life Story," 166).

Robinson wrote that Smith, after acknowledging the incident, claimed he had propositioned Nancy because he "wished to ascertain whether she was virtuous or not, and took that course to learn the facts!" (Bennett 1842, 246). But the Rigdon family would not accept such an explanation. They were persuaded that the rumors about the prophet's polygamy doctrine had been confirmed. The issue continued to be a serious source of contention between the two church leaders until Smith's death in 1844. According to John Rigdon, Sidney told the family that Smith "could never be sealed to one of his daughters with his consent as he did not believe in the doctrine" ("Life Story," 167). Rigdon preferred to keep his difficulties with Smith private, but Bennett's detailed disclosures made this impossible.

A Mormon newspaper, *The Wasp*, printed on 20 July a number of sworn statements by prominent Nauvoo citizens affirming Joseph Smith's "high moral character" and declaring him not guilty of any of Bennett's published accusations. Orson Pratt would not sign the letter, nor would Sidney Rigdon or George W. Robinson. A public meeting was called on 22 July to obtain an "expression of the public mind in reference to the reports gone abroad, calumniating the character of Pr[esident] Joseph Smith." A resolution presented by Wilson Law[9] and published in the 1 August 1842 *Times and Seasons* declared "That, having heard that John C. Bennett was circulating many base falsehoods respecting a number of the citizens of Nauvoo, and especially against our worthy and respected Mayor, Joseph Smith, we do hereby manifest to the world that so far as we know him [he is] a good, moral, virtuous, peaceable and patriotic man."

The Nauvoo Saints must have been shocked when "two or three" persons, including Orson Pratt, voted against the proposed resolution. The minutes of the meeting do not record Pratt's explanation for his vote, but as soon as he finished speaking, Smith jumped to his feet and said to Pratt: "Have you personally a knowledge of any immoral act in me toward the female sex, or in any other way?" "Personally, toward the female sex," Pratt replied, "I have not." Pratt elaborated, but his comments were again not recorded. After Pratt's rebuttal, William Law, Heber C. Kimball, and Hyrum Smith bore "testimony of the iniquity of those who had calumniated Pres. J[oseph] Smith's character" (TS 3 [1 Aug. 1842]: 869).

The refusal of Pratt, Rigdon, and Robinson to certify his "high moral character" no doubt infuriated Smith. Addressing the Saints on 25 August, he admonished the Twelve and others to "support the character of the Prophet, the Lord's anointed." He lashed out at "O[rson] Pratt and others of the same class [who] caused trouble by telling stories to people who would betray me, and they must believe these stories because his Wife told him so!"[10] "And as to all that Orson Pratt, Sidney Rigdon, or George W. Robinson can do to prevent me," the prophet concluded, "I can kick them off my heels, as many as you can name" (Ms History, 29 Aug. 1842).

Three hundred eighty elders, responding to Smith's plea for support, volunteered for assignments to "disabuse the public mind in relation to the false statements of Dr. J. C. Bennett."[11] To provide them with ammunition, the church press printed on 31 August a special edition of "Affidavits and Certificates, Disproving the Statements and Affidavits Contained In John C. Bennett's Letters." To discredit Sarah Pratt's accusations, the publication included a 23 July 1842 letter from Stephen A. Goddard to Orson Pratt which claimed that while Sarah was staying with the Goddards in October 1840 "from the first night until the last, with the exception of one night, it being nearly a month, the Dr. was there as sure as the night came." The letter described the alleged Bennett/Pratt relationship in lurid detail: "One night they took their chairs out of doors and remained there as we supposed until 12 o'clock or after; at another time they went over to the house where you now live and came back after dark, or about that time. We went over several times late in the evening while she lived in the house of Dr. Foster, and were most sure to find Dr. Bennett and your wife together, as it were, man and wife."

The special edition included a sworn statement from Goddard's wife, Zeruiah, that "their conduct was anything but virtuous, and I know Mrs. Pratt is not a woman of truth, and I believe the statements which Dr. Bennett made concerning Joseph Smith are false, and fabricated for the purpose of covering his own iniquities, and enabling him to practice his base designs on the innocent." Hancock County sheriff J. B. Backenstos also provided a sworn affidavit testifying that during the previous winter (1841-42) he had accused Bennett of "having an illicit intercourse with Mrs. Orson Pratt . . . when said Bennett replied that she made a first rate go." But Backenstos's statement may be dismissed as slander—during the winter mentioned, Orson was in Nauvoo, and Sarah sick and pregnant with their daughter Celestia Larissa.

Years later, when totally disaffected from Mormonism, Sarah gave her account of the Goddard incident. She claimed that when she confronted Mrs. Goddard about her published accusations, "She began to sob. 'It is not my fault,' she said. 'Hyrum Smith came to our house, with the affidavits all written out, and forced us to sign them. *Joseph and the Church must be saved*, said he. We saw that resistance was useless, they would have ruined us; so we signed the papers.' "[12] Unlike most "officially certified apostates," the Pratts refused to leave Nauvoo. Orson wrote in the 2 September 1842 *Wasp* that, contrary to rumor, he had not "renounced 'Mormonism,' left Nauvoo, &c." He elaborated in the article that he had not turned against the church, though privately and publicly assailing Smith, because "the lustre of truth cannot be dimmed by the shadows of error and falsehood." Pratt confirmed his determination to stay near the church two weeks later in the 26 September *Wasp* when he asserted that he and Sarah were not "preparing to leave and expose Mormonism" but intended to make "NAUVOO OUR RESIDENCE, AND MORMONISM OUR MOTTO."

Though the Pratts and Rigdons refused to denounce Mormonism, Bennett's serialized expose continued to pose a threat to Smith. The church press provided a protective canopy for the prophet by continually denouncing Bennett's accusations, especially those linking Smith to polygamous behavior. The *Times and Seasons* on 1 September 1842, for example, editorialized that "the public mind has been unjustly abused through the fallacy of Dr. Bennett's letters" and reminded readers that the church's rule for marriage was "that one man should have one wife; and one woman, but one husband."

Six months pregnant, Emma Smith also defended her husband from charges of polygamy. In a 5 September 1842 letter to Illinois governor Thomas Carlin, who on 2 August had signed an order for Smith's arrest and delivery to Missouri officials on the Boggs charges, Emma and other Relief Society sisters petitioned for executive clemency. Emma argued that Bennett was an "unvirtuous man and a most consummate scoundrel, a stirrer up of sedition, and a vile wretch unworthy of the attention or notice of any virtuous man." She condemned his "bare-faced, unblushing falsehoods" and contrasted her husband as a "man of integrity, honesty, truth, and patriotism. We have never, either in public or private, heard him teach any principles but the principles of virtue and righteousness" (HC 5:147).

Both to confirm his public stance and to further portray Bennett as a licentious scoundrel, *Times and Seasons* editor Joseph Smith on 1 October 1842 explained: "We have given the above rule of marriage [monogamy] as the only one practiced in this church, to show that Dr. J. C. Bennett's 'secret wife system' is a matter of his own manufacture." Smith's denial, supported in petition by the Relief Society and individual Nauvoo citizens, served as sufficient evidence to most Mormons that Bennett, not Smith, was the moving force behind the polygamy stories.

Bennett, stripped of his Mormon power base and accused in the church press of deviant acts including "adultery, fornication, embryo infanticide and buggery" ("Bennettiana"), approached the Pratts and Rigdons for testimony corroborating his accusations against Smith. On 10 January 1843 he wrote a letter to Sidney and Orson, explaining that he hoped to collaborate with Missouri authorities to extradite Smith. "We shall try [him] on the Boggs case, when we get him into Missouri," Bennett wrote. "The war goes bravely on; and, although Smith thinks he is now safe, the enemy is near, even at the door. He has awoke the wrong passenger" (HC 5:250-51).

Bennett had underestimated the loyalty of Rigdon and Pratt. After Rigdon passed the letter to him, Pratt delivered it immediately to Smith. Though Smith was concerned over Bennett's impending actions, he was elated with Pratt's allegiance.[13] Two days later on 20 January Smith called a meeting of the First Presidency and Quorum of the Twelve to consider Pratt's case. According to the official minutes, Smith made what some apostles may have found to be a startling announcement: "As there was not a quorum when Orson Pratt's case came up before[,] he was still a member–he had not legally been cut off." Quorum president Brigham Young added that all he personally had against Orson "was when he came home he loved his wife better than David," a cryptic reference to Smith. Smith, speaking of Sarah Pratt's accusations, then turned to Orson. "She lied about me," he said. "I never made the offer which she said I did."

Even in these intimate councils of the church Smith had to hide his involvement in plural marriage. Hyrum Smith, in attendance at the 20 January meeting, was not yet aware of his brother's polygamy. Joseph could not have admitted his involvement without disillusioning Hyrum, who was strongly opposed to the idea. Sarah Pratt was not invited to the proceedings at which her husband's church membership was reconsidered and never retracted her statements. Yet one hour after the adjournment of the 20 January meeting, the Pratts were rebaptized in the Mississippi by Joseph Smith. Afterwards, according to the minutes, "Orson received the Priesthood and the same power and authority as in former days."[14]

By mid-February 1843 Nauvoo seemed as tranquil as the frozen Mississippi. The Pratts had been rechurched. Smith had met with the Rigdon family, who "expressed a willingness to be saved. Good feelings prevailed, and [Joseph and Sidney] again shook hands together" (ibid., 270).[15] But beneath the apparent calm, rumors about Smith and polygamy would not rest. In a 21 February address he described "the saints grumbling." "If the stories about Jos. Smith are true," he said, "then the stories of J. C. Bennet are true about the Ladies of Nauvoo"–ladies who "are [said] to be wifes to Jos Smith. Ladies[,] you know whether it is true[.] no use of living among hogs without a snout" (Smith Diary, 21 Feb. 1843).

Yet on 4 March Smith was secretly sealed to nineteen-year-old Emily Partridge. Four days later he was sealed to her twenty-three-year-old sister, Eliza. And one week later the 15 March 1843 *Times and Seasons* reported: "We are charged with advocating a plurality of wives, and common property. Now this is as false as the many other ridiculous charges which are brought against us. No sect has *a greater reverence for the laws of matrimony* or the rights of private property; and we do what others do not, we practice what we preach."

By mid-fall 1843 Smith had been sealed to at least seven other women: Almira Woodward Johnson (m. 5 April 1843), Lucy Walker (m. 1 May 1843), Helen Mar Kimball (m. May 1843), Flora Woodworth (m. May 1843), Rhoda Richards (m. 12 June 1843), and Maria and Sarah Lawrence (m. late summer or fall 1843).[16]

NOTES

1. William Moore Allred, born near Nashville, Tennessee, 24 December 1819,

converted to Mormonism in 1832. He married Sarah Pratt's sister Orissa Bates 9 January 1842.

2. Allred to Bennett (Bennett 1842, 46). The serious illness of Orissa B. Allred is documented in William Allred's journal.

3. The expletive, probably "whore," is omitted from the *Sangamo Journal*, 1 Aug. 1842.

4. Wilford Woodruff observed in his 10 September 1842 journal: "There was a counsel of the *Twelve* held for four days with Elder *Orson Pratt* to labour with him to get him to recall his sayings against Joseph & The Twelve but he persisted in his wicked course & would not recall any of his sayings which were made in public against Joseph & others sayings which were unjust & untrue. The Twelve then rejected him as a member of their quorum & he was cut off from the Church. Dr John Cook Bennet was the ruin of Orson Pratt" (Kenney 1983-85, 2 187).

5. Boggs (1792-1860), elected lieutenant governor of Missouri in 1832, became governor upon resignation of Daniel Dunklin in 1836. He issued the infamous Mormon "extermination order" in October 1838. The attempt on Boggs's life occurred 6 May 1842.

6. Though an August date is often used for this incident, Bennett reported that it occurred on the day of Ephraim Marks's funeral (9 April 1842). This earlier date seems to be supported by the difficulties Smith and Rigdon were having during this time. For example, the prophet dictated a letter to Rigdon on 12 May "concerning certain difficulties, or surmises which existed" (HC 5:6). The next day Smith received back from Rigdon a letter and walked to the post office to talk with Rigdon concerning "certain reports put in circulation by Francis M. Higbee about some of Elder Rigdon's family" (HC 5:8). On 28 June Smith and Bishop George Miller visited the Rigdon family and "had much conversation about John C. Bennett, and others, much unpleasant feeling was manifested by Elder Rigdon's family, who were confounded and put to silence by the truth" (HC 5:46). A 1 July 1842 letter Rigdon wrote to Smith also dramatizes this conflict: "I write this in the greatest confidence to yourself and for your own eye and no other . . . I am your friend and not your enemy as I am affraid you suppose. I want you to take your horse and carriage on tomorrow and take a ride with me out to the Prarie." Rigdon stressed secrecy: "Say not a word to any person living but to Hiram only. [A]nd no man shall know it from me" (Smith Collection).

7. Smith's interest in Nancy Rigdon had apparently been noticed by her father during the Kirtland years. Clark Braden testified that a "bitter quarrel between Rigdon and Smith shortly before they left Kirtland was because Smith wanted to have Nancy Rigdon a girl of 16 sealed to him" (Braden 1884, 202). William C. Smith (not Joseph's brother) added that "I went to school with Athalia Rigdon, and there was talk among the boys about sealing. I think there was difficulty between Joseph Smith and Rigdon with reference to having Rigdon's daughter sealed to Smith" (ibid., 391).

8. Bennett obtained a copy of the letter and published it in the 19 August 1842 *Sangamo Journal*. In the 27 August 1842 *Wasp*, Sidney Rigdon wrote: "I am fully authorized by my daughter, Nancy, to say to the public through the medium of your paper, that the letter which has appeared in the Sangamo Journal, making part of General Bennett's letters to said paper, purporting to have been written by Mr. Joseph Smith to her, was unauthorized by her, and that she never said to Gen. Bennett or any other person, that said letter was written by said Mr. Smith, nor in his handwriting, but by another person, and in another person's handwriting. . . . I would further state that Mr. Smith denied to me the authorship of that letter." A copy of this letter labeled, "The Letter of the Prophet, Joseph Smith to Miss Nancy Rigdon," is in the Smith Collection. The letter was printed in HC 5:134-36 with a B. H. Roberts footnote: "It is

not positively known what occasioned the writing of this essay; but when it is borne in mind that at this time the new law of marriage for the Church—marriage for eternity, including plurality of wives under some circumstances—was being introduced by the Prophet, it is very likely that the article was written with a view of applying the principles here expounded to the conditions created by introducing said marriage system."

9. Wilson Law, ironically, along with his brother William and others, became disillusioned with Smith when they became confident he was indeed involved in polygamy. The Laws published the *Nauvoo Expositor*, which in the summer of 1844 publicly exposed Smith's involvement in polygamy.

10. Joseph Smith III, president of the rival Reorganized Church of Jesus Christ of Latter Day Saints, in the mid-1870s quizzed Sarah Pratt on these stories about his father. "Sister Pratt," Smith asked, "it has been frequently told that I dare not come to you and ask you about your relations with [my father], for fear you would tell me things which would be unwelcome to me." "You need have no such fear," Sarah is reported to have replied, "your father was never guilty of any action or proposal of an improper nature in my house, to me, or in my presence, at any time or place. There is no truth in the reports that have been circulated about him in this regard" (Anderson and Hulmes 1952, 69-71). But Smith was disinclined to believe any evidence connecting his father with polygamy. In her account of the visit Sarah said: "I saw that he was not inclined to believe the truth about his father, so I said to him: 'You pretend to have revelations from the Lord. Why don't you ask the Lord to tell you what kind of a man your father really was?'" (Wyl 1886, 61).

11. Letters were arriving from missionaries requesting information to combat Bennett's claims. An example is an undated letter (probably July 1842) from Apostle John E. Page, who was in Pittsburg: "The disclosures of Bennett has done much to injure the cause of the Kingdom here the people are anxiously looking for the full and effectual downfall of Mormonism through a Judas of a Bennett—it becomes you and Brothers Young and Kimball to show your selves men of the God of Israel this once to put down the slanders of Bennett and Martha Brotherton. . . . The people believe that Bennett is a villian and effectually exposing villians—But the thinking Public are looking for S[idney] Rigdon and his daughter, O[rson] Pratt and wife, the Higbees and others to finish the work of Death to Mormonism" (Joseph Smith Collection).

12. The Goddard story had serious problems that even Sarah did not point out. Bennett had been appointed 4 October 1840 to work with Smith on drafting the Nauvoo Charter. On this same day he was also selected as a delegate to lobby for passage of the bill through the state legislature at Springfield, nearly one hundred miles distant. That Bennett could draft the complicated documents, make the necessary trips to Springfield, and be with Sarah Pratt every night except one during a one-month period seems improbable. In addition, it seems likely that had Bennett and Sarah been involved in a sexual liaison as public as the Goddard story implies, objections would have been raised when Smith called him to be "assistant president" six months later. Furthermore, despite the numerous cases of church action against sexual sins brought before the Nauvoo High Council, Sarah Pratt's name is never mentioned.

Fabricated stories designed to protect both individuals and institutions in Nauvoo are seen elsewhere. Sidney Rigdon in the 18 June 1845 *Messenger and Advocate* reported that Parley P. Pratt, in speaking of the means by which church leaders should sustain Smith, advised that "we must lie to support brother Joseph, it is our duty to do so." Not only were church leaders willing to violate the law to promote polygamy, they did not hesitate to blacken the character of individuals who threatened to expose the secret practice of plural marriage.

Sarah Pratt was not the only woman to suffer from this policy. The 27 August 1842 *Wasp*, for example, branded Martha H. Brotherton a "mean harlot," and Nancy Rigdon suffered the same treatment after she opposed Smith's polygamous proposals. Stephen Markham, a close friend of Smith, certified in the 31 August 1842 "Affidavits" that he saw Nancy Rigdon in a compromising situation with Bennett. He claimed "many vulgar, unbecoming and indecent sayings and motions" passed between them and testified that he was convinced they were "guilty of unlawful and illicit intercourse with each other." George W. Robinson, on Nancy's behalf, countered with a sworn statement on 3 September 1842 (Bennett 1842, 252) that Markham was lying. Explaining that he was present on the occasion Markham referred to, he pointed out that Nancy was sick and that "Dr. John C. Bennett was the attending physician." Sidney Rigdon also swore out a refutation and employed an attorney to sue Markham. Bennett in his book (p. 248) added that "the young men in the city came forward and gave certificates against Markham, stating that they believed Markham willfully and maliciously lied to injure the character of Miss Rigdon, and to help Smith out of the dilemma."

After Joseph Smith's death in 1844, Orson Hyde attempted to further blacken Nancy Rigdon's character in order to tarnish her father's claim to church leadership. Her conduct was "notorious in this city," Hyde charged; she was "regarded generally, little, if any better, than a public prostitute." He defended the prophet's actions toward her as efforts to "reprove and reclaim her if possible" (Hyde 1845, 27-29).

Jane Law, wife of Smith's counselor William Law, was also blacklisted for rejecting Smith's polyandrous proposal. Mrs. Law said she was told by the prophet in 1844 that "the Lord had commanded that he should take spiritual wives, to add to his glory." She added that "Joseph had asked her to give him half her love; she was at liberty to keep the other half for her husband" (Young 1876, 61). Her husband wrote in a 20 January 1887 letter to the *Salt Lake Tribune* that after her rejection, Smith considered the couple apostates. "Jane had been speaking evil of him for a long time . . . slandered him, and lied about him without cause," Law reported Smith as saying. But Law, like Orson Pratt, Sidney Rigdon, and George W. Robinson, would not suffer a woman he viewed as innocent to be unjustly slandered. "My wife would not speak evil of . . . anyone . . . without cause," he noted; "Joseph is the liar and not she." In addition to defending the honor of his wife, Law insisted that Sarah Pratt was a "good, virtuous woman."

13. Because Rigdon had given the letter to Pratt instead of to him, Smith suspected his counselor's motives. Though the evidence was weak, Smith continued to accuse Rigdon of collusion with Bennett on various occasions throughout the fall of 1843. Rigdon always maintained that "as there seems to be a foolish notion that I have been engaged with J. C. Bennett, in the difficulties between him and some of the citizens of this place, I merely say in reply to such idle and vain reports that they are without foundation in truth" (*Wasp*, 23 July 1843).

14. In 1878, before an audience of RLDS Mormons, Orson Pratt was reported to have based his 1842 difficulties on "a wicked source, from those disaffected, but as soon as he learned the truth he was satisfied" (MS 40 [16 Dec. 1878]: 788). Both Bennett and Sarah Pratt were "disaffected" at the time, but so were numerous other possible sources, including Sidney Rigdon, Oliver Olney, George W. Robinson, Francis Higbee, Chauncy Higbee, Nancy Rigdon, and Martha Brotherton.

15. Less than six weeks later Smith was again charging Rigdon with being an accessory with Bennett to "destroy me and this people." Smith threatened to publish withdrawal of Rigdon's fellowship in the *Times and Seasons*. Rigdon answered, "I can assert in truth, that with myself and any other person on this globe there never

Four

POLYANDRY – A TEST?

Many Mormons have stressed that when Joseph Smith approached married women with polyandrous proposals he was merely testing their faith or loyalty. In Sarah Pratt's case, for example, the *New York Herald*, 14 September 1877, reported: "It is said that the Prophet admitted to [Pratt] the attempt he made on his wife's virtue, but that it was only done to see whether she was true to her absent husband." In several other cases Smith "tested" an apostle by asking him for the hand of his wife. Church president Wilford Woodruff recounted the test of Apostle John Taylor: "The Prophet went to the home of President Taylor, and said to him, 'Brother John, I WANT LEONORA.' " Taylor was stunned, but after walking the floor all night, the obedient Elder said to Smith, "If GOD wants Leonora He can have her." Woodruff concluded: "That was all the prophet was after, to see where President Taylor stood in the matter, and said to him, Brother Taylor, I dont want your wife, I just wanted to know just where you stood" (Whitaker, 1 Nov. 1890).

A similar "test" was evidently required of Apostle Heber C. Kimball. Kimball's biographer, Stanley B. Kimball, recounts the incident: "Joseph demanded for himself what to Heber was the unthinkable, his Vilate. Totally crushed spiritually and emotionally, Heber touched neither food nor water for three days and three nights and continually sought confirmation and comfort from God." Finally, after "some kind of assurance," Heber "took Vilate to the upper room of Joseph's store on Water Street. The Prophet wept at this act of faith, devotion, and obedience. Joseph had never intended to take Vilate. It was all a test" (Kimball 1981, 93).

Jedediah Grant, second counselor to Brigham Young and father of church president Heber J. Grant, commented on such tests in a Utah sermon delivered on 19 February 1854. "When the family organization was revealed from heaven—the patriarchal order of God, and Joseph began, on the right and on the left, to add to his family, what a quaking there was in Israel." But, asked Grant, "Did the Prophet Joseph want every man's wife he asked for? He did not but in that thing was the grand thread of the Priesthood developed. The grand object in view was to try the people of God, to see what was in them" (JD 2 [19 Feb. 1854]: 13-14).

In some instances, however, Smith's actions went beyond "trying the people." He sought to marry wives of several living men, refusing to recognize their civil marriage. Despite the clause in the canonized 1835 Mormon marriage statement recognizing that "all legal contracts of marriage made before a person is baptized into this church, should be held sacred and fulfilled," Smith viewed as invalid those marriages not sealed by his blessing. As God's earthly agent, he believed he had been given powers that transcended civil law. Claiming sole responsibility for binding and unbinding marriages on earth and in heaven, he did not consider it necessary to obtain civil marriage licenses or divorce decrees. Whenever he deemed it appropriate he could release a woman from her earthly marriage and seal her to himself or to another with no stigma of adultery.

This thinking is similar, in part, to the revolutionary "spiritual wifery" philosophy of Emanuel Swedenborg (1688-1772). Swedenborg, an eminent Swedish scientist who turned to theology in middle age, wrote a number of books setting forth "heavenly doctrines" which he claimed were based on biblical teachings interpreted by him through direct communication with the spiritual world. "Two souls which grew up together before life are bound to find each other again on earth," he wrote; "in heaven as on earth there are males and females. Man was made for woman and woman for man. Love must unite them eternally, and there are marriages in heaven" (Cairncross 1974, 174-75).

William Hepworth Dixon, describing the Americanization of spiritual wifery, discussed the "theory of Spiritual Wives" as pronounced by Joseph Smith's New York contemporaries, the Perfectionists: "The theory is, that a man who may be either unmarried before the law or wedded to a woman whom he cannot love as a wife should be loved, shall have the right, in virtue of a higher morality, and a more sacred duty than the churches teach him, to go out among the crowd of his female friends, and seek a partner in whom he shall find some special fitness for a union with himself." When he finds such a "bride of the soul," he has the right to court her, "even though she may have taken vows as another man's wife, and of entering into closer and sweeter relations with her than those which belong to the common earth." The Perfectionists taught that all previous "vows on his part and on her part [were] to this end thrust aside as so much worldly waste" (Dixon 1868, 1:88-89).

New England proponents of spiritual wifery in the 1830s were asking such pointed questions as: Does a true marriage on earth imply a true marriage in heaven? Can there be a true marriage of the body without a binding covenant for the soul? Is not the real marriage always that of the soul? Are not all unions which are of the body only, false unions? Dixon noted that leaders of the movement proclaimed that "all true marriages are good for time and for eternity; . . . all other combinations of the two sexes, even though they have [been] sanctioned by the law and blessed by the

42

Church, are null and void" (ibid., 1:94). Erasmus Stone, a prominent Perfectionist leader, taught that "all arrangements for a life in heaven may be made on earth; that spiritual friendships may be formed, and spiritual bonds contracted, valid for eternity" (Ellis 1870).

In many aspects the Perfectionists' theology paralleled Joseph Smith's 1840-44 teachings. His 21 May 1843 diary, for example, records a public address in which he said, "We have no claim in our eternal comfort in relation to Eternal things unless our actions & contracts & all things tend to this end." William Clayton's 16 July 1843 journal notes Smith preaching "that a man must enter into an everlasting covenant with his wife in this world or he will have no claim on her in the next" (Tanner and Tanner). Yet Smith went a step farther than either Swedenborg or the Perfectionists by advocating what he termed "celestial marriage" – a mixture of eternal marriage and polygamy.

Mary Elizabeth Rollins, married to non-Mormon Adam Lightner since 11 August 1835, was one of the first women to accept the "celestial marriage" teachings of the prophet. "He was commanded to take me for a wife," she declared in a 21 November 1880 letter to Emmeline B. Wells. "I was his, before I came here," she added in an 8 February 1902 statement. Brigham Young secretly sealed the two in February 1842 when Mary was eight months pregnant with her son, George Algernon Lightner. She lived with Adam Lightner until his death in Utah many years later. In her 1880 letter to Emmeline B. Wells, Mary explained: "I could tell you why I stayed with Mr. Lightner. Things the leaders of the Church does not know anything about. I did just as Joseph told me to do, as he knew what troubles I would have to contend with."[1] She added in an 1892 letter to John R. Young: "I could explain some things in regard to my living with Mr. L. after becoming the *Wife of Another*, which would throw light, on what *now* seems mysterious – and you would be perfectly satisfied with me. I write this, because I have heard that it had been commented on to my injury."

Sarah M. Kimball, a prominent Nauvoo and Salt Lake Relief Society sister, was also secretly approached by Smith in early 1842. Despite her solid 1840 marriage to non-Mormon Hiram Kimball, Sarah later recalled how Smith taught her "the principle of marriage for eternity, and the doctrine of plural marriage. He said that in teaching this he realized that he jeopardized his life." But, Sarah added, God had "instructed him to teach it with commandment, as the Church could travel (progress) no further without the introduction of this principle" (Jenson, *Historical Record*, 6 [May 1887]: 232). Sarah, however, rejected Smith's polyandrous proposal, asking him to "teach it to someone else." Although she kept the matter quiet, her husband and Smith evidently had difficulties over the incident. On 19 May 1842, at a Nauvoo City Council meeting, Smith jotted down and "threw across the room" a revelation to Kimball which declared that "Hiram Kimball has been insinuating evil, and formulating evil opinions" against the prophet, which if he does not desist from, he "shall be accursed" (HC 5:12-13). Sarah remained a lifetime member of the church and lifelong wife to Hiram Kimball, who eventually joined the church and was killed in a steamship explosion on a mission to Hawaii.

Nancy Marinda Johnson, sister of apostles Luke and Lyman Johnson, married Orson Hyde in 1834. A year before Hyde returned from Jerusalem in 1843, Marinda was sealed to Smith (in April 1842), though she lived with Orson until their divorce in 1870.[2] In another instance, Josephine Lyon Fisher, born to Windsor P. Lyon and Sylvia P. Sessions on 8 February 1844, less than five months before Smith's martyrdom, related in a 24 February 1915 statement her mother's deathbed testimony of 1882: "She then told me that I was the daughter of the Prophet Joseph Smith, she having been sealed to the Prophet at the time that her husband Mr. Lyon was out of fellowship with the Church."[3] Prescindia Huntington married Norman Buell in 1827 and had two sons by him before accepting Mormonism in 1836. She was sealed to Smith by her brother Dimick on 11 December 1841, though she continued to live with Buell until 1846, when she left him to marry Heber C. Kimball.

Prescindia's sister, Zina D. Huntington, lived in the Smith home. Henry B. Jacobs married the twenty-year-old Zina in March 1841. According to family records, when the Jacobs asked Smith why he had not honored them by performing their marriage, allowing John C. Bennett to officiate instead, he replied that "the Lord had made it known to him that she [Zina] was to be his Celestial wife" (Cannon, "History," 5). Believing that "whatever the Prophet did was right, without making the wisdom of God's authorities bend to the reasoning of any man" (ibid.), the devout Jacobs consented for the six-months-pregnant Zina to be sealed to Smith on 27 October 1841. Though sealed to Smith for eternity, she continued her connubial relationship with Jacobs. On 2 February 1846, pregnant with Henry's second son, Zina was resealed by proxy to the murdered Joseph Smith and in that same session was "sealed for time" to Brigham Young. Faithful Henry B. Jacobs stood as an official witness to both ceremonies (ibid., 7).

This polyandrous triangle became even more complex. Zina and Henry lived together as husband and wife until the westward-bound Saints reached Mt. Pisgah, Iowa. At this temporary stop on the pioneer trail, Brigham Young announced "it was time for men who were walking in other men's shoes to step out of them." "Brother Jacobs," he advised, "the woman you claim for a wife does not belong to you. She is the spiritual wife of brother Joseph, sealed up to him. I am his proxy, and she, in this behalf, with her children, are my property. You can go where you please, and get another, but be sure to get one of your own kindred spirit" (Hall 1852, 43-44).

Young then called Jacobs on a mission to England. Witnesses to his departure commented that he was so ill they had to "put him on a blanket and carry him to the boat to get him on his way" (Cannon, "Short Sketch").

Though his health returned, his spirits remained low. On 27 August 1847 his missionary companion and brother-in-law, Oliver Huntington, received a letter from his wife informing the two missionaries that "Zina had gone to Salt Lake City to live with President Young's family" (Firmage). Oliver dashed off a letter to Zina, lamenting that "Henry is here and herd the letter. He says all is right, he don't care. He stands alone as yet. I have had almost as much trial about you as he has. I have had to hear, feel and suffer everything he has – If you only knew my troubles you'd pitty me."

Henry returned from his mission and settled in California. But he was still in love with Zina, now a plural wife of Brigham Young. His letters to her were frequently heartrending. On 2 September 1852 he wrote: "O how happy I should be if I only could see you and the little children, bone of my bone, flesh of my flesh." "I am unhappy," Henry lamented, "there is no peace for poor me, my pleasure is you, my comfort has vanished. . . . O Zina, can I ever, will I ever get you again, answer the question please." In an undated valentine he added: "Zina my mind never will change from Worlds without Ends, no never, the same affection is there and never can be moved I do not murmur nor complain of the handlings of God no verily, no but I feel alone and no one to speak to, to call my own. I feel like a lamb without a mother, I do not blame any person or persons, no – May the Lord our Father bless Brother Brigham and all purtains unto him forever. tell him for me I have no feelings against him nor never had, all is right according to the Law of the Celestial Kingdom of our God Joseph."

One might ask why a man so obviously in love with his wife would give her up to another. Oliver Huntington, writing of this incident in his autobiography, explained: "Zina's husband took to himself another woman before he had returned from England to the Bluffs . . . and [Zina] chose a guardian, who could supply her with whatever she wanted, which she could not get, this supply came from the Church. She became the wife of Brigham Young." Brigham and Zina's only child clarified the incident further: "President Young told Zina D. if she would marry him she would be in a higher glory" (ibid., 15). Brigham himself provided the clearest insight into this situation in an 8 October 1861 General Conference statement on divorce: "There was another way – in which a woman could leave a man – if the woman preferred – another man higher in authority & he is willing to take her. & her husband gives her up – there is no Bill of divorce required in the case it is right in the sight of God" (Beck Notebooks, vol. 1).[4]

Zina Diantha Huntington Jacobs Smith Young was not the only woman sealed in a polyandrous relationship to Brigham Young. Augusta Adams Cobb, baptized a Mormon in 1832, was a stalwart church member in the Boston area. But her husband was not converted. Returning to Boston in the fall of 1844 after an extended visit to Nauvoo, Augusta was quoted in the 22 December 1847 *Boston Post* as having declared to her husband that she loved Brigham Young and, "live or die, she was going to live with him at all hazards." She returned to Nauvoo and her husband successfully sued for divorce. But church leaders had obviously not recognized her civil marriage in the first place; she and Brigham Young had been secretly sealed on 2 November 1843.

"Gentile Law," with its civil marriage, was publicly denounced as early as 1847 by Orson Pratt in a sermon recorded by Wilford Woodruff: "As all the ordinances of the gospel Administered by the world since the Aposticy of the Church was illegal, in like manner was the marriage Cerimony illegal." Thus, according to Pratt, "all the world who had been begotton through the illegal marriage were bastards not Sons & hence they had to enter into the law of adoption & be adopted into the Priesthood in order to become sons & legal heirs to salvation" (Kenney, 3 [27 Aug. 1847]: 260).[5] Elenore McLean, twelfth wife of Apostle Parley P. Pratt, amplified this theology in a 23 November 1869 newspaper interview in the *New York World*. In an 1857 Arkansas dispute, Elenore's legal husband, Hector, murdered her extralegal Mormon husband, Parley. Trying to clear up the confusion of the polyandrous relationship, she dismissed her legal marriage: "The sectarian priests have no power from God to marry; and a so-called marriage ceremony performed by them is no marriage at all" (Pratt 1975, 233).

Elenore was on safe Mormon ground theologically; her source could have been the published writings of her brother-in-law, Orson Pratt. In his church-sponsored *The Seer*, Pratt had explained in 1853: "Marriages, then among all nations, though legal according to the laws of men, have been illegal according to the laws, authority, and institutions of Heaven." As a result, Pratt went on, "all the children born during that long period, though legitimate according to the customs and laws of nations, are illegitimate according to the order and authority of Heaven" (p. 47).

Even Mormon marriages prior to the fall of 1835, when priesthood authority began to be evoked in marriage ceremonies, were adjudged invalid. Joseph Smith's own marriage to Emma Hale 18 January 1827 by Squire Tarbill qualified as "illegal according to the law of heaven." John D. Lee, a member of the secret Council of Fifty and an adopted son of Brigham Young, later commented, "About the same time the doctrine of 'sealing' was introduced . . . the Saints were given to understand that their marriage relations with each other were not valid." That new-found awareness that "they were married to each other only by their own covenants," according to Lee, opened up some interesting possibilities: "If their marriage had not been productive of blessing and peace, and they felt it oppressive to remain together, they were at liberty to make their own choice, as much as if they had not been married" (Lee 1877, 146-47).

Lee, though a hostile witness at the time of this narrative, is supported by earlier accounts of Mormon marriage customs in Nauvoo. Increase

McGee and his wife, Maria, a couple who participated in sacred temple rites and later wrote about the experience, viewed the ceremonies as "the commencement of the Law of god, and the laws of the land are no more binding on us; all our former ties of marriage, &c., are all now cut asunder, and we are all thrown loose upon the world as if never married." Thus "it is now the woman's privilege to choose whom she sees fit; if she likes the one she had been living with, she can keep him; if not, she is at liberty to ship him and take another; and it is the man's privilege to have one, two, four, ten, or twenty, according to his standing in the church." The couple thus clarified the "object a man has in getting more than one wife": "He is to be promoted through all eternity, according to this theory, by his posterity, which are the subjects of his dominion; and of course the more wives, the more numerous his posterity" (1847, 16.)[6]

Emphasis on posterity formed the framework for Smith's concept of the "Kingdom of God." His friend Benjamin F. Johnson recalled, as an elderly patriarch, that "the Prophet taught us that Dominion & power in the great Future would be Comensurate with the no[.] of 'Wives Childin & Friends' that we inherit here and that our great mission to earth was to Organize a *Nucli* of *Heaven* to take with us. To the increace of which there would be no end" (Zimmerman 1976, 47). Smith, viewing earthly and heavenly ordinances as inextricably intertwined, considered himself "God's earthly agent." After establishing a secret 1844 organization, the Council of Fifty, to promote in part his U.S. presidential candidacy, the prophet was clandestinely crowned a "King, Priest, and Ruler Over Israel on Earth" (Quinn 1980, 163-97). His kingdom, like Old Testament kingdoms, was patriarchal in nature. Salvation for women depended on their being sealed to a "Lord" – a worthy man.

Orson Pratt, eventually recognized as the "Apostle of Polygamy" for his spirited defenses of the principle, published the first theological discussion on the necessity of a woman's being sealed to a worthy man in order to receive heavenly exaltation: "You will clearly perceive from the revelation which God has given that you can never obtain a fulness of glory without being married to a righteous man for time and for all eternity." To fail to do so meant "losing the privilege of enjoying the society of a husband in eternity. You forfeit your right to an endless increase of immortal lives. And even the children which you may be favored with in this life will not be entrusted to your charge in eternity; but you will be left in that world without a husband, without a family, without a kingdom." Mormon marriage theology relegated those with marital failures to the role of "servants and angels" (Pratt 1854, 140).

Steeped in such philosophy, married Mormon women such as Mary Elizabeth Lightner, Sylvia Sessions, Prescendia Buell, Zina D. H. Jacobs, Augusta Cobb, and Elenore McLean were persuaded that their non-Mormon or Mormon laymen husbands could not take them to the highest degree of the Celestial Kingdom. A Mormon male of hierarchical rank, his feet firmly planted in the priesthood, seemed a more sure ticket to heaven.

1. After her sealing, or marriage, to Smith, Mary Lightner had seven more children by Adam Lightner. It was not unusual for Smith to encourage his polyandrous wives to remain with their legal husbands. Joseph Kingsbury wrote that he served as a surrogate husband for the prophet: "I according to Pres[ident]. Joseph Smith & Council & others, I agreed to stand by Sarah Ann Whitney [sealed to Smith 27 July 1843] as though I was supposed to be her husband and a pretended marriage for the purpose of shielding them from the enemy and for the purpose of bringing about the purposes of God" (p. 5).

2. Faulring 1987, 396; see also Quinn, "Prayer Circles," 98. According to Nancy Hyde's testimony during the 1860s, however, she was sealed to Smith in May 1843 (Bachman 1975, 333).

Smith was also sealed by proxy to Mary Ann Frost, wife of Apostle Parley P. Pratt, on 6 February 1846. She had had difficulty accepting Pratt's polygamy and had become alienated from him. Parley wrote in the diary of plural wife Belinda Marden on 11 March 1851 that "By mutual concent of parties and by the advise of President Young [Mary Ann was] sealed to Joseph Smith [the deceased president of the church] for Eternity and to her former husband [Parley] for time, as proxy." Similarly, in 1870 Apostle Amasa Lyman, excommunicated for "teaching false doctrine," was left by one of his wives, who was afterwards sealed to Smith. Her daughter recorded that Caroline Partridge Lyman "felt she must have the protection and the security of the Priesthood in her children's lives. . . . Evidently in her dire circumstances she felt that the Prophet was the only secure anchor to be sealed to" (Lyman 1958, 280).

3. Josephine L. Fisher statement to Andrew Jenson, 24 Feb. 1915. On 12 October 1905 Angus M. Cannon discussed this incident with Joseph Smith III and his son Frederick. In response to the elder Smith's inquiry, "where is the issue in evidence of my father's having married plural wives," Cannon described "one case where it was said by the girl's grandmother that your father has a daughter born of a plural wife. The girl's grandmother was Mother Sessions, who lived in Nauvoo and died here in the valley. Aunt Patty Sessions," according to Cannon, "asserts that the girl was born within the time after your father was said to have taken the mother" (Cannon, "Statement").

The question of whether Joseph Smith cohabited with his wives has long intrigued Mormons. Emily Partridge said she "roomed" with him (*Complainants*, 364, 367, 394), and Melissa Lott Willis testified she was his wife "in very deed" (Bailey 1952, 98-100). The fact that Emma Smith so strongly opposed her husband's polygamy implies she was concerned about the possibility of physical rather than spiritual relationships. But those who disbelieve Smith's involvement in polygamy raise a significant issue: Where are the children? Lucy Walker, sealed to Smith on 1 May 1842, explained that because of his "hazardous life he lived in constant fear of being betrayed by those who ought to have been true to him" (Kimball, "Recollections," 41). However, Lucy lived in Smith's home, under Emma's watchful eye. Sarah Ann Whitney did not. She was sealed to Smith with her parents' permission on 27 July 1842. In an 18 August 1842 letter to the Whitneys, Smith, hiding from Missouri law enforcement officials, detailed his problems in getting to see Sarah Ann without Emma's knowledge. "My feelings are so strong for you since what has pased lately between us . . . if you three would come and see me in this my lonely retreat, it would afford me great relief, of mind, if those with whom I am allied, do love me, now is the time to Afford me succor . . . the only thing to be careful is to find out when Emma comes then you cannot be safe, but when she is not here, there is the most perfect safety."

Mary Elizabeth Lightner provided further perspective. "I knew he had three children," she said in a 1905 statement. "They told me. I think two of them are living today but they are not known as his children as they go by other names." Though the matter is highly speculative, these three mentioned children may be Josephine L. Fisher, Zebulun Jacobs (b. 2 Jan. 1842), and Mary Lightner's own son, George Algernon (b. 22 March 1842). Zina H. Jacobs and Mary Lightner were both in advanced stages of pregnancy when Smith was sealed to them. Oliver Buell (b. 1838-39), son of Prescindia Huntington Buell, is also considered by some to be a possible son of Joseph Smith, though he was born before the prophet was sealed to his mother on 11 December 1841 (Brodie 1975, 301-302).

4. Young's theology came from Joseph Smith. Wilford Woodruff wrote in his 2 June 1857 journal: "Brigham Young Said Joseph taught that when a womans affections was entirely weaned from her husband that was Adultery in spirit. Her Affections were Adulterated from his. He also said that there was No law in Heaven or on Earth that would Compel a woman to stay with a man either in time or Eternity." When asked what would happen if a woman did not wish to go with a high priest who claimed her, Young replied: "You will find then that any man who gets a glory & exaltation will be so beautiful that any woman will be willing to have him if it was right – & whereever it is right for the woman to go thare she will be willing to go for all those evils will vanish to which we are subject in this life" (Kenney 1983-85, 5: 55-56).

5. Pratt added in 1873: "I said their [non-Mormon] baptisms are illegal. Now let me go a little further, and say that the ordinance of marriage is illegal among all people, nations and tongues, unless administered by a man appointed by new revelation from God to join the male and female as husband and wife" (JD, 16 [31 Aug. 1873]: 175).

6. A similar account is found in a contemporary letter: "The Saints are carrying on amongst themselves worse than ever, the council had declared all marriages null and void giving either party leave to choose for themselves if they agree to live together, then the man has the right to as many more wives as he can get to live with but his first wife is mistress of all" (Hardin to Warren, 12).

7. For a complete discussion of Mormon polyandry, see Van Wagoner 1985.

Five

"If a Man Espouse a Virgin"

Perhaps the most disturbing aspect of the Bennett scandal for Joseph Smith was that it kept him from preaching plural marriage publicly. Exactly four weeks after his 1 October 1842 denunciation of polygamy in the *Times and Seasons*, another publication from the church press was released. *The Peace Maker*, a thirty-seven-page booklet, skillfully articulated scriptural and theological justifications for polygamy. Udney Hay Jacob announced in the preface that "the author of this work is not a Mormon, although it is printed by their press. . . . But the public will soon find out what he is, by his work." An intriguing ending to the treatise suggested that "the question is not now to be debated whether these things are so; neither is it a question of much importance who wrote this book? But the question, the momentous question is: *will you now restore the law of God on this important subject, and keep it?*"[1]

Coming on the tail of John Bennett's lurid spiritual wifery/polygamy accusations against Smith, *The Peace Maker*'s call for a restoration of polygamy caused a stir in Nauvoo. Oliver Olney expressed what must have been an often thought though seldom expressed opinion: "If the pamphlet was not written by the authorities of the Church, it by them was revised in Jacobs name" (1843, 10). But Smith responded to the uproar by saying that the work was published "without my knowledge," adding "had I been apprised of it, I should not have printed it[,] not that I am opposed to any man enjoying his privileges, but I do not wish to have my name associated with the authors, in such an unmeaning rigmarole of nonsense, folly and trash" (TS 4 [1 Dec. 1842]: 32).

Despite Smith's denial, it is difficult to understand how such a controversial work could have been typeset and published in the *Times and Seasons* office without his knowledge. Smith was, in fact, editor of the newspaper, and apostles John Taylor and Wilford Woodruff worked in the office. And though his own brother Hyrum decried the publication as coming "from beneath" (Lee 1877, 246), Smith's own denunciation of the work was not nearly as emphatic. Some may have even concluded that his willingness in allowing a man to "enjoy his privileges" was a cryptic approval of polygamy. It is possible, as John D. Lee later suggested, that Smith commissioned Jacob to put forth his work as a "feeler among the people to pave the way for celestial marriage" (ibid.).

If the *Peace Maker* was intended to evaluate the reaction of Nauvoo Saints towards polygamy, it was not the first such test. Helen Mar Kimball Whitney, the fifteen-year-old plural wife of Smith and daughter of Apostle Heber C. Kimball, recounted in 1882 another trial balloon for polygamy remembered by her mother: "On a certain Sabbath morning, previous to the return of the Apostles from Europe, in 1841, [Joseph] astonished his hearers by preaching on the restoration of all things, and said that as it was anciently with Abraham, Isaac, and Jacob, so it would be again, etc. He spoke so plainly that his wife, Emma, as well as others were quite excited over it. Seeing the effect his sermon had upon them, he consoled them in the afternoon by saying that the time of which he had spoken might be further off than he anticipated" (Whitney, "Plural Marriage," 11).

Joseph Lee Robinson, who was in attendance that day, later remembered Smith's discussing possible difficulties missionaries could encounter in "Turkey or India or to a people where it was lawfull to have several wives where they practiced Poligamy." Smith envisioned a Muslim asking, "I have five wives and I love one equally as well as I do the other and now what are the laws in that land, can I bring my five wives there and enjoy them as well as I can here, said the Prophet yes, the laws in Zion are such that you can bring your wives and enjoy them as well as there."

But Smith had underestimated the extent of the opposition of Nauvoo women, especially his wife. When he "went to his dinner," Robinson wrote, "as it might be expected several of the first women of the church collected at the Prophet's house with his wife [and] said thus to the Prophet Joseph O mister Smith you have done it now it will never do it is all but Blassphemy you must take back what you have said to day it is outragious it would ruin us as a people." So in the afternoon session Smith again took the stand, according to Robinson, and said, "Brethren and Sisters I take back what we said this morning and leave it as though there had been nothing said" (pp. 23-24).

Smith's denials of polygamy were accepted at face value by most Saints. But Emma so strongly suspected her husband of practicing it that she enlisted support from other anti-polygamy women to keep track of him. Joseph Lee Robinson wrote of one such alliance. Angeline, wife of his brother Ebenezer, "watched Brother Joseph the Prophet[,] had seen him go into some house that she had reported to Sister Emma the wife of the Prophet[.] it was at a time when she was very suspisious and jealous of him for fear he would get another wife." Robinson alleged that Emma was so angry she "said she would leave and was making preparations to go to her People in The State of New York it came close to breaking up his family."[2]

The Smiths' bitter differences over polygamy reached a peak in early 1843. Eliza Roxcy Snow, "Zion's Poetess," had been living in the Smith home since 14 August 1842. Her sealing to Smith two months earlier on 29 June had been kept secret from Emma. Apparently Emma later found out about the relationship, for Eliza abruptly moved into the Jonathan Holmes residence on 11 February 1843 (Beecher 1975, 402). Eliza's absence from the Smith home evidently left a void in the prophet's life. Within two weeks he had focused his attention on two other women living in his home.

Emily and Eliza Partridge, youthful daughters of deceased church bishop Edward Partridge, had been living in poverty after moving to Nauvoo in early 1840. Emma Smith invited Emily to live in the Smith home to care for the Smiths' baby, Don Carlos, who was born 13 June 1840. Eliza Partridge joined the family a short time later. Emily later wrote that in the spring or summer of 1842 Joseph Smith approached her about polygamy. "I . . . shut him up so quick," she said, "that he said no more to me until the 28th of Feb. 1843, (my nineteenth birthday)" (Young, "Life," 185). On this date Smith approached her privately, saying, "Emily, if you will not betray me, I will tell you something for your benefit." When he asked her if she would burn a private letter he wanted to send to her, Emily replied that she could not accept it from him. But she reconsidered. On 4 March 1843 Smith sent a "friend to plurality," Mrs. Elizabeth Durfee, with a message. When Partridge asked the envoy what Smith wanted, Durfee replied "she thought he wanted me for a wife." At a clandestine meeting later that evening at the Heber C. Kimball home, Emily later recounted, Smith advised her that "the Lord had commanded him to enter into plural marriage, and had given me to him, and although I had got badly frightened, he knew I would yet have him, so he waited till the Lord told him." Emily agreed to Smith's proposal and "was married there and then."[3]

Emily subsequently explained that though she did not know it at the time, her older sister Eliza had also been approached by Elizabeth Durfee, who "introduced the subject of *spiritual wives* as they called it in those days."[4] The older Partridge girl was sealed to Smith on 8 March 1843. Emma Smith knew nothing of these relationships at the time, but two months later Smith apparently convinced his wife to let him be sealed to the girls with her blessing. According to Emily's account, "Emma had consented to give Joseph two wives, if he would let her choose them for him, and she chose E[liza] and myself. . . . I do not know why she gave us to him, unless she thought we were where she could watch us better than some others, outside of the house" (Jenson, *Historical Record* 6 [July 1887]: 226). "To save family trouble," Emily added in an 1887 account of the matter, "Brother Joseph thought it best to have another ceremony performed. Accordingly on the 11th of May, 1843, we were sealed to Joseph Smith a second time, in Emma's presence" (Young, "Life," 185).

Emily is probably incorrect on the date of the second sealing. On 11 May, Emma Smith left Nauvoo at 10:00 a.m. for Quincy, Illinois, and did not return for four days. Unless the ceremony was performed at an early hour, she could not have been in attendance. Moreover James Adams,[5] a Sangamo County probate judge who performed the second sealing, did not arrive in Nauvoo from Springfield until 21 May. The sealing most likely occurred two days later. Smith's journal entry for 23 May reads: "At home. in conversation with Judge Adams, and others." In discussing the impact of the event, Emily later noted that "Emma seemed to feel well until the ceremony was over . . . [but] before the day was over she turned around or repented of what she had done and kept Joseph up till very late in the night talking to him." This closely matches William Clayton's journal entry for 23 May: "Pres[iden]t. stated to me that he had had a little trouble with sis. E[mma] he was asking E[liza] Partridge concerning [Joseph] Jackson['s][6] conduct during Prest.['s] absence & E[mma] came up stairs. he shut to the door not knowing who it was and held it. She came to the door & called Eliza 4 times & tried to force open the door."

Smith may not have provided his scribe with all the details of this situation. What, for example, was the source of Emma's irritation? Did finding Joseph and Eliza privately together bring back jealous memories of Fanny Alger or Eliza R. Snow? Or did Emma discover that Smith's relationship with Eliza Partridge was more than "spiritual?" Emma had not been told about her husband's first sealing to the Partridge girls. Perhaps she had been similarly misled regarding the real purpose of the second sealing as well.

There is evidence to suggest that on at least one other occasion Smith convinced one of his would-be young wives to accept polygamy by persuading her that it was a "spiritual order and not a temporal one." Helen Mar Kimball, fifteen-year-old daughter of Apostle Heber C. Kimball, reported that Smith told her: "If you will take this step, it will insure your eternal salvation & exaltation and that of your father's household & all of your kindred." "This promise was so great," Helen felt, "that I willingly gave myself to purchase so glorious a reward" (Whitney, "Retrospection"). "I thought through *this life* my time will be my own," she wrote in a letter to be opened after her death, "the step I now am taking's for eternity alone" (ibid.). But she reportedly had misinterpreted Smith's intent. She confided to a close friend in Nauvoo: "I would never have been sealed to Joseph had I known it was anything more than ceremony. I was young, and they deceived me, by saying the salvation of our whole family depended on it" (Lewis 1848, 19). If this ruse were used to convince Emma Smith to accept the Partridge girls as "spiritual wives," her dismay at finding her husband and Eliza Partridge together in an upstairs room the day of the sealing would be understandable.

Emily Partridge wrote that from that day forth Emma became a bitter enemy of the girls. "She wanted us immediately divorced, and she seemed to think that she only had to say the word and it was done" (Whitney, "Plural Marriage," 15). Furthermore, Emily wrote, Emma "kept close watch of us. If we were missing for a few minutes, and Joseph was not at home, the house was searched from top to bottom and from one end to the other, and if we were not found, the neighborhood was searched until we were found." Emma soon reached her limit of tolerance. Emily wrote that Emma called the two girls to her room, where they found a subdued prophet with Emma. "Joseph was present, looking like a martyr. Emma said some very hard things – Joseph would give us up or blood should flow. She would rather her blood would run pure than be polluted in this manner."

Insisting that Smith and the girls "promise to break our covenants that we had made before God," Emma told the prophet that "she would cease to trouble us, and not persist in our marrying some one else." The promises were made, Emily wrote, and "Joseph came to us and shook hands with us, and the understanding was that all was ended between us." The girls went downstairs while Joseph and Emma remained in the upper part of the house. When Smith came down, Emily noted, he "looked as if he would sink into the earth." Declaring "my hands are tied," he left the room. Emma came in "on his track," as Emily put it, and asked, "Emily, what did Joseph say to you?" "He asked me how I felt," Partridge replied. "You might as well tell me," Emma insisted, "for I am determined that a stop shall be put to these things, and I want you to tell me what he says to you." The feisty Emily responded, "I shall not tell you, he can say what he pleases to me, and I shall not report it to you, as there has been mischief enough made, by doing that. I am as sick of these things as you can be."

The Partridge sisters did not remarry until after Smith's death,[7] but they did move from the Smith home shortly after the confrontation, and Emily said she only spoke to the prophet once before his murder in 1844. Ironically, sometime after the Partridges left, the prophet was sealed to two other young women living in his home. Emily Partridge noted that "[Emma] afterwards gave Sarah and Maria Lawrence to him, and they lived in the house as his wifes. I knew this" (Young, "Life," 186).[8]

Emma was not the only Smith strongly opposed to polygamy. Joseph received almost as much opposition from his brother Hyrum as from Emma. After citing an anti-polygamy passage from the Book of Mormon (2 Jac.) in his 14 May 1843 public denouncement of the practice, Hyrum "Said there were many that had a great deal to say about the ancient order of things Solomon & David having many wifes & Concubines – but its an abomination in the Sight of God. . . . If an angel from heaven should come and preach such doctrine, [you] would be sure to see his cloven foot and cloud of blackness over his head" (Levi Richards Journal, 14 May 1843).

The following day Hyrum joined William Law, William Marks, and perhaps others in a conspiracy to ferret out evidence of Smith's polygamous relationships. William Clayton recorded in his 23 May diary a conversation with Heber C. Kimball "concerning a plot that is being laid to entrap the brethren [involved in polygamy] . . . by bro H[yrum], and others." Hyrum related to Marks that "he did not believe in it [polygamy] and he was going to see Joseph about it, and if Joseph had a revelation on the subject, he would believe it" (Newell and Avery 1984, 141).

Before he had a chance to talk with Joseph, however, Hyrum ran into Brigham Young. Young reported in an 1866 address that the two sat down together on fence rails piled on the Masonic Hall lot. According to Young, Hyrum said he knew that "you and the twelve know some things that I do not know. I can understand this by the motions, and talk, and doings of Joseph, and I know there is something or other, which I do not understand, that is revealed to the Twelve. Is this so?" The canny Young, aware of Hyrum's entrapment plans, replied: "I do not know any thing about what you know, but I know what I know."

But Hyrum would not be denied: "I have mistrusted for a long time that Joseph has received a revelation that a man should have more than one wife, and he has hinted as much to me, but I would not bear it. . . . I am convinced that there is something that has not been told me." Young requested Hyrum to "sware with an uplifted hand, before God, that you will never say another word against Joseph and his doings, and the doctrines he is preaching to the people." After Hyrum consented, Young revealed: "Joseph had many wives sealed to him. I told him the whole story, and he bowed to it and wept like a child, and said 'God be praised.' He went to Joseph and told him what he had learned, and renewed his covenant with Joseph" (Young, Unpublished Address).

Evidently it was at this time that Smith explained to Hyrum the full meaning of "celestial marriage." Hyrum's first wife, Jerusha Barden, had died on 13 October 1837. Smith explained: "You can have her sealed to you upon the same principle as you can be baptized for the dead." "What can I do for my second wife?" Hyrum asked. "You can also make a covenant with her for eternity and have her sealed to you by the authority of the Priesthood," the prophet advised. Hyrum discussed the ordinance with his living wife, Mary Fielding Smith, and she responded, "I will act as proxy for your wife that is dead and I will be sealed to you for eternity myself for I never had any other husband. I love you and I do not want to be separated from you nor be forever alone in the world to come" (Ms History, 8 April 1844).

Less than two months later Hyrum became the catalyst for Smith's receiving the key revelation on "celestial marriage" (D&C 132). On 12 July the brothers, along with William Clayton, were in Smith's office discussing

Emma's opposition to polygamy. Hyrum still harbored concerns that polygamy was adulterous. Charles Smith, a Nauvoo elder, later said that Hyrum told the Elders' Quorum in the winter of 1843-44 "that the doctrine of Plurality of Wives had bothered him considerably and he felt constrained to ask wherein Abraham, Moses, David & others could be justified before God in practicing this to him repugnant doctrine—He asked his brother the Prophet Joseph to ask the question of the Lord—Joseph did so and the Revelation given 12 July 1843 was the answer" (St. George Record).

The new revelation called for the restoration of biblical polygamy, integrated within the framework of sealing for time and eternity. All marriages not sealed by the power of the priesthood were "of no efficacy, virtue, or force in and after the resurrection." Those persons sealed under this new law were advised that they would come forth in the first resurrection and, in the life after death, would inherit thrones, kingdoms, principalities, powers, and dominions. Announcing that a throne was prepared for Smith "in the kingdom of my Father, with Abraham your father," the revelation thus described "the law of the priesthood": "If any man espouse a virgin, and desire to espouse another, and the first give her consent, and if he espouse the second, and they are virgins, and have vowed to no other man, then he is justified: he cannot commit adultery." Yet "if one or either of the ten virgins, after she is espoused, shall be with another man, she has committed adultery, and shall be destroyed; for they are given unto him to multiply and replenish the earth."

This emphasis on procreation became the basis for the Mormon concept of humanity's progress to divinity. All of Smith's Nauvoo doctrinal innovations fell into place around this new teaching. Smith explained that God was an exalted man and that mortal existence was a testing ground for men to begin progress toward exalted godhood. Salvation became a family affair revolving around a husband whose plural wives and children were sealed to him for eternity under the "new and everlasting covenant."

According to this developing theology, the family extended backward as well as forward in time. Smith had already taught that the Saints had spiritual obligation towards unenlightened dead ancestors and friends in the 15 August 1840 funeral of Elder Seymour Brunson. Discussing the new principle of "baptism for the dead," Smith had said that "people could now act for their friends who had departed this life, and that the plan of salvation was calculated to save all those who were willing to obey the requirements of the law of God" (JH, 15 May 1840). Plank by plank, the theological framework for the new eternal Mormon social order continued to build upon the numerous revelations and ordinances advanced by Smith. The Nauvoo temple became the foundation for this "restoration of all things," the 12 July 1843 revelation on "celestial marriage" (D&C 132) the capstone.

Because Smith had begun to practice polygamy earlier than 1843, Mormon leaders after his death concluded that the revelation was given as early as 1831 and merely written down on 12 July 1843. A more reasonable explanation is that while Smith may have justified biblical polygamy at an early period in his life, the revelation on celestial marriage was a document contemporary to 12 July 1843. Smith's journal entry for the day pointedly says: "Received a Revelation in the office in presence of Hyrum & Wm Clayton." And the 25 August 1843 entry in the *History of the Church* reads: "My brother Hyrum in the office conversing with me about the new revelation upon celestial marriage."[9] Furthermore, Smith's nephew, Joseph F. Smith, declared in an 1878 Salt Lake City speech that "when the revelation was written, in 1843, it was for a special purpose, at the request of the Patriarch Hyrum Smith, and was not then designed to go forth to the church or to the world. It is most probable that had it been then written with a view to its going out as a doctrine of the church, it would have been presented in a somewhat different form." Smith gave as evidence of his conclusion the fact that "there are personalities contained in a part of it which are not relevant to the principle itself, but rather to the circumstances which necessitated its being written at that time" (JD 20 [7 July 1878]: 29).

One of the personalities mentioned in the revelation is Emma Smith. The intent of the revelation was obviously to convince her to accept what she had been resisting. William Clayton, in an 1874 affidavit, reported that Hyrum had asked Joseph on 12 July 1843, "If you will write the revelation on celestial marriage, I will take it and read it to Emma, and I believe I can convince her of its truth, and you will hereafter have peace." Joseph, knowing better the extent of her opposition, replied, "You do not know Emma as well as I do." Hyrum pleaded, "The doctrine is so plain, I can convince any reasonable man or woman of its truth, purity and heavenly origin." So the prophet agreed to dictate the revelation to Clayton. After three hours, Smith commented that "there was much more that he could write on the same subject, but what was written was sufficient for the present" (Jenson, *Historical Record* 6 [July 1887]: 226).

It was not sufficient for Emma. Hyrum returned a short time later after delivering the document to her and said "he had never received a more severe talking to in his life . . . Emma was very bitter."[10] Perhaps Emma resented the revelation's threatening tone. Verse 52 directed "mine handmaid, Emma Smith," to "receive all those that have been given unto my servant Joseph." "If she will not abide this," the "commandment" warned, "she shall be destroyed." Adding insult to injury, the revelation directed Emma to "forgive my servant Joseph his trespasses; and then shall she be forgiven her trespasses against me."

Though Emma's "trespasses" are not spelled out, Clayton's 23 June 1843 diary suggests a relevant concern of the prophet's. Smith told Clayton that Emma was "disposed to be revenged on him for some things[;] she thought that if he would indulge himself she would too." Evidently sometime prior to this date Smith had offered his wife a surrogate husband to compensate for his plural wives but later had second thoughts. Perhaps Smith thought Emma had her eye on William Clayton. On 29 May Clayton wrote in his diary that Smith asked him "if I had used any familiarity with E[mma]. I told him by no means & explained to his satisfaction."

Considerable light on this obscure situation is shed by the 12 July revelation. Verse 51 contains a commandment "unto mine handmaid, Emma Smith, your wife, whom I have given unto you, that she stay herself, and partake not of that which I commanded you to offer unto her; for I did it, saith the Lord, to prove you all, as I did Abraham, and that I might require an offering at your hand, by covenant and sacrifice." Verse 54 directs Emma to "abide and cleave unto my servant Joseph and to none else." Though Smith may have been suspicious of Clayton, his deeper concern appears to have been directed toward his counselor William Law. Joseph H. Jackson, a non-Mormon opportunist who gained the confidence of Smith in Nauvoo, recorded in an 1844 expose of Mormonism: "Emma wanted Law for a spiritual husband" because Joseph "had so many spiritual wives, she thought it but fair that she would at least have one man spiritually sealed up to her and that she wanted Law, because he was such a 'sweet little man' " (p. 20).

Emma's threat to "be revenged and indulge herself" may have been merely a warning to the prophet to give up polygamy. Though Smith and Law had serious difficulties in 1844 over Smith's polyandrous proposals to Law's wife, Jane, there is no evidence to suggest that Law and Emma were ever anything more than friends. Furthermore, Law in 1887 denied his involvement in a "spiritual swop": "Joseph Smith never proposed anything of the kind to me or to my wife; both he and Emma knew our sentiments in reaction to spiritual wives and polygamy; he knew that we were immovably opposed to polygamy in any and every form." Law did confirm, however, that the stories came about because "Joseph offered to furnish his wife Emma with a substitute for him, by way of compensation for his neglect of her, on condition that she would forever stop her opposition to polygamy and permit him to enjoy his young wives in peace and keep some of them in his house and to be well treated etc." ("Mormons in Nauvoo").

If the purpose of the 12 July revelation was to convince Emma to accept the plural wives her husband had previously taken, it failed. The revelation would became the law of the church in 1852, despite the destruction of the original copy. On 12 July 1843, after Hyrum returned from being rebuked by Emma, the revelation was read to several other church leaders. Towards evening Bishop Newel K. Whitney asked Joseph if he could make a copy of the document. William Clayton noted that "it was carefully copied the following day by Joseph C. Kingsbury." A few days later Smith related to Clayton and several others that, according to Clayton, "Emma had so teased, and urgently entreated him for the privilege of destroying [the revelation], that he became so weary of her teasing, and to get rid of her annoyance, he told her she might destroy it[,] and she had done so, but he had consented to her wish in this matter to pacify her, realizing that he knew the revelation perfectly, and could rewrite it at any time if necessary" (Jenson, *Historical Record* 6 [July 1887]: 226). It is unlikely that Emma was told a copy of the revelation had been made.

Brigham Young in Salt Lake City later recounted his version of the story: "Emma took that revelation, supposing she had all there was[,] . . . went to the fireplace and put it in, and put the candle under it and burned it, and she thought that was the end of it, and she will be damned as sure as she is a living woman" (JD 17 [9 Aug. 1874]: 159). Emma's version, as later recalled by William McLellin from an 1847 conversation with her, differs considerably. She said that one night after she and Smith had gone to bed, "he told her that polygamy would be the ruin of the church. He wanted her to get the revelation and burn it. But she refused to touch it, even with tongs." McLellin said that Smith then got out of bed and burned the revelation himself (McLellin to Smith).

The purported revelation-burning incident may have occurred the same evening the document was first written. Clayton recorded in his 13 July 1843 journal that Smith called him "into his private room with E[mma] and there stated an agreement they had mutually entered into[.] they both stated their feelings on many subjects & wept considerable. O may the Lord soften her heart that she may be willing to keep and abide by his Holy law." Whatever transpired in their personal conversations during this period, Emma remained unconvinced of the correctness of polygamy, and Smith continued to take additional wives without her knowledge or consent. Three days after he and Emma had entered into their "agreement," Smith provided a window into the situation in an address in which he "preached . . . concerning a mans foes being they of his own house" (Joseph Smith Diary, 15 July 1843). Apparently Emma had uncovered additional evidence that the prophet had taken other women to wife without her knowledge. While Emma was on a trip to St. Louis, Lucy Walker, a seventeen-year-old "dining room girl" living in the Smith home, had been sealed to Smith by William Clayton on 1 May 1843.[11] The next morning, prior to Emma's afternoon arrival at the steamboat landing, Clayton noted Smith had spent the morning riding with sixteen-year-old Flora Woodworth, an activity which was probably noticed by others as well.[12] Eliza R. Snow described in her 20 July 1843 journal a visit from an angry woman—evidently Emma Smith. "Her appearance," Snow wrote, "very plainly manifested the perturbation of her mind."

Incidents evoking Emma's anger and jealousy multiplied. On 16 August Clayton noted in his journal that Smith told him "since E[mma] came back from St. Louis she had resisted the P[riesthood] in toto & he had to tell her he would relinquish all for her sake. She said she would [have] given him E[mily] and E[liza] P[artridge] but he knew if he took them she would pitch on him & obtain a divorce & leave him. He however told me he should not relinquish any thing." Five days later, after Smith had promised to "relinquish all," Clayton noted a confrontation he had had with Emma in his 21 August diary. He explained that Emma had produced two letters to Smith she had discovered in her husband's pockets and wanted to know if Clayton had delivered them. Clayton recorded, "I had not done it. I satisfied her I had not. They appeared to be from E[liza] R. Snow . . . E[mma] seemed vexed and angry." Two days later Smith dropped Emma off at the Lucian Woodworth home while he attended to some business at the temple. Clayton noted in his 23 August diary that Smith told him when he returned to pick Emma up "she was demanding the gold watch of F[lora]," the Woodworth's daughter. (Smith had given a similar watch to Eliza R. Snow.) Emma was furious. Smith told Clayton that he "reproved her for her evil treatment [but] on the way home she abused him much & also when he got home. He had to use harsh measures to put a stop to her abuse but finally succeeded."

Emma's position should be viewed in perspective. She loved her husband and desired the exclusive relationship he had promised her in their 1827 marriage covenant. Furthermore, she was thirty-nine years old—no longer a young woman—and found herself competing for her husband's affections with younger women. Utah Mormons have traditionally shown little sympathy to Emma because of her rejection of plural marriage and her refusal to go west with Brigham Young and his followers. Emily Partridge, closer to Emma's circumstances than most, displayed remarkable empathy for her in her 1883 diary: "After these many years I can truly say; poor Emma. She could not stand polygamy, but she was a good woman, and I never wish to stand in her way of happiness and exaltation. I hope the Lord will be merciful to her, and I believe he will. . . . Perhaps she has done no worse than any of us would have done in her place. Let the Lord be the judge."

NOTES

1. Jacob's scriptural and literary background was known to church leaders. Two years earlier he had written a book on baptism and sent an extract to Joseph Smith's close friend Oliver Granger, requesting that he show it to "your Printer, & to Joseph Smith, and to Sidney Rigdon, and let them refute it if they can" (Jacob to Granger, 3 March 1840). Jacob joined the church in 1843 and died in Salt Lake City in 1860. In a 5 March 1851 letter to Brigham Young, Jacob said he wrote the *Peace Maker* "for the citizens of the United States, who professed to believe in the bible." He also added that it served as an "apology for this people [Mormons] who were accused by them of Polygamy." For a complete discussion of the *Peace Maker* controversy see Foster 1974, 21-34, and Foster 1981, 174-77.

2. Robinson Journal, 49. Robinson added that Smith was so upset over the incident that he had a talk with Angeline, but "she would not give him any satisfaction, and her husband [Ebenezer] did not reprove his wife, and it came to pass, the Prophet cursed her severely, but they thought it would not take effect because he the Prophet was angry." This late 1841 incident appears to be the reason for Smith's abrupt release of Ebenezer Robinson as *Times and Seasons* editor.

Respecting Emma's use of the Relief Society to curtail polygamy, Emily P. Young noted: "She took occasion from the President to work upon the sister's feelings, and cause them to betray their brethren who were in polygamy and in that way brought about much trouble for Joseph and his true hearted brethren" (Young, "Incidents").

3. The Partridge account, except where noted otherwise, is from Emily Dow Partridge Young's "Autobiographical Sketch."

4. Elizabeth Davis Durfee was sealed by proxy to Joseph Smith on 22 January 1846 in the Nauvoo Temple (Quinn, "Prayer Circles," 88).

5. James Adams (1783-1843) became a Mormon in 1840. An intimate friend to Joseph Smith, he was in the first group of Endowment Council initiates on 4-5 May 1842. He was also an early polygamist, sealed to Roxena Repshire on 11 July 1843. Smith anointed him to the office of patriarch in the fall of 1843 (Walgren 1982, 121-36).

6. Jackson, a newcomer to Nauvoo, was a non-Mormon opportunist who passed himself off, according to Smith's diary, as a Catholic priest but said that he told Joseph he was a fugitive from justice.

7. Emily later married Brigham Young; Eliza married Apostle Amasa Lyman.

8. Maria (1823-1847) and Sarah (1826-1872) Lawrence, seventeen- and nineteen-year-old Canadians, were the daughters of Edward and Margaret Lawrence. Considering Emma's strong reaction to the Partridge girls' relationship with her husband, it seems unlikely that she would have willingly consented to another pair of sealings. Evidence for her having done so is secondhand. The statement of Lucy Walker, who was sealed to Smith on 1 May 1843, is typical: "I can also say that Emma Smith was present and did consent to Eliza and Emily Partridge. Also Maria and Sarah Lawrence being sealed to her husband. This I had from [Joseph's] own lips, also the testimony of [Emma's] niece. Hyrum Smith's Eldest daughter, my brother Loren's wife, said to me that Aunt Emma told her this, as well as the young ladies themselves" (Kimball, "Recollections," 13).

9. Apostle Orson Pratt, in statements given in the 1850s, made it perfectly clear that this revelation did not come until 1843. In 1853 he explained that "in the early rise of this church, the Lord gave no command unto any of His servants authorizing them to take more than one wife, but on the contrary, said unto them that they should give heed to that which was written in the book of Mormon." Therefore, Pratt pointed out, early Mormons "were under the strictest obligations to confine themselves to one wife, until a commandment came to the contrary, which the Lord did not see proper to give unto any of them, until about thirteen years after the first organization of the church [1830]" (*The Seer* 1:30). Seven years later, in 1859, Pratt reaffirmed the date of 1843 for the revelation. "Thirteen years after the publication of the Book of Mormon [1830]," he said, "the same Prophet that translated the Book of Mormon received a revelation upon marriage, which commanded certain individuals in this Church to take unto themselves a plurality of wives for time and all eternity, declaring that it is a righteous principle and was practiced by inspired men in times of old" (JD 6 [24 July 1859]: 362).

Apostle John Taylor, one of the earliest to accept plural marriage in Nauvoo, also understood the revelation on "celestial marriage" to have been first given in 1843.

In a 6 November 1869 letter to the *Deseret Evening News*, responding to U.S. vice-president Schuyler Colfax's accusation that the original Doctrine and Covenants denounced polygamy, Taylor noted that the Marriage Section was "published in the appendix to the book of Doctrine and Covenants long before the revelation concerning Celestial Marriage was given. . . . The revelation on polygamy was given in 1843."

10. Clayton's 12 July 1843 journal entry states: "after it was wrote Prests. Joseph & Hyrum presented it and read it to E[mma]. who said she did not believe a word of it and appeared very rebellious."

11. In a court deposition, Lucy testified that "Emma Smith was not present" at the sealing and "did not consent to the marriage; she did not know anything about it at all" (*Complainants*, 374).

12. Clayton in a 16 February 1874 statement (*Historical Record*, 6 [July 1887]: 225) identifies Flora Woodworth as a plural wife of Smith.

THE *NAUVOO EXPOSITOR* AND MARTYRDOM

The revelation on celestial marriage confused and divided the church as had no other single event. Growing public awareness of the revelation in the summer of 1843 further polarized a church already divided into two camps—the handful of people secretly introduced to Joseph Smith's private polygamous teachings and the much larger faction that accepted at face value the public denunciations of the practice. The tension over the issue was summed up in an 8 September 1843 letter by Charlotte Haven. This Mormon Nauvoo resident wrote of rumors that "plurality of wives is taught in the Bible, that Abraham, Jacob, Solomon, David, and indeed all the old prophets and good men, had several wives, and if right for them, it is right for the Latter Day Saints." But Haven, like most Saints, rejected this logic: "I cannot believe that Joseph will ever sanction such a doctrine" (Mulder and Mortensen 1967, 126).

Those uninitiated into the inner circles of the church had good reason to feel as Charlotte Haven did about polygamy. On 5 October 1843 Smith made his most pointed denunciation of plural marriage. Willard Richards, keeper of Smith's personal journal, recorded on this date: "instruction to try those who were preaching teaching or [crossed out in the original: "practicing"] the doctrine of plurality of wives on this Law. Joseph forbids it, and the practice thereof.—No man shall have but one wife."[1] Four months later, in the 1 February 1844 *Times and Seasons*, Joseph and Hyrum Smith co-authored a letter which "cut off from the Church for his iniquity" Hyrum Brown, a Mormon in Michigan who was "preaching polygamy and other false and corrupt doctrines." And the 15 March *Times and Seasons* printed a letter from Hyrum responding to charges that a man having a "certain priesthood" may have as many wives as he pleases. "There is no such doctrine taught," Hyrum argued, "neither is there any such thing practiced here. And any man that is found teaching privately or publicly any such doctrine is culpable, and will stand a chance to be brought before the High Council, and lose his license and membership also."

It was not only lay members who were caught in this web of apparent deception; some church leaders were equally befuddled. During a 12 August 1843 meeting of the Nauvoo High Council, Dunbar Wilson "made inquiry in relation to the subject of a plurality of wives, as there were rumors about respecting it, and he was satisfied there was something in those remarks, and he wanted to know what it was" (Shook 1914, 97). Joseph Smith, who was ill, was not at the meeting. His brother Hyrum requested a short adjournment and crossed the street to his home, where he picked up his copy of the 12 July revelation. Thomas Grover, another member of the council, later testified that Hyrum read the document to the group and said: "Now, you that believe this revelation and go forth and obey the same shall be saved, and you that reject it shall be damned" (ibid., 98). But several prominent church leaders, including the prophet's second counselor William Law, Nauvoo stake president William Marks, and High Council members Leonard Soby and Austin A. Cowles could not see the hand of God in the revelation.

Law, a prominent Nauvoo businessman, was solidly devoted to Smith until mid-1843. During the Bennett scandal, he quickly came to Smith's defense, reassuring the Saints that church leaders did not condone "spiritual wifery" or any such behavior. Smith held his counselor in such high esteem that he included him in the first small group of male initiates to the endowment ceremony in May 1842. And Law rendered much moral and financial support to a discouraged Smith when Missouri officials were attempting to extradite him on the Boggs case.

By early 1843, however, Law began to waver in his commitment to Smith. Initial difficulties between the two centered on business matters. William and his brother Wilson owned considerable real estate in upper Nauvoo. Smith, as trustee-in-trust for the church, owned nearly all of the mosquito-infested Mississippi bottom lands. The influx of Mormon converts to Nauvoo created stiff business competition between Smith and the Law brothers. Smith did not hesitate to use his ecclesiastical leverage to tilt real estate sales in his direction. His 13 February 1843 journal entry, for example, notes his counsel that "those who come here having money and purchased without the church & without council Must be cut of[f]." A month later he admonished a group of newly arrived English Saints to purchase property only from him. "We can beat all our competitors in lands, price and everything. . . . The lower part of the town is most healthful. In the upper part of the town are the merchants, who will say that I am partial, &c; but the lower part of the town is much the most healthful; and I tell you in the name of the Lord" (HC 5:356-57). The 20 December 1843 *Nauvoo Neighbor* requested that "all the brethren . . . when they move into Nauvoo[,] consult President Joseph Smith, the trustee in trust, and purchase their lands of him." Such statements by Smith greatly influenced the real estate market, making it difficult for the Laws to sell their property.[2]

But a deeper source of the Laws' disaffection was their detestation of polygamy. In an 1887 interview William explained that Hyrum Smith had shown him the revelation on "celestial marriage" in the fall of 1843. "Hyrum gave it to me in his office," Law said, and "told me to take it home and read it, and then be careful with it, and bring it back again." He and Jane "were just turned upside down by it" ("Mormonism in Nauvoo"). William took the document directly to the prophet and commented that it was in contradiction to the Doctrine and Covenants. Smith noted that the section on marriage in the Doctrine and Covenants was "given when the Church was in its infancy, when they were babes, and had to be fed on *milk*, but now they were strong and must have *meat*. He seemed much disappointed in my not receiving the *revelation*," William wrote. "He was very anxious that I would accept the doctrine and sustain him in it. He used many arguments at various times afterward in its favor" (Shook 1914, 126).

Law's refusal to accept polygamy was compounded in the prophet's eyes by Law's lending a sympathetic ear to Emma Smith in her opposition to the principle. In an 1885 affidavit Law testified that Smith had told him in 1843 that "he had several wives sealed to him, and that they afforded him a great deal of pleasure . . . [but] Emma had annoyed him very much about it." According to Law, Emma had also complained to him about "Joseph keeping his young wives in her house and elsewhere, and his neglect of her" (ibid.). This closeness between Law and the prophet's wife gave rise to rumors and caused bouts of jealousy for the prophet. When, two days after Law's excommunication, Emma left Nauvoo and traveled downriver, the 23 April 1844 *St. Louis Republican* reported, "Joe Smith . . . has turned his wife out of doors for being in conversation with a gentleman of the Sect which she hesitated or refused to disclose." Though Emma had only gone to Saint Louis on a short shopping trip, the rumors about her and William Law obviously upset Joseph. One day after her departure, according to Smith's own account, he gave a group of men a "history of the Laws' proceedings, in part, in trying to make a difficulty in my family" (HC 6:343).[3]

Though no evidence exists to show that the relationship between Emma Smith and William Law was anything more than platonic, it posed enough difficulties that the prophet was cited in the 17 June 1844 *Nauvoo Neighbor* Extra as blaming "all the sorrow he ever had in his family" upon "the influence of Wm Law." The friendship between Law and Emma Smith may have been the reason that the prophet refused to seal Law to his wife, Jane. Hyrum Smith suggests such a possibility as recorded in the 12 June 1844 journal of William Clayton: "Law wanted to be sealed [to his wife] & J[oseph] told him he was forbid—which begun the hard feeling." Alexander Neibaur, a close friend of the prophet, related in his 24 May journal that Smith told him "Mr. Wm Law—wisht to be Married to his Wife for Eternity Mr Smith said would Inquire of the Lord, Ansered no because Law was [an] Adulterous person." Hyrum Smith, according to the 17 June 1844 *Nauvoo Neighbor* Extra, also accused Law of adulterous behavior.

The accusations of adultery against Law may have been for the purpose of discrediting him in the eyes of the Saints. No adultery charges were mentioned during his excommunication proceedings in April 1844. One day previous to the Neibaur journal entry, however, Law had filed a suit against Smith in Hancock County Circuit Court, charging the prophet with living with Maria Lawrence "in an open state of adultery" from 12 October 1843 to 23 May 1844. Smith commented on the charges the next day in Sunday services, noting that such accusations were not new to him. "Another indictment has been got up against me," he said. "I had not been married scarcely five minutes, and made one proclamation of the gospel, before it was reported that I had seven wives. . . . What a thing it is for a man to be accused of committing adultery, and having seven wives, when I can only find one" (ibid., 408-11). Smith, who had been sealed to Maria and Sarah Lawrence in the summer or early fall of 1843, had himself appointed legal guardian of the two orphan girls on 4 June 1844, two weeks after Law's charges were filed. He also decided on the fourth of June, after discussing the matter with several church leaders, to prosecute "Laws and Fosters for perjury, slander, &c. . . . in behalf of Maria Lawrence" (ibid., 427).

Law's charge of adultery against the prophet was apparently his final attempt to get Smith to abandon polygamy. On 8 January 1844, nearly five months before filing the suit, Law noted in his journal that he had told the prophet in an emotional street encounter that "polygamy was of the Devil and that [Smith] should put it down."[4] Law's son Richard later added that his father, "with his arms around the neck of the Prophet, was pleading with him to withdraw the doctrine of plural marriage[,] . . . with tears streaming from his eyes. The Prophet was also in tears, but he informed [Law] that he could not withdraw the doctrine, for God had commanded him to teach it, and condemnation would come upon him if he was not obedient to the commandment" (pp. 507-10).

Smith told Law during this encounter that he was excluded in the future from the Endowment Council and that he was dropping him from the First Presidency as well. Law did not take the dismissal lightly. "I confess I feel ennoyed very much by such unprecedented treatment," he wrote in his 8 January journal, "for it is illegal, inasmuch as I was appointed by revelation (so called) first [and was sustained] twice after by unanimous voice of [crossed out in the original: "the"] general Conference." But Law felt "relieved from a most embarrassing situation. I cannot fellowship the abominations which I verily know are practiced by this man, consequently, I am glad to be free of him."

Church leaders attempted a reconciliation with Law, but he insisted that polygamy first be purged from the church. On 18 April 1844 Law and his wife Jane and brother Wilson were excommunicated for "unchristianlike conduct." Ten days later they and other dissidents founded a separatist church, declaring Smith a fallen prophet. The group issued a prospectus for an opposition newspaper, *The Nauvoo Expositor*, 10 May 1844. Nauvoo citizens were forewarned that the paper would advocate repeal of the Nauvoo Charter,[5] foster religious tolerance and freedom of speech, censure gross moral imperfections, and oppose union of church and state in Nauvoo civil government. The publishers promised "to give a full, candid, and succinct statement of FACTS, AS THEY REALLY EXIST IN THE CITY OF NAUVOO—fearless of whose particular case the facts may apply."

Smith was concerned enough over the promised disclosures that he sent Sidney Rigdon to try to persuade Law to discontinue the publication of the paper. But Law remained firm, noting in his 13 May journal that he had told Rigdon "if they wanted peace they could have it on the following conditions. That Joseph Smith would acknowledge publicly that he had taught and practised the doctrine of plurality of wives, that he brought a revelation supporting the doctrine, and that he should own the whole system (revelation and all) to be from Hell." Law further wrote in his journal that "[Joseph] ha[s] lately endeavored to seduce my wife and ha[s] found her a virtuous woman."[6]

Less than three weeks later, on 7 June, Law wrote in his journal: "This day the Nauvoo Expositor goes forth to the world, rich with facts, such expositions as make the guilty tremble and rage. . . . 1000 sheets were struck and five hundred mailed forthwith." Though the paper contained a short story, some poetry, and a few news items copied from eastern newspapers, its pervasive theme was opposition to polygamy. Claiming in its "Preamble, Resolutions and Affidavits, of the Seceders from the Church at Nauvoo" that the gospel as originally taught by Joseph Smith was true, the *Expositor* charged that Smith was a fallen prophet who had introduced doctrines that were "heretical and damnable in their influence." The preamble resolved that because Joseph and Hyrum Smith and other unnamed church leaders had "introduced false and damnable doctrines into the Church, such as plurality of Gods above the God of this universe, and his liability to fall with all his creations; the plurality of wives, for time and eternity," they should be denounced as apostates.

Another reference in the preamble to doctrines "taught secretly, and denied openly," referred more specifically to polygamy. Sylvester Emmons, non-Mormon member of the Nauvoo City Council and editor of the *Expositor*, acknowledged in a brief introductory statement the presence in Nauvoo of "a system which, if exposed in its naked deformity, would make the virtuous mind revolt with horror; a system in the exercise of which lays prostrate all the dearest ties in our social relations—the glorious fabric upon which human happiness is based—ministers to the worst passions of our nature and throws us back into the benighted regions of the dark ages." Along with the excessive editorializing, the paper provided evidence from William Law,

Jane Law, and Austin Cowles that Hyrum Smith had read to them the revelation sanctioning polygamy. The *Expositor* warned: "We intend to tell the
whole tale."

Nauvoo citizens were furious when the paper hit the streets. Smith's
retrospective defense to Governor Thomas Ford was that "people were indignant, and loudly called upon our city authorities for redress of their griev-
ances, which, if not attended to[,] they themselves would have taken the
matter into their own hands, and have summarily punished the audacious
wretches, as they deserved" (HC 6:581).[7] Church leaders responded immediately. On Saturday, 8 June 1844, the day following the issuance of the
Expositor, the city council met for over six hours in two sessions. They met
again Monday, 10 June, for more than seven hours.

Saturday's meetings were devoted to a discussion of the character
and conduct of the publishers. William Law and Robert Foster in particular
were condemned for "oppressing the poor, counterfeiting, theft, conspiracy
to murder, seduction, and adultery." The 19 June *Nauvoo Neighbor's* account
of the meeting explained that Hyrum Smith "referred to the revelation, read
to the High Council of the Church, which has caused so much talk about a
multiplicity of wives; that said revelation was in answer to a question concerning things which transpired in former days, and had no reference to the
present time." And the prophet was quoted as having said, "They make it a
criminality for a man to have a wife on the earth while he has one in heaven."
He added that "the order [was] in ancient days, having nothing to do with
[t]he present times."

The question of what to do about the newspaper was addressed on
Monday. Joseph Smith, Nauvoo mayor, read aloud the editor's "Introductory"
and argued that the paper was a "nuisance–a greater nuisance than a dead
carcass." He urged the council to pass legislation for stopping the opposition
press. The group responded by passing an ordinance "concerning Libels,"
resolving that any persons who "shall write or publish, in said city, any false
statement, or libel any of the Citizens, for the purpose of exciting the public
mind against the chartered privileges, peace, and good order of said city"
shall be "deemed disturbers of the peace" (Nauvoo City Council, 10 June
1844).

With the law to back them, the city council, without identifying
specific statements which were considered libelous, next discussed ways to
silence the press. Councilor John Taylor, editor of the church's newspaper,
the *Times and Seasons*, spoke the feeling of the group: "We are willing they
should publish the truth; but it is unlawful to publish libels. The *Expositor* is
a nuisance, and stinks in the nose of every honest man" (HC 6:445). Hyrum
Smith added that he thought the best way to suppress the publication was to
smash the press and scatter the type. After an emotion-filled afternoon, the
city council resolved that the *Nauvoo Expositor* and its printing office were a

"public nuisance . . . and the Mayor is instructed to cause said printing establishment and papers to be removed without delay, in such manner as he shall direct" (ibid., 448). Smith ordered the city marshal to "destroy the printing press from whence issues the *Nauvoo Expositor* and pi the type of said printing establishment in the street, and burn all the *Expositors* and libelous handbills found in said establishment" (ibid.).

The destruction of the press caused an uproar in surrounding non-Mormon communities. Six days after the press had been destroyed, Smith issued a public proclamation from the mayor's office, explaining that the paper had aimed to destroy "the institutions of the city, both civil and religious. Its proprietors are a set of unprincipled scoundrels, who attempted in every possible way to defame the character of the most virtuous of our community." He insisted on "the correctness of our conduct in this affair." "We appeal," wrote the prophet, "to every high court in the state, and to its ordeal we are willing to appear at any time that his Excellency, Governor Ford, shall please call us before it" (ibid., 484-85).

The next day, Smith and others were arrested for inciting a riot—"destroying the *Nauvoo Expositor* press." They were released later that afternoon after a hearing before judge Daniel H. Wells, who would become a Mormon in two years. Fearful of reprisals from the non-Mormon element in the area, Smith declared martial law in the city. On 21 June, Governor Ford sent a letter to the mayor and city council asking for statements from "well-informed and discreet persons, who will be capable of laying before me your version of the matter," and requesting that the council receive from him "such explanations and resolutions as may be determined on."

Ford, however, was dissatisfied with Smith's description of the situation. "Your conduct," he declared, "was a very gross outrage upon the laws and the liberties of the people. [The paper] may have been full of libels, but this did not authorize you to destroy it." After taking Smith to task over what he viewed as constitutional violations, Ford announced that he would "have to require you and all persons in Nauvoo accused or sued to submit in all cases implicitly to the process of the courts and to interpose no obstacles to an arrest either by writ of habeas corpus or otherwise" (Ford 1854).

But the Smiths were fearful of placing themselves in Ford's hands. "We dare not come," Joseph wrote to the governor on 22 June. "Writs, we are assured, are issued against us in various parts of the country. For what? To drag us from place to place, from court to court, across the creeks and prairies, till some bloodthirsty villain could find his opportunity to shoot us" (HC 6:539-40). Notifying Ford that he intended to travel to Washington, D.C., to present his case before President Tyler, Smith crossed the Mississippi into Iowa on the evening of June 23. The next day, however, he changed his mind and returned to Nauvoo. He sent a letter to Ford offering to "come to you at Carthage on the morrow, as early as shall be convenient for your *posse* to escort us into headquarters, provided we can have a fair trial, not be abused nor have my witnesses abused, and have all things done in due form of law" (ibid., 550).

But the Smiths were never brought to trial. In the early afternoon of 27 June, a large mob of men with blackened faces overpowered the small force assigned by Governor Ford to guard the prisoners in the Carthage Jail. Joseph and Hyrum Smith were shot to death in the second story bedroom.

NOTES

1. When incorporating Joseph Smith's journal into the *History of the Church*, Apostle George A. Smith, a cousin, altered this passage to reflect later Mormon thinking: "Gave instructions to try those persons who were preaching, teaching, or practicing the doctrine of plurality of wives; for, according to the law, I hold the keys of this power in the last days; for there is never but one on earth at a time on whom the power and its keys are conferred; and I have constantly said no man shall have but one wife at a time, unless the Lord directs otherwise" (HC 6:46).

2. Smith initially described Commerce as "so unhealthful, very few could live there" (HC 3:375). Despite Smith's enthusiasm and efforts to drain the swampy lowlands, widespread sickness prevailed throughout the entire Nauvoo period (Arrington 1976, 141-42).

3. Wilson Law also caused trouble for Smith by printing "Buckeye's Lamentation For Want of More Wives" poems in the *Warsaw Message*, an anti-Mormon newspaper. The 7 February 1844 issue published the first "piece of doggerel," as Joseph Smith described it:

> And 'tis so here, in this sad life—
>   Such ills you must endure—
> Some *priest* or *king*, may claim your wife
>   Because that you are poor.
> A *revelation* he may get—
>   Refuse it if you dare!
> And you'll be damned *perpetually*,
>   By our good *Lord* the *Mayor*.
> But if that you yield willingly,
>   Your daughters and your wives,
> In *spiritual marriage* to our POPE,
>   He'll bless you all your lives. . . .
> This is the secret doctrine taught
>   By Joe and the *red rams*—
> Although in public they deny—
>   But then 'tis all a sham. . . .
> He sets his snares around *for ALL,*—
>   And VERY SELDOM FAILS
> To catch some thoughtless PARTRIDGES,
>   SNOW-birds or KNIGHT-ingales!

4. William Law's diary is in private hands. The portions cited here are from Cook 1982.

5. The group felt Smith thumbed his nose at the law by abusing the *habeas corpus* rights of the charter to escape answering the Boggs charges in Missouri.

6. Joseph H. Jackson added that shortly after 15 January 1844 the prophet "informed me, in conversation, that he had been endeavoring for some two months, to get Mrs. William Law for a spiritual wife. He said that he had used every argument in his power, to convince her of the correctness of his doctrine, but could not succeed" (Jackson 1844, 19). Alexander Neibaur's diary of 24 May 1844 offers Smith's account of the situation: "Mr Wm Law—wisht to be Married to his Wife for eternity Mr. Smith said would Inquire of the Lord, Answered no because Law was a Adulterous person. Mrs Law wanted to know why she could not be Married to Mr Law Mr S[mith] said would not wound her feeling by telling her, some days after Mr Smith going toward his Office Mrs. Law stood in the door beckoned to him more the once did not Know whether she bekoned to him went across to Inquire yes please to walk in no one but herself in the house. [S]he drawing her Arms around him if you wont seal me to my husband Seal myself unto you. [H]e Said stand away & pushing her Gently aside giving her a denial & going out."

7. For an excellent discussion of the events surrounding the destruction of the *Expositor,* see Oaks 1965.

Seven

FOLLOWING THE BRETHREN

Some Mormon observers were convinced that the deaths of the Smith brothers was evidence of divine retribution, the act of an angry God. William Law, who had left Nauvoo after the destruction of his *Nauvoo Expositor*, wrote in a 20 July 1844 letter to a friend, "While the wicked slay the wicked I believe I can see the hand of a blasphemed God stretched out in judgment, the cries of innocence and virtue have ascended up before the throne of God, and he has taken sudden vengeance" (Law to Hill). And Sidney Rigdon wrote, "If Joseph sinned[,] which he did, the Lord has cut him off from his stewardship . . . he contracted a whoring spirit and . . . the Lord smote him for this thing" (*Latter Day Saints' Messenger and Advocate*, Jan. 1845).

Contrary to the views of those who saw in it the doom of the Mormon movement, the martyrdom of Joseph and Hyrum Smith, though disruptive to the Mormon community for a time, actually unified the Saints.[1] Sidney Rigdon, the only surviving member of the First Presidency, returned to Nauvoo shortly after the Smiths' deaths and presented himself to the Saints as "guardian" of the church "to build [it] up to Joseph as he had begun it." But he was rejected as an interim president by the majority of Mormons in favor of the leadership of the Quorum of the Twelve under Brigham Young. Rigdon's continued efforts to make himself the rallying standard for Mormonism resulted in his excommunication in the fall of 1844. Returning to Pittsburg, he attempted to gather about him leaderless remnants of the Mormon community.

Rigdon began to publicly denounce polygamy in his *Latter Day Saints' Messenger and Advocate* shortly after he left Nauvoo. Referring to the Quorum of the Twelve as the "Spiritual Wife Fraternity," he reasoned in the 15 October 1844 issue that "it would seem almost impossible that there could be found a set of men and women, in this age of the world, with the revelations of God in their hands, who could invent and propogate doctrines so ruinous to society, so debasing and demoralising as the doctrine of a man having a plurality of wives." Decrying the "transactions of the secret chambers," he announced that "the Twelve and their adherents have endeavored to carry on this spiritual wife business in secret." Moreover, he added, they "have gone to the most shameful and desperate lengths to keep it from the public.

First, insulting innocent females, and when they resented the insult . . . would assail their characters by lying." Rigdon vented his dismay at the deceptive practices of church leaders: "How often these men and their accomplices stood up before the congregation, and called God and all the holy Angels to witness, that there was no such doctrine taught in the church; and it has now come to light."

Church leaders in Nauvoo denounced Rigdon's accusations. "Wo to the man," the 15 November 1844 *Times and Seasons* warned, "who will thus willfully lie to injure an innocent people! The law of the land and the rules of the Church do not allow one man to have more than one wife alive at once." But Rigdon knew better, and he was determined to make his knowledge public. On 6 April 1845, the fifteenth anniversary of the founding of Mormonism, he had himself ordained president of the Church of Christ. His call for a reformation based on the principles of the Kirtland church appealed to a few former Mormons, including his son-in-law George W. Robinson, former apostle William McLellin, Nauvoo dissenter Oliver F. Olney, and anti-polygamous Nauvoo Stake high councilman Austin Cowles.

Though the group was short-lived, its attack on polygamy was zealous. "Did the Lord ever tell any people," Rigdon asked in the 15 February 1845 issue of the *Messenger and Advocate*, "that sleeping with their neighbor's wives and daughters had any thing to do with preparing the way of the Savior's coming[?]"[2] His expose of Nauvoo polygamy was confirmed by former member of the First Presidency William Law in the spring of 1845 when Law and William McLellin arrived at a 16 February Kirtland conference of Rigdon's followers. Addressing the congregation, Law "settled the question forever on the public mind," Rigdon wrote, "in relation to the spiritual wife system, and the abominations concerning it." Law reported that "Joseph Smith and others had attempted to get him into it, and in order to do so had made him acquainted with many things about it" (*Messenger and Advocate*, 15 March 1845).

Despite his long-standing opposition to polygamy, and published condemnations of the practice, Rigdon would be accused of introducing the system within his declining congregation. Apostle Parley P. Pratt turned Rigdon's accusations against him in a 1 July 1845 letter in the British *Millennial Star*, warning the Saints to "beware of seducing spirits, and doctrines of devils, as first introduced by John C. Bennett, under the name of 'spiritual wife' doctrine; and still agitated by the Pittsburg Seer, and his followers under the same title." Apostle John Taylor, editor of the 15 November 1844 *Times and Seasons*, published a letter from "An Old Man of Israel" which denounced the "sham quotations of Sidney Rigdon and his clique, under the 'dreadful splendor' of 'spiritual wifery' which is brought into the account as graciously as if the law of the land allowed a man a plurality of wives."

There is no solid evidence that Rigdon ever advocated polygamy.[3] His son John maintained that Rigdon "took the ground no matter from what source it came whether from Prophet seer revelator or angels from heaven [that] it was a false doctrine and should be rejected" (Rigdon, "Life Story," 184). Yet accusations linking Rigdon to polygamy and insinuating that his daughter Nancy was a prostitute undermined his status as the only surviving member of the First Presidency. Few people took his leadership claims seriously; he never attained a large following. John Rigdon later noted that his father "was not a leader of men . . . the Mormon church . . . made no mistake in placing Brigham Young at the head of the church . . . if Sidney Rigdon had been chosen to take that position the church would have tottered and fallen" (ibid.).

Rumors of polygamy followed another prominent leader of post-martyrdom Mormonism, James Jesse Strang, a multi-talented New Yorker with a background similar to Joseph Smith's own. Though never a member of the Mormon hierarchy, the resourceful Strang claimed himself Smith's successor on the strength of a 9 June 1844 letter he said he had received from the prophet. "If evil befall me," the letter promised, "thou shall lead the flock to pleasant pastures." Early in August 1844 Strang declared that an angel had appeared to him at the "very hour" of Smith's death on 27 June 1844 and had ordained him the prophet's successor. Several prominent followers of the prophet, impressed by the charismatic similarities of the two men, joined with the Strangites.[4] Establishing his disciples on Beaver Island in Lake Michigan, Strang had himself crowned "King James the First" on 8 July 1850. Theatrically inclined George J. Adams placed a metal crown on Strang's head and draped across the shoulders of the king-to-be a bright red robe which had served as a stage prop. Amidst the pomp and ceremony Strang read to the congregation for the first time his "Book of the Law of the Lord," a portion of which he claimed was a translation of the "plates of Laban," part of the Book of Mormon record.

Strang, like Joseph Smith, publicly denounced polygamy. The king's private posture, however, also like the prophet's, radically differed from his public position. Former Mormon apostle John E. Page, a follower of Strang, wrote, "We have talked hours, yea, even days with President Strang, and we find to our utmost satisfaction that he does not believe in or cherish the doctrine of polygamy in any manner, shape, or form imaginable whatever" (Fitzpatrick 1970, 74). To underscore his opposition, Strang published the following official denial in the 12 August 1847 *Voree Herald*: "I have uniformly and distinctly discarded and declared heretical the so-called 'spiritual wife system' and everything connected therewith." Yet one year later he took his first plural wife, Elvira Eliza Field, who traveled about the country with him masquerading as his male secretary, "Charlie Douglass." While the community on Beaver Island eventually reached seven hundred members, only about twenty families were polygamous. Strang himself had five wives and four-teen children. And like Smith, he too came to a violent end. On 16 June 1856, Thomas Bedford, a Beaver Island resident who had been publicly whipped on Strang's direction, fatally shot the king.

Initially Joseph Smith's family may have supported Strang's succes-sion claims. For example, the July 1846 *Voree Herald* contained a certificate endorsing Strang, reportedly prepared by the prophet's brother William and signed by the entire Smith family, except Emma, Smith's widow. More than fifty years later the certificate was repudiated in the *Saints' Herald*, the official voice of the Reorganized Church of Jesus Christ of Latter Day Saints (RLDS). Regardless of the authenticity of the Smith family statement, the Strangite movement proved to be the fertile soil in which the RLDS church germi-nated.[5]

Opposition to polygamy motivated three influential members of Strang's congregation to withdraw from the group. Jason W. Briggs, Henry H. Deam, and Zenas H. Gurley, Sr., directed on 6 April 1853 the "New Organization of the Church of Jesus Christ of Latter Day Saints," which eventually became The Reorganized Church of Jesus Christ of Latter Day Saints. For a period of seven years, from 1853 to 1860, Jason W. Briggs, as president of the Quorum of Twelve Apostles, presided over the movement. In 1860, Joseph Smith III, the eldest son of Joseph Smith, Jr., became the first president of the RLDS church.

In his 6 April 1860 acceptance speech, delivered in the presence of his mother, young Joseph left no doubt as to where he stood on polygamy. "There is but one principle taught by the leaders of any faction of this people that I hold in utter abhorrence," he announced; "that is a principle taught by Brigham Young and those believing in him." Elaborating on his hatred of polygamy, the young prophet attested: "I have been told that my father taught such doctrines. I have never believed it, and never can believe it. If such things were done, then I believe they never were of Divine authority. I believe my father was a good man, and a good man never could have promulgated such doctrines" (Tullidge 1880, 608-11).

Opposition to polygamy and other militant theocratic innovations attributed to his father became the hallmark of the leadership of Joseph Smith III.[6] His opposition to such practices probably originated with his mother. Though evidence indicates that Emma possessed intimate knowledge of not only polygamy but also Endowment Council and Council of Fifty matters, she did not pass this information down to her children. Robert Flanders, an RLDS historian, has pointed out that "while it seems evident that Emma taught her children Christian principles and virtues, she never talked much to them of the old church and its affairs. There is no indication that she prej-udiced them in any way, although she did maintain in them respect for their father." Flanders sees the "ignorance later shown by Joseph and Alexander about church history" as evidence that "their mother had been for the most part silent on the subject" (1954, 11).

The reality of her husband's polygamous relations undoubtedly evoked painful memories for Emma. It may be that she refused to give tongue to memory simply because she could not face the shadows of the past. Emma, like her son Joseph, spent a lifetime struggling to bring honor and respectability to the Smith name. An admission that Joseph was a polygamist was impossible for both of them.

Emma, in an April 1867 interview with a Reorganite elder, Jason W. Briggs, would not even admit to a personal knowledge of her husband's revelation on "celestial marriage" (Shook 1914, 185-86). Her sons, shying away from what must have been a very sensitive subject, apparently never asked her about their father's involvement in polygamy, despite the urgings of many to "ask your mother, she knows." In 1879, however, Joseph and Alexander "decided to present to her a few prominent questions, which were penned and agreed upon." Emma responded to the questions as follows: "Q. What about the revelation on polygamy? Did Joseph Smith have anything like it? What of spiritual wifery? A. There was no revelation on either polygamy, or spiritual wives. There were some rumors or something of the sort, of which I asked my husband. He assured me that all there was to it was that, in a chat about plural wives, he had said, "Well, such a system might possibly be, if everybody was agreed to it, and would behave as they should; but they would not; and besides, it was contrary to the will of heaven." No such thing as polygamy, or spiritual wifery, was taught, publicly or privately, before my husband's death, that I have now, or ever had, any knowledge of. Q. Did he not have other wives than yourself? A. He had no other wife but me; nor did he to my knowledge ever have. Q. Did he not hold marital relation with women other than yourself? A. He did not have improper relations with any woman that ever came to my knowledge. Q. Was there nothing about spiritual wives that you recollect? A. At one time my husband came to me and asked me if I had heard certain rumors about spiritual marriages, or anything of the kind; and assured me that if I had, that they were without foundation; that there was no such doctrine, and should never be with his knowledge, or consent. I know that he had no other wife or wives than myself, in any sense, either spiritual or otherwise" ("Last Testimony," 289-90).

Emma's interview with her sons was not published until after her death. This led to speculation from some Utah Mormons that the entire interview was a sham. But the document accurately portrayed the public posture of both Emma and Joseph Smith. Irrefutable evidence in letters and journals of Smith's closest Nauvoo associates, particularly William Clayton and Emily Partridge, portray the contradictory private and public positions of the prophet and his wife. Even statements by founding RLDS churchmen dispute the Smiths' public posture by affirming the prophet's practice of polygamy.

Some have admitted that Joseph Smith became involved in polygamy but later tried to disentangle himself from the practice. Brigham Young conceded in 1866 that "Joseph was worn out with it, but as to his denying any such thing I never knew that he denied the doctrine of polygamy. Some have said that he did, but I do not believe he ever did" (Unpublished Address). But Smith's niece, Mary Bailey, writing in 1908 said that her uncle finally "awoke to a realization of the whole miserable affair [and] . . . tried to withdraw from and put down the Evil into which he had fallen" (Newell and Avery 1984, 179). Prominent early leaders of the RLDS church also shared this viewpoint. Isaac Sheen, who became affiliated with the RLDS movement in 1859 and edited the church periodical *Saints' Herald*, wrote in the first issue of that paper (March 1860) that though "Joseph Smith taught the spiritual-wife doctrine," he "repented of his connection with this doctrine, and said it was of the devil." Former Nauvoo stake president William Marks, a close friend of Emma, wrote in a July 1853 letter to the *Zion's Harbinger and Baneemy's Organ* that he met with the prophet a short time before his death. "We are a ruined people," Marks quoted Smith; "this doctrine of polygamy, or Spiritual-wife System, that has been taught and practiced among us, will prove our destruction and overthrow. I have been deceived . . . it is wrong; it is a curse to mankind, and we shall have to leave the United States soon, unless it can be put down, and its practice stopped in the Church." Marks said that Smith ordered him "to go into the high council, and I will have charges preferred against all who practice this doctrine; and I want you to try them by the laws of the Church, and cut them off, if they will not repent, and cease the practice of this doctrine . . . I will go into the stand and preach against it with all my might, and in this way, we may rid the Church of this damnable heresy." But Smith was killed shortly after this conversation, and when Marks related what Smith had said, his testimony "was pronounced false by the Twelve and disbelieved."

Much later in his life, after his mother's death, Joseph III seems to have modified his earlier position on the origins of Mormon polygamy. "I believe that during the later years of my father's life," he postulated in an 1879 address, "there was in discussion among the elders, and possibly in practice, a theory like the following: that persons who might believe that there was a sufficient degree of spiritual affinity between them as married companions, to warrant the desire to perpetuate that union in the world to come and after the resurrection, could go before some high priest . . . pledging themselves while in the flesh unto each other for the observance of the rights of companionship in the spirit." Once this idea of spiritual or eternal marriage began to spread, young Smith theorized, "lines between virtue and license hitherto sharply drawn, grew more and more indistinct; spiritual companionship if sanctioned by a holy priesthood, to confer favors and pleasures in the world to come, might be antedated and put to actual test here. . . .

From this, if one, why not two or more, and plural marriage, or the plurality of wives was the growth" (Tullidge 1880, 798-800).[7]

Despite his personal animosity towards Brigham Young, young Joseph maintained close ties with his Mormon cousins. In a 20 January 1886 letter to Utah cousin John Henry Smith, he wrote: "As the son of Joseph Smith, I have a son's right, independent of any religious obligation, to see that the name of my sire is not burdened with shame, obloquy, or unjust censure." He related that after seriously considering joining the Mormons as a young man in 1853, he was told "by the voice of revelation, not to have anything to do with polygamy, except to oppose it." "If father had more wives than one," he wrote, "it does not affect the rule given to the Church. It proves nothing only that he was a transgressor against the rule, and the civil law. From my view polygamy could not and never did emanate by command from God. It had [an]other source. Hence, Joseph Smith was not justified in its practice; nor is the practice defensible from the consideration that he did so."

In a 29 April 1905 letter to Sidney Rigdon's son John, Joseph clarified his position: "Whether my father was or was not the one through whom the practice was introduced into the church and was or was not guilty of practicing it, both the dogma and the practice were contrary to the Bible, Book of Mormon, and the revelations given to the church." The younger Smith felt "under no obligation to take his [father's] practice or his teaching of the dogma, if he did so practice or teach, as evidence of its divinity; nor was I under obligation to either teach or practice it."

Though the movements founded by Sidney Rigdon, James Jesse Strang, and other minor historical figures were of brief duration, the RLDS church continues to grow today.[8] But the most powerful leader to emerge from the chaos surrounding Joseph Smith's 1844 death was Brigham Young. He, as president of the Quorum of the Twelve Apostles, became the standard-bearer for the continuance of the revolutionary developments Smith had introduced to faithful members of the church after his 1839 escape from Liberty Jail. At the center of those policies lay polygamy. Young and select members of the Twelve began in the fall of 1844 to marry secretly the widowed plural wives of Joseph Smith. As the Nauvoo Temple neared completion, all women known to have had a polygamous relationship with Smith were resealed to him by proxy. Zina D. H. Jacobs Smith Young related that at the time of these eternal sealings, each of Smith's plural wives was given the opportunity to be sealed to the church leader of her choice "for time" (Firmage).

Church leaders knew by 1845 they could not remain in Nauvoo much longer. The surrounding non-Mormon community was whipped to a fever pitch by the anti-Mormon element. They wanted the Mormons out of the state. The Saints, who had heard those rumblings before in Ohio and Missouri, made plans to leave Illinois. Their magnificent temple, which could be seen for miles up and down the Mississippi, became a beehive of activity day and night as church leaders sought to introduce the Mormon temple endowments to the general church membership. By mid-February an advance party of Mormons vacated the city and crossed the frozen Mississippi into Iowa. Within a year Nauvoo, which had been renamed "The City of Joseph," was a virtual ghost town.

NOTES

1. In a 1 March 1845 letter Isaac Scott wrote of this confusion: "The Church is now divided, and part go for Sidney Rigdon and William Law, the only Presidents left the Church. The other part hold to the Twelve, who arrogate to themselves the authority to lead the Church" (Mulder and Mortensen 1958, 155). For background on events surrounding the succession of Joseph Smith, see Quinn 1976.

2. Though Rigdon did not mention Smith's polygamous proposals to his daughter Nancy, a follower, J. Gibson Divine, apparently did in the 15 March 1845 *Messenger and Advocate*: "I now ask if it is not a system of oppression to lead a man, standing at the head of a family of interesting children, into a covenant to obey every revelation or every order coming from a certain source, asking no questions, and in a few days after one of his daughters to be demanded as a *wife* for a married man, and not a question to be asked by the father."

3. Peter Hess, a follower of James Strang, recounted in a 14 December 1846 letter to Strang a second-hand story that during a September 1846 conference in Antrim, Pennsylvania, "Mr. Rigdon had introduced a System of Wifery or the Battle Axe System or free or common intercourse with the women" (Gregory 1981, 61). But Ebenezer Robinson, who was Rigdon's counselor in Antrim, wrote in 1886 that Rigdon did not practice polygamy there (ibid.). Furthermore, Rigdon claimed a 4 March 1866 revelation answering a question raised by a follower, Stephen Post, which announced: "I the Lord say unto my servant Stephen that the system of polygamy as had among a people who were called after my name was not of me. . . . I never gave to Joseph Smith nor any other man authority to introduce in my name that system as had among that people in any of its forms as a pretended spiritual relation or otherwise" (Post to Adams, 16 May 1866).

4. In addition to George J. Adams, John E. Page, William Marks, George Miller, and William Smith, John C. Bennett also became a follower of Strang. The king had written to Bennett on 9 March 1846 offering him a position in his organization. At Voree, Wisconsin, Strang's "Garden of Peace," Bennett became "the Prime Minister for the Imperial Primate of the Order of the Illuminati"–Strang's chief advisor. But, as in Nauvoo, his sexual adventures got him into difficulties. The "Minutes of a High Council Meeting held Oct. 4, 1846 to investigate certain charges against J.C. Bennett" report that Moses Smith brought charges against him for "Teaching False Doctrine such as Polygamy & concubinage and attempting to carry them into practice." In the same minutes, Willard Griffiths testified that "Bennett was about to exalt him and wished him to fill a certain quorum and by doing what he was directed he would become a father of a tribe." Griffiths further testified that when he asked Bennett concerning illicit intercourse, Bennett "told him there was no harm in it, [he] wanted good FUCKERS" (emphasis in original). Griffiths added that Bennett also taught him "that it was no harm for married men to have intercourse with other women." Griffiths was a high priest and Bennett told him that when women came to him for confession "he would have good chance to have connection with them" (Strang Papers). Bennett was not excommunicated from the Strangites until the summer of 1847.

5. Mormon church leaders, in addition to denouncing Sidney Rigdon, also attacked Strang through the pages of their English newspaper, *The Latter-day Saints' Millennial Star*. Typical of the shrill Mormon rhetoric of the day was the portrayal of Strang as the "successor of Sidney Rigdon, Judas Iscariot, Cain (the brother and murderer of Abel) and Co. Envoy Extraordinary and Minister Plenipotentiary of His Most Gracious Majesty Lucifer the I, assisted by his allied contemporary advisors, John C. Bennett, William Smith [a brother of Joseph], G. J. Adams, and John E. Page [former member of the Council of Twelve]" (Fitzpatrick 1970, 149-50).

6. In a revealing 1883 letter to E. L. Kelley, Joseph Smith III detailed his reason for discounting the evidence supporting his father's polygamy. "I have been ambitious of but one thing," he wrote: "to prove by the logic of conduct that my father was not a bad man. When my duty was made plain, and I was directed to the Reorganization already begun, I found its policy in some things, I thought at fault—notably the admission that my father taught polygamy. I found no proofs sufficient . . . to prove it to me. I adopted a different theory, and was at first much decried for it. It was charged as being the result of *pride in family name*. I think, however, I have disproved that statement. If not it will be proved by and by."

7. Joseph III's anti-polygamy position may have stemmed from both his mother and his uncle William Smith. Not only was the mercurial William Smith involved with John C. Bennett's scandalous Nauvoo behavior, but in mid-1844 he, along with George J. Adams and Samuel Brannan, introduced polygamy to Mormons in New England. After church leaders were sent to the area to try to reverse the damage the actions of the trio had caused, Smith returned to Nauvoo where on 17 August 1845 he openly advocated polygamy in a public gathering of the Saints. William Clayton in his journal of this date wrote that Smith "intimated in strong terms that [the Twelve] were practising such things in secret but he was not afraid to do it openly." His frankness and instability resulted in his excommunication on 19 October.

William lapsed into the same patterns when he joined the Strangites. Both he and John C. Bennett were excommunicated for immorality in the summer of 1847. Shortly afterwards, Smith formed his own church in northern Illinois. But his followers saw his polygamy as a coverup for promiscuity. Isaac Sheen, who severed himself from the movement in early 1850, referred to William as a "hypocritical libertine." "He professed the greatest hostility to the plurality wife doctrine," Sheen noted, yet "he told me that he had a right to raise up posterity from other men's wives. He said it would be an honor conferred upon them and their husbands, to allow him that privilege, and that they would thereby be exalted to a high degree of glory in eternity." Sheen insisted that Smith offered his wife to him "on the same terms that he claimed a partnership in other men's wives" (Isaac Sheen to editor, *Cincinnati Daily Commercial*, 22 May 1850).

Despite his involvement in polygamy within the framework of three separate Mormon factions, William was able to write to his nephew, Joseph Smith III: "Neither your father nor any member of the Quorum of the Twelve ever said any thing to me about [the] Plural marriage Revelation either before or Since your fathers death—up to the time of my Seperation from that Quorum which took place in September 1845 up to the time I was driven out of Nauvoo by the Bloody Danites" (Hutchins 1977, 81).

By this time, however, William Smith was old, ill, and financially dependent on his nephew. He was therefore willing to accept such directives as Joseph III gave to him in a 11 March 1882 letter as he was preparing a book about his involvement in Mormonism: "I have long been engaged in removing from Father's memory and from the early church, the stigma and blame thrown upon him because of Polygamy; and have at last lived to see the cloud rapidly lifting. And I would not consent to see further blame attached, by a blunder now. Therefore, Uncle, bear in mind our standing today before the world as defenders of Mormonism from Polygamy, and go ahead with your personal recollections. . . . If you are the wise man I think you to be, you will fail to remember anything [but] referring lofty standard of character at which we esteem these good men. You can do the cause great good; you can injure it by vicious sayings" (Launius 1988, 112).

8. In 1983 the RLDS posture on polygamy was modified. This position, detailed in a paper by official church historian Richard P. Howard, suggests polygamy was practiced by "some of the participants of the church in Nauvoo . . . [but] does not claim that Joseph Smith, Jr., was directly responsible for the practice of polygamy himself, or that it was among the authorized beliefs and practices of the church at Nauvoo" (*Saints' Herald*, 15 Dec. 1983). See Howard 1983.

Eight

ANNOUNCING THE PRACTICE

As the advance companies from Nauvoo began regrouping at Sugar Creek, Iowa, people lowered their guard and discussed polygamy more openly. Eliza R. Snow, now one of Brigham Young's plural wives, noted in a February 1846 diary entry that "we felt as tho' we could breath more freely and speak one with another upon those things where in God had made us free with less carefulness than we had hitherto done." Another of Young's wives, Zina, then visibly pregnant with her legal husband Henry Jacobs's child, remembered of the Sugar Creek Camp: "We there first saw who were the brave, the good, the self-sacrificing. Here we had now openly the first examples of noble-minded, virtuous women, bravely commencing to live in the newly-revealed order of celestial marriage. 'Woman; this is my husband's wife!' Here, at length, we could give this introduction without fear of reproach, or violation of man-made laws" (Tullidge 1877, 369).

After crossing Iowa, the Mormons wintered in the Council Bluffs/Winter Quarters area near present-day Omaha, Nebraska. Plans and preparations were undertaken during the winter of 1846-47 which allowed a vanguard company of pioneers to travel west in the spring. They arrived in the Great Salt Lake Valley on 24 July 1847. Upper California, as the region was then called, was Mexican territory until the 1848 Treaty of Guadalupe Hidalgo annexed it to the United States. Brigham Young, perhaps anticipating the results of the Mexican War, had informed U.S. president James K. Polk in the summer of 1846, while the Mormons were still in Iowa, "As soon as we settle in the great basin we design to petition for a territorial government bounded on the north by the British and on the south by Mexican domains and east and west by the summits of the Rocky and Cascade Ranges."

Church leaders actually intended to establish a Mormon theocratic kingdom, based on the leadership of a pre-designated Council of Fifty, independent of U.S. government interference. Pragmatic considerations, however, forced church leaders to give temporary allegiance to the United States. The Council of Fifty acted as a shadow government; council members often doubled as officials in the territorial hierarchy. John M. Bernhisel was selected by the Council of Fifty to pursue territorial status in Washington. Soon thereafter, Thomas L. Kane, a friend to Mormonism with political savoir-faire, advised: "You are better without any government from the hands of Congress than with a Territorial government. The political intrigues of government officers will be against you. . . . You do not want corrupt political men from Washington strutting around you."[1] Church leaders took his advice, and Almon Babbitt was dispatched to the nation's capital with a statehood petition. Brigham Young was to be governor of the state, his first counselor, Willard Richards, secretary of state, and his second counselor, Heber C. Kimball, chief justice. But federal officials were not in the mood to allow Mormons full control over their own affairs, as they had enjoyed in Nauvoo. Utah was granted territorial status on 9 September 1850.

Once established in the Great Basin, church leaders were less concerned about hiding polygamy than they had been in Illinois. "That many have a large number of wives," U.S. Army officer John W. Gunnison, leader of a government survey crew to Utah, noted in 1850, "is perfectly manifest to anyone residing among them, and indeed, the subject begins to be more openly discussed than formerly" (pp. 66-67). Brigham Young first publicly announced his own polygamous practices on 4 February 1851. "I have more wives than one," he declared to the territorial legislature; "I have many and I am not ashamed to have it known" (Kenney 4 [4 Feb. 1851]: 12).

The privilege of plural marriage in Utah was extended to a much broader segment of the Mormon community than at Nauvoo. Phineas Cook, a Mormon millwright, left an interesting account of Young's invitation to take a second wife. Preparing to move south to the Sanpete Valley to establish a mill at Young's direction, Cook told Brigham that his "wife was nearly tired out and we wanted to get away as soon as we could. He said he had the advantage of me, for when his women got tired, he could take them home and change them for fresh ones." Later that evening when the two were engaged in private discussion, Young told him that "he wanted me to get all the wives I wanted, and it was his council that I should do so" (Kunz, 87).

Though the Mormons were living in isolation, hundreds of miles from other settlements, their polygamous behavior became increasingly apparent to the outside world. Apostle John Taylor, for example, husband to fifteen wives, defensively argued in July 1850 during a public discussion in Boulogne-sur-Mer, France, that "we are accused of polygamy, and actions the most indelicate, obscene and disgusting, such that none but a corrupt and depraved heart could have contrived. These things are too outrageous to admit of belief. . . . I shall content myself by reading our views of chastity and marriage, from a work published by us, containing some of the articles of our faith" (Shook 1914, 184).

Polygamy-related public relations in far-away France were difficult enough; in Utah they were nearly impossible. In 1851 federal officials arrived in Salt Lake City to administer the new territorial government and immediately clashed with church leaders. Mormons, viewing the easterners as political hacks, refused to cooperate with them. Unable to wrest political control from the Mormon hierarchy, four of the officials left the territory and returned to Washington. A 19 December 1851 letter from the four to U.S. president Millard Fillmore complained that the church was "overshadowing and controlling the opinions, the actions, the property, and . . . the lives of its members; usurping and exercising the functions of legislation and the judicial business of the Territory." In addition, claimed the federal officials, the Mormons openly sanctioned and defended "the practice of polygamy, or plurality of wives" ("Report of Messrs.").

The report of the officials, though discounted by the Mormons, made it difficult to continue disguising polygamy. To counter negative publicity on Mormon issues, Brigham Young sent his counselor Jedediah M. Grant east to coordinate church public relations. As part of his campaign Grant penned three extensive letters and submitted them to the *New York Herald*. The only letter of the three published (9 March 1852) denied charges of treason and other alleged Mormon crimes and defended polygamy.[2] James G. Bennett, editor of the *Herald*, unimpressed with Mormon rhetoric on the issues, particularly polygamy, took Grant to task in an editorial. W. W. Phelps, erstwhile Mormon editor and apologist, came to Grant's aid, engaging Bennett in a verbose debate in the columns of the paper. "Of two evils," Phelps wrote, "a Mormon chooses neither but goes in for all good and more good; which, if, as Solomon said, a good wife is a good thing, then the more you have the more good you have" (Ferris 1856, 250).[3] On 15 July 1852 Phelps wrote, "The constitution has no power over religion, neither has Utah's Congress. . . . The federal authorities have no control over morality–that belongs to the good old book, the word of the Lord" (*New York Herald*, 15 July 1852).

Utah's appointed representative in Congress, John M. Bernhisel, was incensed at the indelicacy of Phelps's letter.[4] He wrote Brigham Young on 14 August that conditions for statehood were improving "until this inconsiderate and untimely letter made its appearance, reviving former prejudices and adding fresh fuel to the fire which had burned so furiously for several months." With his finger on the national pulse, Bernhisel feared that "so far as considering us a religious people, very many here and elsewhere, regard us among the most immoral and licentious beings on the face of the globe. . . . I therefore beg, entreat and implore Judge Phelps, as an elder brother, to write no more letters nor dialogues on this subject, upon which the nation is so sensitive."[5]

Jedediah M. Grant, in his printed letter to the *Herald*, had intimated he was going to ask Apostle Orson Pratt to "publish an exposition of the *Peculiar Doctrine*" of polygamy. The levelheaded Bernhisel advised Brigham Young in his 14 August letter that "no such publication had better be made, for the public mind is exceedingly sensitive on that subject, not at all prepared to receive it, and its effect would be decidedly injurious." Church leaders, however, evidently felt that the time was right to go public with the doctrine they had been denying for nearly two decades. Brigham H. Roberts, prominent Mormon historian, theologian, and church leader, theorized in his retrospective analysis of the decision that the church "owed it to frankness with the world to make the official proclamation." He pointed out that many Mormons were in doubt as to what course they should pursue. "In the absence of an official announcement it had become a source of embarrassment." Women particularly were in a difficult position, Roberts noted, "for their standing must have become equivocal had [the announcement] been much longer delayed" (Roberts 1930, 4:57-58).

Orson Pratt, widely respected among Mormons for his theological insight, was selected to introduce the doctrine officially during a church conference on 29 August 1852. Pratt announced that he had unexpectedly been called upon to address the crowd on the subject of "a plurality of wives." Denying that the practice had been instituted to "gratify the carnal lusts and feelings of man," he argued that its chief purpose was to provide righteous men and women the opportunity to have "a numerous and faithful posterity to be raised up and taught in the principles of righteousness and truth." After citing scriptural evidence that biblical prophets practiced polygamy, Pratt speculated that Jesus' relationship with Mary, Martha, and Mary Magdalene may have been polygamous.

Pratt next asserted that four-fifths of the world believed in a plurality of wives. The practice could provide an opportunity for every Mormon woman to be a wife and mother. Monogamy, reasoned Pratt, invited immorality. Prostitution could be prevented "in the way the Lord devised in ancient times; that is, by giving to his faithful servants a plurality of wives." Realizing the possibility of a political backlash, Pratt concluded: "I believe they will not under our present form of government (I mean the government of the United States), try us for treason for believing and practicing our religious notions and ideas. I think, if I am not mistaken, that the Constitution gives the privilege to all the inhabitants of this country, of the free exercise of their religious notions, and the freedom of their faith, and the practice of it. . . . And should there ever be laws enacted by this government to restrict them from the free exercise of this part of their religion, such laws must be unconstitutional" (*Deseret News, Extra,* 14 Sept. 1852).

After Pratt's discourse, Young took the stand and explained the circumstances surrounding the preservation of Joseph Smith's revelation on "celestial marriage." He announced that the document "contains a doctrine, a small portion of the world is opposed to; but I can deliver a prophecy upon it. . . . It will sail over, and ride triumphantly above all the prejudice and priest-craft of the day; it will be fostered and believed in by the more intelligent portions of the world, as one of the best doctrines ever proclaimed to any people" (ibid.).

Despite that optimistic forecast, church leaders recognized the difficulties in convincing the non-Mormon populace of the divine origin of Smith's revelation. They hoped to counter the inherent bias against polygamy through publishing a periodical defending it. Two weeks after his public announcement, editor Orson Pratt was on his way to Washington, D.C., to establish *The Seer*. He announced in the first issue of the magazine that it would expound "the views of the Saints in regard to the *ancient Patriarchal Order of Matrimony, or Plurality of Wives*, as developed in a Revelation, given through JOSEPH the SEER." Though Pratt's efforts with the publication were herculean, it would not sell. It was Bernhisel's dire predictions of negative public reaction to polygamy that proved prophetic rather than Young's.

European Mormons were evidently aghast at the church's announcement of polygamy. English missionary Thomas D. Evans noted that the Saints had "heard nothing of that principle, and it brought on a great deal of persecution." His future wife, Priscilla Merriman of Tenby, England, related a scene which may have been typical of the reaction. One of the Mormon girls in her branch had come to her "with tears in her eyes" asking if it were true "that Brigham Young has ninety wives?" (Carter 1958-75, 14:270, 282). Thomas B. Stenhouse, also a Mormon missionary at the time, later wrote that during the first six months polygamy was preached 1,776 British Saints left the church (1873, 202).[6]

Most Utah Mormons were aware that church leaders were secretly practicing polygamy long before it was publicly admitted. Thus the official announcement in Salt Lake City was not nearly so devastating as in Europe. In Utah polygamy-related problems arose both from the federal government's opposition to the practice and from the belief that Utah's territorial government was controlled by Mormon despots. The passage of the Democrat-sponsored Kansas-Nebraska Act in 1854, granting popular sovereignty on slavery in Kansas and Nebraska, unleashed a flood of opposition to the Democratic party, culminating in the organization of the Republican party, which demanded that polygamy and slavery, "twin relics of barbarism," be purged from American society. Democratic chair of the Senate Committee on Territories Stephen A. Douglas, not wishing to imply support of polygamy by the party's support of slavery, declared on 12 June 1856 that the Mormons were a traitorous group whose allegiance to Young superseded their commitment to the country. He proposed the "absolute and unconditional repeal of the Organic Act—blotting the territorial government out of existence—upon the ground that [the Mormons] are alien enemies and outlaws, denying their allegiance and defying the authorities of the United States" (G. Larson 1971, 22-23).

Despite Douglas's barrage, the Democratic party continued to advocate popular sovereignty. In the words of 1857 Democratic president-elect James Buchanan, territories and states should be "perfectly free to form and regulate their domestic institutions in their own way subject only to the constitution of the United States" (Richardson 1896-99, 5:431). Brigham Young was in complete agreement. "It is not the prerogative of the President of the United States," he argued in 1856, "to meddle with this matter, and Congress is not allowed, according to the Constitution, to legislate upon it. . . . If we introduce the practice of polygamy it is not their prerogative to meddle with it." Young was determined to make Utah "a sovereign State in the Union, or an independent nation by ourselves" (JD 4 [31 Aug. 1856]: 40).

In the pre-Civil War paranoia of the late 1850s, Young's rhetoric was interpreted as treasonous. President Buchanan, after receiving a 30 March 1857 resignation letter from Utah judge W. W. Drummond, became convinced the Mormons were in a state of full rebellion. The ex-judge complained that Mormons looked only to Brigham Young for leadership, were bound by secret oath to resist the laws of the country, employed a body of enforcers to kill those who opposed Mormon rule, destroyed the Utah Supreme Court records, harrassed federal officials, and slandered the American government on a daily basis.

Drummond's inflammatory letter, underscoring as it did similar complaints of polygamy and anti-American sentiment from other territorial officials, prompted Buchanan to action. Fearful of Mormon secessionary action, he appointed a new slate of territorial officials for Utah, providing them with a military escort of some 2,500 soldiers. He defended his actions in his December 1857 message to Congress by declaring that Brigham Young's power was "absolute over both church and state." Declaring that he felt bound to "restore the supremacy of the Constitution and laws within its limits," Buchanan said he felt "confident of the support of Congress, cost what it may, in suppressing the insurrection and in restoring and maintaining the sovereignty of the Constitution and laws over the Territory of Utah" (Richardson 1896-99, 5:454-56).

Church leaders in Utah failed to anticipate Buchanan's severe reaction, expecting him to be more understanding of their position than his hard-driving opponent, John C. Fremont. Respecting the president's position on polygamy, Brigham Young, in a 25 March 1857 letter to Apostle John Taylor, had written: "It is currently reported that President Buchanan fondles or has administered kindly to six or more 'Cyprians' [prostitutes] and may not be so severe in his legislative enactments against the Polygamists of Utah. . . . Had the helm of state been put into the hands of Fremont the pot would have boiled over a little sooner."

When the Saints were informed during a 24th of July celebration in Big Cottonwood Canyon that a U.S. Army of occupation was on its way to the territory, fear gripped the people. Young felt compelled to use his gubernatorial powers to declare martial law. "Our opponents have availed themselves of prejudice existing against us to send out a formidable host to accomplish our destruction," he declared. Noting that no investigating committee was sent to the territory, Young argued that the action "compels us to resort to the great first law of preservation and stand in our own defense, a right guaranteed to us by the genius of the institutions of our country and upon which the government is based" (Young Ms History, 15 Septe. 1857).

Ultimately "Buchanan's Blunder," as Mormons and other critics irreverently termed the military occupation of the territory, cost nearly $15 million. After initial resistance, the Mormon populace acquiesced to the intrusion of imposed officials and troops, and the outbreak of Civil War in 1861 diverted the federal government's attention from the "Mormon problem." But it was only a temporary reprieve. The church would not be relieved of government pressure to abandon polygamy until the early 1900s.

NOTES

1. Wilford Woodruff quoting Kane, in JH, 26 Nov. 1849; see also Kenney 3 (26 Nov. 1849): 496.

2. All three letters were published in pamphlet form by the church. Copies were sent to influential politicians, including President Fillmore, and to major newspapers.

3. Phelps, a noted toastmaster, made this same statement in a toast on "Mormonism and Marriage," MS 14 (24 July 1852): 643.

4. Bernhisel's philosophy on marriage is an interesting study in itself. Celibate until age forty-four, he married a forty-year-old widow with six children in 1845. The following year he married six plural wives. But shortly before his initial departure for Washington he reverted to monogamy with his youngest wife, though not formally divorcing the others. While he accepted polygamy in principle, he opposed its open promulgation and practice. For a treatment of his position, see Van Wagoner and Walker 1982, 15-18.

5. Bernhisel remained sensitive to such letter writing throughout his tenure. On 14 December 1854 he wrote to Young: "I wish that those brethren who indulge in the thoughtless practice of writing letters on the subject of poligamy . . . would cease to do so. These letters find their way into the newspapers, and aggravate and perpetuate that deep rooted and bitter prejudice which is operating so much to our injury" (LDS Archives).

6. B. H. Roberts, however, disagreed that polygamy was at the root of the excommunications. Citing the excommunication figure 2,164 for the six months preceding the announcement on plural marriage, he viewed the action as having only minimal effect on church membership (1930, 4:58-59).

WOMEN IN POLYGAMY

Contrary to popular nineteenth-century notions about polygamy, the Mormon harem, dominated by lascivious males with hyperactive libidos, did not exist. The image of unlimited lust was largely the creation of Gentile travelers to Salt Lake City more interested in titillating audiences back home than in accurately portraying plural marriage. Newspaper representatives and public figures visited the city in droves seeking headlines for their eastern audiences. Mormon plural marriage, dedicated to propagating the species righteously and dispassionately, proved to be a rather drab lifestyle compared to the imaginative tales of polygamy, dripping with sensationalism, demanded by a scandal-hungry eastern media market.

The stark reality behind the headlines and head shaking was an essentially puritanical Mormon marriage system. Brigham Young explained the purposes of plural marriage to a 14 July 1855 Mormon audience: "God never introduced the Patriarchal order of marriage with a view to please man in his carnal desires, nor to punish females for anything which they had done; but He introduced it for the express purpose of raising up to His name a royal Priesthood, a peculiar people" (JD 3 [14 July 1855]: 266).

Young insisted that polygamy was not something he would have sought of his own volition and testified that the time Joseph Smith advised him to take a plural wife "was the first time in my life that I had desired the grave" (ibid.). John Taylor, one of the earliest apostles to accept polygamy, agreed that taking a second wife had not been an easy matter. "I had always entertained strict ideas of virtue," he commented, "and I felt as a married man that this was to me . . . an appalling thing to do. . . . Nothing but a knowledge of God, and the revelations of God . . . could have induced me to embrace such a principle as this. . . . We [the Twelve] seemed to put off, as far as we could, what might be termed the evil day" (Roberts 1965, 100).

Another prevalent nineteenth-century misconception about Mormon polygamy was that women were dehumanized by the practice. In reality, polygamous wives lived lives similar to those of other frontier women. Despite several notable exceptions who attained success in business, mercantile, literary, and medical careers, most Mormon women remained in the domestic sphere; they were not exploited for their income-earning capacity as trades-people or factory workers. In interviews with the children of 155 plural wives, the Charles Redd Center for Western Studies at Brigham Young University has discovered that only twelve percent of their mothers ever worked outside the home after marriage. Most of those who did were teachers, nurses, mid-wives, housekeepers, and seamstresses. Thirty-six percent of the women sup-plemented their family's income by selling farm produce, taking in boarders, washing clothes, or selling breadstuffs, quilts, or rag rugs (Embry, "Economic Role," 6-7).

Mormon polygamy, unlike plural marriage in other cultures, devel-oped rapidly and without long-term cultural shaping. Since the number of wives permitted was never defined some men married beyond their means. Though the first wife's consent was supposedly required by scripture, it was not always sought or willingly given. Courtship manners were not well estab-lished, and accounts of older men "making fools of themselves" over young girls are seen occasionally. The rules of wooing depended on the individuals involved: interest could be initiated by the man, the prospective wife, or even the first wife who felt it was her religious duty to do so.

As no set patterns of living arrangements evolved in Mormon polyg-amy, personality conflicts often influenced such matters. In some households— Brigham Young's being probably the most obvious example—all wives lived under the same roof. But this could be a source of jealousy and frustration. Consequently husbands usually tried to provide separate dwellings for each woman. If wives lived in the same community husbands usually alternated days or nights with each family. Some men were fair to the minute; others favored their more agreeable or younger wives and spent more time with them. When wives lived far apart husbands sometimes visited branches of their family only a few times each year.

Plural wives, like their husbands, viewed polygamy as a practical and honorable means for providing marriage and motherhood to thousands of women who may have otherwise remained unmarried in a monogamous world. Church leaders pronounced over and over that plural marriage coun-tered various social evils. Above all they stressed that the principle was com-manded by God to raise a righteous generation. Mormons nearly always entered polygamy because they believed it was essential to their salvation, that God required it of them. "Maney may think it verry strainge that I would consent for my dear husband[,] whome I loved as I did my own life and lived with him for years[,] to take more wives," wrote Sarah D. Rich, wife of Apostle Charles C. Rich. "This I could not have done if I had not believed it to be right in the Sight of god, and believed it to be one principal of his gospel once again restored to earth, that those holding the preasthood of heaven might by obeying this order attain to a higher glory in the eternal world" (Arrington 1974, 288). Annie Clark Tanner was similarly certain that "women would never have accepted polygamy had it not been for their religion. The principle of Celestial Marriage was considered the capstone of the Mormon religion. Only by practicing it would the highest exaltation in the Celestial Kingdom of God be obtained" (Tanner 1976, 1-2).

Despite constant exhortation from the pulpit to live the principle of polygamy and the resulting group pressure to conform, most men remained monogamous. The percentage of polygamous households varied considerably from community to community—depending on the enthusiasm of the local church leaders in promoting the practice. The most comprehensive study to date, detailing forty 1880 Mormon towns, found that almost 40 percent of St. George households were polygamous compared to 11 percent in nearby Harrisburg/Leeds. In Rockville only 10 percent was polygamous, while 67 percent of Orderville was. In South Weber, north of Salt Lake City, 5 percent practiced polygamy, compared to nearly 30 percent in Bountiful. Other studies found a 15 percent incidence in Springville, while 63 percent of Mormon men in the Mexican colonies had more than one wife (Bennion 1984, 30-31; Logue 1984, 10; Nelson 1983, 57).[1]

In addition, polygamous men often married only one additional wife, evidently just enough to satisfy the letter of the law. Stanley Ivins's 1956 demographic study (using a sample of 6,000 families), pointed out that of the 1,784 polygamous men in the group, 66.3 percent married only two wives, 21.2 percent married three, 6.7 percent married four, and a scant 5.8 percent married five or more women.

Although defenders of Mormon polygamy stress that the principle was intended for religious rather than sexual purposes, plural wives tended to be much younger than their husbands. A 1987 study completed by the Charles Redd Center for Western Studies at Brigham Young University found that 60 percent of the 224 plural wives in their sample were under the age of twenty. The man was usually in his early twenties when he married his first wife, who was in her late teens. When he took a second wife he was generally in his thirties and his new wife between seventeen and nineteen years of age. Men who married a third wife were commonly in their late thirties. The average age of third wives was nineteen as were fourth wives whose husbands by then were between thirty-six and forty-five (Embry 1987, 34-35).

Though polygamous families were always a minority, most Mormons viewed the practice as the model lifestyle. Church leaders deftly twisted the guilt in the hearts of Saints who were less than enthusiastic about engaging in the practice. "If any of you will deny the plurality of wives," Brigham Young was quoted in the 14 November 1855 Deseret News, "and continue to do so, I promise that you will be damned." His colorful counselor, Heber C. Kimball, the husband of forty-three wives and father of sixty-five children, went so far as to promise aging Mormon men that polygamy would bring them a renewal of youth. "I have noticed," he commented, "that a man who has but one wife, and is inclined to that doctrine, soon begins to wither and dry up, while a man who goes into plurality looks fresh, young, and sprightly" (JD 5 [6 April 1857]: 22). Portly apostle George A. Smith poked fun at non-polygamists by calling them a "poor narrow-minded, pinch-backed race of men, who chain themselves down to the law of monogamy, and live all their days under the domination of one wife" (JD 3 [6 April 1856]: 291).

No period of Mormon history demonstrated a devotion to polyga-mous duty more than the two-year-period from 1856 to 1857, known as the Mormon Reformation. This movement, led by Brigham Young's fiery coun-selor Jedediah M. Grant, stressed cleanliness, confession, repentance, self-sufficiency—and plural marriage. Stanley S. Ivins, a prominent student of polygamy, noted that during this two-year period, sixty-five percent more polygamous marriages were contracted than at any other two-year period in Mormon history (Ivins 1956, 231). "All are trying to get wives," Wilford Woodruff wrote fellow apostle George A. Smith, "until there is hardly a girl 14 years old in Utah, but what is married, or just going to be" (JH, 1 April 1857). A Salt Lake City woman writing to her friend wondered "if the refor-mation has taken as much effect where you are, as it has here in regard to getting more wives. If it has, and your husband is a true Saint, I might pos-sibly be obliged to send the comforting words of 'grin and bear it' to you. . . . Indeed this is the greatest time for marrying I ever knew" (Ellsworth 1974, 38).

The belief that polygamy was divinely sanctioned was no guarantee against marital problems. Mormon sociologist Kimball Young, in a study of 175 polygamous marriages, rated 53 percent as "highly successful" or "rea-sonably successful," 25 percent as "moderately successful," and 23 percent as troubled by "considerable" or "severe conflict" (1954, 56-57). More recent studies have revealed that at least 1,645 divorces were granted by Brigham Young during the period of his presidency (Campbell and Campbell 1978, 5). It is not known, however, the extent to which polygamy was a factor in these cases. D. Michael Quinn's study of the Mormon hierarchy indicates that of the seventy-two General Authorities who entered plural marrige, thirty-nine were involved in marital breakups, including fifty-four divorces, twenty-six separations, and one annulment. Many of these church leaders, however, were married to numerous wives, thereby substantially increasing the possi-bility for broken marriages.[2]

The extent of Mormon divorce was a concern to Brigham Young. During the millennial fervency of the Reformation many Saints had entered into unsatisfactory marriages. In an 1858 address Young argued, "It is not right for the brethren to divorce their wives the way they do. I am deter-mined that if men don't stop divorcing their wives, I shall stop sealing" (JH, 15 Dec. 1858). Though upset about the frequency of divorce, Young did not require unhappy women to stay with their husbands. His advice to a woman seeking counsel was to "stay with her husband as long as she could bear with him, but if life became too burdensome, then leave and get a divorce" (President's Office Journal, 5 Oct. 1861). He suggested in an 1861 address that "when a woman becomes alienated in her feelings and affections from her husband, it is his duty to give her a bill and set her free." In an unusual moral definition, he declared it "would be fornication for a man to cohabit with his wife after she had thus become alienated from him." There was another church-approved way in which a woman could leave a man — if the woman preferred a man *higher in authority*," Young explained, "and he is willing to take her and her husband gives her up. There is no bill of divorce required, in [this] case it is right in the sight of God" (Beck Notebooks).

Mormon men were under a lifetime moral obligation to care for their ex-wives. "For a man to seek a divorce is almost unheard of," Apostle George Q. Cannon noted when explaining the legal and religious safeguards for divorced women. "The liberty upon this point rests with the woman, and as regards a Separation, if her position should become irksome, or distasteful to her, even, and she should desire a Separation, not only is the man bound to respect the expressal of her wish to that effect, but he is bound also to give her and her offspring a proportionate share of his whole property." Divorced families had an economic claim upon a man, according to Cannon, "from which he is never completely absolved" (Cannon 1879, 36).

Some have argued that marital discord in Mormon polygamous marriages was no greater than in the monogamous American populace. Others, however, have disagreed. George S. Tanner, prominent Utah educator and polygamous son, reasoned: "I doubt there was a woman in the church who was in any way connected with Polygamy who was not heartsick. . . . They would not admit it in public because of their loyalty to the church and their brothers and sisters." Tanner was persuaded that "the women try to be brave, but no woman is able to share a husband *whom she loves* with one or more other women. . . . Only a few of the women involved in polygamy asked for a divorce simply because it was not a popular thing to do" (Campbell and Campbell 1978, 14-15). Mrs. Hubert Howe Bancroft, a prominent visitor to Salt Lake City in 1880, commented on the ability of polygamous women to maintain appearances. She observed that Mormon women viewed polygamy as "a religious duty and schooled themselves to bear its discomforts as a sort of religious penance, and that it was a matter of pride to make everybody believe they lived happily and to persuade themselves and others that it was not a trial; and that long life of such discipline makes the trial lighter" ("Inner Facts," 18).

Predictably, observations from women living polygamy varied as widely. "If anyone in this world thinks plural marriage is not a trial," Sadie Jacobson said, "they are wrong. The Lord said he would have a tried people" (1972, 292). "I want to testify," said her sister-wife Becky Jacobson, "that I have been happy and blessed as a polygamist wife. . . . Any sacrifice we made for each other was rewarded ten-fold. . . . We learned to worship together, sorrow together, play and rejoice together, to unselfishly pool all our resources for the good of the family" (ibid.).

Ada and Vady Hart, though experiencing jealous bouts over their shared husband, felt that these feelings "were the work of the devil who was trying to destroy the Lord's work." When they would find themselves "out of harmony" the two wives would "fast and pray" in order to "get the right spirit again" (Embry, "Effects," 58). At the other end of the patience spectrum was the tongue-in-cheek quip attributed to a daughter of Jedediah M. Grant: "Polygamy is alright when properly carried out—on a shovel" (Shook 1914, 208). Contemporary diary and letter accounts of polygamous relationships generally present a less-than-glowing picture of polygamy. Positive testimonials are most often seen in public or retrospective accounts. Church members, recognizing that the eyes of the world were upon them, may have been inclined to put forth a sanitized "storybook polygamy" publicly rather than portraying the real hardships involved in trying to live the practice.

The paradox of women publicly supporting plural marriage while privately suffering from it is demonstrated in the lives of such prominent Mormon women as Emmeline B. Wells and Martha H. Cannon. Wells, wife of Daniel H. Wells of the First Presidency, editorialized in the *Women's Exponent* that plural marriage "gives women the highest opportunities for self-development, exercise of judgment, and arouses latent faculties, making them more truly cultivated in the actual realities of life, more independent in thought and mind, noble and unselfish" (Godfrey et al. 1982, 16). Yet Emmeline's marriage to Daniel was unhappy. "O, if my husband could only love me even a little and not seem to be perfectly indifferent to any sensation of that kind," she wrote in her 30 September 1874 diary. "He cannot know the craving of my nature; he is surrounded with love on every side, and I am cast out. . . . O my poor aching heart when shall it rest its burden only on the Lord. . . . Every other avenue seems closed against me."[3] On their twenty-second wedding anniversary she wrote in her diary, "Anniversary of my marriage with Pres. Wells. O how happy I was then how much pleasure I anticipated and how changed alas are things since that time, how few thoughts I had then have ever been realized, and how much sorrow I have known in place of the joy I looked forward to" (10 Oct. 1874). The autumn years of Emmeline's life brought a bittersweet unexpected reunion with her erstwhile husband. Wells, now seventy-six, became attentive to the sixty-two-year-old wife he had essentially ignored for nearly four decades. After his death in 1891, she wrote, "Only memories, only the coming and going and parting at the door. The joy when he came the sorrow when he went as though all the light died out of my life. Such intense love he has manifested towards me of late years. Such a remarkable change from the long ago—when I needed him so much more" (24 March 1891).

Dr. Martha Hughes Cannon, twenty-seven-year-old resident physician at Deseret Hospital in Salt Lake City and later the first female state senator in the United States, became the third plural wife of fifty-year-old Angus Cannon, Salt Lake City stake president and one of Deseret Hospital's directors. Government pressure to stamp out polygamy and a too-often-absent husband made Martha's marriage less than enviable. Forced to leave Salt Lake frequently to prevent her husband's arrest for practicing polygamy, she described her marriage as "a few stolen interviews thoroughly tinctured with the *dread of discovery.*" In a 3 February 1888 letter to her husband while she was in Europe, she wrote that the trials of polygamy would be unendurable without "a thorough knowledge from God, that the *principle* for which we are battling and striving to maintain in purity upon the earth is ordained by Him, and that we are chosen instruments in His hands to engage in so great a calling." She added that "even with this assurance grounded in one's heart, we do not escape trials and temptations, grievious at times in their nature."

Martha was acquainted with several monogamous families and yearned for an exclusive relationship. She described such a marriage as "a joy and comfort to witness, where the wife and Mother is proud and happy in the devotion of a noble husband, while he in turn is equally contented and happy in the possession of the partner he has chosen for life; while at *home* in each other's association is where their greatest joys are centered."[4] "Oh for a home!" she lamented in a 30 December 1891 letter to Angus: "A husband of my own because he is my own. A father for my children whom they know by association. And all the little auxiliaries that make life worth living. Will they ever be enjoyed by this storm-tossed exile. Or must life thus drift on and one more victim swell the ranks of the great unsatisfied!"

Marital satisfaction proved an elusive dream for Martha. Though she noted in a letter to her husband that she "would rather spend one hour in your society, than a whole lifetime with any other man," near-constant lack of money and a husband occupied with other family, church, and civic responsibilities resulted in the collapse of their marriage. "How do you think *I* feel," she angrily wrote to her husband, "when I meet you driving another plural wife about in a glittering carriage in broad day light? [I] am entirely out of money—borrowing to pay some old standing debts. I want *our* affairs *speedily* and *absolutely* adjusted—after all my sacrifice and loss you treat me like a dog—and parade others before my eyes—I will not *stand* it."

She wrote on another occasion, "Will you send remitance— coal— flour etc etc . . . to say nothing of winter clothing essential to growing children. I find myself inadequate to *entirely* support them while they have a so-called 'handsome magn[i]fic' father living." Eventually Martha found her husband's inattention insufferable: "I should have appreciated the interest you should have felt more than the money—Tis the *little* things you could have done and not the larger things you could *not*, that has estranged us. . . . I will never feel as I *once* did. And you are to blame—so little[,] had you helped[,] would have alleviated this."

In a 3 February 1888 letter to her husband, Martha Cannon explained that had she not believed living in plural marriage would have enabled her to "associate with the elect in eternity," she would "undoubtedly have given plural marriage a wide berth except perhaps as first wife." But the adjustment required of the first wife in switching from monogamy to polygamy was perhaps the most difficult of all. After years of an exclusive relationship with a husband, having to share him with other women was a trial for any Mormon woman. Some, like Emma Smith, opposed their husbands' taking additional wives. In such instances the man had two options. Either he could respect his wife's wishes and remain monogamous, or he could, as Joseph Smith did, ignore her objections and take plural wives without her consent.[5]

Kimball Young reported an account of a Mormon elder in St. George who was asked why he never entered polygamy when so many of his peers had. "She wouldn't let me," he nodded towards his wife. "I told him," she reported, "that if he ever took another wife, when he brought her in the front door I would go out the back. And when I told his mother what I said she told me, 'If I had only a quilt, you would be welcome to half of it when you left him'" (1954, 123). A novel though unsuccessful attempt to get a second wife was initiated by an elder from southern Utah. Young reported that the fearful man hesitated to ask permission of his feisty wife. "Finally, he told her he had had a revelation to marry a certain girl and that in the face of such divine instructions, she must give her consent." He had obviously underestimated the ingenuity of his wife, who announced the next morning that she had received a revelation to "shoot any woman who became his plural wife" (ibid.). He remained monogamous.

Prominent Lehi settler Isaac Goodwin also lived monogamously and would have it no other way. "I have a kingdom of my own," he told adventurer John Codman in 1878, "without polygamy: this old lady, seven children, and thirty-three grandchildren." He then explained his philosophy in detail: "I believe in the doctrine for those who like it, but God never required it of me. Matrimony is a "straight and narrrow path." I like to go it alone. Now you hang a plummet down from the wall and let it drop between two women. Each of them will say it swings nearer the other one than toward her. I might be straight up and down like that plummet, and though the women mighn't say anything, both of them would think I was leaning the wrong way from her. So much for *two* women. Now hang yourself like a plummet in a circle of half a dozen, and then you can make some calculation what kind of a time you would have through life" (p. 200).

96

Pressures to live polygamously, however, were compelling to Mormon males desirous of advancement in church position. Apostle John Taylor was told by Joseph Smith to take a second wife, and when Taylor hesitated, Smith spelled out the consequences of failure to enter polygamy: "'Elder Taylor, have you concluded to enter into that principle and observe the counsel that you have received?' I told him I was thinking about it very seriously, when he replied, 'Unless that principle is observed and acted upon, you can proceed no further with the full fellowship of God'" (Cannon, "Statement," 24). Hints to take additional wives were not always subtle. In 1875 Apostle Wilford Woodruff announced, "We have many bishops and elders who have but one wife. They are abundantly qualified to enter the higher law and take more, but their wives will not let them. Any man who permits a woman to lead him and bind him down is but little account in the church and Kingdom of God" (Cowley 1909, 490).

When government anti-polygamy pressure intensified in the 1880s, President John Taylor received several revelations which further pressured monogamists. In calling monogamist Seymour B. Young to the Council of Seventies in a 13 October 1882 revelation, he stipulated that Young would first have to "conform to my law . . . it is not meet that men who will not abide in my law shall preside over my Priesthood." The next day, in a meeting of the First Presidency and Quorum of the Twelve, Taylor related that Joseph Smith had once said to him: "If we do not keep the same law that Our Heavenly Father has we cannot go with him. . . . A man obeying a lower law is not qualified to preside over those who keep a higher law" (Kenney 8 [14 Oct. 1882]: 126). In 1884 Taylor reported another revelation which urged monogamists to resign ecclesiastical offices in the church (Abraham H. Cannon Journal, 6 April 1884).[6]

Church leaders went so far as to threaten monogamist men with excommunication and loss of their one wife in the afterlife to more obedient polygamists. During an 1873 meeting at Paris, Idaho, Brigham Young said that a "man who did not have but one wife in the Resurrection that woman will not be his but [be] taken from him & given to another" (Kenney 7 [31 Aug. 1873]: 152.)[7] Francis M. Lyman, eventual president of the Quorum of the Twelve, remarked in 1883 that "Celestial marriage is for the fulness of the glory of god. it is the crowning glory. a man has no right to one wife unless he is worthy of two . . . [T]here is no provision made for those who have had the chance & opperternity and have disregarded that law. Men who disregard that law are in the same situation as if they broke any other law. they are transgressors" ("Remarks").

An 1883 letter to church president John Taylor asked if a man "having a wife sealed to him over the alter, and lives faithful, and is not successful in getting another. Will the one he has be taken from him?" Taylor's secretary responded, "A person cannot reject that principle without eternal loss to himself. . . . Those who reject and fight against this law of heaven would do well to have a care lest the anger of god fall upon them" (William Marsden to George Reynolds, 19 Nov. 1883; Reynolds to Marsden, 26 Nov. 1883).[8] Marriner W. Merrill, in the early 1880s, called Andrew L. Hyer to preside over the seventies quorum in Richmond, Utah. "But first you've got to take another wife," Merrill warned. Though Hyer did not want to, he changed his mind after Merrill threatened to cut him off from the church (Embry, "Richardson," 4).

David John, a member of the Utah Stake presidency for thirty years, recorded in his 1884 journal that the First Presidency (consisting of John Taylor, George Q. Cannon, and Joseph F. Smith) said that "Celestial Marriage" was "binding on all the Latter-day Saints and no man was entitled to the right of Presiding without abiding this law." According to John, the officials added that "If Bro. Wm. W. Cluff and Abraham [sic] Hatch and other leading men had gone into this order 18 months or more ago Zion would today have been upon a higher place than now" (p. 421). Neither Summit Stake president Cluff nor Heber Stake president Hatch entered polygamy. William Forman, a bishop in Hatch's stake, noted in his 11 March 1884 diary that during a local priesthood meeting Hatch said it took Wilford Woodruff forty years to obey the Word of Wisdom, the church's health code, and it would probably take him (Hatch) that long to live polygamy. Forman added that Hatch "feels quite important and says he is not going to resign."

Women who opposed the "patriarchal marriage system" were publicly condemned for failure to "follow counsel." Ellen Clawson wrote to a friend during the Mormon Reformation, "Some of the brethren here have to take more wives, whether they want to very bad or not, and Bro. [Heber C.] Kimball says those that havn't but one, she rules, and he makes so much fun of them, that they are ashamed, and get another as quick as they can" (Ellsworth 1974, 38). Brigham Young browbeat recalcitrant females in an 1856 address: "Let the father be the head of the family . . . and let the wives and the children say amen to what he says, and be subject to his dictates, instead of their dictating the man, instead of trying to govern him" (JD 4 [21 Sept. 1856]: 55).

Some women, however, would not bend to such patriarchal directive. Such a woman was Sarah M. Pratt. Her husband, Orson Pratt, following his own 1842 difficulties over plural marriage, came, like many Mormons, to hold a larger-than-life image of polygamy. "Instead of a plurality of wives being a cause of sorrow to females," he wrote, "it is one of the greatest blessings of the last dispensation: it gives them the great privilege of being united to a righteous man, and of rearing a family according to the order of heaven." Instead of remaining single or marrying a "wicked man who will ruin her and her offspring," a woman in plural marriage "can enter a family where peace and salvation reign . . . where the head of the family stands forth as a patriarch, a prince, and a savior to his whole household; where blessings unspeakable and eternal are sealed upon them and their generations after them; where glory is eternal and her joy is full" (Pratt 1853-54, 155-56).

But Pratt's first wife, Sarah, did not view polygamy so idealistically. She insisted that the first wife "should be it, and resented her husband's affections toward his other wives" ("Elizabeth Ivins"). Being away from home on church assignment was a hallmark of dedication for Mormon males, and during the years 1839-68, Orson Pratt was absent from his home for a total of nearly eleven years. Thirteen children were born during this period. Death took many, and other hands than Orson's usually buried them. Most of the happy times found him absent as well. Sarah learned to get by, rearing the children with little help from their father.

Ultimately Pratt's preoccupation with church work and his habit of marrying much younger women dealt a fatal blow to his relationship with Sarah. After returning from England in early 1868, the fifty-seven-year-old man began courting a sixteen-year-old girl who would become his tenth wife on 28 December 1868. At fifty-one, Sarah could no longer bear children, and she had come to resent bitterly Pratt's relationships with women younger than their oldest daughter. In an 1877 interview she lashed out at him. "Here was my husband," she said, "gray headed, taking to his bed young girls in mockery of marriage. Of course there could be no joy for him in such an intercourse except the indulgence of his fanaticism and of something else, perhaps, which I hesitate to mention" ("Orson Pratt's Harem").

Sarah could not have been fully aware of the workings of polygamy when she first let Orson take additional wives in Nauvoo. Few women—or men—were. Sarah half-heartedly went along with the system for nearly a quarter of a century, as her son Arthur put it, "from an earnest, conscientious desire to do what was right as a Mormon, and to please a husband whom she loved with all the strength of her nature" (*Anti-Polygamy Standard*, Feb. 1882, 81). But because of her earlier difficulties with Joseph Smith in Nauvoo, she was never converted to polygamy.

Sarah explained, ten years after the fact, that her marriage to Pratt finally came to an abrupt end on 12 March 1868, when he announced his intent to equalize his time spent with each wife. "I believed," Sarah said, "when he decided to enter upon the practice of polygamy, that he did so not from any violence of individual passion, but from sheer fanaticism." Orson told her that he considered it "his duty to take other women besides myself to wife," but that "this would make no difference in his affection for me, which would continue pure and single as it had ever been." This did not prove to be the case, according to Sarah, as indicated by Orson's eventual desire to spend equal time with his other wives. "By and by he told me that he intended to put these five women on an exact equality with me," Sarah later remembered, by spending "a week with one, a week with another, and so on, and that I should have the sixth week! Then patience forsook me," Sarah claimed; "I told him plainly that I wouldn't endure it. I said, 'If you take five weeks with your other women you can take the sixth with them also.'"[9]

She meant what she said. When Orson refused to reconsider his equal-time plan, she turned a cold shoulder to both him and the church. Because of her high profile as an outspoken anti-polygamous wife of a church leader, numerous individuals interviewed her, and in one interview in the mid-1870s she castigated polygamy as the "direst curse with which a people or a nation could be afflicted. . . . It completely demoralizes good men, and makes bad men correspondingly worse. As for the women—well, God help them! First wives it renders desperate, or else heart-broken, mean-spirited creatures; and it almost unsexes some of the other women, but not all of them, for plural wives have their sorrows too" (Froiseth 1884, 38-40).

Even those first wives who seemed to adjust well to polygamy often suffered quietly. Artemesia Snow, wife of Apostle Erastus Snow, complained frequently to him of the difficulties of raising her children in a house filled with other wives and their children while he was away on church activity. "You often ask how we enjoy ourselves," she wrote to her absent husband; "we enjoy ourselves as well as we can under existing circumstances[;] we have a large family of little children and many different kinds[;] it is not very pleasant having so many kinds of children and so many different mistresses." She lamented that they did not have a father with them: "I become more and more satisfied every day of my life that it is no way to bring up children, and I think that you would be convinced of that fact if you were at home a few evenings from sunset till dark and hear the music of the four babies[,] saying nothing of the others[,] to join in and help them a little. [W]e often wish you were hear to hear them but we will try and stand it till you come home and then we will poke you up with hot blocks" (A. Larson 1971, 270).

Mary Ann Angell Young, Brigham Young's second wife, was a patient, uncomplaining woman.[10] But even she reportedly remarked to a friend, "God will be very cruel if he does not give us poor women adequate compensation for the trials we have endured in polygamy" (*Anti-Polygamy Standard*, Aug. 1882, 36). The highly favored Emmeline Free Young experienced, as Mary Ann put it, "the torments of the damned" over being displaced by Brigham's younger wife, Amelia Folsom. When a friend asked one of Mary Ann's daughters if it did not grieve her mother to see Young's devotion to his new wife, she replied, "Mother does not care. She is past being grieved by his conduct, but, on the other hand, it gives her most intense satisfaction to see Emmeline suffer as she does. She can understand now what mother had to undergo in past years. In fact, all the women are glad that Emmeline is getting her turn at last" (ibid.).

Phebe Woodruff, first wife of Apostle Wilford Woodruff, also shared the ambivalent feelings of Mormon women in polygamy. Called upon to defend the principle in a mass meeting of Mormon women, Phebe bore testimony that "If I am proud of anything in this world, it is that I accepted the principle of plural marriage, and remained among the people called 'Mormons' and am numbered with them to-day." A few days later in a conversation with a long-time friend she was asked, "How is it Sister Woodruff that you have changed your views so suddenly about polygamy? I thought you hated and loathed the institution." "I have not changed," was her response: "I loathe the unclean thing with all the strength of my nature, but Sister, I have suffered all that a woman can endure. I am old and helpless, and would rather stand up anywhere, and say anything commanded of me, than to be turned out of my home in my old age which I should be most assuredly if I refused to obey counsel" (ibid., June 1882, 20).

Zina D. Jacobs Smith Young, plural wife of Brigham Young, was another strong public advocate of polygamy, who, like Phebe Woodruff, harbored private feelings different from her public posture. In the 1876 women's mass meeting Zina proclaimed, "The principle of plural marriage is honorable. It is a principle of the gods, it is heaven born. God revealed it to us as a saving principle; we have accepted it as such, and we know it is of him for the fruits of it are holy. Even the Savior, himself, traces his lineage back to polygamic parents" (Jenson 1901, 1:698-99). However, when a woman whose husband had taken a second wife went to Zina in great anguish of mind to ask, "Does the fault lie in myself that I am so miserable; or is the system to blame for it?" Zina reportedly replied, "Sister, you are not to blame, neither are you the only woman who is suffering torments on account of polygamy. There are women in this very house [Brigham Young's] whose hearts are full of hell, and in that room . . . is a woman who has been a perfect fury ever since Brother Young married Sister Amelia Folsom. Brigham Young dare not enter that room or she would tear his eyes out. It is the system that is to blame for it, but we must try and be as patient as we can" (*Anti-Polygamy Standard*, Jan. 1882, 75).

By this time Zina had nearly forty years of polygamous experience. Though she was an apologist for the system, she realized the practical difficulties in making plural marriages successful. "Much of the unhappiness found in polygamous families is due to the women themselves," she was quoted in the 19 November 1869 *New York World*. "They expect too much attention from the husband, and because they do not get it, or see a little attention bestowed upon one of the other wives, they become sullen and morose, and permit their ill-temper to finally find vent." Zina felt that "a successful polygamous wife must regard her husband with indifference, and with no other feeling than that of reverence, for love we regard as a false sentiment; a feeling which should have no existence in polygamy."

Vilate Kimball, first wife of Heber C. Kimball, also recognized the value of romantic distance in a plural marriage. Counseling an unhappy plural wife, she advised the woman that "her comfort must be wholly in her children; that she must lay aside wholly all interest or thought in what her husband was doing while he was away from her" and be as "pleased to see him when he came in as she was pleased to see any friend" (Cooks 1884, 5-6). A polygamous wife basing her relationship on romantic love often found the emotional foundation of marriage weakened by jealousy. Women who were not overly fond of their husbands in a romantic sense seemed to make the easiest adjustment to the situation. As in Puritan society, where marriage and family ties were also important, "there were strong proscriptions against the development of very strong emotional bonds between spouses; husband and wife were supposed to like each other, but not too much" (Cohen 1959, 113).

Church leaders, recognizing the emotional trauma that polygamy could induce, encouraged plural wives to focus their attentions on their children and on church and community activities. But as the church sought economic independence from the gentile invasion of Utah territory, women were counseled to involve themselves in such projects as teaching, medicine, writing, telegraphy, agriculture, mercantile enterprises, and a wide variety of home industries including silk production as well. Though the demands of mothering and maintaining a household kept most women from pursuing employment outside the home, one researcher has pointed out that "some women may have welcomed polygamy as a great boon, as it decreased some of the demands and divided the duties of the wife role, allowing them more time to develop personal talents" (Casterline 1974, 80-81).

Martha Cannon once wryly commented on a seldom-noted advantage of being a plural wife: "If her husband has four wives," she said of a hypothetical Mormon woman, "she has three weeks of freedom every month" (*San Francisco Examiner*, 8 Nov. 1896). Of course this apparent advantage was the flip side of polygamy's major disadvantage. As Annie Clark Tanner concluded after thirty years as a plural wife, the "companionship between husband and wife in polygamy could not be so close as in monogamy. There was more independence on both sides in polygamy. . . . Monogamous marriages are by far the more successful. They give security and confidence, and these are the requirements for happiness" (Tanner 1976, 272).

Though polygamy reduced the exclusivity of marital relationships, it greatly improved the cohesiveness of the larger Mormon community. Group violation of what had been conventional behavioral norms served to weld the Saints into in a new fraternity of people—a "peculiar people," as they were fond of calling themselves—united in their opposition to government interference in marriage practices. This militant separateness lasted nearly fifty years. In the end, however, federal government opposition to Mormon polygamy put a stop to plural marriage. At the beginning of the twentieth century, the Saints began the tortuous process of re-emerging into mainstream American society.

Notes

1. Leonard J. Arrington and Davis Bitton cite a lower figure. They estimate 5 percent of Mormon males (generally church leaders), 12 percent of Mormon women, and 10 percent of Mormon children were from polygamous households (1979, 199). Some statements have suggested that the number was as low as 3 percent, but these estimates are usually based on figures given during the Reed Smoot hearings when a lower percentage was politically advantageous to the church. Stanley S. Ivins in his analysis estimated 15-20 percent of Mormon families in Utah were polygamous (1956, 230).

2. These eighty-one failures in 400 marriages represent a 20 percent level (Quinn 1973, 248-91).

3. For treatments of Emmeline B. Wells's life, see Madsen 1982, and Rasmussen and Dushku, in Burgess-Olson 1978, 457-78.

4. The Martha H. Cannon letters cited in this work are all from the Angus M. Cannon Collection. For a treatment of the life of Martha H. Cannon, see "Martha H. Cannon," in Burgess-Olson 1978, 385-97.

5. The process for exempting a wife from the "law of Sarah" had been outlined in the 1843 revelation on celestial marriage (D&C 132:65). When cross-examined during the Reed Smoot hearings, church president Joseph F. Smith gave the official position on the necessity of a wife's consent: "A. The condition is that if she does not consent the Lord will destroy her, but I do not know how he will do it. Q. Is it not true that . . . if she refuses her consent her husband is exempt from the law which requires her consent. A. Yes; he is exempt from the law which requires her consent. She is commanded to consent, but if she does not, then he is exempt from the requirement. Q. Then he is at liberty to proceed without her consent, under the law. In other words, her consent amounts to nothing? A. It amounts to nothing but her consent" (1:201).

Orson Pratt also explained this clause in his writings on celestial marriage: "When a man who has a wife, teaches her the law of God, and she refuses to give her consent for him to marry another according to that law, then, it becomes necessary, for her to state before the President the reasons why she withholds her consent; if her reasons are sufficient and justifiable and the husband is found in the fault, or in transgression, then, he is not permitted to take any step in regard to obtaining another. But if the wife can show no good reason why she refuses to comply with the law which was given unto Sarah of old, then it is lawful for her husband, if permitted by revelation through the prophet, to be married to others without her consent, and he will be justified, and she will be condemned, because she did not give them unto him, as Sarah gave Hagar to Abraham, and as Rachel and Leah gave Bilhah and Zilpah to their husband, Jacob" (1853-54, 41).

6. Though this revelation was not published in English versions of the D&C, it was included as section 137 in the German editions of 1893 and 1903 and also as section 137 in the Danish edition of 1900. For background on this revelation, see Heber J. Grant discourse in *Conference Reports*, Oct. 1922, 2-3, and Kenney 8 (13-14 Oct. 1882): 126-27.

7. Two years earlier on 24 October 1871, Young expressed what seems the opposite point of view when he explained that "a Man may Embrace the Law of Celestial Marriage in his heart & not take the Second wife & be justified before the Lord" (Kenney 7 [24 Oct. 1871]: 31).

8. Reynolds's postscript adds this semi-official approval to his response: "I have read your letter to Pres. Taylor."

9. *New York Herald*, 18 May 1877. Orson Pratt also discussed this situation in an 1878 letter to Sarah: "You once, professedly, believed in the sealing ordinances, according to the revelation on marriage for eternity. You, at several times, did put the hands of others into my hand, and did give them to me as wives, immediately before the marriage ceremony was pronounced. Those women I took with all confidence, and with your consent. After several years had elapsed, I proposed to you, to commence living upon principles of greater equality in regard to my attentions: this proposition you positively rejected; and you further said, that if I introduced this equality, you would never live with me again, in time, nor in eternity. This was a hard and grievous trial to me: but believing . . . my proposition to be, not only right, but duty, I firmly concluded to follow my convictions, though it should be at the sacrifice of life itself."

10. Brigham Young married Miriam Works in 1824. She died in 1832, and two years later he married Mary Ann Angel. Though Brigham Young is usually depicted as the husband of twenty-seven wives, he was actually married to fifty-six and fathered the same number of children. Many of the wives, however, were spiritual charges with no connubial relationship (Jessee 1979).

"TWIN RELICS OF BARBARISM"

In 1852, when the Mormons announced their practice of polygamy to the world, there were no federal laws prohibiting it. But national opposition based on moral and religious objections quickly grew. War provided only a brief respite. Many Mormons viewed the Civil War as divine retribution for the government's refusal to provide redress for the Saints' losses in Missouri and Illinois. As war fever swept the country, church leaders predicted the nation's collapse. "It seems that many [easterners] are looking with some hope," Brigham Young wrote to Utah congressman William H. Hooper, "apparently not yet realizing that the corruption of the nation has sealed its doom . . . the people whom the very great majority have striven to obliterate, will step forward and sustain the falling banner and continue to honor the Heaven inspired constitution bequeathed to us [as] so rich a legacy by our forefathers" (G. Larson 1971, 28). Apostle John Taylor, too, anticipated that the nation would be "shaken to its center and . . . continue to fall and to crumble until it is no more" (JD 11 [11 Dec. 1864]: 26).[1] When the government emerged from the Civil War essentially intact, however, the country refocused on the abolition of Mormon polygamy.

Clergymen, women's leaders, newspaper editors, and federal appointees raised their voices demanding legislative action to wipe out polygamy in Utah. The Salt Lake evangelical ministry attacked plural marriage with particularly rabid ferocity. Local ministers provided the media with much anti-Mormon propaganda to "keep the Mormon question *in* the American press and Utah *out* of statehood" (G. Larson 1971, 53).[2]

Public reaction towards plural marriage was reflected in the 14 March 1860 *House Report* on a proposed anti-polygamy bill. "Whatever differences of opinion may exist as to whether marriage is a civil or a canonical contract," the bill declared, "the whole civilized world regards the marriage of one man to one woman as being alone authorized by the law of God, and that while the relation of husband and wife exists, neither can be lawfully married to another person." Referring specifically to Utah, the report expressed shock at the "open and defiant license which, under the name of religion and latitudinous interpretation of our Constitution, has been given to this crime in one of our Territories."

During debate on the issue, Illinois congressman McClernand expressed a typical sentiment against plural marriage. "As to polygamy," he argued, "I charge it to be a crying evil; sapping not only the physical constitution of the people practicing it, dwarfing their physical proportions and emasculating their energies, but at the same time perverting the social virtues, and vitiating the morals of its victims." He aligned the system with political despotism, which he reasoned "invariably begets among the people who practice it the extremes of brutal bloodthirstiness or timid and mean prevarication. . . . It is a scarlet whore. It is a reproach to the Christian civilization; and deserves to be blotted out" (*Congressional Globe*, 36th Congress, 1st session, 1860, 1514).

The idea that polygamy would result in genetic abnormalities was a common one. A presentation at the New Orleans Academy of Sciences in 1861 "demonstrated" physical abnormalities prevalent in the "new race" of polygamists: "The yellow, sunken, cadaverous visage; the greenish-colored eye; the thick, protuberant lips, the low forehead; the light, yellowish hair, and the lank, angular person, constitute an appearance so characteristic of the new race, the production of polygamy, as to distinguish them at a glance. The older men and women present all the physical peculiarities of the nationalities to which they belong; but these peculiarities are not propogated and continued in the new race; they are lost in the prevailing type."[3]

Numerous legislative packages were drafted in Congress to prevent this "new race" from taking hold. It was not until the Republican administration of Abraham Lincoln, however, that lawmakers passed the first of many bills which attempted to legislate polygamy out of existence. President Lincoln, a follower of the Mormon saga since his early experience with the church in Illinois, initially seemed content to let the Mormons be, despite the Republican party platform. During the early years of the Lincoln administration Mormon journalist T. B. H. Stenhouse asked the president what course he intended to pursue respecting the Mormons. "When I was a boy on the farm in Illinois," he replied, "there was a great deal of timber on the farms which we had to clear away. Occasionally we would come to a log which had fallen down. It was too hard to split, too wet to burn and too heavy to move, so we plowed around it. That's what I intend to do with the Mormons" (Nibley 1974, 369).[4] But church leaders feared Lincoln's administration. Brigham Young, as reported by Wilford Woodruff, prayed "daily that the Lord will take away the reigns of government of the wicked rulers & put it into the hands of wise good [men]." In addition to dramatically reducing the size of Utah territory on three separate occasions, Lincoln ordered an army of California volunteers to occupy Utah in 1861. Specifically responding to the sending of troops to Utah, Brigham Young further added that the "feelings of Abe Lincoln is that [President James] Buchanan tried to destroy the mormons & Could not. Now I will try my hand at it" (Kenney, 5 [11 Dec. 1861]: 605-06).

Young worried about Lincoln's intent. "I believe Abe Lincoln does intend to bring destruction upon this people if he Can and has the power," he said during a political meeting (ibid., 609).

Young's fears were not entirely correct, however. Lincoln did not wish to destroy the Mormon people, only to prevent their practice of polygamy. His wishes were fulfilled through the legislative efforts of Vermont congressman Justin Morrill. Morrill, a devout anti-polygamist, had failed on numerous occasions to secure passage of legislation before Lincoln signed the Morrill Anti-bigamy Act into law on 1 July 1862. The intent of this legislation was to "punish and prevent the practice of polygamy in the Territories of the United States and to disapprove and annul certain acts of the territorial legislature of Utah."

Despite the successful passage of this legislation, church leaders felt that it ultimately would have no effect on them. They were convinced that the Civil War would usher in the Millennium, and they would become the political salvation of the American government. Brigham Young, addressing the Utah territorial legislators on 19 January 1863, said that though "we are called the State Legislature," the time will come when "we shall be called the Kingdom of God." Young felt sure that while "our government is going to pieces, the time will come when we will give laws to the nations of the earth. . . . We should get all things ready, and when the time comes, we should let the water on the wheel and start the machine in motion" (JH, 19 Jan. 1863). John Taylor agreed: "The Almighty has established this kingdom with order and laws and everything pertaining thereto . . . that when the nations shall be convulsed, we may stand forth as Saviours . . . and finally redeem a ruined world, not only in a religious but in a political point of view" (JD 9 [13 April 1862]: 342).

Despite all the clamor about the Morrill Act, it remained essentially a dead issue for nearly five years. It might have remained that way indefinitely had not the Mormons been anxious to see the law removed from the books. In early 1867 the Utah territorial legislature sent a petition to the U.S. Congress requesting that the Morrill Act be repealed since "the judiciary of the Territory has not up to the present time, tried any case under said law though repeatedly urged to do so by those who have been anxious to test its constitutionality" (G. Larson 1971, 61). But federal officials viewed the Mormon move as an attempt to legitimize polygamy. They sought answers through the House Judiciary Committee as to why the law was not being enforced in Utah. Investigation revealed that the absence of aggressive judges committed to the anti-polygamy campaign had caused the law to be "practically a dead letter in the Territory of Utah" (*House Reports*, 39th Congress, 2nd session. no. 27, 1867).

Nearly all probate judges in Utah were Mormon bishops, unlikely to convict polygamists for practicing what they themselves believed to be the "law of God." The position of the church was that the Morrill Act was unconstitutional, a violation of the First Amendment which included a provision that "Congress shall make no law respecting an establishment of religion or prohibiting the free exercise thereof." Though a few legal scholars supported the position of the Saints, their voices were drowned out by the overwhelming majority who opposed the practice.

Though the federal government's primary Utah focus appeared to be on erradicating polygamy, Mormon allegiance to church leaders, which eclipsed loyalty to the country, was the chief underlying concern of politicians. Vice-President Schuyler Colfax, after visiting Salt Lake City in the fall of 1869, argued that "it is time to understand whether the authority of the nation or the authority of Brigham Young is the supreme power in Utah; whether the laws of the United States or the laws of the Mormon Church have precedence within its limits" (*New York Independent*, 2 Dec. 1869).

A series of bills was presented to Congress in the late 1860s in an attempt to strengthen the Morrill Act, although none became law. To get around the problem of Mormon judges, the Cullom Bill was introduced. Under the provisions of this legislation, the appointive power of the Utah governor was to be expanded to include not only local judges but sheriffs and notaries as well. Probate courts were to be denied criminal jurisdiction, and believers in plural marriage were to be excluded from jury duty in polygamy-related court cases. Wives would be permitted to testify against husbands, fines and punishments were prescribed, and polygamists were barred from holding political office, voting, or becoming naturalized.

Debate over the proposed Cullom Bill caused considerable stir throughout the country. Some, remembering the exhorbitant cost of the Utah Expeditionary Force, were afraid that the government might make an additional attempt to use military force to settle the Mormon question. Others were content to let polygamy run its course. "Mormon polygamy we think may be safely left to the corrective power of advancing civilization," the *New York Sun* editorialized; "The building of the Union Pacific Railroad has struck it a blow the effects of which it can escape only by flight to some remoter region" (in MS 32 [8 March-12 April 1870]: 151-210).

As on previous occasions when their beliefs were assailed, however, Mormon resolve was strengthened by opposition. On 13 January 1870 nearly three thousand Mormon women gathered in the Salt Lake Tabernacle to protest the Cullom Bill. Though the meetings were orchestrated by the Mormon hierarchy, observers, who viewed Mormon women as meek subservients in their husbands' harems, were surprised by their spunk. The meeting was "perhaps one of the grandest female assemblages in all history," a reporter for the *New York Herald* reported. "We venture to say," he added, "that whatever may be the individual reader's opinion of the merits or demerits of Mormon institutions, it will not be denied that Mormon women have both brains and tongues. Some of the speeches give evidence that in general knowledge in logic and in rhetoric the so-called degraded ladies of Mormondom are quite equal to the Women's Rights women of the East" (in MS 32 [8 March 1870]: 151). One month later, on 14 February, Utah became the second territory to grant female suffrage, a move that dramatically strengthened Mormon voting power.

Despite the controversy, the Cullom Bill passed the House on 23 March. Mormon leaders were terribly disappointed. At a mass meeting on 31 March, a memorial to Congress was adopted by "citizens of Salt Lake City." "We . . . are believers in the principle of plural marriage or polygamy," the petition declared, "not simply as an elevating social relationship and a preventive of many terrible evils which afflict our race, but as a principle revealed by god, underlying our every hope of eternal salvation and happiness in heaven." Encouraging the Senate to reject the Cullom Bill, the petitioners expressed the predicament they would be in should the bill become law. "It gives us no alternative," they argued, "but the cruel one of rejecting God's command and abjuring our religion, or disobeying the authority of a government we desire to honor and respect" ("Memorial").

Various lobbying efforts kept the Cullom Bill from reaching the Senate floor. But President Ulysses S. Grant, riding his post-Civil War popularity, personally favored a strong-arm approach in dealing with the "Mormon menace." General J. Wilson Shaffer, who had won recognition in re-establishing federal control in the southern states, was appointed governor of Utah, and James B. McKean became chief justice. Both appointees accepted their position with the same sense of mission they had followed in helping abolish slavery, the "first relic of barbarism."

McKean immediately trained his sights on Brigham Young, indicting the church president on charges of "lascivious cohabitation." The judge made no attempt to cover the fact that the issue was in reality "Federal Authority against Polygamic Theocracy." He announced that "The Government of the United States, founded upon a written constitution, finds within its jurisdiction another government claiming to come from God—*imperium in imperio*—whose policies and practices are in grave particulars, at variance with its own. The one government arrests the other in the person of its chief and arraigns it at the bar. A system is on trial in the person of Brigham Young" (*Salt Lake Tribune*, 9 Oct. 1871).

McKean's plans were shattered by the 15 April 1872 *Englerecht* decision of the U.S. Supreme Court which denounced the method of jury selection in the case. "Jury unlawfully drawn; summons invalid; proceedings ordered dismissed; decision unanimous, all indictments quashed," the 16 April 1872 *Salt Lake Herald* tersely reported. President Grant, who felt that the federal government had been embarrassed by the *Englerecht* decision, in his 1872 message to Congress called for "the ultimate extinguishment of polygamy." In February 1873 he outlined the necessary legislation, and on 23 June 1874 the Poland Law gave U.S. district courts in Utah exclusive civil and criminal jurisdiction, thus limiting probate courts to estate and divorce settlement.

Despite the Poland Law, church leaders were elated over what they viewed as victories in the defeat of the Cullom Bill and the Supreme Court's ruling in *Englerecht*. They were convinced that their position on plural marriage was sound and would be vindicated in court action. In mid-1874, church leaders met with the U.S. attorney in Salt Lake City and agreed to arrange a test case to determine the constitutionality of the anti-polygamy laws. George Q. Cannon, Utah's territorial delegate to Congress and second counselor to Brigham Young, felt that there was "universal belief" among Mormons that the polygamy law was unconstitutional. He correctly observed that "many eminent lawyers, both in and out of Congress" also held this position (Cannon Letterbooks, 10 Jan. 1879). The individual selected to be the "test balloon" was Young's personal secretary, avowed polygamist George Reynolds, who reported in his 21 October 1874 diary that Cannon approached him on the street and told him he had been selected for the case.

Reynolds was indicted for bigamy in October 1874 by a grand jury. Proving him guilty was a difficult task though he provided witnesses himself. His second wife, Amelia Jane Schofield, was eventually subpoenaed and admitted to her polygamous marriage. Though Reynolds was found guilty, the conviction was overturned by the territorial supreme court on grounds of irregularity in empaneling the jury. In a second trial one year later, Reynolds was again found guilty, on the basis of the testimony of his plural wife given in the first trial. Chief justice Alexander White's charge to the jury in the second trial became the basis for the U.S. Supreme Court's eventual ruling against Reynolds. "In matters of opinion, and especially in matters of religious belief," White argued, "all men are free. But parallel with and dominating over this is the obligation which every member of society owes to that society; that is, obedience to the law" (*Deseret Evening News*, 10 Dec. 1875).

Church leaders sought and ultimately obtained an appeal to the U.S. Supreme Court. On 6 January 1879 chief justice Waite, in the landmark decision *Reynolds v. the United States*, delivered the opinion which upheld the Utah territorial court decision, first by declaring that Congress had the right to legislate territorial law, and second by upholding the 1862 Morrill Act. "Laws are made for the government of actions," he declared, "and while they cannot interfere with mere religious belief and opinions, they may with practices." Waite argued that allowing a religious organization to go against society's established behavioral norms would have the effect of making the "professed doctrines of religious belief superior to the law of the land and in effect to permit every citizen to become a law unto himself. Government could exist only in name under such circumstances" (*United States*, 166-68).

In essence, *Reynolds* settled the question of whether religious belief could be accepted as justification for an act made criminal by the law of the land. Mormons, as the articulate George Q. Cannon put it, afterwards viewed "the Supreme Court of the United States on one side and the Lord on the other" (Cannon 1879, 6).[5]

The initial Mormon reaction of shock and disbelief at the court's decision quickly turned to defiance. An obvious conflict between the law of God and the law of the land existed in the minds of church leaders. Yet Mormon scripture strongly denounced civil disobedience. "Let no man break the laws of the land," an 1831 revelation had commanded, "for he that keepeth the laws of God hath no need to break the laws of the land. Wherefore, be subject to the powers that be" (D&C 58:21-22). A 2 August 1833 revelation had further explained that "that law of the land which is constitutional, supporting that principle of freedom in maintaining rights and privileges, belongs to all mankind, and is justifiable before me" (ibid. 98:5-6). On 17 August 1835 the entire church voted to accept as its "Declaration of Belief" the principle that "we believe that all men are bound to sustain and uphold the respective governments in which they reside" (ibid. 134:5).

Despite the ideals expounded in these scriptures, Mormons ignored *Reynolds* and continued their practice of polygamy. "The fools seem to think it is an easy thing to Measure arms with the Lord of Hosts," Mormon poet Charles Walker wrote in his 6 December 1879 journal; "the Step they are now taking will bring stife, anarchy, misery, and bloodshed upon the Nation. Meanwhile the Saints are as calm as a summer's morning, and not a soul seems to care or to be the least concerned about the infamous decision of the Supreme Court of the United States of America" (Larson and Larson 1980, 1:474). Quorum of the Twelve president Wilford Woodruff went a step farther in a public letter to the church. "Now Latter-day Saints, what are we going to do under the circumstances?" he wrote; "God says, 'we shall be damned if we do not obey the law.' Congress says 'we shall be damned if we do' . . . Now who shall we obey? God or man? My voice is that we will obey God" (Woodruff, "Epistle").[6]

Acting church president John Taylor in a 13 June 1879 interview with the *New York Tribune* denounced chief justice Waite's opinion as "so much bosh." Asked what effect he thought the court's decision would have on the Mormons, Taylor replied, "I don't know that it will have any effect except to unite us and confirm and strengthen us in our faith" (Hollister). Taylor saved his strongest words for the Saints. In October 1879 General Conference, after accusing Congress of a "shameless infraction of the Constitution of the United States," he thundered: "God will lay his hand upon this nation . . . there will be more bloodshed, more ruin, more devastation than ever they have seen before. . . . We do not want them to force upon us that institution of monogamy called the social evil. We won't have their mean-ness, with their foeticides and infanticides, forced upon us" (JD 20 [8 Oct. 1879]: 319-20).

Despite the defiant position of Taylor and other church leaders after Brigham Young's 1877 death, there is some evidence in the decade preceding his demise that Young may have been waning in his support for polygamy as had Joseph Smith during the last year of his life. Government opposition was not the only difficulty with polygamy. Many Mormons had entered polyg-amy, particularly during the Mormon Reformation of the mid-1850s, because they had been led to believe the Millennium was imminent. When this event was not forthcoming, many found themselves in unsatisfactory marriages which they wished to have Young dissolve. These divorces greatly disturbed him. In 1876 he closed the Endowment House on Temple Square, where most polygamous sealings were taking place. It was during this period that he apparently first began advising church leaders to marry only one wife.[7] In 1871 Young reversed his previously held position that polygamy was essen-tial to reaching the highest degree of heaven by announcing that "a man may embrace the law of celestial marriage in his heart and not take the second wife and be justified before the Lord" (Kenney 7 [24 Sept. 1871]: 31).[8]

Other church leaders evidently did not support Young's revised posi-tion. Apostle Joseph F. Smith, son of the martyred Hyrum Smith, announced to an 1878 assembly of Mormons: "Some people have supposed that the doc-trine of plural marriage was a sort of superfluity, or non-essential to the sal-vation or exaltation of mankind. In other words, some of the Saints have said, and believe, that a man with one wife, sealed to him by the authority of the Priesthood for time and eternity, will receive an exaltation as great and glorious, if he is faithful, as he possibly could with more than one. I want here to enter my solemn protest against this idea, for I know it is false" (JD 20 [7 July 1878]: 28).

Even more emphatic than the statements of Joseph F. Smith in stress-ing continued polygamy were those of the church's most militant polyga-mist, President John Taylor. Pressures both from within and without the church during the 1880s were working to influence Taylor to abandon the practice of polygamy. To put to rest any rumors that he might do so, he defiantly argued from the pulpit that "the people of the rest of the country are our enemies" and "we must not yield to them. . . . When they enact tyrannical laws, forbidding us the free exercise of our religion, we cannot submit. God is greater than the United States. And when the Government conflicts with Heaven, we will be ranged under the banner of Heaven and against the government." "Polygamy," Taylor insisted, "is a divine institu-tion. It has been handed down direct from God. The United States cannot abolish it. No nation on earth can prevent it, nor all the nations of the earth combined. I defy the United States. I will obey God" (*Salt Lake Tribune*, 6 Jan. 1880).

1. These statements were viewed by government leaders as evidence of lack of loyalty to the United States. Territorial governor Harding, who listened to such speeches or read them in the *Deseret News*, thought church authorities were guilty of treason. Reporting to Secretary of State William H. Seward on 3 September 1862, he noted that church leaders constantly taught that "the government of the United States is of no consequence; that it lies in ruins; [and] the prophecy of Joseph Smith is being fulfilled to the letter." Harding explained that Smith's prophecy predicted the government would be destroyed and that the Saints would step in and "enjoy the possession of the land and also what is left of the ruined cities and desolated [places]." Mormons, according to Harding, believed Zion would be built up not only in Utah, but "the Great Center of their power and glory, is to be in Missouri [where] the Saints under the lead of their prophet, were expelled years [ago]" (G. Larson 1971, 28).

Long after the Civil War had ended, church leaders still considered the event a divine act of retribution. Wilford Woodruff, for example, after reading an account of lives lost and monies expended during the war, noted in his 5 March 1885 journal: "This shows the inspired Man what it costs a Nation to Kill the Prophets and Apostles & shed the Blood of the Lords Anointed" (Kenney 8 [5 March 1885]: 307).

2. Since the First Amendment to the Constitution guaranteed religious freedom, anti-polygamy factions branded plural marriage as unreligious. Representative Cullom of Illinois, for example, argued that "polygamy has gone hand in hand with murder, idolatry, and every secret abomination." Cullom claimed that "instead of being a holy principle, receiving the sanction of Heaven, it is an institution founded in the lustful and unbridled passions of men, devised by Satan himself to destroy purity and authorize whoredom" (*Congressional Globe*, 41st Congress, 2nd session, 17 Feb. 1870: 1373).

Representative Ward of Illinois argued against the Mormon position that God had "commanded" polygamy, making it a valid religious tenet. "The God that sacrifices women to the lusts of men under the form of a plurality of wives is a God that I do not worship," he declared. Ward compared Mormon practices to other unfortunate beliefs: "It is in the name of religion that the widow mounts the funeral pyre in India. It is in the name of religion that helpless infants are sacrificed in the waters of the Ganges. It was in the name of religion that thousands of human beings were sacrificed to the Aztec gods upon the bloody altars of Mexico" (*Congressional Record*, 43rd Congress, 1st session, 2 June 1874: 447).

3. Paper presented by Samuel A. Cartwright and C. G. Forshey, based primarily on quotations from the report of U.S. Army Assistant Surgeon Robert Bartholow, "Effects and Tendencies of Mormon Polygamy in the Territories of Utah" (in Ivins 1956, 238).

4. See Brigham Young's account of this story in JD 10 (4 June 1864): 306.

5. Cannon had earlier attributed the expansion of Mormonism to the fact that the church practiced polygamy. "All the prosperity, seemingly, that we enjoy," he advocated, "has been bestowed upon us since the proclamation of that principle and its adoption by us into our faith and practice. There has been an almighty power hedging us round about and encircling us from that day until the present time" (JD 14 [11 June 1871]: 165-66). After the Reynolds decision was announced, Cannon, who was in Washington, D.C., saw little protection for the Saints other than God. Writing to John

Taylor on 8 January 1879, he lamented that the justices "appear willing to leave us to our fate, or the fate our enemies would mete out to us. Now it is up to the Lord to preserve us" (Cannon Letterbooks).

6. Woodruff had previously declared in 1879: "The Congress of 1862, and the supreme judges of 1879, in their acts and decisions, have taken a dangerous and fearful step; their acts will rap the very foundation of our government, and it will be rent asunder, and the God of heaven will hold them responsible for these things" (MS 41 [21 April 1879]: 243.

7. Apostle John Henry Smith remembered Young's counsel on this matter: "President Young once proposed that we marry but one wife" (Anthon H. Lund Journal, 10 Jan. 1900).

8. Young's position on this matter fluctuated. Two years later, he announced that a "man who did not have but one wife in the Resurrection that woman will not be his but [be] taken from him & given to another" (Kenney 7 [31 Aug. 1873]: 152).

Eleven

"PRISONERS FOR CONSCIENCE'S SAKE"

In spite of their leaders' public defiance of the 1879 U.S. Supreme Court ruling, many Mormons were uneasy about living in opposition to constitutional law. Some presumed that God would shortly intervene and that their opponents would be overthrown. Wilford Woodruff, soon-to-be president of the Quorum of Twelve Apostles, received a revelation on 26 January 1880 supporting this position. "Woe unto the nation or house or people who seek to hinder my people from obeying the patriarchal law of Abraham, which leadeth to celestial glory," the revelation warned, "for whosoever doeth these things shall be damned, saith the Lord of hosts, and shall be broken up and wasted away from under heaven by the judgments which I have sent forth. . . . And thus, with the sword, and by bloodshed, and with famine and plagues and earthquakes and the thunder of heaven, and the vivid lightnings shall this nation and the nations of the earth be made to feel the chastening hand of Almighty God."[1]

In the spring of 1880 senior apostle John Taylor, during a session of General Conference, sought continued church support for defying the Supreme Court ruling: "Has God given us a law? Yes! Have they made a law to punish us for obeying His law? Yes. All right we will get along and do the best we can, but we won't forsake our god[;] and all those who are willing to abide by the law of god signify it by raising the right hand" (*Deseret News Weekly*, 12 May 1880). Reportedly the vote of support for Taylor's proposal was unanimous. As the government stance became more threatening, Taylor reiterated the Mormon position. "Polygamy is with us a matter of revelation," he was quoted in the 12 November 1880 *Deseret News Weekly*, "also a natural law which rules the lives of millions on this globe. One sure thing is that we will not surrender polygamy." "Though they may imprison or kill most Mormons," he was quoted in the 25 February 1885 *Deseret News Weekly*, "there will always be somebody left to carry on the work." But he warned the Saints not to rebel openly against the "powers that be." He advised them to observe God's laws but with no "bloodshed, no rendering evil for evil."

Leaders of the monogamist Reorganized Church of Jesus Christ of Latter Day Saints proposed a compromise to U.S. president Rutherford B. Hayes which they hoped would avert bloodshed on the polygamy issue.

They suggested that he appoint Joseph Smith III as governor of Utah, reasoning that such a move would launch a missionary campaign in the territory which would encourage a grassroots anti-polygamy revolt in the church (G. Larson 1971, 93). Predictably, the RLDS suggestion was not implemented and leaders of some denominations were far less concerned about shedding Mormon blood. Prominent eastern minister DeWitt Talmage, for example, argued that "Mormonism will never be destroyed until it is destroyed by the guns of the United States Government. . . . If the Mormons submit to the law—all right. If not, then send out troops . . . and let them make the Mormon Tabernacle their headquarters, and with cannons of the biggest bore, thunder into them the seventh commandment" (*Deseret News*, 13 Oct. 1880).

President Hayes, who had visited Utah in September 1880, made several strongly worded suggestions to Congress in December. "Polygamy will not be abolished," he argued, "if the enforcement of the law depends on those who practice and uphold the crime. It can only be suppressed by taking away the political power of the sect which encourages and sustains it." He recommended that the "right to vote, hold office and sit on juries in the Territory of Utah be confined to those who neither practice nor uphold polygamy" (Richardson 1896-99, 7:606). Hayes's 1881 successor, James A. Garfield, who in his inaugural address said that polygamy "offends the moral sense of manhood," also urged congressional action against polygamy, as did Chester A. Arthur, who assumed the presidency on Garfield's assassination. During his first annual message to Congress on 6 December 1881, Arthur reviewed the previous executive and legislative actions against polygamy, noting that the "existing statute for the punishment of this odious crime, so revolting to the moral and religious sense of Christendom, has been persistently and contemptuously violated ever since its enactment." He argued that the Mormon practice of polygamy "imposes upon Congress and the Executive the duty of arraying against the barbarous system all the power which under the constitution and the law they can wield for its destruction" (ibid., 57).

Arthur found a strong supporter for his anti-polygamous posture in Vermont senator George Edmunds. After visiting Utah in 1881, the senator reported his findings in the January 1882 *Harper's Magazine*. "It is the object of the Mormons," he explained, "as shown by repeated and persistent efforts, to set up for themselves and maintain an exclusive political domination in the Territory of Utah, and to so frame and administer laws as to encourage rather than repress polygamy." Edmunds correctly assessed: "These people have plainly seen that once established as a State in the Union, their domestic concerns, including polygamy and every revolting practice which they might choose to set up, would be absolutely beyond the legal reach of the people of other States."

An aggressive drive for Utah statehood later that year was virtually ignored by Congress, which was considering Senator Edmunds's proposed anti-polygamy bill, an amendment to the Morrill Anti-bigamy Act of 1862. On 16 February the Senate passed Edmunds's legislation, laying legal groundwork for court action against Mormons not only for the difficult-to-prosecute offense of polygamy but also for the more easily substantiated "unlawful cohabitation." The Edmunds Act was intended to disfranchise polygamists and make them ineligible for public office and jury duty. All voter registration would be cancelled by the act, and all elective offices would become vacant. In addition, not only would amnesty be offered to polygamists who complied with specific conditions but children born to plural marriages prior to 1 January 1883 would be declared legitimate.[2]

House debate on the bill began on 13 March. Apostle John Henry Smith, sent to Washington to lobby against the act, followed the action closely, as did Utah congressional delegate George Q. Cannon, who would lose his seat if the bill became law. Apostle Smith, who described Senator Edmunds as a man with the "face of a monkey" who "looks to me as if he would take the cat's paw to put in the fire," was greatly dismayed on 14 March when the House passed the bill by a vote of 199 to 42 (Pusey 1982, 135). "The Republicans were filled with venom," Smith wrote in his 14 March journal, "and were bent upon the accomplishment of their purpose. . . . God our Father must judge these men for their evil design and [I] doubt not he will do so in his own due time."

President Arthur signed the Edmunds Act into law on 22 March and appointed a five-man Utah Commission to oversee new elections, as prescribed by the act. Two weeks later, in General Conference addresses, church president John Taylor left no doubt in the minds of observers what his position would be respecting the new law. "Let us treat it," he said in one speech, "the same as we did this morning in coming through the snow storm [and] put up our coat collars (suiting the action to the word) and wait till the storm subsides. After the storm comes sunshine. While the storm lasts it is useless to reason with the world; when it subsides we can talk to them" (Roberts 1965, 360-61). "We shall abide all constitutional law, as we always have done," he added, "but while we are godfearing and lawbiding and respect all honorable men and officers, we are no craven serfs, and have not learned to lick the feet of oppressors." Taylor clearly demarcated the Mormon course of action: "We will contend, inch by inch, legally and constitutionally, for our rights as American citizens, and for the universal rights of universal man" (JD 23 [9 April 1882]: 67).

President Taylor also recorded a revelation on the matter. In response to the question, "Is the law of Celestial Marriage a law given to this nation or to the world," Taylor dictated the "word of the Lord" on the subject. "Concerning the course taken by the United States," the document reads, "they have a right to reject this law themselves . . . but it is contrary to the provisions of the constitution, which is the supreme law of the land, for them to prohibit you from obeying it. Therefore abide in my law which I have revealed unto you, saith the Lord God, and contend for your rights by every legal and constitutional method" (Taylor Collection).

As the legal wheels set in motion by the Edmunds Act began to turn slowly, disruption of Mormon life became extensive. Scores of federal officials were brought into the territory to conduct "cohab hunts," and bounties were offered for information leading to the arrest of polygamists. Mormons not wishing to give up their plural wives and children faced dismal options—legal prosecution, a life in hiding on the "Mormon underground," or complete exile. Despite the bravado demonstrated by the "cohabs," as polygamists were called, those who did not submit to arrest had to be constantly on the move. Women and children were left to provide for themselves as best they could. Secret codes were employed in letters and messages, and children were taught to be evasive under questioning so as not to give away the details of polygamous relationships.

When marshals came to Lehi, Utah, young Ed Ross had been prepared by his elders. Questioned as to the whereabouts of his grandfather William Clark, he replied, "He has gone as far as you can run north, and as far as you can run west with your mouth full of chicken manure" (Watkins Interview). Agnes W. Roskelley approached the matter more seriously. She simply taught her sons "that they didn't know what their name was; they didn't know where they lived; they didn't know who their dad or mother was" (Embry 1987, 22).

Mormons were angered at what they deemed inconsistent interpretations of the law as well as violations of their civil and religious rights. "The paramour of mistresses and harlots, secure from prosecution, walks the streets in open day," they argued in a 2 May 1885 petition to President Grover Cleveland, and "no United States official puts a spotter on his 'trail,' or makes an effort to drag his deeds of guilt and shame before a judge and jury for investigation and punishment." Noting the persecution heaped upon Mormon polygamists in Utah and surrounding states, the petitioners pointed out that " 'Spotters' and spies dog their footsteps. Delators thrust themselves into bedchambers and watch at windows. Children are questioned upon the streets as to the marital relations of their parents. Families are dragged before commissioners and grand juries, and on pain of punishment for contempt, are compelled to testify against their fathers and husbands." The treatment, the polygamists felt, was not only demeaning but immoral: "Modest women are made to answer shamefully indecent questions as to the sexual relations of men and women. Attempts are made to bribe men to work up cases against their neighbors. Notoriously disreputable characters are employed to spy into men's family relations." Furthermore, the petitioning Mormons complained, "contrary to good law," those accused of crime were considered guilty until proven otherwise. "Trial by jury in the Territories is no longer a safeguard against injustice to a Mormon accused of crime," they argued; "accusation is equivalent to conviction. Juries are packed to convict, and if they fail to find a verdict against the accused when he is a Mormon, insult and abuse are heaped upon them by the anti-Mormon press. Men, fearful of not obtaining justice in the courts, are avoiding arrest, believing no fair and impartial trial can be had under existing circumstances" (*Salt Lake Tribune*, 3 May 1885).

Many Mormon men on the underground hid near or within their own homes. Hidden compartments and cellars—"polygamy pits" as they were called—secreted men who had scurried for cover when an unexpected knock was heard at the parlor door. But as lawmen became more numerous and sophisticated it became more difficult to escape. Francis W. Kirkham's diary account of the 8 December 1886 arrest of his father provides a poignant description of a successful polygamy raid: "How vividly the picture presents itself to me. Pa was expecting John who was staying in the tithing yard to call him at about 4 oclock in the morning, & of course when he heard a knock at about that hour he said, 'All right John I'll be there.' Imagine his surprise when a stranger accosted him by saying, 'I arrest you in the name of the law.' I was laying in the next room, & I was perspiring with excitement. Of course the household was soon up. My mother started a fire & soon had some warm tea for one of the Deputies who was sick [drunk]. . . . Pa was summoned to court & he being true to his religion was taken to the Utah Pen on March 21 1887" (pp. 12-15).

James Kirkham and nearly 1,000 other Mormon men and a few women were jailed for polygamy, "unlawful cohabitation," or both.[3] These "prisoners for conscience sake" were incarcerated in locations as widespread as Arizona, Michigan, South Dakota, and Idaho. The majority were jailed in the Utah Territorial Penitentiary on the present site of Sugar House Park (2100 South 1400 East) in Salt Lake City. Considering the bitterness between Mormons and anti-polygamists, it is surprising that only one life was lost during this intense period of prosecution. Polygamist Edward M. Dalton was killed in 1886 by a pursuing deputy marshal (Dix 1973).

Twenty-seven-year-old Rudger Clawson was the first person to be tried under the Edmunds Act, a distinction that added to his stature as a folk hero among the Mormons.[4] On 24 April 1884 he was indicted by a grand jury for polygamy, arrested, and released on $3,000 bail. In October his case came before the docket of Judge Charles S. Zane. Widely recognized as a fair and impartial judge, Zane became the major judicial force in the government actions against polygamists. Although he viewed the Mormon marriage system as a violation of basic moral standards, he demonstrated considerable leniency towards those who were willing to obey the law and abandon plural marriage.

Clawson appeared in Zane's court one month after the judge had taken office. Refusing to compromise his integrity, the fiery Mormon would not plead guilty. The court subpoenaed both Clawson's mother and his plural wife Lydia Spencer to testify, but they could not be found. Other testimony was less than convincing, and the jury dismissed the case. That evening, however, Lydia was apprehended by federal deputies and the case was retried. She initially refused to testify, but, after spending a night in jail under threat of indefinite imprisonment, she agreed to cooperate.

On 3 November 1884 Clawson appeared before Zane's bench for sentencing. When asked why judgment should not be pronounced, he retorted, "I very much regret that the laws of my country should come in conflict with the laws of God, but whenever they do I shall invariably choose the latter." Clawson explained that "the law of 1862 and the Edmunds Law were expressly designed to operate against marriage as practiced and believed in by the Latter-day Saints. They are therefore unconstitutional, and of course cannot command the respect that a constitutional law would."

Zane leaned back in his chair and contemplated the response for more than a minute before speaking. "While all men have a right to worship God according to the dictates of their own conscience, and to entertain any religious belief that their conscience and judgment might reasonably dictate," he pronounced, "they have not the right to engage in a practice which the American people, through the laws of their country, declare to be unlawful and injurious to society" (*Deseret News*, 3 Nov. 1884). Clawson's declaration that he believed it right to violate the law resulted in a stiff sentence of three and one-half years in prison and a $500 fine for polygamy, plus an additional six months and $300 for unlawful cohabitation.[5]

As the Utah penitentiary population gradually became predominantly Mormon, polygamy sentences became a mark of status and honor.[6] Frequently Mormon wards staged elaborate social functions in honor of the departing or returning "cohab." But early prisoners for polygamy found prison life difficult. After the new "fresh fish" was processed, the prisoner found himself in the company not only of polygamists but also of common criminals. Rudger Clawson found this introduction uncomfortable – sixty men gathered around him and "stood gazing like wild beasts ready to pounce upon their prey and devour it" (Bashore 1979, 28). "Oh! the awful Scene that met My Eyes," John Lee Jones wrote of his first night in a cell. "I could precive dark ugly Visiages in human Shape each one was sucking a dirty Pipe the smoak darkened the cell till you could Scarsely distinguish anything inside. The dense clouds of smoak imited from the Pipes turned me heart Sick." And the cells were less than clean. "We looked around or rather groped our way to one corner of the Cell," Jones wrote, "where we found an empty dirty bunk with some Straw in it & torn or tattered Bed Tick. One of the inmates informed us that was our Bunk to Sleep in" (Jones Diary, 73-75).

Rudger Clawson's first night was, in his own words, "oppressive to a degree almost maddening." The stench of tobacco was overwhelming; the noise from throat clearing, spitting, and prisoners' screaming in their sleep prevented him from sleeping at all. The bedbugs were so thick that Clawson reported "a man could write his name with the blood of bugs by pressing his finger against them as they crawled along the wall" (Bashore 1979, 31). James Kirkham, on the eve of his release from the prison, celebrated the occasion by spending most of the night on a bedbug hunting expedition. "Such a night I shall never forget," he wrote: "we spent the whole of the time fighting bedbugs. We killed by actual count 249" (Kirkham Diary, 19 Aug. 1887).

As increasing numbers of polygamists entered the prison system, they were initiated into the "brotherhood" by being required to entertain the group singing a song, dancing a jig, making a speech, or performing some other outlandish act. But whereas comraderie helped lift their spirits at times, prison life was rarely so jovial. Abraham H. Cannon, son of George Q. Cannon, noted that during his 1886 stay at the prison the men had been complaining for several days about the poor quality of coffee sent to them. "On being mentioned to the Warden," Cannon wrote in his diary on 28 May 1886, "he said that a bottle of carbolic acid had accidentally been dropped into the coffee, and the kettle in which the drink was made had not been cleaned out for some time. But this had now been remedied." Cannon had other culinary complaints. "The bread for two days has been so sour that we could scarcely eat it. Radishes that were sent in last night were so tough that they could scarcely be eaten, and lettuce sent in the night previously was nearly covered with worms. It is something new for us to receive anything green to eat from the Penitentiary ranch, but it would be better to have it in an eatable condition."

Abraham's father, George Q. Cannon, was the federal officials' most-wanted polygamist. His commanding presence, as well as President Taylor's advanced age and Joseph F. Smith's "exile" in Hawaii, caused the elder Cannon to be considered "the power behind the throne." Cannon surrendered himself in 1888 to show that "the leading men are willing to suffer but not to concede."[7] His experiences with prison life, well documented in his journal, seem more pleasant than those of others. During his initial processing, he specifically requested no special "favors that would embarrass [prison officials] by calling forth attacks from our enemies" (Cannon 1947, 396). However, Warden Arthur Pratt, anti-polygamous son of Apostle Orson Pratt, allowed Cannon numerous advantages, including keeping his cell door open when he wished. After one week of prison life, Cannon told a new arrival, Reddick Allred, that "he would not miss [the prison experience] for anything" ("Diary of Reddick Allred," 354). Cannon made good use of the duration of his sentence, collaborating on a biography of Joseph Smith with his sons, writing magazine articles, organizing a Sunday school and teaching a Bible class, acquiring an organ for the prison, entertaining hundreds of visitors, and having his picture taken in "prison stripes."

Few prisoners were able to make as much of jail stays. For many, the hours with little to do added new dimensions to their meaning of eternity. One commented: "At morning I long for the evening/At evening I long for the day" (Bashore 1979, 40). Rudger Clawson, who endured the longest sentence of any polygamist, wrote that "one day so nearly resembles another in every particular as almost to create confusion in the mind . . . one long, tedious, never-ending day—a living death" (ibid.).

Not all polygamists were as willing as Clawson to suffer imprisonment and financial hardship. Orson P. Arnold became the first Mormon to renounce polygamy in order to escape judicial action. Judge Zane fined him $300 but did not impose a prison sentence. Individuals who followed suit were strongly criticized by church leaders. The most prominent Mormon dissenter from that official line was John Sharp, bishop of the Salt Lake City twentieth ward. "I acted according to the dictates of my conscience," he later explained, "and just as in all wisdom I should have acted. . . . I do not renounce my religion or any part thereof. I simply give up the practice of polygamy, because the United States law forbids my indulging in it any longer. As long as I am a citizen of the United States I do not see how I can do otherwise."[8]

Sharp's law-abiding position came under intense criticism from both the church-owned *Deseret News* and high-ranking church leaders. The 19 September 1885 *News* lamented that Sharp had missed the "one opportunity of his life" to sustain a principle he believed divine. Joseph F. Smith, hearing of the situation while in Hawaii, wrote to George Q. Cannon on 12 November 1885, "I am truly sorry for br. John Sharp. . . . I can see no way for him but repentance, and a full acknowledgement of his error and a full return to the responsibilities devolved upon him by reason of the covenants he had made." But Smith acknowledged this might be impossible, complaining that "the material of which martyrs were made in olden times has become very scarce in these latter days in the civilized world."

Five days after his court appearance Sharp was interviewed by his ecclesiastical superior, acting Salt Lake Stake president Joseph E. Taylor.[9] Asked to resign as bishop, Sharp refused. A short time later the Salt Lake high council decided that Sharp had rendered himself ineligible to retain his office. He appealed the decision to the First Presidency, who supported the high council's finding. The response of church leaders to John Sharp's course of action fully conformed to their opinion of the amnesty clause in the Edmunds Act. "A premium is placed on perfidy and heartless villainy," the *Deseret News* editorialized on 27 January 1885, "by offering amnesty to polygamists who will throw their manhood to the dogs and enter the ranks of the debased by discarding their helpless and dependent wives and children, an alternative that death itself would not induce a true Latter-day Saint to accept."

Despite the harshness of their language, church leaders desperately sought alternatives for polygamist Saints. In January 1885 President Taylor, with his counselor Joseph F. Smith and others, traveled to southern Arizona to examine the possibility of Mormon polygamy in Mexico. When the group reached California, Taylor received word that federal officials had ordered his arrest. Despite the danger, he returned to Salt Lake City on 27 January 1885. Five days later he preached his last public sermon, declaring that he would submit to arrest "if the law would only be a little more dignified." That night he disappeared from public view and went into hiding.

With many leaders on the underground, church activities were severely limited. General Conferences, usually held in Salt Lake City, were scheduled in outlying areas. Federal officials haunted these conferences, hoping to arrest polygamists who might attend. By the end of 1888 federal marshals had swooped down on nearly every community in Utah and southern Idaho looking for "cohabs." Those polygamists who expected quick divine intervention in resolving their predicament were sadly disappointed.

NOTES

1. This unpublished revelation, often called "A Revelation to Wilford Woodruff in the Wilderness," was received by Woodruff in an area some forty miles from Sunset, Arizona, and recorded in his journal (Kenney 7 [26 Jan. 1880]: 546, 615-21). It was accepted as the "word of the Lord" by John Taylor and the Quorum of the Twelve the following April.

2. For a discussion of the church's position towards the amnesty clause, see Allen 1980. The Utah Commission is treated extensively in Poll 1939 and 1958, and Grow 1954.

3. In July 1889, Utah territory's district attorney reported 970 convictions and 106 acquittals for violations of federal laws during the years 1885-89. The following year church leaders would claim that 1,300 Mormons had been imprisoned for these types of offenses (Driggs 1988, 120).

4. Clawson and Joseph Standing, missionary companions in Varnell's Station, Georgia, were attacked by a mob on 21 July 1879. Standing was shot to death trying to escape. When the mob turned its attention to Clawson he calmly folded his arms, faced the men, and said, "Shoot." Reportedly, his composure so unnerved the mobsters that he was allowed to go free (Nicholson 1886).

5. Clawson was pardoned on 12 December 1887 by President Grover Cleveland. Two weeks later he was set apart as a stake president in Brigham City. Ten years later he became a forty-one-year-old apostle, and in 1921 he began a twenty-two-year assignment as president of the Quorum of the Twelve.

6. George Q. Cannon vividly expressed this point in a 1 September 1886 essay in *The Juvenile Instructor*: "What is the use of punishment if it does not punish?" he argued. "Any attempt to degrade a man is a miserable failure if he accepts the intended degradation as an honor." Adding that the Mormon prisoners do not view themselves as criminals but rather as religious martyrs, Cannon insisted that the Saints esteemed them "sufferers for righteousness the defenders of the great and sublime

principle of religious liberty." Even their enemies and persecutors, according to Cannon, are "forced to acknowledge that with all the machinery of punishment at their control they cannot make the Latter-day Saints bow to their wishes. This utter inability to bring the people to their terms causes them to boil with rage."

7. Marshal E. A. Ireland on 8 February 1886 offered a $500 reward for information leading to Cannon's arrest. Federal officers made numerous raids on church offices and Cannon's places of residence in an effort to capture him. President Taylor, concerned for his counselor's safety, sent him to Mexico to negotiate a land contract. En route he was apprehended by federal marshals near Humbolt Wells, Nevada. The returning party occupied a stateroom in the rear of one of the railroad cars. During a night-time restroom trip, Cannon stepped outside the rear of the car to assess the possibilities of escape. The train lurched; he was thrown from the car and later recaptured in a dazed condition, bleeding profusely from a badly broken nose.

Boasts were made that Cannon would be imprisoned for life and that he would be sent to a distant prison where his condition would be made "unbearable." On the advice of President Taylor and with the approval of his bondsmen, Cannon returned to the underground and forfeited a $45,000 bond. After considerable effort in Washington, Cannon's son Frank, an eventual U.S. senator from Utah, was able to gain an audience with President Grover Cleveland and persuade him to replace punitive federal judges in Utah with more lenient ones. As part of this agreement, George Q. Cannon voluntarily appeared before Judge Elliott Sandford and pleaded guilty to two charges of "unlawful cohabitation." He was fined $450 and sentenced to 175 days in prison.

8. See accounts in *Deseret News*, 14 April, 20 July, and 21 Sept. 1885; *Salt Lake Tribune*, 19 Sept., 7 Nov. 1885. This situation is extensively covered in Allen 1980, 149-74.

9. Sharp's stake president, Angus M. Cannon, was then serving time in the penitentiary for "unlawful cohabitation." A short time before his imprisonment, Cannon had declared in stake conference, "When a man professing to be a Latter-day Saint will cower before our enemies and beg for mercy, forgetting or renouncing the promises of God, he considered him a contemptible hypocrite" (Allen 1980, 169). Under the circumstances it is not difficult to see why Sharp's ecclesiastical leaders were less than sympathetic towards his position.

Twelve

PAVING THE WAY TO STATEHOOD

The determination of the federal government to eradicate plural marriage eventually forced the church to capitulate. Polygamists resisted as long as they could. When attempts to overturn various pieces of anti-polygamy legislation failed, church leaders began pursuing a variety of other equally ineffective measures to maintain plural marriage. When federal raids made shambles of Mormon communities in the mid-1880s, for example, George Q. Cannon suggested to President Taylor that polygamists burden the courts by surrendering en masse, pleading that "the laws of congress conflict with my sense of submission to the will of the Lord, I now offer myself, here, for whatever judgment the courts of my country may impose" (Van Wagoner and Walker 1982, 53-54).

A less dramatic solution was for polygamists to move in great numbers to remote areas. During the final years of Brigham Young's administration, when the polygamy issue first began to heat up, church leaders established settlements in areas they thought beyond reach of government harassment. In the three-year period from 1876 to 1879, more than one hundred new settlements were founded outside Utah, mostly in Arizona, Nevada, Wyoming, and Colorado. These settlements, essentially efforts to expand Mormon influence, became havens for fleeing polygamists in the mid-1880s.

The first Mormon expedition to Mexico in 1875 also sought suitable areas for settlement, and serious colonization began in the mid-1880s. In early 1884, President John Taylor instructed stake president Christopher Layton to move his congregation from Saint Joseph, Arizona, to Mexico to escape the harassment of government authorities. Taylor and other church leaders visited southern Arizona and northern Mexico in 1885 and again encouraged polygamous Saints to move south of the border. They first chose a spot near Casa Grande in Chihuahua. After purchasing land word was sent "by mail or by messengers, it was grapevined to remotest hamlets in the Region. In St. Johns, Snowflake, Sunset, Luna, Smithville in Arizona, in Savoy, Socorro and other locations in New Mexico and even in many towns in Southern Utah troubled men heard the message and were moved to go in search of the promised land" (Embry 1987, 23).

By the end of 1885 hundreds of Mormon colonists were pouring into Chihuahua in northern Mexico. "Our affairs in Mexico for opening settlements for our people, are quite satisfactory at present," L. John Nuttall, secretary to the First Presidency, wrote to his son. "When the United States find they have not got us in a corner, and cannot prey upon us, they may see that the business of crushing out Mormonism is not likely to be successful as they had anticipated." The Mormon population in Mexico continued to grow. In less than a decade more than three thousand Saints had estabished eight polygamous colonies in Mexico—six in Chihuahua and two in Sonora. Though polygamy was outlawed by the Mexican states where the Saints settled, enforcement of the laws by Mexican officials was virtually nonexistent.[1]

Other polygamous colonizers moved north to the Canadian province of Alberta. Charles Ora Card, president of Cache Stake in Logan, Utah, had been instructed by John Taylor to seek out a place of "asylum and justice" in Canada. On 27 April 1887 he selected a place for a settlement on Lees Creek, Alberta—the present site of Cardston. Polygamy was outlawed by Canadian law as definitely as by American and Mexican statutes. Utah leaders in 1888 sent to Ottawa a three-man delegation consisting of Charles O. Card and apostles Francis M. Lyman and John W. Taylor to defend Mormon polygamy to Prime Minister John A. MacDonald. The contingent made an appeal on behalf of polygamous Saints in Alberta to bring their plural families into the province. "We would respectfully ask the government of the Dominion of Canada," their lengthy written petition began, to allow polygamists "an abiding place in peace in Canada where they can provide for their families, educate their children, and not be compelled to cast them off and subject them to the charities of a cold world, thus breaking faith with their tender and devoted wives, innocent children and with God our Eternal Father, from whose hand we received them" (Carter 1953, 2:80-83).

Though the Canadian government was pleased to have the industrious Saints colonize the sparsely settled plains of western Alberta, Prime Minister MacDonald made it clear that Mormon polygamy would not be tolerated in Canada. But the Mormon premise that God had commanded them to enter plural marriage led them to view polygamy as a "higher law," thereby justifying their disobedience of Mexican and Canadian statutes as they had earlier justified their disobedience to Illinois state law forbidding polygamy.[2]

A far more convenient means than colonization for obtaining release from government pressures would have been statehood. Church leaders recognized that entry into the union would reduce federal control over their domestic affairs. Though a congressionally approved constitution would certainly outlaw polygamy, local administrative and judicial officials could see to it that anti-polygamy laws would be lightly enforced or conveniently ignored. Federal officials, aware of this possibility, consistently rebuffed statehood bids. Government leaders continued to pressure church leaders to issue a statement abandoning plural marriage. George Q. Cannon rejected the Cleveland administration's November 1885 attempt to obtain such a statement, insisting that even if the First Presidency issued such a manifesto, the Saints would not accept it. "If they did," he noted, "and we were to repudiate this principle our church would cease to be the Church of God, and the ligaments that bind it together would be severed" (Quinn 1985, 31).

Statehood became such an important goal for Mormon leaders that they sometimes resorted to bribery to help pave the way. In January 1885 all three members of the First Presidency and several apostles joined in two days of discussion on a private railroad car en route to Cheyenne, Wyoming. The group decided to send Apostle Brigham Young, Jr., and *Deseret News* editor-in-chief Charles W. Penrose on a mission east to try to place $20,000 of church funds where such a sum would help "get U[tah] in U[nion]" (Seifrit 1983). The apostles could not find viable takers and the mission failed. Trying another avenue, George Q. Cannon was sent to Washington, D.C., in an effort to gather political support for statehood. The former congressman visited each member of the cabinet and paid three visits to President Cleveland. Cannon returned from the trip convinced that Utah polygamists should leave the territory until statehood could be obtained. He believed the exiles could then return to a state government that would either allow polygamy or be soft on interpreting laws against the practice.[3]

Congressional debate on the newly proposed Edmunds and Tucker bills in 1886 provided vivid headlines for Utah's newspapers, and the debates in Congress and in the press intensified rumors that church leaders might be considering the abandonment of plural marriage. Many feared President Taylor would initiate such action; others prayed that he would. On 11 January 1886 he received an anonymous letter from a member of the latter—and perhaps predominant—camp. "You are hidden away and cannot know the true feelings of our people," the writer charged: "The people say that you and Cannon and Smith have run away and left the masses to go to the penitentiary or humiliate themselves before the courts. . . . You will force men to go to the pen when you will not go yourselves." Though the writer did not want to see President Taylor in prison, he pleaded with him to "Save us from division and contention within and reproach from without. We appealed to the highest tribunal as a last resort but this did no good, now what can we do?" Seeing the abandonment of polygamy as the only possible solution to the church's difficulties, the letter urged Taylor, if he did not want to "take the responsibility of doing away with polygamy," to "order an election of all the people and let them say Yes or No without fear or hindrance, and you will see for yourself how they feel, and you will be exonerated from all blame" (Taylor Collection).

President Taylor, however, was adamant in his refusal to capitulate on the plural marriage issue, predicting that government harassment would eventually decrease. Apostle Abraham H. Cannon recorded in his 28 March 1886 journal that Taylor received a revelation which stated that "God was satisfied with the sacrifice made by the people in this crusade and that he would now turn [government] wrath aside." Six months later, while Taylor was being hidden in the John W. Woolley home in Centerville, the church president received one of the most controversial revelations in the history of Mormonism. He had petitioned the Lord respecting the possibility of giving up plural marriage. "All commandments that I give must be obeyed," he was answered, "unless they are revoked by me or by my authority and how can I revoke an everlasting covenant for I the Lord am everlasting and my everlasting covenants cannot be abrogated nor done away with but they stand forever." The message was absolutely clear: "I have not revoked this law nor will I for it is everlasting and those who will enter into my glory must obey the conditions thereof, even so amen."[4] Three months later, on 19 December 1886, seventy-eight-year-old John Taylor took as a plural wife twenty-six-year-old Josephine Roueche (Quinn 1985, 30).

In early January 1887 a proposal for a state constitutional convention was drafted by church agents in Washington, D.C. John W. Young, counselor to the Quorum of the Twelve, prominent businessman and promoter, and son of Brigham Young, headed the lobbying efforts of a group composed of John T. Caine, Utah delegate to Congress; Franklin S. Richards, church attorney; and Richards's non-Mormon legal associate, George Ticknor Curtis. These politically astute observers had witnessed the passage of the Edmunds Bill in early 1886 and recognized the danger the impending passage of the more extreme Tucker Bill would pose for the church and Utah citizens alike.

J. Randolph Tucker, chair of the House Judiciary Committee, drafted the Tucker Bill as a substitute for the Edmunds Bill. The Tucker Bill not only provided for escheatment of church property but proposed that federal officials not be required to prove marriage in polygamous relationships, a modification posing far greater legal entanglements for polygamists than previous legislation. Another worrisome area of the bill was its threat to destroy the church's political influence by making all offices in the territory appointive rather than elective, potentially placing law enforcement agencies under complete control of the non-Mormon element.

The church lobby in Washington saw little hope of defeating the Tucker Bill once it reached the House floor. They were successful for a time in keeping the bill in committee but recognized the inevitability of passage. George T. Curtis, the non-Mormon member of the lobby, informed the First Presidency of their seemingly hopeless position. "I am perfectly convinced that public opinion has become so crystallized on what is called 'the Mormon question,'" he wrote on 23 January, "that it is idle to expect to modify or change it." Curtis saw polygamy as politically doomed: "I have never known anything in the course of my life that presented such a phenomenon. In the ante-bellum period, when the whole country was so much excited about slavery, there were great and powerful States interested in defending it, which could combine for that purpose; and throughout the North there were at least large masses of people who, before actual war had begun, cordially and heartily stood by the South." But the Saints, said Curtis, were without allies— "you are a mere handful of people; 150,000 against 50 or 60 millions, and those millions have made up their minds that polygamy shall be exterminated."

The lobby felt the only hope for defusing the explosive situation was to offer some Mormon concession. Without consulting the First Presidency, the group drafted an amendment to the Tucker Bill. This resolution proposed that the effective date of the bill be postponed for six months after passage. During this period a constitutional convention would be held in Utah Territory. If the proposed constitution, accepted by Utahns, prohibited polygamy, as the agents anticipated, the Tucker Bill would be withheld until Congress had examined the constitution and determined whether Utah should be granted statehood. Members of the lobby presented the newly drafted resolution to House Democrat William L. Scott of Pennsylvania, who had been opposing the Tucker Bill. Scott submitted the amendment, but it was not well received by the House. Members recognized the long-standing Mormon opposition to anti-polygamy legislation and viewed the church effort as a ploy to buy time.

While the Tucker bill was being debated in committee, John W. Young took the Scott Amendment to President Grover Cleveland. Young argued that polygamy could never be eliminated without Mormon cooperation and that passage of the Tucker Bill without the Scott Amendment would only anger Mormons and strengthen their resolve. Cleveland, who felt favorably disposed toward the Mormon situation, had sought on several occasions to resolve the polygamy issue. In the Scott Amendment he saw a glimmer of hope that the standoff between the government and the church might end. But church president John Taylor, upon receiving word of the conditions of the amendment, ordered his agents to "go slow" (Jack to Young). Taylor feared that any indication of concession on his part would be interpreted as a step towards surrendering plural marriage. "It will not do for us," he wrote to the church's agents on 27 January 1887, "after enduring what we have for the sake of our religion and its principles, to put ourselves in a position where our words and actions may be construed into a surrender of that for which we have ever contended" (Taylor/Cannon to Caine/Young).

Church agents strove behind the scenes to effect a compromise between the First Presidency and government officials. On 15 February 1887 the House Judiciary Committee completed work on the Edmunds-Tucker Bill, a compromise of two bills in committee, which passed both houses of Congress in quick order. John W. Young once again met with President Cleveland. The president was "entirely satisfied with the wording of the Scott Amendment," Young wired the First Presidency; he said "no good man could ask for more" (Young to Jack). The amendment, Young concluded, could be viewed as a peace overture from the president of the United States to Utahns.

Young's telegram reached President Taylor on 27 February 1887, shortly after the church president had been informed of the death of his wife Sophie. "If Scott amendment will satisfy President Cleveland," the mourning church leader telegraphed Young, "it will be acceptable to us. If it shall become law [I] see no objections to people carrying out its provisions." He added, however, that acceptance of the amendment in no way should imply that the church was altering its position on plural marriage. "We desire it distinctly understood," he noted, that "we accept terms of Scott amendment as a political necessity, and that in doing so we neither yield nor compromise an iota of our religious principles" (Taylor to Jack).

President Cleveland allowed the Edmunds-Tucker Bill to become law without his signature on 3 March 1887, and the Scott Amendment was defeated. But church agents in Washington were encouraged by Cleveland's support of the amendment and pressed church leaders for their support of an anti-polygamy constitution for Utah. In April 1887, President Taylor, still in hiding, announced to the church by letter that henceforth he would deny recommends for plural marriages. "The Church is now passing through a period of transition, or evolution," he wrote: "Such periods appear to be necessary in the progress and perfecting of all created things, as much so in the history of peoples and communities as of individuals. These periods of transition have most generally their pains, perplexities and sufferings" (Clark 1965-75, 3:127).

Shortly after the reading of President Taylor's letter to a General Conference of the church, a territorial convention was called to draft a state constitution. John Taylor and George Q. Cannon both endorsed the drafted constitution, which declared polygamy a misdemeanor. Church leaders began an immediate campaign to see that the constitution was accepted by the Saints. On 7 July 1887 Cannon urged all local church leaders to vote for the state constitution, declaring that in so doing they "would not offend God nor violate his laws" (L. John Nuttall Journal). Members of the Quorum of the Twelve were sent on short-term missions to convey this message to the Mormon populace. To encourage popular support for Utah statehood on a national level, church leaders sought to "secure the press of the country" by placing large cash payments with major newspapers. Apostle Heber J. Grant noted in his 12 August 1887 diary that "President Cannon stated that the parties with whom they were negotiating could secure . . . the leading papers of New York and other cities, to write articles in favor of our admission to the union for the sum of $74,000 cash and an additional $70,000 after we are admitted" (Lyman 1981, 160-61.)[5]

President John Taylor, the longtime champion of plural marriage, did not live to see either the overwhelming acceptance of the state constitution on 1 August or eventual statehood. He died at the Roueche home in Kaysville on 25 July. "Few men have ever lived who have manifested such integrity and such unflinching moral and physical courage," George Q. Cannon and Joseph F. Smith eulogized in the 26 July 1887 *Deseret News*. They lamented that Taylor had been "killed by the cruelty of those officials who have in this Territory misrepresented the government of the United States."

The anti-Mormon *Salt Lake Tribune* came to the defense of the government officials in its 27 July issue. "George Q. Cannon and Joseph F. Smith seized upon the opportunity presented by the death of a worn-out old man," the paper reported, "to grossly slander some gentlemen whose only crime has been their efforts to perform their official duties under their oaths." The *Tribune* took issue with the charging of John Taylor's death to the persecution of federal officials: "There has not been one moment during the past two and a half years that John Taylor could not have shaken all fear of Federal officials by simply appearing before the District Court and promising to henceforth obey the laws."

On 3 August the Quorum of the Twelve met to discuss the leadership void left by Taylor's death. The meeting did not go smoothly. Several of the apostles took advantage of the opportunity to lodge complaints against the actions of George Q. Cannon, who had essentially been running the church during Taylor's years of declining health (see John Henry Smith Journal, 3 Aug. 1887, 20-26 March 1888). Difficulties again broke out during the October 1887 conference week. Apostles Moses Thatcher, F. M. Lyman, Heber J. Grant, and John Henry Smith demanded explanations from Cannon on actions he had taken on several matters without consulting the quorum. The meeting remained in session until 2:00 A.M. before most objections were finally resolved.

On 20 March 1888 Wilford Woodruff, president of the Quorum of the Twelve and next in line for the church presidency, called the Twelve together and suggested that it was "about time to organize the First Presidency." Controversy again sparked the meeting, however. Several apostles opposed George Q. Cannon's serving in the First Presidency, and both Heber J. Grant and Moses Thatcher objected to Wilford Woodruff's leadership on grounds that the aging apostle would lack the resilience to handle the pressure of anti-polygamy actions launched by the federal government. Tension was so great during this period that Woodruff remarked to his secretary that "he would about as soon attend a funeral as one of our council meetings" (L. John Nuttall Diary, 27 Feb. 1889). It was not until 7 April 1889, nearly two years after John Taylor's death, that members of the quorum were united enough to sustain Wilford Woodruff as the fourth president of the church, and contrary to Grant's and Thatcher's opinion, the eighty-two-year-old Woodruff proved to be the man of the hour. His administration solved the long-standing difficulties with the federal government by issuing the "Wilford Woodruff Manifesto," setting the wheels in motion for 1896 Utah statehood.

NOTES

1. Mexican statutes, after 1884, prohibited polygamy. Mexican law also refused to recognize marriages performed elsewhere unless they were "valid according to the laws of the country" in which they took place. See Quinn 1985, 17; Jorgenson and Hardy 1980, 18. Though church leaders often made statements suggesting they were ignorant of Mexican anti-polygamy laws, they had been apprised of such opposition in early 1885 by church agent John W. Young. In a 21 May letter to apostles Brigham Young, Jr., and Moses Thatcher, who were in Mexico, he warned that a member of the Mexican Congress had advised him not to raise the issue of Mormon polygamy in that country because "there was a very plain congressional law on the subject." The 14 November 1895 *Salt Lake Tribune* reminded Mormon leaders that nowhere in North America could they legally practice polygamy. Moreover, when giving newly appointed Juarez stake president Anthony Ivins instructions on 5 October 1895, President George Q. Cannon told him, "If you have occasion to meet Porfio Diaz, President of Mexico, we want you to tell him that we are NOT practicing polygamy in Mexico" (H. G. Ivins, 5).

2. Most Mormon polygamists in Canada brought only one of their plural wives across the border. Few, if any, plural marriages in Alberta were performed until after 1890. For a specific treatment of plural marriage in Canada, see Embry 1985. For general treatment of Alberta settlement, see Wilcox 1950 and Lee 1968.

3. George Q. Cannon was the architect of much of the church's official position respecting late nineteenth-century polygamy. For example, President Joseph F. Smith in an 11 April 1911 telegram to Senator Reed Smoot noted that "Prest. Cannon was the first to conceive the idea that the Church could consistently countenance polygamy beyond confines of the republic where there was no law against it, and consequently he authorized the solemnization of plural marriages in Mexico and Canada after manifesto of 1890" (Smoot Collection).

4. A copy of this uncanonized revelation is in the John Taylor Letter File, LDS Archives; see also discussion in chapter 17.

5. In 1888 the arrangement with subsidized newspapers was expanded. Church agent Alexander Badlam informed Hiram Clawson of his activities in this area: "I was compelled to come here [from Washington, D.C. to New York City] and proceed to Boston and four or five other New York and New England cities to see some newspaper men and pacify them a little which I will do cheerfully for they have in almost every instance done handsomely with us, in fact I am proud of this branch of our labors as good results have come through from our efforts. The puritanical and sectarian press here have been looked after and their material interest consulted in so handsome and economical a manner that you must pardon me for reference again to it. . . . When a certain question [statehood] comes up properly before Congress I am satisfied it will have strong support, where formerly enmity existed" (Lyman 1981, 173).

Thirteen

THE WILFORD WOODRUFF MANIFESTO

The framers of the Edmunds-Tucker Bill intended their legislation to destroy the Mormon theocratic system. Though polygamy was the war cry of these and other lawmakers, a 15 February 1885 *Salt Lake Tribune* article hit on a more basic motivation for opposition to plural marriage. "The essential principle of Mormonism is not polygamy at all," the paper warned, "but the ambition of an ecclesiastical hierarchy to wield sovereignty; to rule the souls and lives of its subjects with absolute authority, unrestrained by any civil power." Utah's non-Mormon governor, Caleb West, echoed this point in an 1888 letter: "In the Mormon policy established and governing the people of this Territory since its settlement, the unity of the Church and state is perfect and indissoluble. It is based upon the complete, and absolute control of a priesthood. . . . This priesthood not only rules the Church, it governs the state."[1]

Regulations of the Edmunds-Tucker Bill declared that marriages not publicly recorded were felonies, that wives could be forced to testify against husbands, and that children of plural marriages would be disinherited. Female suffrage was abolished, and a test oath was administered which disfranchised all polygamists and prohibited them from jury service or political office. The most serious stipulation of the bill, however, was the threat to dissolve the legal entity of the church corporation and to confiscate all church property in excess of $50,000.

On 30 July, the day after President John Taylor was buried, the government initiated the legal moves necessary to destroy the economic base of the church. The U.S. attorney general filed suits in the Utah Supreme Court against both the church corporation and the Perpetual Emigrating Fund Company. The church answered the suits by affirming that its status as a corporation had already been dissolved on 1 July 1862 by the Morrill Anti-Bigamy Law. The church testified that Trustee-in-Trust John Taylor had disposed of all church property, except enough to pay its debts, on or before 28 February 1887. This property, with the exception of Temple Square, the church president's office, the church farm in Salt Lake City, and several Indian farms, had been secretly deeded to various trusted individuals throughout the church.

When hearings on the issue began on 17 October 1887, the church unsuccessfully sought to force the case to the U.S. Supreme Court. In the meantime, on 5 November, Marshal Frank H. Dyer was appointed receiver of the church's estate and began immediately taking over the escheated property.

Church leaders, scattered over much of the western United States and Mexico, were confident that once their case came before the U.S. Supreme Court, the property would be returned. In the meantime they continued their efforts towards achieving Utah statehood. In January 1888 the Utah territorial legislature enacted a bill prohibiting polygamy and requiring all marriages to be publicly recorded in the appropriate county clerk's office. Pressures to abandon polygamy mounted, both from within and outside the church. Some Saints argued that if church leaders had in fact discontinued approving plural marriages, a public announcement of such practice should be made for its public relations value.

Non-Mormon friends of the church advised abandonment of polygamy. L. John Nuttall, a secretary to the First Presidency, noted in his journal of 19 December 1888 a letter to President Woodruff from "friends in the East," asking church members to "conform their lives to the Laws of Congress." The letter endeavored to show "reasons why the church should openly renounce the practice of Polygamy in the future, [or] until the time comes when the saints can again practice that principle of their religion unmolested." After lengthy discussion in the Quorum of the Twelve, "the brethren were very emphatic in opposing or accepting such a measure, [which] they felt had not come from the right source." Woodruff then said, "You have spoken right. Had we accepted this proposition the Lord would have rejected us." In words echoing the 1886 revelation of President John Taylor, Woodruff added, "The doctrine of plural marriage has come to stay for all time" (John Henry Smith Journal, 20 Dec. 1888).[2]

President Woodruff was confident that the situation would be resolved either by a favorable Supreme Court decision or by attainment of statehood. In a 26 February 1889 letter to James Q. Broadhead, a legal consultant to the church, Woodruff commented on the legal brief Broadhead had prepared in defense of the church's position: "I never read a more forcible and unanswerable argument in my life upon any subject. It certainly will require something more than sophistry of unprincipled men to override that iron bulwark of constitutional and fundamental law which you have placed before them." Woodruff was convinced that the Supreme Court could not possibly, in the face of unassailable argument, "attempt to escheat and confiscate the real and personal property of the Latter-day Saints. If they do, I tremble for my country."

Woodruff wrote of his hope for Utah statehood to his good friend William Atkin on 18 March 1889: "We are now, politically speaking, a dependency or ward of the United States; but in a State capacity we would be freed from such dependency, and would possess the powers and independence of a sovereign State, with authority to make and execute our own laws." President Woodruff then reflected on his oft-quoted expectation that the federal government would soon collapse: "We would, in the event of the disruption of the general government, be independent of all earthly powers and clothed with legal as well as divine authority to assume the position in the earth god has designed or may design us to fill in such an event."[3]

For all the firmness of his hopes, Woodruff, unlike his predecessor John Taylor, did not desire to antagonize the government through defiant actions or inflammatory public rhetoric while the question of statehood was being debated. The issue was so sensitive during his administration that he reprimanded assistant church historian Andrew Jenson on 6 August 1887 for publishing a list of the known plural wives of Joseph Smith. "We do not think it is a wise step to give these names to the world at the present time in the manner in which you have done in this 'Historical Record.' Advantage may be taken of their publication and in some instances, to the injury, perhaps, of families or relatives of those whose names are mentioned." Woodruff, though not in attendance at the April 1888 General Conference, went so far as to instruct the senior apostle present, Lorenzo Snow, that "if anyone attempted to speak about polygamy to throw his hat at him." Snow either forgot or ignored the advice, and popular Rudger Clawson, just released from prison, defended the doctrine before conference attendees. "We were considerably annoyed," Woodruff later wrote to two church leaders, "not to say mortified, at the want of care which was manifested in cautioning the brethren who spoke not to touch on topics that at the present time, were likely to rouse prejudice" (Woodruff to Richards/Penrose).[4]

In efforts to reduce even further the frictions against Utah statehood, Woodruff began refusing permission for plural marriages shortly after he organized the First Presidency in April 1889. He did not inform his first counselor, George Q. Cannon, of this decision until the fall. Asked by a stake president what to do about plural marriages, Cannon recorded in his 9 September diary that Woodruff said, "I feel that it is not proper for any marriages of this kind to be performed in the territory at the present time." Cannon then noted that Woodruff had "intimated, however, that such marriages might be solemnized in Mexico or Canada." Cannon wrote that this was the "first time that anything of this kind has ever been uttered to my knowledge, by one holding the keys" (Quinn 1985, 36).

A feeling was developing among many that the church was finally bowing to government demands on polygamy. This feeling was enhanced on 20 October 1889 when Woodruff was quoted in the *Salt Lake Tribune* as saying, "I have refused to give any recommendations for the performance of plural marriages since I have been President . . . and have instructed that they should not be solemnized." One week later, in the 27 October 1889 *Salt Lake Herald*, Woodruff was asked, "What is the church attitude toward the law prohibiting polygamy?" Woodruff replied, "We mean to obey it. We have no thought of evading or ignoring it. We recognize the laws as binding upon us. I have refused to give any recommendations for the performance of plural marriage since I have been President."

John W. Young and other influential individuals sought during this tense period to influence Woodruff to make a more pointed official announcement that he was no longer authorizing plural marriages. After Young met with Woodruff and church attorneys, at least one individual feared the church president had been converted to Young's position. L. John Nuttall, secretary to the First Presidency, noted in his 24 November journal, "When Pres' Woodruff commenced talking to me this evening I felt he had become converted and [I] actually trembled[,] for I knew such had not been Pres. Woodruff's feelings before." Woodruff sought guidance from his counselors, but both refused to advise him on the issue. Apostle Abraham H. Cannon wrote in his 19 December 1889 journal that Woodruff "laid the matter before the Lord." "The answer came quick and strong," he observed of Woodruff's 24 November revelation: "The word of the Lord was for us not to yield one particle of that which He had revealed and established. He had done and would continue to care for His work and those of the Saints who were faithful, and we need have no fear of our enemies when we were in the line of our duty. We are promised redemption and deliverance if we will trust in god and not in the arm of flesh."

On the eighty-fourth anniversary of the birth of the prophet Joseph Smith, 23 December 1889, Mormons observed a church-wide day of fasting and prayer, seeking God's intervention on their behalf. Church leaders issued an appeal to the nation for greater understanding and tolerance. President Woodruff, viewed by some of his colleagues as a better fisherman than administrator, was keenly aware of the precarious position of the church at the close of 1889. He wrote in his journal on New Year's Eve: "Thus Ends the year 1889 And the word of the Prophet Joseph Smith is beginning to be fulfilled that the whole Nation would turn aginst Zion and make war upon the Saints. The nation has never been filled so full of lies against the Saints as to Day. 1890 will be an important year with the Latter Day Saints & American nation" (Kenney 9 [31 Dec. 1889]: 74).

Woodruff's statement was prophetic. On 19 May 1890 the Supreme Court's decision in *The Late Corporation of the Church of Jesus Christ v. United States* upheld the seizure of church holdings by the federal government. Perhaps feeling polygamy's days were numbered, Woodruff secretly authorized at least twenty-three plural marriages between December 1889 and 7 June

1890 (Quinn 1985, 41). At the same time church leaders initiated several tactics designed to promote statehood and thus to save the church from the effects of the government's legal maneuverings. On the advice of the leaders of both major U.S. political parties, church authorities began to disband the church-sponsored People's Party and encouraged the Saints to divide along national party lines. In elections held in February, the local non-Mormon Liberal Party won most of the Salt Lake City offices. For the first time in Salt Lake City's history, political control of the Mormon city fell into "gentile" hands.

The church suffered a staggering blow later that same month when the Supreme Court upheld the constitutionality of the Idaho test oath which disfranchised Idaho Mormons. Utah Liberals immediately sought the disfranchisement of all Mormons in their territory, sending Robert Baskin to the nation's capital with a quickly drafted document patterned after the Idaho law. This legislation, which became known as the Cullom-Strubble Bill, was intended to strip all Utah Mormons of their rights as American citizens.

Church leaders quickly formulated opposition to the Cullom-Strubble Bill. In April, Woodruff declared that no plural marriages could occur "even in Mexico unless the contracting parties or at least the female has resolved to remain in that country" (Abraham H. Cannon Journal, 10 April 1890),[5] and on 3 May the *Deseret Evening News* editorialized that "the practice of polygamy has been suspended if not *suppressed*." In addition to the rhetoric, a defense fund was organized, and George Q. Cannon headed a Washington delegation to lobby against passage of the bill. Professional lobbyists Judge Jeremiah M. Wilson and A. B. Carlton, former chair of the Utah Commission, were also hired to advance the church's position. Frank J. Cannon, a personal emissary of his father, George Q., sought audience with several influential Republicans. Secretary of State James G. Blaine, a friend of the senior Cannon, granted an interview. "The Lord giveth, and the Lord taketh away," Blaine prophetically remarked at the conclusion of the discussion. "Wouldn't it be possible for your people to find some way—without disobedience to the commands of God—to bring yourselves into harmony with the law and institutions of this country?" "Believe me," the astute politician added, "it's *not* possible for any people as weak in number as yours, to set themselves up as superior to the majesty of a nation like this. We may succeed this time, in preventing your disfranchisement; but nothing permanent can be done until you 'get into line.' "[6]

Blaine drafted a statement which he urged church leaders to adopt. Apostle Abraham H. Cannon noted in his 12 June diary that Woodruff "showed me a paper which Secretary of State Blaine had prepared for the leading authorities of the Church to sign in which they make a virtual renunciation of plural marriage." Cannon found that his "feelings revolt[ed] at signing such a document." Others apparently felt the same way, and the document was not endorsed by church leaders. Meanwhile the Utah Commission, which had recommended that all Mormons, whether polygamists or not, be disfranchised, issued a 22 August 1890 "Annual Report" to the Department of the Interior pointing out that "authoritative and explicit" disavowal of polygamy had been made by church leaders. The commission felt that these statements would be accepted by most Mormons without question and a "settlement of the much discussed 'Mormon question' would soon be reached." More disconcertingly, however, the report noted "forty-one male persons . . . have entered into the polygamic relation, in their several precincts, since the June revision in 1889."

This report spelled trouble for church leaders who had publicly stated that they were no longer approving plural marriages. And time was running out in Washington. Frank J. Cannon returned from the capital and informed President Woodruff that he had repeated to prominent congressional leaders the promise his father had made that "something will be done." He emphasized that it was George Q. Cannon's promise that made it possible for the Cullom-Strubble Bill to be "held back – with the certainty that it would never become law if we met the nation half way." "To be very plain with you," young Cannon told the church president, "our friends expect, and the country will insist, that the Church shall yield the practice of plural marriage." "I had hoped," Woodruff sadly responded, "we wouldn't have to meet this trouble this way. You know what it means to our people. I had hoped that the Lord might open the minds of the people of this nation to the truth . . . Our prophets have suffered like those of old, and I thought that the persecutions of Zion were enough – that they would bring some other reward than this" (Cannon and Higgins 1911, 103-11).

On 3 August 1890 President Woodruff and several others began a 2,400-mile trip to visit the Saints in Utah, Wyoming, Colorado, New Mexico, and Arizona. The eighty-three-year-old leader was able to see firsthand the terrible circumstances of polygamist Saints. Shortly after returning from this extensive trip, Woodruff and George Q. Cannon left Salt Lake City for California. The Republican Party had recently come to power with the election of Benjamin Harrison, and church leaders discussed the Mormon position with Republican power brokers in San Francisco. They conferred with Judge Morris M. Estee, Republican National Chair, sometime-church-agent Isaac Trumbo, U.S. senator Leland Stanford, Henry Biglow of the *San Francisco Examiner*, and several others. The meetings were crucial not only for the church but for officials of the Republican Party who knew Mormons held a potential balance of political power in several western states. Estee promised Republican support for Utah statehood but affirmed that "sooner or later" the church would have to make an official announcement "concerning polygamy and the laying of it aside." George Q. Cannon, writing of Estee's comments in his 12 September 1890 diary, worried about the "difficulty there was in writing such a document—the danger there would be that we would either say too much or too little" (Quinn 1985, 43).

Woodruff and Cannon arrived back in Salt Lake to find an 18 September telegram from the church's Washington agents informing them that the Utah Commission's unfavorable report to the Secretary of the Interior would likely result in the passage of more explicit disfranchisement bills. The report compelled a decisive response. Three days later, on 24 September, Woodruff and Cannon met with counselor Joseph F. Smith and three members of the Council of the Twelve "upon an important subject." A member of the Presiding Bishopric, John E. Winder, later said that when Woodruff entered the meeting he commented that he had not slept much during the night. "I have been struggling all night with the Lord," he related, "about what should be done under the existing circumstances of the church." Laying some papers on a table, he said, "Here is the result" (ibid., 44). George Q. Cannon added in his 24 September diary: "This whole matter has been at President Woodruff's own instance. He has felt strongly impelled to do what he has, and he has spoken with great plainness to the brethren in regard to the necessity of something of this kind being done. he has stated that the Lord had made it plain to him that this was his duty, and he felt perfectly clear in his mind that it was the right thing" (ibid.).

Frank J. Cannon, who was apparently invited to the 24 September meeting, later described the setting. "The portraits in oils of the dead presidents, martyrs, and prophets of the Church, looked down on us from the facade of a little gallery." Standing against the backdrop of the paintings, Woodruff appeared to be "so old and other-worldly," Cannon remarked, "that he seemed already of their circle rather than ours. . . . He had called the brethren together (he said) to submit a decision to their consideration, and he desired from them an expression of their willingness to accept and abide by it."

Woodruff provided a brief history of the sufferings of the polygamous Saints in opposition to government regulations and declared that the courts had decided "against us." He then pointed out, according to Frank Cannon's account, that "Brother George Q. Cannon, Brother John T. Caine, and the other brethren who had been in Washington, had found that the situation of the church was critical. Brother Franklin S. Richards had advised that our last legal defense had fallen." With "broken and contrite spirit," President Woodruff "had sought the will of the Lord, and the Holy Spirit had revealed that it was necessary for the church to relinquish the practice of that principle for which the brethren had been willing to lay down their lives."

After a brief period of silence, Woodruff asked the group for individual reactions. "The matter is now before you," he said "I want you to speak as the Spirit moves you." When no one spoke, Woodruff asked his counselor George Q. Cannon to respond. After his supportive comments, several men asked questions. Did this decision mean the absolute cessation of plural marriage? Would they be required to discontinue living with their plural wives and families? According to the account of Frank J. Cannon, the answer to both of these questions was yes.[7] Woodruff explained that church agents in Washington saw no other solution to the problem and "that it was the will of the Lord; that we must submit." "I saw their faces flush and then slowly pale again – and [then] the storm broke," Cannon reported. "One after another they rose and protested, hoarsely, in the voice of tears, that they were willing to suffer 'persecution unto death' rather than to violate the covenants which they had made 'in holy places' with the women who had trusted them."

After each man had had the opportunity to express himself, George Q. Cannon again addressed the group. He reviewed the long unsuccessful efforts of the church's legal department and concluded that as "citizens of a nation, we were required to obey its laws. And when we found, by the highest judicial interpretation of statute and constitution that we were without grounds for our plea of religious immunity, we had but the alternative either of defying the power of the whole nation or of submitting ourselves to its authority." Cannon declared himself "willing to do the will of the Lord. And since the Prophet of God, after long season of prayer, had submitted this revelation as the will of the Lord, he was ready for the sacrifice" (Cannon and Higgins 1911, 96-98).

That afternoon Woodruff dispatched a press release to the Associated Press in Chicago. The following day he sent a similar telegram to Utah's congressional delegate John T. Caine and to First Presidency secretary L. John Nuttall in Washington. Nuttall labored the following week to print and distribute more than a thousand copies of the press release to "the President, Cabinet, Senate & House of Reps & other leading men." Denying the Utah Commission's report that plural marriages were still being encouraged and solemnized, Woodruff announced the policy change that had long been sought by government officials: "Inasmuch as laws have been enacted by Congress forbidding plural marriages, which laws have been pronounced constitutional by the court of the last resort, I hereby declare my intention to submit to those laws, and to use my influence with the members of the Church over which I preside to have them do likewise. . . . And now I publicly declare that my advice to the Latter-day Saints is to refrain from contracting any marriage forbidden by the laws of the land."

NOTES

1. Caleb West to Department of the Interior, Oct. 1888, in G. Larson 1971, 245. West was not alone in this opinion. "The government of Utah to-day has no semblance to republican government," Senator Bayard had declared during 1882 debate on

the Edmunds Act. "All that was intended to be conserved of republican institutions and theory has been displaced by a system of theocracy. And therefore for the purpose of obtaining the spirit and meaning and principle of republican government it is necessary that the theocracy shall be displaced" (*Congressional Record*, 47th Congress, 1st session, 13 [1882]: 1202-1203.)

2. At the dedication of the Manti Temple on 17 May 1888, Woodruff proclaimed that "we are not going to stop the practice of plural marriage until the coming of the son of man" (John Henry Smith Journal).

3. Atkin, the founder of a one-family village at Bloomington (near St. George), Utah, on several occasions provided Woodruff with refuge to escape U.S. marshals. Grace Atkin Woodbury recalled that Woodruff, an avid outdoorsman, to escape detection would often go hunting in a sunbonnet and Mother Hubbard dress. During a three-month period at the home in 1887, the eighty-year-old apostle made more than forty visits to the Atkin pond. This slough near the Virgin River, surrounded by cattails and rushes, not only made for good fishing and duck hunting but served as an excellent hiding place when federal marshals were in the vicinity. On one such occasion Woodruff was alerted, and the Atkin family quickly loaded him, his bed roll, food and water, books, and his fishing tackle into a large boat. Grace Woodbury recalled that "when the danger was passed, William [Atkin] went out to the pond, made a noise like a duck and Woodruff quacked back in reply" (Mulder and Mortensen 1958, 411-15).

4. Clawson boldly announced in his conference talk that "If the gospel is worth anything to us it is worth everything. There is no sacrifice we can make for it that should be too great. We should be willing to go to prison for the truth." He reminded the congregation that he had been willing: "In 1884 I was convicted and sentenced to prison for keeping a commandment of God. . . . I was sentenced to four years imprisonment, and was incarcerated three years and one month. I saw 300 of my brethren enter the penitentiary for similar reasons and 220 of them emerged from prison while I was there. I feel none the worse for my experience. My testimony is stronger than ever. It is pleasing to God for men to go to prison under an unjust law rather than act contrary to their covenants. The brethren who were imprisoned exhibited great patience in the midst of the worst class of criminals. It was better for them to do this than to enter into an agreement not to serve God" (*Deseret News*, 7 April 1888.)

5. Angus M. Cannon, brother of George Q. Cannon and president of the Salt Lake Stake, in 1888 testimony before a U.S. commissioner explained that the church no longer "sanctioned" plural marriages. When asked when such practices had been discontinued, he replied, "It must be a year I think, very near a year, not quite, since persons applying have been refused." To the question, "Has this refusal been since the death of President Taylor only," Cannon replied, "I have understood that it existed before his death, but I was not conscious of it. I had no occasion to sign any marriage recommends for some time" ("Report of Utah Commission," 24 Sept. 1888). Wilford Woodruff reported in the 20 October 1889 *Salt Lake Tribune* that President Taylor refused to recommend plural marriages "since the Edmunds-Tucker Law [3 March 1887]."

An example of Woodruff's refusal to allow a plural marriage is his 2 June 1889 letter to Ammon M. Tenney in Diaz, Mexico. "It is a very delicate matter, on which you write," the church president penned, "to be made the subject of correspondence between yourself and me, under existing circumstances." "Prudence and precaution" were advised by Woodruff, "especially in regard to my own acts in relation thereto." Tenney's request was refused: "I have deemed it wise and best for the present to advise the Saints to . . . await patiently His providences for our relief. . . .

I am somewhat familiar with your circumstances . . . and am constrained to say that I think it will be wise for you not to take the step proposed at present, but rather carefully watch over the interests and guard the blessings and bear the burdens you already have, until the Spirit of the Lord shall direct otherwise."

6. Frank J. Cannon's account in this treatment is taken from Cannon and Higgins 1911. Cannon, though friendly towards Mormonism at this time, was excommunicated 14 March 1905 for "unchristianlike conduct and apostasy." As editor of the *Salt Lake Tribune*, Cannon unleashed a barrage of critical editorials against church leaders, particularly President Joseph F. Smith. For details on the life of Frank J. Cannon, see Van Wagoner and Walker 1980, 44-48.

7. If Cannon correctly reported the answer to this second question, church leaders soon changed their position. Six days following the release of the Manifesto, during a Quorum of the Twelve meeting, Apostle Francis M. Lyman said: "I endorse the Manifesto, and feel it will do good. I design to live with and have children by my wives, using the wisdom which God gave me to avoid being captured by the officers of the law." And during a 1 October quorum meeting Apostle John Henry Smith said: "I cannot feel to say that the Manifesto is quite right or wrong. It may be that the people are unworthy of the principle and hence the Lord has withdrawn it. I cannot consent to cease living with my wives unless I am imprisoned" (Abraham H. Cannon Journal, 30 Sept., 1 Oct. 1890). For further discussion of the unresolved issue of post-Manifesto cohabitation, see ibid., 19 Oct. 1891.

Fourteen

INTERPRETING WOODRUFF

Mormon reaction to the "Wilford Woodruff Manifesto," as the press release subsequently became known, was mixed. Apostle Abraham H. Cannon noted in his 26 September 1890 diary that there was "considerable comment and fault-finding among some of the Saints." Many longtime church members, steeped in the philosophy that plural marriage was essential for the highest degree of exaltation, wondered about the eternal consequences of the announcement. Just four years earlier George Q. Cannon, in a powerful 1 May 1885 editorial in *The Juvenile Instructor*, had warned against the "Vain and delusive hope" that the "people of god" would renounce plural marriage. "To comply with the request of our enemies," he adamantly argued, "would be to give up all hope of ever entering into the glory of God, the Father, and Jesus Christ, the Son." Cannon denounced the "costly bargain" which the Saints were asked to make: "So intimately interwoven is this precious doctrine with the exaltation of men and women in the great hereafter that it cannot be given up without giving up at the same time all hope of immortal glory."

The absence of the signatures of First Presidency counselors George Q. Cannon and Joseph F. Smith on the Manifesto also concerned some Saints. Others wondered why the document began with the unusual "To Whom It May Concern" rather than the authoritative "Thus Saith the Lord" usually associated with revelatory pronouncements. Skepticism outside Mormonism, considering past difficulties, was not surprising. The 26 September 1890 *Salt Lake Tribune* commented, "We cannot resist the thought that this was not prompted by President Woodruff at all, but that it was prompted by shrewd men in the Church, and that the object is purely political." The same editorial charged that George Q. Cannon had probably persuaded Woodruff to issue the Manifesto as a smoke screen which would "give the country an idea that we had abandoned polygamy because of our respect for the laws." On 27 September the *Tribune* declared that the "manifesto was not intended to be accepted as a command by the President of the Church, but as a little bit of harmless dodging to deceive the people of the East."

Territorial governor Arthur L. Thomas, a strong critic of Mormon polygamy, also viewed the Manifesto skeptically. "The general sentiment is a hope it is in good faith," he was quoted in the 30 September *Deseret News*, "but many things lead to doubt." He noted that the statement "does not come in the usual channel" and that while submission to the law was advised, "there is no injunction to obey the laws." He added that the Manifesto did not address the question of unlawful cohabitation, nor did it say whether "polygamy is wrong or the law is right." The 2 October *Tribune* summed up the reaction: "No Gentile in Utah believes [the Manifesto] is to be what it purports to be, or what the outside world believes it to be."

But to the church press the meaning of the Manifesto was clear. "Anyone who calls the language of President Woodruff's declaration 'indefinite,' " the *Deseret Evening News* editorialized on 30 September, "must be either exceedingly dense or determined to find fault. It is so definite that its meaning cannot be mistaken by any one who understands simple English." On 3 October the paper added, "Nothing could be more direct and unambiguous than the language of President Woodruff, nor could anything be more authoritative." As to his part in the press release, Woodruff wrote in his 25 September journal: "I have arrived at a point in the History of my life as the President of the Church of Jesus Christ of Latter Day Saints where I am under the necessity of acting for the Temporal Salvation of the Church. The United State[s] Governme[n]t has taken a Stand & passed Laws to destroy the Latter day Saints upon the Subje[c]t of poligamy or Patriarchal order of Marriage. And after praying to the Lord & feeling inspired by his spirit I have issued the following Proclamation which is sustained by My Councillors and the 12 Apostles" (Kenney, 9 [25 Sept. 1890]: 113-14).

As to its text, the Manifesto contained several incorrect statements. For example, the plural marriages claimed by the Utah Commission and denied in the text of the Manifesto have since been well documented. And there were only three apostles present at the 24 September council meeting to sustain President Woodruff's statement: Marriner W. Merrill, F. D. Richards, and Moses Thatcher (Marriner Wood Merrill Diary, 6 Oct. 1890).[1] Full acceptance by the First Presidency and Quorum of the Twelve did not take place until 2 October and not until after three days of lengthy debate. Apostle John Henry Smith related that apostles Lorenzo Snow, Franklin D. Richards, Moses Thatcher, and Francis Lyman immediately approved the Manifesto when the full quorum met on 30 September. But others, including Smith himself, "were not fully clear upon it" (John Henry Smith Journal, 30 Sept. 1890). Outspoken apostle John W. Taylor, though acknowledging "the hand of the Lord" in the action, remained unsettled on the issue. "My father when President of the Church," he said, "sought to find a way to evade the conflict between the Saints and government on the question of plural marriage, but the Lord said it was an eternal and unchangeable law and must stand" (Abraham H. Cannon Journal, 30 Sept. 1890).

An especially difficult issue to resolve was the matter of continued cohabitation with plural wives. Frank J. Cannon thought Woodruff initially viewed the Manifesto as forbidding future cohabitation, but George Q. Cannon, during a 7 October meeting of church leaders, stressed that "a man who will act the coward and shield himself behind the Manifesto by deserting his plural wives should be damned." Woodruff himself added: "This Manifesto only refers to future marriages and does not affect past conditions. I did not, could not, and would not promise [the nation] that you would desert your wives and children. This you cannot do in honor" (ibid., 7 Oct. 1890).

Another unsettled matter was whether the Manifesto was to be presented to the Saints for a sustaining vote in General Conference. Abraham H. Cannon noted in his 2 October journal that "some felt that the assent of the Presidency and Twelve to the matter was sufficient without committing the people by their votes to a policy which they might in the future wish to discard." This controversy was not resolved until 5 October. Abraham H. Cannon noted in his journal that a telegram from Representative John T. Caine was read to the assembled church leaders, indicating that the government "could not accept President Wilford Woodruff's Manifesto without its acceptance by the conference as authoritative against the statements of the Utah Commission and Governor A. L. Thomas."

The next day George Q. Cannon, while addressing the assembled Saints in General Conference, used Doctrine and Covenants 124:49 as the basis for his plea to have the Manifesto accepted by the church. He eloquently argued that when God gives a commandment and the Saints are hindered from carrying it out by "their enemies"—in this case the United States government—then it is for God to accept their offering and to require that they no longer live the commandment. After Cannon had spoken, Woodruff took the stand and assured his followers that he had not acted hastily in the matter. "The step which I have taken in issuing the Manifesto has not been done without earnest prayer before the Lord. . . . It is not wisdom for us to make war upon sixty-five million people. It is not wisdom for us to go forth and carry out this principle against the laws of the nation and receive the consequences. This is in the hands of the Lord and He will govern and control it" (Cowley 1909, 570-71).

Following the remarks by Cannon and Woodruff, Orson F. Whitney, a talented poet, musician, and a future apostle, then read the Manifesto to the assembled Saints. Silence prevailed until someone from the gallery called for a second reading. After this request was granted, Quorum of the Twelve president Lorenzo Snow moved that the declaration be accepted as "authoritative and binding." Many of the thousands in attendance abstained from voting. Apostle Marriner W. Merrill noted in his 6 October diary that the motion was "carried by a weak voice, but seemingly unanimous." Future events were to show that assent of church leaders and laymen was anything but unanimous, however. "We were all greatly astonished," plural wife Lorena Eugenia Washburn Larsen recalled. "It seemed impossible that the Lord would go back on a principle which had caused so much sacrifice, heartache, and trial." Describing what must have been the anguish of many Saints, she added: "I thought that if the Lord and the church authorities had gone back on that principle, there was nothing to any part of the gospel. I fancied I could see myself and my children, and many other splendid women and their families turned adrift, and our only purpose in entering it, had been to more fully serve the Lord. I sank down on [my] bedding and wished in my anguish that the earth would open and take me and my children in. The darkness seemed impenetrable" (Bergera 1977).

Others, however, evidently felt the light had finally come. Annie Clark Tanner, who like many other women had endured an unhappy marriage as second wife, recorded that when she first heard of the Manifesto, "a great relief came over me. . . . At that moment I compared my feelings of relief with the experience one has when the first crack of dawn comes after a night of careful vigilance over a sick patient. At such a time daylight is never more welcome; and now the dawn was breaking for the Church. I suppose its leaders may have realized, at last, that if our Church had anything worthwhile for mankind, they had better work with the government of our country rather than against it" (Tanner 1976, 130).

The question of whether the Manifesto was a divine manifestation or a political ruse designed to "beat the devil at his own game" has long been a subject of debate. George Q. Cannon, during the 6 October General Conference, explained to the Saints: "We have waited for the Lord to move in the matter; and on the 24th of September, President Woodruff made up his mind that he would write something, and he had the spirit of it. He had prayed about it and had besought God repeatedly to show him what to do. At that time the Spirit came upon him, and the [Manifesto] was the result" (*Conference Reports*, Oct. 1890). Woodruff himself, in a 20 August 1891 meeting of the First Presidency, church lawyers, and some apostles, said, "Brethren, you may call it inspiration or revelation, or what you please; as for me, I am satisfied it is from the Lord" (Quinn 1985, 50).

But many church leaders viewed the Manifesto as purely a political proclamation. Apostle Marriner W. Merrill, for example, noted in his diary, "I do not believe the Manifesto was a revelation from God but was formulated by Prest. Woodruff and endorsed by His counselors and the Twelve Apostles for expediency" (in Bitton, *Guide*, 238). And counselor Joseph F. Smith, responding to Heber J. Grant's 21 August 1891 question about whether the Manifesto was a revelation, answered, "No." Smith explained that he

146

regarded the document as inspired given the conditions imposed by the government on the church. But "he did not believe it to be an emphatic revelation from god abolishing plural marriage" (Quinn 1985, 83). However, Woodruff, despite subsequent contradictory actions, said on 21 October 1891 that "the manifesto was just as authoritative and binding as though it had been given in the form of 'Thus saith the Lord' " (ibid., 51).

Whatever inspired the document, the Manifesto did not produce the abrupt about-face in the church's position that Mormons today tend to imagine. Both John Taylor and Wilford Woodruff had already begun authorizing fewer plural marriages. Woodruff declared in 19 October 1891 court testimony: "After I was appointed president of the Church I looked the question over and . . . was convinced that . . . plural marriage would have to be stopped in this church altogether; it was not ourselves, who were suffering, but a large portion of the people, who had not entered into it." He further testified that "after I was made president of the church—I did not advocate the principle . . . it was upon that ground that I issued that manifesto, by I will say, as I viewed it, by inspiration: I believed it was my duty."

Woodruff, perhaps more pragmatic and certainly less combative than John Taylor, recognized the necessity of changing the church's public position on polygamy. Continued opposition to the government was clearly foolhardy. The government had both the power and the resolve to destroy the church's influence in the territory if it did not publicly capitulate on the polygamy issue.

Woodruff defended his actions in several public statements. His sermon to a group of Logan Saints, reported in the 7 November 1891 *Deseret Evening News*, posed the issue in the form of a question: "Which is the wisest course for the Latter-day Saints to pursue—to continue to attempt to practice plural marriage with the laws of the nation against it and the opposition of sixty millions of people, and at the cost of the confiscation and loss of all the temples, and the stopping of all the ordinances therein, both for the living and the dead, and the imprisonment of the First Presidency and Twelve and the head[s] of families in the church . . . or after doing and suffering what we have through our adherence to this principle to cease the practice and submit to the law?" Woodruff insisted that the Lord had shown him "by vision and revelation exactly what would take place if we did not stop this practice. He has told me exactly what to do, and what the result would be if we did not do it." The church president was adamant about the revealed nature of the decision: "I should have let all the temples go out of our hands; I should have gone to prison myself, and let every other man go there, had not the God of heaven commanded me to do what I did do."

Woodruff's anticipation of the Millennium undoubtedly influenced his timing in issuing the Manifesto. He was convinced that maintaining church temples, where ordinances for the living and the dead could be performed, was "more important than continuing the practice of plural marriage for the present" (Marriner Wood Merrill Diary, 6 Oct. 1890).[2] Mormons had long been taught that Joseph Smith established the "Kingdom of God" to prepare for the imminent second coming of Christ. The political kingdom, as embodied in the Council of Fifty, had ceased to function. If Woodruff allowed the spiritual kingdom, the church, to be sacrificed for plural marriage, there would be no organization left to prepare for Christ's coming.

Still there were definite political dimensions to the Manifesto as well. Public statements to the contrary, the First Presidency privately counseled that plural marriage was not to be abandoned nor were polygamists to discontinue connubial relationships with their plural wives. Though some church leaders, such as Lorenzo Snow, began living with only one wife, most continued to violate the unlawful cohabitation statute. And until 1904 scores of new plural marriages were authorized and performed in Mexico, Canada, and even in the United States.

Byron Harvey Allred was evidently one of the first individuals permitted to marry a plural wife after the Manifesto. He and his first wife brought to the October 1890 conference a woman he had intended to take as a plural wife. The adoption of the Manifesto placed them in a difficult position, and they sought counsel from the First Presidency. President Woodruff explained that because of the agreement entered into by the Manifesto, no more plural marriages would be solemnized in the United States and suggested that Allred go where polygamy could be practiced without violating the law. Joseph F. Smith, who was also present, advised Allred that "many Saints had already moved to Mexico for that very purpose, and others were going" (Allred 1968, 199).

Though polygamy was illegal in the area of Mexico where Mormons had settled, Mexican officials, as previously noted, did not enforce such regulations.[3] As church president, Joseph F. Smith later explained how President Woodruff avoided duplicity in authorizing new plural marriages outside of the United States. In an 11 April 1911 telegram to Senator Reed Smoot, Smith, who served in the First Presidency longer than any other man, verified that "Prest. Cannon was the first to conceive the idea that the Church could consistently countenance polygamy beyond confines of the republic where there was no law against it, and consequently he authorized the solemnization of plural marriages in Mexico and Canada after manifesto of 1890" (Smoot Collection).[4] Walter M. Wolfe, former Brigham Young Academy faculty member, in testimony before the Senate Committee on Elections and Privileges, during the 1904 Reed Smoot hearings, explained how the system worked. For example, Ovena Jorgensen, a student at Brigham Young Academy in 1898, went with her prospective husband, William C. Ockey, to request President Woodruff's permission to marry polygamously. Brushing them aside with a wave of his hand, the church president said "he would have nothing to do with the matter, but referred them to President George Q. Cannon." They were given a letter from Cannon to President Anthony W. Ivins of the Juarez Mexico Stake and were subsequently married by him in Mexico (*Proceedings* 4:11).

A handful of plural marriages performed in Mexico were apparently approved by President Woodruff in the month following the announcement of the Manifesto. But in November he temporarily stopped signing recommends because, according to Abraham H. Cannon's 2 November 1890 diary, "one young man [Christian F. Olsen] who recently had this privilege, came back and allowed the knowledge of it to go out, and thus put the church in danger." Yet some statements by the church president himself, as well as by other members of the First Presidency, promoted both continued cohabitation and new plural marriages in the church. During a joint First Presidency and Quorum of the Twelve meeting on 2 April 1891, for example, Woodruff announced that "the principle of plural marriage will yet be restored to this church, but how or when I cannot say" (Quinn 1985, 61).

Furthermore, during a 7 October 1891 meeting of church leaders with stake presidents and bishops, Joseph F. Smith advised: "God will not justify you in kicking out your families and stultifying yourselves in the eyes of all good men. We do not want you to leave your wives because of the Manifesto. Tell your people to take care of their families just as they have always done" (Abraham H. Cannon Journal, 7 Oct. 1891). Cannon further observed the proceedings of a joint meeting of the Quorum of the Twelve and First Presidency later that day. "We got to the point where we realized that polygamy is no longer a law of the church," he wrote, "and so far as our present families are concerned, we must support and honor them; though if we live with them it is at our peril" (ibid.).

Church authorities and lay members, familiar with the private statements of the First Presidency, were shocked when they read the October 1891 testimony of their leaders before the Master in Chancery. Seeking to obtain the return of the church's escheated property, Woodruff, Cannon, and Smith all testified that not only had polygamy ceased, but cohabitation was discontinued. Woodruff's testimony was particularly pointed. Asked what was his "object and purpose in issuing the manifesto," he testified that "It was to announce to the world that the plural marriage had been forbidden by the church and that it could not be practised hereafter." His testimony was explicit: "Q. State whether or not it would be contrary to the law of the church, for any member of the church to enter into or contract a plural marriage. A. It would be contrary to the laws of the church. Q. What would be the penalty? A. Any person entering into plural marriage after that date, would be liable to become excommunicated from the church. Q. Do you understand that that language was to be expanded and to include the further statement of living or associating in plural marriage by those already in the status? A. Yes, sir; I intended the proclamation to cover the ground, to keep the laws—to obey the law myself, and expected the people to obey the law. . . . Q. Was the manifesto intended to apply to the church everywhere? A. Yes, sir. Q. In every nation and every country? A. Yes, sir; as far as I had a knowledge in the matter. Q. In places outside of the United States as well as within the United States? A. Yes, sir; we are given no liberties for entering into that anywhere. . . . Q. Unlawful cohabitation, as it is named, and spoken of, should also stop, as well as future polygamous marriages? A. Yes, sir, that has been the intention. Q. And that has been your views and explanation of it? A. Yes, sir, that has been my view."

Charles Walker, a colorful St. George poet, commented on Woodruff's testimony in his 20 October 1891 journal: "This announcement by him as Pres. of the Church has caused an uneasy feeling among the People, and some think he has gone back on the Revealation on Plural Marriage and its covenants and obligations" (Larson and Larson 1980, 2:723). Several church leaders viewed the situation similarly. But at a 12 November meeting of church leaders, Woodruff explained his stance. Apostle Abraham H. Cannon recorded in his journal that Woodruff said "he was placed in such a position on the witness stand that he could not answer other than he did. Yet any man who deserts and neglects his wives or children because of the Manifesto should be handled on his fellowship." Cannon concluded that "our talk resolved itself into this[:] that men must be careful to avoid exposing themselves to arrest or conviction for violation of the law and yet they must not break their covenants with their wives."[5]

The First Presidency's public interpretation of the Manifesto differed consistently from their private feelings. In a 5 February 1899 interview with the *New York Herald*, President George Q. Cannon explained if a man's wife was barren, he might "go to Canada and marry another wife. He would not be violating our laws, and would not be in danger of prosecution unless the first wife should follow him there from Utah and prefer a charge of bigamy against him. He might go to Mexico and have a religious ceremony uniting him to another that would not violate our law." But the issue involved more than "barren wives." Discussing a particular case before the Quorum of the Twelve the following year, Cannon reviewed what had been the church's posture respecting "new polygamy" after the Manifesto. "When the Manifesto was issued," he explained, "we did not pledge ourselves to abandon our plural wives, nor even to cease to perform plural marriages outside of the government; and when our people get the idea that we have bound ourselves to the whole world they manifest ignorance. A man may go to some countries and not violate their laws by taking a plural wife and living in plural marriage" (JH, 16 Aug. 1900). First Presidency secretary George F. Gibbs subsequently wrote that "President Woodruff's manifesto . . . was not intended to apply to Mexico, and did not, as the church was not dealing with the Mexican government, but only with our own government" (Quinn 1985, 49).

The casuistry of Mormon leaders was obviously self-protective. As guardians of the church, they were motivated to defend the religious institution and its tenets, including plural marriage, at all costs. This commitment to plural marriage had repeatedly dictated situational responses to ethical dilemmas since the early 1830s. Apostle Matthias F. Cowley, in testimony before the Council of the Twelve on 10 May 1911, articulated the rationale for such duplicities: "I have always been taught that when the brethren were in a tight place that it would not be amiss to lie to help them out. One of the Presidency of the Church made the statement some years ago . . . that he would lie like hell to help his brethren" (Minutes).

Whether inspiration or political expediency or, more probably, both prompted the Manifesto, the action lessened tensions with the government and hastened statehood. With the church publicly opposing polygamy, the government had no reason to continue to punish polygamists. Judge Charles S. Zane, who had so firmly prosecuted polygamists prior to the Manifesto, demonstrated in his court decisions that he intended to uphold the law but not to carry out a vendetta against the church. He adopted a policy of leniency with those brought before him and supported general amnesty for those previously convicted.

One polygamist who benefited from the relaxation of government prosecution was Charles L. Walker. Reporting to Beaver judge James A. Miner on 13 September 1892, he listened as the clerk read the indictment "charging me with the *crime* of unlawfull cohabitation against the peace and *dignity* of the People of the. US &c." Walker pleaded "guilty to the charge," but promised to obey the law in the future, after which the judge remarked, "Mr. Walker I shall dismis your case with costs." Walker said that he was "in embarresed circumstances and could not pay the costs." The judge replied that he would consider the case overnight and pronounce sentence in the morning. Standing before the judge the next day, Walker detected "a rougish twinkle in his eye" which he interpreted as "an omen of good." "Mr. Walker," the judge declared, "I have considered your case, and I shall dismiss you with a fine of 6 cents." Walking to the clerk's desk, the relieved man laid down a dime. When told there was no change, Walker replied, "keep the 4 cents . . . in interest against the U.S." (Larson and Larson 1980, 2:749-50).

Such lenient judicial rulings against Mormon polygamists upset many of the church's enemies. But the action ultimately ushered in a new era of positive Mormon/non-Mormon relationships. Much of the improved political atmosphere can be directly traced to church leaders' newly formed allegiance with the Republican party and the willingness of many Gentiles to accept Mormonism minus polygamy.

1. The Manifesto was incorrect on several other points as well. Though Woodruff may have not been teaching or advocating polygamy, his counselors and several apostles were. As the 3 October 1890 *Salt Lake Tribune* wryly noted: "Our recollection is that [Woodruff] says he knows nothing of such marriages. That is, he personally has not given his written consent to them. He was not present at the marriages. No one has told him since. Hence, he knows nothing of them."

Regarding the Manifesto's explanation of why the Endowment House was torn down, the 2 October *Tribune* correctly noted that the claim that the "Endowment house was torn down because there were to be no more plural marriages, no one believes at all; because, on point of fact, the Endowment House had been raided by United States Marshals and was considered contaminated. It was on dangerous ground and was liable to be seized by the receiver in the escheat cases. It was so public that it was impossible to carry on the usual business without danger of discovery, and in the meantime, the Logan Temple had been completed. Finally, as was testified to in the cases before Judge Anderson last autumn, such a place was not necessary for the celebration of plural marriages." In addition, the work generated by demolishing the building served as an effective public works project for unemployed Mormons brought to the city to improve the Mormon position at the voting polls.

Perhaps Woodruff's most interesting claim in the statement was that he was submitting to the laws of the land which forbade polygamy. The U.S. Supreme Court in 1879 had declared the anti-polygamy legislation of 1862 constitutional. Eleven years passed before the church began professing obedience to the law.

2. Woodruff is considered the "Father of Mormon Temple Work." For details on this aspect of his life, see Van Wagoner and Walker 1980, 398-99.

3. Church president Heber J. Grant noted in a 15 November 1935 letter to Katherine H. Allred that "for a period of time after the issuing of the manifesto, plural marriages were performed in Mexico, the officials of the Mexican government expressing the desire that more Mormon children should be born in that Republic, as the Mormons were the best citizens of Mexico."

4. On 21 April 1911, George F. Gibbs, secretary to the First Presidency, wired Smoot that "the use of [Canada] was a mistake on our part, please strike it out, as the word 'Mexico' only should be used" (Smoot Collection).

5. Woodruff had always held this view. In a May 1882 letter to Moses Franklin Farnsworth he had counseled: "Concerning your families, I think it would be wisdom for our brethren to have one wife under the roof where he lives, if his circumstances will permit it. But we do not intend to cast off any of our wives and children because of the Edmunds bill, or any other Bill, but to exercise what prudence and wisdom we can in these matters" (Carter 1958-75, 3:194-96). In his 3 October 1885 journal Woodruff wrote: "I would *rather be shot* dead in the Streets or struck with lightening than to Desert my children Break my Covenants turn my wives into the Street" (Kenney, 8 [3 Oct. 1885]: 337); see also ibid., 520.

POST-MANIFESTO POLYGAMY

Prior to 1890, when President Woodruff met with Republican leaders in San Francisco, the majority of Mormons supported the Democratic party on national issues. But in the mid-1880s, during President Grover Cleveland's Democratic administration, George Q. Cannon warned in a letter to Cleveland's emissary George L. Miller that the harshness with which his administration was dealing with the Mormons would "act disastrously upon the future prospects of the party." Cannon stressed that Mormons were, "with very few exceptions, Democrats," and that they held the political power in Utah, Idaho, and Arizona and were "not to be despised in Nevada and Colorado." Reminding officials that Mormons numbered nearly 250,000, Cannon hoped that the Democrats would "appreciate their value" and seek their favor rather than oppress them (Lyman 1981, 60-61).

Mormon hope for Democratic support of Utah statehood gradually waned. After Cleveland signed on 27 February 1889 the omnibus bill squelching Utah's statehood bid, Utah congressman John T. Caine lamented the action in a letter to George L. Miller. "I believe the Democratic party by its cowardice on the Mormon question through its refusal to admit Utah with an anti-polygamy constitution has lost the control of four states which the Mormon people could have given it, viz. Utah, Idaho, Arizona, and Wyoming." The Mormons "have always been true to the Democratic party," Caine added, "but the party when in power did not appreciate them and failed to take advantage of the strength which they could have given it" (ibid., 223-24).

Early in 1890 President Woodruff sent his counselor George Q. Cannon to Washington, D.C., to try again to obtain Democratic support for Utah statehood. The Democrats provided no aid. Cannon, who during his congressional service had sat on the Democratic side of the floor, switched his allegiance to the Republican party. Cannon's son Frank, an ardent Republican, succeeded in mid-May 1890 in obtaining Republican support for opposing passage of the Cullom-Strubble Bill. The elder Cannon was optimistic that the "Republican party are becoming more favorably impressed with regard to the importance of securing Mormon votes and influence" (Abraham H. Cannon Diary, 10 July 1890). A shrewd politician, Cannon immediately began to lobby other church leaders to support the Republicans. His son Abraham noted in his 31 July 1890 diary, "The Democrats when they had the power to do us good were afraid, and betrayed us so that now we feel as though the Republican party should be tried to see if they will be fair to us."

When Presidents Woodruff and Cannon returned from California in September 1890 with word of support from Republican leaders, church allegiance soon shifted towards that party. Two days before the 10 June 1891 dissolution of the Mormon-controlled People's Party, Apostle Abraham H. Cannon worried in his journal about the "danger of our people all [giving their allegiance to the] Democrats. . . . It is felt that efforts should be made to instruct our people in Republicanism and thus win them to that party."

Cannon also recorded the revealing comment made by his colleague in the First Presidency Joseph F. Smith that "We have received the strongest admonition from our Republican friends that we must not allow this Territory to go strongly Democratic." Announcing that church leaders had "favored John Henry [Smith]'s going on the stump so as to convince the people that a man could be a Republican and still be a saint,"[1] second counselor Joseph F. Smith admonished: "I wish more of the Apostles belonged to this party and would sign the rolls. The Republicans will stand by their friends, which the Democrats have not done and I believe they will yet grant us amnesty if we encourage them to believe this may become a Republican state. I know many prominent men of this party who are today our friends and who are working in our interests, but I do not know a single Democrat who is helping us. Such men as Blaine, Clarkson, Stanford, and Estee are deeply interested in our affairs and desire to do us good" (ibid., 9 July 1891).[2]

Church leaders publicly urged the Saints to join the political party of their choice. However, to counterbalance Democratic strength in the territory, authorities decided that "men in high authority who believed in Republican principles should go out among the people, but that those in high authority who could not endorse the principles of Republicanism should remain silent" (ibid., 15 June 1891).[3]

The Republican party responded to this newfound Mormon allegiance by pressing for the amnesty of polygamist Saints convicted under the Edmunds and Edmunds-Tucker acts. During the summer of 1891 a petition drafted by Joseph F. Smith and his cousin John Henry Smith was sent to U.S. Republican president Benjamin Harrison. Signed by the First Presidency and ten members of the Quorum of the Twelve, the paper explained the origin of the Manifesto and said that the Mormon people had "in the most solemn manner accepted [it] as the future rule of their lives. . . . As shepherds of a patient and suffering people," the petition concluded, "we ask amnesty for them and pledge our faith and honor for their future" (Clark 1965-75, 3:229-31).

An amnesty proclamation was issued on 4 January 1893. After citing the various anti-bigamy laws, the report of the Utah Commission, and the previous pardon given to some individuals guilty of illegal cohabitation, President Harrison granted a full amnesty and pardon to all persons "liable to the penalties of said act by reason of unlawful cohabitation under the color of polygamous or plural marriage, who have, since November 1, 1890, abstained from such unlawful cohabitation." He specified, however, that the amnesty was based on the condition that in the future those who had been pardoned must obey the law or be "vigorously prosecuted" (*Proceedings* 1:19).

The Utah Commission continued the liberalizing trend on 19 July by ruling that reformed polygamists would again be allowed to vote. Shortly thereafter the escheated church property was returned. President Grover Cleveland, elected to a second term, eventually broadened the amnesty proclamation of Benjamin Harrison. However, church officials soon demonstrated that they held the practice of plural marriage in greater esteem than they did their pledge to the government. With the exception of Lorenzo Snow, who cohabited only with his youngest wife, not a single apostle or member of the First Presidency discontinued connubial relationships with plural wives.

Apostle Abraham H. Cannon recorded several comments in his diary from a 1 April 1892 discussion of the proposed amnesty petition. According to Cannon, Lorenzo Snow stated that "when the Manifesto was issued we had no idea that it was to effect our cohabitation with our wives, but Pres. Woodruff and his brethren who were on the witness stand before the Master in Chancery, were forced to go further in their testimony than we anticipated, or we would have been placed in a worse position than we were before the Manifesto was issued." Apostle Moses Thatcher added, "I have yet to meet the first man among all the eminent men with whom I have conversed upon our question who feels that our past family relations should be disrupted."

Heber J. Grant, later to become president of the church, clearly described the situation, as again noted in Cannon's 1 April 1892 diary entry. "I remember Pres. Woodruff saying that the Manifesto would never apply to our living with our wives, and he would see them damned and in hell before he would agree to cease living with his wives or advise any other person to do so." Grant personally felt "that if we had taken the manly stand and had said we will continue to live with and honor our present wives but will cease marrying in the future, we would have fared better; but now I cannot see any chance of our ever being permitted to live with our wives in freedom again."

Though the 1891 petition for amnesty did not specifically pledge conformity to the law, the grants of amnesty from Presidents Harrison and Cleveland clearly assumed such.[4] Still, eleven General Authorities, including Heber J. Grant, fathered seventy-six children by twenty-seven plural wives during the years 1890-1905 (Cannon 1978, 31). Though Grant had children by only one wife after 1890, he pled guilty to a charge of unlawful cohabitation in 1899 and was fined $100 (*Salt Lake Tribune*, 9 Sept. 1899). In addition he later reportedly sought permission from President Joseph F. Smith to marry Fanny Woolley as a post-Manifesto plural wife.[5] Smith refused Grant's request. Thus the future church president became one of the few members of the hierarchy who neither took a post-Manifesto plural wife nor sealed others in plural marriages.[6]

Few authorized plural marriages occurred during the first three years after the Manifesto.[7] Many church members who continued to believe that plural marriage was essential to their exaltation approached President Woodruff requesting that exceptions be made in their cases. Most petitioners were simply told that the First Presidency could do nothing for them at present. But polygamy was authorized for those who were willing to travel to Mexico. Authorization was usually given by George Q. Cannon, who had initially proposed that plural marriages continue to be performed in Mexico. Woodruff, now nearing ninety, evidently preferred a system of "plausible deniability" wherein he allowed his younger counselors to direct the new polygamy so that as church president he could not be directly linked to the activities.[8]

Cannon and Joseph F. Smith sent couples wishing to be married to Mexican church leaders Alexander F. MacDonald or Apostle George Teasdale. In 1895 the First Presidency called Anthony W. Ivins to replace Teasdale as marriage officiator and to serve as the first stake president in Colonia Juarez. Though a monogamist himself, Ivins was authorized during June 1897 meetings with the First Presidency to perform plural marriage sealings. A form letter was discussed which, when presented to Ivins by a couple, would indicate First Presidency approval to seal the marriage. Later, relating that meeting to a son, Ivins explained that George Q. Cannon had taken him aside and said, "Now Brother Ivins, if you have occasion to meet Porfio Diaz, President of Mexico, we want you to tell him that we are NOT practicing polygamy in Mexico" (H. G. Ivins, 5).[9]

In addition, George Q. Cannon also gave Matthias Cowley permission to marry couples polygamously. Cowley's sealings usually took place in the United States. "I was never instructed to go to a foreign land to perform those marriages," Cowley later reported: "President Cannon told me to do these things or I would never have done it" (Minutes of the Quorum of the Twelve, 10 May 1911). After Cannon's death, Joseph F. Smith also sent couples to Cowley (Quinn 1985, 90-91). The total number of church-approved plural marriages between 1890 and 1904 numbered at least two hundred and fifty, but the annual number was apparently never greater than the thirty-three performed in 1903 (Cannon 1983, 29).

A definite increase in plural marriages occurred after Utah statehood was granted in 1896. Mormon leaders had wanted to convince the government that the church was giving up polygamy. But once statehood was attained they hoped plural marriage could again be openly practiced under lenient or amended state laws. Apostle John Henry Smith discussed this in a 3 April 1888 letter to his cousin, Joseph F. Smith. "It looks to me," he wrote two years before the Manifesto, "as if the only chance on that score [statehood] is to give the whole business away [plural marriage], renouncing our faith save for five years and then taking it up again when once inside the great government fold." But the plans of church leaders were anticipated and waylaid. The Utah constitution, drafted in 1895, prohibited polygamy "forever," nomenclature taken from the Utah Enabling Act passed by Congress. The state drafting committee also felt it necessary to insert an amending clause which retained in force after statehood the 1892 territorial anti-polygamy law.

Though the number of plural marriages sanctioned after statehood was small compared to pre-1890 practices, the conflict between church leaders' endorsement of new polygamy and their anti-polygamy public assurances began to cause increased difficulties. The discrepancy led Utah lawmakers in 1898 to include a statute in the criminial code outlawing unlawful cohabitation. More disturbing still to church leaders was a new attack from the press, which accused the church of bad faith in not keeping its pledges.

Wilford Woodruff died on 2 September 1898. His successor, Lorenzo Snow, sent out messages on new polygamy that for many Mormons were nearly as confusing as Woodruff's private and public utterances had been. Predictably, the result was chaotic division within the Quorum of the Twelve and among the church generally. Before performing an October 1898 plural marriage for Joseph Morrell, Apostle Matthias Cowley asked Snow's permission, and later reported that the church president "simply told me that he would not interfere with Brother Woodruff's and Cannon's work" (Minutes of the Quorum of the Twelve, 10 May 1911). Yet Snow sent Apostle John Henry Smith to Mexico in 1901 to tell A. F. MacDonald that "if he was sealing plural wives to men his standing in the Church was in danger" (John Henry Smith Diary, 27 May 1901). Smith delivered the message, threatening MacDonald with excommunication if he did not stop the practice. But MacDonald, like Anthony W. Ivins and Matthias Cowley, was receiving different instructions from Presidents Cannon and Smith. Joseph F. Smith, through a visiting apostle, sent word to MacDonald in September advising him to ignore Snow's threats and continue to seal plural marriages, which he did.

President Snow seemed to be moving slowly in the direction of abandoning polygamy. "The Church has positively abandoned the practice of polygamy . . . in this and every other state," he explained in an 8 January 1900 *Deseret News* editorial. "No one has any authority whatever," he added, "to form a plural marriage or enter into such relation." But several apostles, including Marriner W. Merrill and George Teasdale, "stood firmly in favor of polygamy" when the issue was discussed in a meeting of the apostles two days later (John Henry Smith Diary, 10 Jan. 1900).[10]

Dissension in the ranks of the hierarchy over new polygamy was complicated when a 1900 congressional investigation, instigated to prevent Elder B. H. Roberts from taking his House seat, produced evidence that Roberts and other church leaders had ignored their pledges to the government. Newspapers attacked the Mormons for going back on their word. These accusations disturbed eighty-six-year-old Lorenzo Snow. To clarify his position to other church leaders he announced on 1 January 1900 that any man living with his plural wives was in violation of the law.

Later that month, during a meeting with the Quorum of the Twelve, Snow expressed fears that plural marriages were being sanctioned in the church despite his opposition. "Without reference to anyone present," an account of the meeting reported, he "said that there were brethren who still seemed to have the idea that it was possible under his administration to obtain a plural wife and have her sealed to him. He authorized and requested the brethren present to correct this impression wherever they find it. He said emphatically that it could not be done." George Q. Cannon, the leader most responsible for "back-handed" polygamy, as Reed Smoot's secretary Carl Badger would later call it, moved that Snow's pronouncement be "seconded as the mind and will of the Lord" (ibid., 11 Jan. 1900).

One year later Snow reaffirmed his anti-polygamy sentiments by telling Apostle Brigham Young, Jr.: "God has removed this privilege from the people, and until he restores it, I shall not consent to any man taking a plural wife. . . . There is no such thing as men taking plural wives and keeping it secret. . . . It cannot be done. Has any one of the Apostles a right to seal plural wives to men by reason of former concessions made to them by the Presidency? No, sir, such right must come from me and no man shall be authorized by me to break the law of the land" (Brigham Young, Jr. Journal, 13 March 1901).[11] Mormons who believed that no plural marriages had been authorized by church leaders after the Manifesto found support in the statements of President Snow. But those who were aware of previous official doubletalk viewed Snow's rhetoric as more of the same: a necessity in protecting their domestic life.

Though the marriage record of Anthony Ivins in the Utah State Historical Society Library shows a decrease of marriages performed during Snow's administration, Apostles Matthias F. Cowley, John W. Taylor, Brigham Young, Jr., George Teasdale, Abraham O. Woodruff, Marriner W. Merrill, John Henry Smith, Anthon H. Lund, and perhaps even George Q. Cannon and Joseph F. Smith were involved in sealing plural marriages not only in Mexico but also in Canada and the United States during this period.[12]

Numerous changes shook Mormonism during 1901. George Q. Cannon died in April. Six months later, on 10 October, Lorenzo Snow died.

Meanwhile church leaders unsuccessfully attempted to nullify the unlawful cohabitation section of the Utah criminal code. A measure drafted by prominent Utah County Mormon, Abel John Evans, passed both state houses but was eventually vetoed by Governor Heber M. Wells, one of the thirty-seven children of First Presidency counselor Daniel H. Wells. "I have every reason to believe," Governor Wells warned, "its enactment would be a signal for a general demand upon the National Congress for a constitutional amendment directed solely against certain conditions here; a demand which under the circumstances would assuredly be complied with" (*Proceedings* 1:11).

Joseph F. Smith, who in 1906 would plead guilty to violating the Utah state anti-polygamy law, became sixth president of the church on 17 October 1901. Smith had not only been aware of authorized post-Manifesto marriages—as evidenced by his 1890 advice to Byron Harvey Allred, Sr., and his 11 April 1911 telegram to Reed Smoot[13]—but had personally performed at least one such marriage prior to becoming church president. Smith was strongly critical of the church's polygamy restrictions. "I have no sympathy whatever," he wrote to Anthony W. Ivins on 6 February 1900, "with the prevailing feeling which seems to be leading some to the setting of stakes and fixing of meets and bounds to the purposes and policies of providence in such a way as to establish almost unsurmountable difficulties which may rise up to vex them and others in the future." In August 1900, Smith and Elder Seymour B. Young were at Colonia Diaz during the sealing of Brigham Young Academy president Benjamin Cluff, Jr., to a plural wife, Florence Reynolds. Cluff had previously appealed unsuccessfully to Anthony W. Ivins to marry him and Reynolds without First Presidency approval. He later told a daughter that "Brother Joseph F. Smith told me that I could marry Aunt Florence" (Ingram). Another report described the marriage: "It was very dark and brother Clawson could not see who performed the ceremony. The voice, however, sounded exactly like President Smith's" (LeBaron 1981, 39-40).

The tight restrictions Lorenzo Snow had placed on new polygamy were greatly relaxed during the first three years of Joseph F. Smith's administration. From 1902 to April 1904 at least sixty-three plural marriages were sealed throughout the church. Anthony W. Ivins performed twenty-nine of these (Cannon 1983, 29). In a 7 March 1911 letter to his son, Ivins defended his role in post-Manifesto marriages, "It was not an easy matter to adjust conditions which had existed for nearly 40 years to the new order of things. Family ties had been established, covenants of the most sacred character were entered into, and it was thought that in exceptional cases, where such conditions existed, and people were in Mexico, marriages might be solemnized." He then added an important postscript: "You may depend upon it. I have never performed a marriage ceremony without proper authority." Further evidence that Ivins was acting under authority from Salt Lake City was his 1932 letter to a woman who had been excommunicated for becoming a plural wife after 1904. "I am speaking thus plainly," Ivins wrote, "in order that you may know the truth. . . . The difference between these people [those advocating polygamy after 1904] and myself and others is that we acted with authority from the Church" (H. G. Ivins, 6-7).

That this "authority" included not only George Q. Cannon but also Joseph F. Smith is documented in the journal of Orson Pratt Brown, a bishop in the Mexican colonies. Brown related that during a visit to Salt Lake City he took the marriage records of his father-in-law, Alexander F. MacDonald, who had performed post-Manifesto marriages in Mexico, to President Smith. After thumbing through the book, Smith said to Brown, "all of this work that Brother MacDonald performed was duly authorized by me." He then gave instructions for Brown to keep the record in Mexico so that federal marshals could not recover the document (Brown Journal, 39-40). In addition to Bishop Brown's account, Joseph F. Smith's personal papers in the LDS Archives include numerous signed forms similar to those used by George Q. Cannon to authorize Ivins and others to perform plural marriages.

Within a few months after Joseph F. Smith took office, the fact that polygamy continued began to cause new problems for the church. As early as March 1902 congressional efforts were afoot to pass a constitutional amendment forbidding polygamy and polygamous cohabitation in the United States. Church leaders feared this move and sent a circular letter to stake presidents throughout the church requesting statistical information to support their position that the number of polygamous Saints was decreasing.[14] The First Presidency also sent Apostle John Henry Smith and Ben E. Rich to lobby against the proposed amendment. They were encouraged by President Theodore Roosevelt, who told them he thought "the proposed constitutional amendment should not go through" (Pusey 1982, 187). Other Republican figures, counting on future political support in Utah, also provided assurances that the amendment would not pass.

Meanwhile President Smith continued the familiar pattern, established in Nauvoo, of publicly denying what was being privately practiced. Thus during a First Presidency and Quorum of the Twelve meeting composed predominantly of men who had either married post-Manifesto wives or sealed others in such relationships, Smith could say that no new plural marriages "were taking place to his knowledge in the church, either in the U.S. or any other country." Furthermore, he explained, "it is thoroughly understood and has been for years that no one is authorized to perform any such marriages" (Brigham Young, Jr. Diary, 5 June 1902). During a 19 November 1903 meeting of the Quorum of the Twelve, he claimed "he had not given his consent to anyone to solemnize plural marriages" and "did not know of any such cases" (JH, 19 Nov. 1903). "Does the Mormon Church solemnize or permit plural marriages?" the 3 December 1903 *Salt Lake Tribune* asked Smith. "Certainly not," he replied. "The church does not perform or sanction, or authorize, marriage in any form that is contrary to the laws of the land. The assertion that prominent Mormons practice polygamy is evidently done to mislead the public."

Despite Smith's reassurances that the church did not officially support new plural marriages, monogamist apostle Reed Smoot's 1902 announcement of his candidacy for the U.S. Senate provided a convenient focus for anti-polygamy sentiment. The Salt Lake Ministerial Association objected that an apostle in Congress would violate the principle of separation of church and state. Despite the uproar, Smoot won the nomination and headed east. By the time he reached Washington, however, a national campaign challenging his right to be seated had been mounted against him. Charged with being the front-man for the Mormon hierarchy which "controlled Utah's elections and economy" and was "secretly continuing to preach and permit plural marriages," Smoot faced an uphill struggle to be confirmed. Though Smoot was allowed to take his seat pending results of the investigation, the matter was not resolved for nearly thirty months.

The more than three thousand pages of testimony from witnesses, including President Joseph F. Smith and several apostles, placed the church in an extremely bad light. Senator-elect Smoot summarized the Mormon position of acute embarrassment in a 22 March 1904 letter: "[W]e have not as a people, at all times, lived strictly to our agreements with the Government, and this lack of sincerity on our part goes farther to condemn us in the eyes of the public men of the nation than the mere fact of a few new polygamy cases, or a polygamist before the manifesto living in the state of unlawful cohabitation" (Smoot to Jesse M. Smith).

NOTES

1. The First Presidency had organized a committee to promote Republicanism in the territory. John Henry Smith was called on a personal mission to engage in this activity, but Democrat apostle Moses Thatcher opposed to Smith's activities. Defending his position, Smith annnounced he was "advancing the work of the Lord" by disposing "of the theory that this Territory belonged to the Democrats by divine right" (Abraham H. Cannon Journal, 9 July 1891).

2. For background on the People's Party, see Wilford Woodruff/George Q. Cannon 23 June 1891 interview in the Salt Lake Times, also in Clark 1965-75, 3:211-17.

3. Democrats Moses Thatcher, B. H. Roberts, and Charles Penrose ignored this advice and were eventually censored for their Democratic campaigning. Political differences of opinion in 1896 resulted in Roberts's brief disfellowship and Thatcher's expulsion from the Quorum of the Twelve (see Van Wagoner and Walker 1980, 243-44, 368-70).

The Republican leanings of the First Presidency caused them difficulty in 1892. Their powerful secretary, George F. Gibbs, had written a letter which influenced the outcome of the 1891 Logan municipal elections. Gibbs, in the name of the First Presidency, had been "effective in turning many Democrats from their party to the Republican fold." Presidents Woodruff and Joseph F. Smith later denied authorizing

Gibbs to use their names. "If we have any desire in this matter," they responded in the 25 March 1892 *Deseret News Weekly*, "it is that the people of this territory shall study well the principles of both the great national parties, and then choose which they will join, freely, voluntarily and honestly, from personal conviction. . . . We have no disposition to direct in these matters, but proclaim that, as far as we are concerned, the members of this church are entirely and perfectly free in all political affairs."

4. See Proclamation no. 42, at 27 U.S. stat. 1058 (4 Jan. 1893), and Proclamation no. 14, at 28 U.S. stat. 1257 (25 Sept. 1894), in Jorgensen and Hardy 1980, 8. For full details on the steps leading to amnesty, see G. Larson 1971, 291-92.

5. See Minutes of the Quorum of the Twelve, 10 May 1911; also Heber J. Grant to Heber Bennion, 2 May 1929, Grant Letterbooks.

6. President Wilford Woodruff, John W. Taylor, Brigham Young, Jr., Matthias F. Cowley, George Teasdale, Marriner W. Merrill, Abraham H. Cannon, and Abraham O. Woodruff were post-Manifesto polygamists. In addition, George Q. Cannon, Joseph F. Smith, John Henry Smith, Anthon H. Lund, and Heber J. Grant either approved of or performed plural marriages after 1890. For details of these marriage ceremonies, see Quinn 1985; Cannon 1983; 27-41; and Jorgenson and Hardy 1980, 10-19. The Joseph Eckersley Journal, 2-6 Sept. 1903, implies that Apostle F. M. Lyman was the lone apostle who interpreted the Manifesto as banning new polygamy, and "he was not in harmony with the rest of the Apostles on that subject."

7. Family Group Sheets of Byron Harvey Allred, Sr., Calvert Lorenzo Allred, and Anson Call document three such marriages (LDS Genealogical Archives).

8. Apostle Matthias F. Cowley related in 1911: "President Cannon told me he had the authority from President Woodruff and Brother Joseph F. Smith told me on two occasions that Brother Cannon had the authority and Brother Woodruff didn't want to be known in it" (Minutes of the Quorum of the Twelve, 10 May 1911). Respecting his own position in performing post-Manifesto marriages, Cowley reported, "President Cannon told me to do these things . . . President Snow, did not, he simply told me he would not interfere with Brother Woodruff's and Cannon's work" (ibid.).

The influence of Woodruff's counselors during his administration was made public during an 1895 statement by Apostle John W. Taylor. Abraham H. Cannon noted in his diary on 3 December 1895 that during a Davis (Utah) Stake conference, Taylor "made some remarks which were scarcely proper concerning the mental and physical condition of Pres. Woodruff who was unable, he said, to do the work of the Church without the help of his counselors, 'As well might a baby be placed at the head of the Church as Pres. Woodruff without the aid of Presidents Cannon and Smith'."

9. See also Stanley S. Ivins to Juanita Brooks, 25 Feb. 1955, copy in author's possession.

10. Merrill went so far as to say: "I am aware of the feeling growing among the people that plural families are unpopular. They are growing less. They will never die out. This principle will never be taken from the earth. . . . There are some who think the Church is going back upon the principle I tell them this is not so" (Anthon H. Lund Journal, 9 Jan. 1900).

11. Referring to "former concessions made by the Presidency," Carl A. Badger quoted Joseph F. Smith in his diary for 26 March 1904 as saying that "the Church did not authorize such things but that some of the brethren who hold the authority to do such things refuse to give up their power."

12. The Canadian government, unlike the Mexican government, rigidly enforced its opposition to polygamy. For this reason plural marriage was never as visible in Canada as it was in Mexico.

13. B. Harvey Allred, Jr., noted that his 15 July 1903 plural marriage to Mary Evelyn Clark was approved by a "recommend" Joseph F. Smith had sent to Ivins: "This recommends Brother Byron Harvey Allred as a man worthy to live the United Order with the Saints in Old Mexico" (Allred 1968, 372). The telegram to Smoot is in the Smoot Collection.

14. The survey showed that in 1902 there were only 897 polygamous families, as compared with 2,451 in 1890 (Allen and Leonard 1976, 441). This survey was not conducted without bias, however. Stake presidents who gathered the data were forewarned that it was to the church's advantage to minimize the number of polygamous families. In addition the survey only represented polygamous families in the United States. The hundreds, perhaps thousands, of plural families in Mexico and Canada were excluded by instructions that "in cases where heads of families have . . . gone for the purpose of residing beyond the confines of the republic . . . the polygamic relations, so far as the purpose of this inquiry is concerned, must be regarded as ended" (see First Presidency [Joseph F. Smith, John R. Winder, Anthon H. Lund] to St. George Stake president E. H. Snow, 21 March 1901).

Sixteen

SPOTLIGHTING THE CHURCH –
THE SMOOT HEARINGS

The Smoot Hearings (January 1904 to February 1907) examined far more than the specific charges brought against Smoot. The entire structure of the Mormon church was closely scrutinized by the Senate Committee on Privileges and Elections. A great deal of attention was devoted to the church's commercial and political activities, although post-Manifesto polygamy commanded the center ring throughout the investigation.

President Joseph F. Smith, the first witness called by those protesting against Smoot, was subpoenaed to appear before the investigating committee in early March 1904. His five days of testimony, together with that of other church authorities, confirmed the accusations of critics who claimed church leaders were in violation of laws against polygamous activities. Members of the hierarchy admitted to serious infractions of both church and civil law. President Smith, defending his unlawful cohabitation with his five wives, pleaded for understanding. He explained that he preferred "to meet the consequences of the law rather than abandon my children and their mothers; and I have cohabited with my wives – not openly, that is, not in a manner that I thought would be offensive to my neighbors – but I have acknowledged them; I have visited them" (*Proceedings* 1:129).

Despite Smith's emotional defense for his illegal actions, investigators found his behavior inexcusable. They reminded him of the pledges he had made to secure his personal amnesty and were particularly piqued that he had fathered eleven post-Manifesto children. They frowned upon the church president's rationalization of his post-Manifesto cohabitation in his statement that "since the admission of the state there has been a sentiment existing and prevalent in Utah that these old marriages would be in a measure condoned. They were not looked upon as offensive, as really violative of law; they were, in other words, regarded as an existing fact, and if they saw any wrong in it they simply winked at it" (ibid., 1:130).

Though admitting his own illegal cohabitation, Smith adamantly insisted that since the Manifesto "there has never been, to my knowledge, a plural marriage performed with the understanding, instruction, connivance, counsel, or permission of the presiding authorities of the church, in any

164

shape or form" (ibid., 1:129). Investigators subsequently turned the church inside out to link Smith directly to new polygamy, but the evidence proved inconclusive.

The post-Manifesto plural marriage most talked about in Washington during the hearings was the June 1896 union of Apostle Abraham H. Cannon with Lillian Hamlin. George Q. Cannon had been deeply grieved by the death of his missionary-son David. His sorrow was the more poignant because the young man had not yet married and hence would have no kingdom in the hereafter. Reminded of the leviratic practices of the Old Testament, George Q. Cannon spoke to his son Abraham about "taking some good girl and raising up seed by her for my brother David. . . . He told me to think the matter over, and speak to him later about it. Such a ceremony as this could be performed in Mexico, so Pres. Woodruff has said." Abraham later suggested to his father, in the presence of the entire First Presidency and his uncle Angus Cannon, that the proxy wife should be his cousin Annie Cannon, Angus's daughter.[1] But Abraham's brother, Frank J. Cannon, later indicated that it was David's fiancee, Lillian Hamlin, who was married to Abraham in "fulfillment of the biblical instruction that a man should take his dead brother's wife" (Cannon and Higgins 1911, 176).

Abraham H. Cannon died of meningitis one month after the marriage to Hamlin, so he was beyond reach of the Smoot investigators. But they were after bigger game in Joseph F. Smith, and his alleged complicity in the Cannon marriage offered a way to get at him. Abraham's plural wife Wilhelmina, who had threatened him with divorce on several occasions, told the Senate committee that her husband had admitted to her in early June 1896 his intention to marry Hamlin. According to Wilhelmina's testimony, Cannon left Salt Lake City for Los Angeles by train on 18 June 1896 with Elder and Mrs. Joseph F. Smith, Lillian Hamlin, and others. He returned to Salt Lake City on 1 July, seriously ill. But before his 19 July death Wilhelmina said he admitted to her his marriage to Hamlin.

The Smoot investigations focused on the question of who had married Abraham H. Cannon and Lillian Hamlin. Government investigators suspected Joseph F. Smith. The church president denied involvement in the matter. When *Salt Lake Tribune* editor Patrick H. Lannon prompted John Henry Smith to ask his cousin privately if the charges were true, Joseph F.'s response was again an emphatic "No, sir" (Pusey 1982, 189). When the Senate committee asked the church president who had married the couple, he said he did not know but presumed a marriage had taken place "because they were living together as man and wife." When they asked what inquiry he had made into the situation, the frustrated investigators were told, "I made no inquiry at all." "Did you not have any interest in finding out" whether there had been a marriage, attorney Robert W. Tayler persisted. "Not the least," Smith replied (ibid.).

Even Reed Smoot was nervous about Smith's curious testimony. After the church president returned to Utah in April 1904, Smoot wrote to him that a Mrs. Stanley was going to state before the committee that Lillian Hamlin told her she "was married to Abram H. Cannon by President Jos. F. Smith, at sea etc." In reply, Smith informed Smoot on 9 April, "She simply lied. . . . I have been told by one of her most intimate friends that she herself denies ever having told such a story." To sooth Smoot's concern about the trip Smith explained that "I cannot recall a moment when I was in the presence of Mrs. Cannon that my wife was not with us. My wife was seasick while crossing the channel to Catalina Island, and I was with her during the voyage." Smith suggested that conditions of the trip did not allow for the marriage; the voyage "did not occupy more than two hours and scarcely that long, I think. The boat was filled with excursionists and we all took Deck passage. . . . Hugh J. Cannon, a brother of Abraham's was also in our party and was a witness to all our pastime and enjoyments."

Despite the explanation, Smoot harbored reservations on the matter. Two years later he seemed to be playing the devil's advocate in a 10 May 1906 letter to President Smith. "[Senator Beverage] said that he had just been reading your testimony in relation to the marriage of Abram H. Cannon," Smoot wrote. "He did not understand how you, a member of the First Presidency of the Church, could go on a trip with A. H. Cannon and be introduced to a young lady as his wife and have them occupy the position of husband and wife toward each other, it being six years after the issuance of the Manifesto . . . and not complain of one of the Apostles so acting, and of no action being taken by the Church, unless the Church approved of new marriages or at least allowed them."

Though Cannon family tradition credits Joseph F. Smith with marrying Lillian Hamlin to Abraham H. Cannon outside U.S. jurisdiction during the excursion to Catalina Island, recent evidence tends to suggest an alternative possibility. Historian D. Michael Quinn in his 1985 analysis of post-Manifesto marriages presents intriguing circumstantial evidence that on 17 June 1896 in the Salt Lake Temple Joseph F. Smith sealed Lillian Hamlin to the deceased and previously unmarried David H. Cannon (pp. 83-84). Abraham H. Cannon stood as proxy for his brother in the ceremony and apparently also acted as proxy in fulfilling the request of their father, George Q. Cannon, that he "raise up seed" for David. Eight months after Abraham's death Lillian Hamlin gave birth to a daughter "Marba" (Abram spelled backwards). Although the child was named a benefactor of Abraham H. Cannon's earthly estate, in the Mormon scheme she would be David's daughter in the hereafter.

Thus Joseph F. Smith may have been truthful, if not completely forthcoming, in denying allegations that he had married the couple on the high seas. Though he did perform the marriage, it could have been a proxy sealing uniting a dead man and his fiancee.[2] But government investigators were understandably frustrated with Smith's testimony. Smith himself felt that he had done little to further Smoot's chances for being permanently seated. After the church president's 22 March 1904 testimony, Smoot's secretary Carl Badger recorded in his diary that Smith said over and over to church attorney F. S. Richards, "I am sorry for Reed. I am sorry for Reed" (see also Bergera 1983).

Others were concerned about the testimony given at the hearings as well. Badger wrote to a friend, "I hope our people will look at this matter in its true light; we have got to learn our lessons, and instead of shouting about the opportunity which we have had of teaching our faith to the world, we ought to dot down the unpleasant but obvious fact, that the lesson which the world is learning from the testimony thus far given is, that we have failed to keep our word. I wish our people could come to the conclusion that this investigation has not been wholly creditable to us" (Badger to R. S. Collett, 21 March 1904).

As soon as President Smith arrived back in Utah, pressures began to build for him to make a statement on new polygamy.[3] Reed Smoot, in a 22 March 1904 letter to his colleague E. H. Callister, wished that "President Joseph F. Smith would see his way clear to announce at this coming April Conference that since his visit to Washington he had learned that public sentiment outside of the State of Utah is opposed to a man living in unlawful cohabitation." Smoot hoped "that hereafter" President Smith's "advice would be to the Mormon people to arrange their affairs so as to obey the law, and further, that he himself intends to do so. It is my opinion that if this is not done that there will be considerable trouble ahead for our people."

Callister responded five days later that he did not think making such a statement would be "very wise." "I do not think we will have any more manifesto on the polygamy subject," he reported, "as long as Joseph F. is at the head." But Callister had misread the situation. On 2 April church attorney Franklin S. Richards urged President Smith to say something "to the Conference in regard to the investigations going on in Washington" (Anthon H. Lund Journal, 2 April 1904). Two days later Lund observed in his journal that "we had a counsel meeting in which we discussed the wisdom of saying something to pacify the country. R[udger] Clawson feared that it would do no good but make many hearts ache. He thought that it would be a second manifesto and we had had manifestos enough." But Lund "favored letting the Saints know our status as they are beginning to doubt our sincerity or rather that of Pres. Smith before the investigations committee." In early April the Quorum of the Twelve decided "that we speak to the conference concerning our present conditions and have Pres. Smith make an official declaration that plural marriages should not be celebrated and any one who should undertake to do so would be liable to be cut off from the

Church. Bro. Owen [Woodruff] was much opposed to anything against the principle which had given him birth and which would tend to obliterate it" (ibid., 6 April 1904).

On Sunday, April 7, President Smith did indeed present a "Second Manifesto" to the Saints for their sustaining vote. "Inasmuch as there are numerous reports in circulation that plural marriages have been entered into contrary to the official declaration of President Woodruff, of September 26, 1890," he began, "I, Joseph F. Smith, . . . do hereby affirm and declare that no such marriages have been solemnized with the sanction, consent, or knowledge of the Church of Jesus Christ of Latter-day Saints." President Smith was emphatic in his declaration that plural marriages were prohibited: "If any officer or member of the church shall assume to solemnize or enter into any such marriage he will be deemed in transgression against the church, and will be liable to be dealt with according to the rules and regulations thereof and excommunicated therefrom."

Referring to charges that church leaders were "being dishonest and untrue to our word" respecting the 1891 amnesty, Smith characterized this as "nonsense." The president called for church sanction of the statement: "I want to see today whether the Latter-day Saints representing the church in this solemn assembly will not seal these charges as false by their vote." The conference vote, like the 6 October 1890 vote on the Wilford Woodruff Manifesto, supported the measure (Roberts 1930, 6:401).

Though the 1904 Manifesto sought and obtained Mormon confirmation of President Smith's statements before the Smoot hearings, most Saints knew little of the covert post-Manifesto polygamy that church leaders had been supporting. Public approval of President Smith's statements proved that church members were willing to "follow the Prophet," but close study shows that Smith's Manifesto said nothing new. The utterance, like the Woodruff Manifesto, neither specifically forbade plural marriages outside the United States nor clarified the question of unlawful cohabitation.[4] The Second Manifesto was, in the words of President Smith himself, only a "reconfirmation of the Wilford Woodruff Manifesto" (JH, 6 April 1904, 6).

However, the two statements were interpreted differently. The Wilford Woodruff Manifesto was not intended, by those who issued it, to stop polygamy. Virtually all church leaders, either by action or assent, disregarded the Woodruff Manifesto. President Woodruff himself may have married at least one post-Manifesto wife (Quinn 1985, 62-65). Carl Badger succinctly analyzed the 1890 statement after listening to Joseph F. Smith's Washington testimony. "The truth of the matter," he wrote in a letter, "is that very few of our people have been willing to admit that the Manifesto was a revelation." He further observed that "the leading authorities have not encouraged this view, but rather that the necessities of the cause compelled that we openly give up what we secretly clung to" (Badger to Ed Jenkins, 18 March 1904).

Although the 1904 Smith Manifesto, like the Woodruff Manifesto, was presented as church policy rather than revelation, violators soon learned that fourteen years of ambiguity on the matter had ended; the church was now committed to ending plural marriage.[5]

The first official step after April conference was to brief absent apostles on the recent statement. Quorum president Francis M. Lyman sent identical letters on First Presidency stationery to John W. Taylor, John Henry Smith, Reed Smoot, and undoubtedly others on 5 May 1904, informing them of the official declaration and requesting their "co-operation in emphasizing the same in your private conversations and counsels as well as your public utterances, to the end that no misunderstanding may exist among our people concerning its scope and meaning; but on the contrary, that all may [be] given to distinctly understand that infractions of the law in regard to plural marriage are transgressions against the Church punishable by excommunication" (Lyman Letterbooks).[6]

Francis M. Lyman's 9 July letter to recalcitrant polygamist and apostle George Teasdale was even more pointed: "Every member of our council, must sustain the stand taken by President Smith and must not talk nor act at cross purposes with the Prophet. What has already been done is shaking the confidence of the Latter-day Saints. We are considered as two-faced and insincere. We must not stand in that light before the Saints or the world." Lyman then announced the beginning of an anti-polygamy crusade: "The Presidency hold me responsible to see to it that the members of our council be thoroughly advised that we will not be tolerated in anything out of harmony with the stand taken by President Joseph F. Smith before the Senate Committee on the subject of Plural marriage. We must uphold his hands and vindicate the Church" (Lyman Letterbooks).[7]

Despite the efforts of the church to harmonize official statements with the private posture of its leaders, the government was not through investigating Reed Smoot. His hearings were extended into 1905 and 1906 in hopes that such key witnesses as John W. Taylor, Matthias F. Cowley, Marriner W. Merrill, Anthony W. Ivins, and George Teasdale could be persuaded to testify. Smoot wrote President Smith that several senators were asking why the church did not force Anthony W. Ivins to make the trip. Though Ivins had attended the world's fair in Saint Louis during September 1904, he refused to testify in Washington. Several years later he told a son why he had not gone: "It is none of the Senate's business what the Mormons were doing in Mexico, and further, I refused to perjure myself" (H. G. Ivins, 5).[8]

Apostles John W. Taylor and Matthias M. Cowley were at the top of the government's most-wanted list. Carl Badger blamed much of Smoot's difficulties on the two. "Apostles Taylor and Cowley must come to Washington," he affirmed to a friend. "I think we are greatly indebted to

[Taylor] for all this 'unpleasantness,'—if you can refer to a national scandal as such" (Badger to Ed Jenkins, 16 March 1904).

President Smith sent Taylor a telegram in Raymond, Alberta, requesting that he go to Washington. He refused: "I must ask you to excuse me from complying with your request, both on account of my business interests and my own positive disinclinations to do so." Noting that he was a subject of the Canadian government, Taylor added in his 16 March 1904 letter, "In my official labors as an apostle in the Church, I hold myself entirely subject to your directions, but in a matter so personal and purely political, concocted for the purpose of prying into the domestic relations of men who are in no wise amenable to this class of schemers, nor even to the department of the U.S. government represented by this honorable committee, I must ask to be excused from entering upon a task so humiliating."

Carl Badger was keenly aware of the church's predicament over the refusal of many leading Mormons to appear in Washington. Badger told Smoot that he was discouraged with church leaders and voiced his opinion that "something must be done with those who have violated the pledge against the taking of new wives." Smoot, convinced that the new polygamy was church approved, answered, "Nothing will be done; I believe they were authorized to take the wives" (Badger Journal, 18 Dec. 1904). But the perceptive Badger recognized that the government would not be satisfied until someone paid the price for the church leaders' violation of their pledges. The youthful secretary was especially concerned over the position the church would find itself in if Taylor and Cowley did not soon testify. He wrote to Ed Jenkins on 24 March 1904 that "we are in a bad place. . . . I do not hesitate to say that it will be a shame and a disgrace if they do not come" (Badger Collection).

Church leaders sent Apostle John Henry Smith to Mexico to bring back Cowley, who was known by the pseudonym "Westlake." The wayward apostle could not be found. Angered, Smith ordered church leaders in Mexico to "trace Westlake immediately." The next day he appeared. After a long conversation with John Henry, "Westlake decided he would not go with me," Apostle Smith reported (Pusey 1982, 192). Francis M. Lyman was sent on a similar mission to Canada to bring back John W. Taylor. He too returned empty-handed.[9] President Smith, upon learning that both Cowley and Taylor refused to testify in Washington, wrote to Smoot on 9 April that "Elders Taylor and Cowley have stated their own cases, and they will have to abide the results themselves" (Smoot Collection).[10]

The status of the two apostles was as much discussed in quorum meetings as in Washington. Church attorney Franklin S. Richards urged President Smith as early as 18 April 1904 not to present Taylor and Cowley's names for a sustaining vote in the next conference, advising that "if they did not come and take full responsibility of the conduct to cut them off of the

Quorum, and, if necessary, to excommunicate them" (Badger Journal, 18 April 1904). Badger noted in his 12 February 1905 journal that "from all I can learn, if anything is done with Cowley and Taylor, by the leaders of the Church, it will be because they are forced to do something."

Smoot suffered much pressure from his fellow senators. "If the Church is not guilty of new polygamy, why are the apostles avoiding subpoenas," he was asked, "why are they hiding now?" "Why does the Church sustain them in their positions?" Carl Badger recognized that something would have to happen soon to relieve the pressure on Smoot. "If nothing is done [about Cowley and Taylor] at the October Conference," he wrote to his wife Rose in Utah on 9 April 1905, "I would not be in Senator Smoot's shoes for one million cold cash – to be candid, I would not now" (Badger Collection). Smoot, obviously reaching the same conclusion as his secretary, decided not to support Cowley and Taylor in fall conference when their names were presented to the Saints for a sustaining vote.

Smoot's position with regard to Cowley and Taylor was supported by many church leaders, including Cowley and Taylor themselves. John Henry Smith noted that he and others "favored Taylor and Cowley doing something to ease public sentiment both at home and abroad" (Pusey 1982, 192). According to Taylor's wife Nellie, Cowley and Taylor agreed to tender their resignations in an altruistic gesture designed to help both Smoot and the church. "It was better to smooth things over with the Government," she said, "keep Smoot in the Senate . . . [by] deposing Cowley and Taylor. Then, when conditions were more favorable, the two could be reinstated." This motion was voted unanimously by the Quorum of the Twelve according to her testimony (Samuel W. Taylor 8 Jan. 1936 interview with Nellie E. Taylor, Taylor Collection). Anthony W. Ivins, recognizing the political implications of the Taylor and Cowley resignations, wrote Heber J. Grant when he heard of the action: "It might be all right if it were going to deceive anyone but ourselves. We will be the only ones fooled" (Quinn 1985, 103).

Though Cowley and Taylor submitted their resignations on 28 October, church leaders decided to pocket them until the time was most advantageous to disclose them publicly.[11] The First Presidency made Smoot aware that the resignations could be used to improve his position if needed. Smoot wrote to First Presidency secretary, George F. Gibbs, on 6 December 1905, "I[f] you decide to use resignations do not make them public until I ask advice as to best time to do it" (Smoot Collection). The next day Smoot was notified that "if you think case will be opened again or you are likely to be expelled by all means withhold resignations and do not make mention of them to any person. F. M. Lyman will be here tomorrow when we will telegraph." At 3:55 p.m., on 8 December, Gibbs wired, "F. M. Lyman here. When you become convinced action should not be delayed any longer let us know." Twelve minutes later Gibbs wired again, "Brethren beginning to feel

J. W. Taylor and Cowley should not be sacrificed unless required by C[om-mittee] on P[rivileges] and E[lections] to save you" (Smoot Collection).[12]

Smoot wired the next day that he thought he would not be expelled. He also informed the First Presidency, "I have concluded in my own mind that public announcement of resignations [of Cowley and Taylor] made at this late day would have an unfavorable effect upon the country and Senators," but that he wanted to meet with the president of the United States and "tell him in confidence and—perhaps one or two friends on the committee and ask their advice." Smoot did not feel comfortable having his fellow apostles become scapegoats to "save my expulsion or to save me." "If Taylor and Cowley have done no wrong," he wired the First Presidency, "and their acts meet with the approval of the Brethren for Heavens sake don't handle them but let us take the consequences" (Smoot Collection).

Quorum president Francis M. Lyman wrote back one week later on 15 December to advise, "You may feel at perfect liberty to use the resigna-tions . . . where you need to use them. They were not given for your benefit, but for the relief of the church" (Lyman Letterbooks). Smoot returned to Utah for the Christmas holidays and on 1 January 1906 met with President Smith. Together they agreed that on his return to Washington he would tell President Roosevelt that during Quorum of the Twelve investigations Taylor and Cowley had admitted to taking plural wives since the Manifesto, but that it had been done outside the United States. On his four-day train trip back to the capitol, Smoot changed his mind. "If I went to President Roosevelt and told him Taylor and Cowley had admitted their guilt," he later wrote to President Smith, "the President in his blunt, honest, and personal way would immediately ask me whether they had been excommunicated, and if not, why not." So Smoot, recognizing that Roosevelt would be "displeased with our adopted policy," decided against discussing the situation with the pres-ident.

In early spring, as General Conference neared, influential apostle Charles W. Penrose wrote to Smoot on 9 March asking that he try to extend the Washington investigations until after conference. *"Action may be taken[,] and I believe will[,] then* which ought to be placed in a legitimate way upon the record of your case" (Smoot Collection). Two days later Smoot received a letter, dated 7 March 1906, from Apostle Heber J. Grant, who was in Liverpool, England. "It has been my earnest and constant prayer," the future church president wrote, "that Brothers Taylor and Cowley might be preserved from the shafts of the enemy. I feel sure that if they were sacrificed that it would only be one more concession and that in the near future something else would be demanded" (Smoot Collection).

During conference weekend the Taylor and Cowley resignations were officially accepted on grounds that the two apostles were "out of harmony" with their brethren. The resignations dismayed many Saints who recognized the involvement of a majority of General Authorities in new polygamy and did not accept the "out of harmony" explanation. They instead viewed the much-loved apostles as sacrificial lambs. Anthony W. Ivins noted that in Mexico it was commonly believed "that Brothers Taylor and Cowley were dropped for political reasons only" (Minutes of the Quorum of the Twelve, 10 May 1911). During a 22 July 1909 meeting of the Quorum of the Twelve, some apostles were also openly skeptical about Cowley and Taylor being "out of harmony." Orson F. Whitney reported that "the Saints don't consider that they were out of harmony, but simply a necessary sacrifice." Rudger Clawson modified this view somewhat. "Bros. Taylor and Cowley offered to harmonize themselves with the quorum," he explained, "they admitted they had been out of harmony, but offered to put themselves right." After considerable discussion, quorum president F. M. Lyman snapped, "I want this body of men to understand they did not harmonize themselves with the quorum" (Joseph Musser Journal, 22 July 1909).[13]

After the resignations of Taylor and Cowley, events seemed to flow more smoothly for the church and Senator Smoot. Though the Senate Committee on Privileges and Elections recommended his expulsion, the full Senate, influenced by President Roosevelt, refused to act on the recommendation. Smoot was a senator for thirty years and became chair of the powerful Senate Finance Committee.

Meanwhile the church began the difficult task of convincing the Mormon and non-Mormon populace that polygamy was past history. In 1907, the First Presidency, with unanimous approval from the Saints in General Conference, issued a statement entitled, *An Address: The Church of Jesus Christ of Latter-day Saints to the World*. This sixteen-page document restated the basic beliefs of the church and affirmed that Mormons did not intend to mix politics with religion, were politically loyal to the United States, and did not support polygamy. A clarification was added that those few individuals who continued to practice plural marriage were in defiance not only of civil law but of church law as well. However, these few renegades would prove a perpetual problem for a church anxious to convince a twentieth-century America that Mormons were as anti-polygamous as anyone.

Notes

1. See details of this situation in Abraham H. Cannon Journal, 2 Nov. 1890 and 19, 24 Oct. 1894.

2. Joseph Musser reported a 16 February 1914 meeting in his diary with Apostle F. M. Lyman which sheds light on the Cannon-Hamlin situation. Grilled on his polygamy beliefs, Musser remarked that he "heard one of the members of the 1st Presidency . . . (since dead) justify his son in entering the relation." "Yes," Lyman replied, "Geo. Q. Cannon did bring reproach upon the church in letting Abram H. Cannon get into it. He was responsible for Abram's act. Abram didn't need the girl—

he had a large family, and he destroyed his usefulness in the church. Such men as he, Geo. Q., Apostles Merrill, Teasdale, Cowley, Woodruff and Taylor . . . bro[ugh]t reproach upon the church, and had done wrong."

3. Stanley S. Ivins noted in his 29 November 1934 journal the concerned comments of a post-Manifesto plural wife regarding Smith's testimony: "I met K. K. Steffenson at lunch [about a month ago] and we got to talking about post-manifesto polygamy. His sister was a post-man wife of one of the _____. He said that she had refused to be married by anyone but Pres. Smith and he had married her in the Salt Lake Temple. When he later testified at the Smoot investigation that there had been no authorized post-manifesto plural marriages, she was upset and had her brother, K. K., go to see Pres. Smith about it. He told K. K. to tell his sister that her marriage was O.K., but he had had to say what he did in Washington to protect the Church."

4. Church leaders obviously intended to continue living with their plural wives. Carl Badger reported in his journal that after Smoot wrote the First Presidency in the latter part of 1904 asking that "unlawful cohabitation be given up," he was told to "leave these things alone" (22 Dec. 1904).

5. Compelling evidence that some church members in Mexico were fore-warned of Smith's impending declaration and moved up their dates for plural mar-riages accordingly is discussed by Jorgenson and Hardy 1980, 26.

6. On this same day, Lyman also informed various apostles that permission to perform sealings outside temples was also withdrawn. In a separate letter to John W. Taylor and George Teasdale, he wrote: "As you are aware until within a few years ago the custom prevailed in Canada, Arizona and Mexico . . . to marry for time only on account of the inconvenience and expense of attending a journey to a temple. . . . President Woodruff and President Snow, each in his time, authorized some of the Apostles, and perhaps others, to perform sealings for time and eternity in behalf of young couples of those places, and that this authority has been exercised quite freely until this time." Lyman announced the change in policy: "The council of First Presi-dency and Apostles have now deemed it expedient and wise to withdraw this author-ity from those brethren, leaving it solely in the hands of him who holds the keys thereof, and a resolution to this affect has been unanimously passed by the council" (Lyman Letterbooks).

7. Teasdale was a key figure in post-Manifesto plural marriages. Not only did he marry at least two plural wives himself (see Marriner W. Merrill Journal, 17 May 1900; Anthon H. Lund Journal, 24 Jan. 1904; and Orson Pratt Brown Journal, 39), he encouraged and performed many more such marriages. Had it not been for his age and poor health (he died in 1907), he would likely have been dropped from the quo-rum along with Taylor and Cowley.

8. Reed Smoot in an undated letter to Joseph F. Smith suggests Ivins was likely advised not to go to Washington. "It would seem unwise to me," the senator wrote, "to have brother Ivins come here to testify, and he is the only one who could testify on this point [the alleged George Q. Cannon authorization letters to Ivins]" (Smoot Collection). Abraham O. Woodruff and George Teasdale were definitely urged by President Smith to remain out of the country during the hearings (see Quinn 1985, 100; George F. Gibbs to George Teasdale, 20 Aug. 1904 and 6 Jan. 1905; First Presi-dency [Smith, Winder, Lund] to Teasdale, 2 Nov. 1905—all in Joseph F. Smith Letterbooks).

9. Evidence suggests, however, that John W. Taylor, like Ivins, Woodruff, and Teasdale, was instructed not to go to Washington. Several accounts imply that when F. M. Lyman was in Alberta, Canada, attempting to bring Taylor back, he was

told in a dream not to insist on Taylor's testifying before the Senate committee. See Samuel W. Taylor 8 July 1937 interview with Raymond, Alberta, stake president H. S. Allen, and George Henry Budd to Nellie Todd Taylor, 5 May 1932, both in Samuel W. Taylor Collection. Carl A. Badger's 8 September 1905 journal entry also verifies the Lyman incident.

Regardless of whether Taylor and/or Cowley had been advised against testifying, Smoot was relieved they did not come to Washington. In a 10 May 1906 letter to Joseph F. Smith, he wrote: "From the intimations I have received, I think that it would be just as well for Cowley and Taylor to keep out of the way until the adjournment of congress. Burrows and Owens think that if the case were reopened and Taylor were subpoenaed, that he could give them light upon a great many points" (Smoot Collection).

10. A few days later, on 15 April, Smith wrote Julius C. Burrows, chair of the Senate Committee on Privileges and Elections: "It is with regret, that I inform you of my inability to procure the attendance of Messrs. John Henry Smith, George Teasdale, Marriner W. Merrill, John W. Taylor, and Matthias F. Cowley before the Senate Committee on Privileges and Elections." Explaining that "illness" made it impossible for Smith, Teasdale, and Merrill to testify, Smith concluded, "I am powerless to exert more than moral suasion in the premises" (Clark 1965-75, 4:85-86).

11. Copies of both resignations are in the Smoot Collection.

12. Using code names, Gibbs sent a letter further explaining this action and admonishing, "if you will cast aside for ever all thought of making a sacrifice of zoanthropia [Taylor] and whimper [Cowley] you will begin to see your way brighten, for such a thing cannot be done simply in the hope of avoiding drastic legislation, nor for the purpose of convincing friends that the ziamet [President] is honest" (9 Dec. 1905, Smoot Collection).

13. According to the official minutes, Apostle Charles W. Penrose gave what may be considered a post-1904 view of the "harmony" issue during a 10 May 1911 Quorum of the Twelve meeting: "The charge was made that Brothers Taylor and Cowley were out of harmony with the Twelve with regard to marrying plural wives themselves and encouraging others to take plural wives. They [Taylor and Cowley] said they would answer if they could have five minutes to talk with President Smith, President Smith refused to talk with them and therefore they refused to tell whether they had taken other wives. The question of the scope of the manifesto [Woodruff] was also discussed. The other brethren of the quorum maintained that it covered every place and they [Taylor and Cowley] claimed it referred to the United States. Then the question of their resigning came up. They were out of harmony with regard to plural marriages and they resigned, the matter was kept quiet for a number of months with the hope that they might reconcile themselves with the Brethren later. They seemed to take the ground that they had the right to go ahead and in this were out of harmony."

In fairness to Taylor and Cowley, however, they were not out of harmony with their pre-1904 quorum. Anthony W. Ivins pointed this out in a 29 January 1923 letter to Price W. Johnson: "The view was taken that the manifesto applied only to the United States, and not to Mexico, or other foreign countries" (Ivins Letterbooks, LDS Archives). Furthermore, as previously discussed, a majority of the pre-1904 quorum, as well as the First Presidency, privately supported post-Manifesto polygamy. The only 1890 apostle to view the Woodruff Manifesto with worldwide application was F. M. Lyman, who led the post-1904 efforts of the hierarchy to purge polygamy from the church. Joseph Eckersley explained in his 2-6 September 1903 journal that after stake president Joseph Robinson had written to the First Presidency requesting clarification on post-Manifesto marriages they sent Apostle Matthias Cowley to conduct a conference. Eckersley noted a private conversation with Cowley who informed him of the "feeling of the authorities respecting the 'Woodruff Manifesto' and that Apostle Lyman stood alone on his construction of its meaning and was not in harmony with the rest of the Apostles on that subject."

Seventeen

FOUNDING MORMON FUNDAMENTALISM

The Smoot Hearings and the 1891 testimony of Wilford Woodruff, George Q. Cannon, and Joseph F. Smith before the Master in Chancery had demonstrated that church leaders were capable of obscuring details to protect the church and themselves. At the conclusion of the Smoot Hearings, Carl Badger reflected on his disappointment at the casuistry of members of the Mormon hierarchy. "I believe our honor is more to us than anything on earth," he wrote in a personal letter. "If as a people we had strictly observed the Manifesto, I believe that our example would have challenged the admiration of the world; but we have thought that there is something higher than honesty, and behold our confusion." Badger yearned for "simple honesty, the facts . . . a remedy from which we shrink—but I pray for the last time, I wish it were possible for me to hurl in the teeth of the world the accusation and the boast: While you have been cruel, we have been honest" (Badger to "My Dear Charlie," 22 June 1906, Badger Collection).

Badger was not the only one to view with disappointment the testimony of church leaders. Many recalled the belief of Apostle John Henry Smith, later recanted, that "the [Woodruff] Manifesto is only a trick to beat the devil at his own game" (*Proceedings* 4:13)[1] and saw Joseph F. Smith's 1904 Manifesto and subsequent official statements as more of the same conniving. In the face of past inconsistencies in statements and actions of church leaders, powerful Quorum of the Twelve president F. M. Lyman led the 1904 task force which set about to convince the Saints and others that the church was now intent on suppressing polygamy.

During an 8 December 1906 conference at Colonia Juarez, the heart of post-Manifesto polygamy country, Lyman warned "those who feel that their rights are curtailed who cannot obtain the privileges which belong to them. We do not want men to trouble us. The Bishop & High Council must take care of such characters if necessary cast them out. No plural marriages are to be permitted. No man in the world is authorized to solemnize such marriages" (Anthony W. Ivins Journal, 8 Dec. 1906). Lyman consistently warned members of his quorum that "it was the duty of the 12 to instruct people where we visit that plural marriages have ceased" (ibid., 7 July 1909). He even went so far as to make a public example of a friend who unwisely claimed to have entered into an unauthorized plural marriage. The quorum president instigated ecclesiastical and civil actions which resulted in the man's excommunication and imprisonment.

In 1909 church authorities established a committee consisting of apostles Lyman, John Henry Smith, and Heber J. Grant to investigate new polygamy.[2] The group was authorized to "call into council" anyone suspected of encouraging plural marriage (George F. Richards Diary, 14 July 1909). The majority of summoned witnesses were uncooperative and evasive. Lyman commented during one such cross-examination that "he answers just like the other brethren who are in the same position. . . . One would think these brethren had rehearsed their pieces" (Joseph Musser Journal, 22 July 1909). But some spoke their mind. The bishop of the Grantsville (Utah) Ward, for example, argued that "no matter what policy the church may adopt if the Lord will reveal to a man that he should take a plural wife & indicate the way that he can get in it, it is all right for him to take her" (Anthony W. Ivins Journal, 20 Sept. 1909).

By mid-1910 church leaders had recognized a need for an official policy for dealing with new polygamists. In an 8 September Quorum of the Twelve meeting Reed Smoot proposed that "all new cases should be excommunicated from the church and that action should be taken at once. Also that the church should not retain any man taking a plural wife after the Manifesto in a church position where people were asked to support him" (Smoot Journal, 8 Sept. 1910, Smoot Collection). Smoot again proposed the plan on 27 September. But his fellow apostles "thought that a wholesale slaughter should not be made of those who were induced to take plural wives by Taylor, Cowley, Woodruff and Merrill before Pres Smith's declaration of April 1904, but drop them as fast as conditions will permit without making a great stir about it" (ibid., 27 Sept. 1910).

Joseph F. Smith, who was ill, had not been involved in quorum meetings in which disciplinary measures for new polygamists had been discussed. Smoot visited the ailing church president on 28 September and urged him to make a public statement in the upcoming General Conference "to prove to our people we are sincere in our opposition to new polygamy" (ibid., 28 Sept. 1910). During a quorum meeting on 5 October, the apostles spent two hours discussing what to do with known post-Manifesto polygamists. Smoot again proposed dropping them from their church positions, but his motion would not carry. First Presidency counselor Anthon H. Lund suggested at least that they not present for a sustaining vote at the coming General Conference the leadership of the church's auxiliary organizations in order to "avoid presenting any such person." The quorum agreed upon the wording of a circular letter to be sent to all stake presidents instructing excommunication for anyone "who advises, counsels, or entices any person to contract a plural marriage . . . as well as those who solemnize such marriages, or those who enter into such unlawful unions" (Clark 1965-75, 4:210).

The 8 October *Salt Lake Tribune* sent out a shockwave when it listed more than two hundred Mormon men, including six apostles, who had taken post-Manifesto wives. President Anthon H. Lund, addressing General Conference later that day, called attention to the numerous accounts of new polygamy being reported. He stressed that plural marriage was against the rules of the church, then read the letter of instructions the quorum had prepared for stake leaders. Joseph F. Smith, speaking after Lund, cited his 1904 manifesto. "After the Church had spoken thus plainly," he said, "we took it for granted that none of its members would be found disobeying its voice. But in the face of this action, emphasized repeatedly in private and public by us, and by the apostles as well, we now find that some person or persons have assumed authority to solemnize plural marriages, and that men and women have entered into polygamous relations through having been married under such pretended authority." Without providing names, he announced that "some of the violators of this official action of the Church have been tried on their fellowship, and have been excommunicated. But there are rumors afloat (and some of these rumors appear to be well founded) that there are still others equally guilty, and it is to such cases that we desire to direct your attention" (ibid., 217-18).

Over the weekend the demand for the Saturday *Tribune* was so great that the paper reissued the list of new polygamists on Monday with a few added names. The editor of the paper sarcastically explained that he wished to publish the revised list of two hundred twenty names "to bring it to the attention of Apostle Francis M. Lyman, who at Logan recently declared ecclesiastical war against this class of men, whom he designated as 'skullduggers.' " "In this list alone," the paper continued, "is furnished enough to keep the president of the twelve busy disciplining and excommunicating while we look up some more cases for him." The paper considered the church's efforts to purge polygamy insincere. "Apostle Lyman's recent little splurge of indignation was no more and no less than a bluff—which fooled nobody in particular, and least of all The Tribune."

The accusations of the Salt Lake City paper were of special concern to Reed Smoot, who would soon have to return to Washington and face President Taft and other government leaders. Though the First Presidency and Quorum of the Twelve on 8 November had decided to remove from ecclesiastical positions men who had taken post-Manifesto wives, Smoot worried about President Smith's less-than-enthusiastic endorsement of the measure (John Henry Smith Journal, 8 Nov. 1910). On 15 November the senator and F. M. Lyman met with the First Presidency to clarify the issue. Smoot noted in his diary that church leaders were in essential agreement that "All cases between the Woodruff manifesto and 1904 should be dealt with according to the circumstances and if drawn into by Apostles they would not be excommunicated but would be relieved of all positions in the church where the people were asked to vote for them." President Smith withheld his approval on the latter point until the following day but then appeared to agree.

Two of the new polygamists listed in the 8 October *Salt Lake Tribune* were ex-apostles Matthias Cowley and John W. Taylor. At the time of their resignations both men presumed that when the storm had blown over they would be reinstated to their former positions. One of Taylor's plural wives told a son that in 1905 Joseph F. Smith had said to both men, "You brethren are called upon to make this sacrifice, but you will lose nothing from it. When things quiet down you will be reinstated" (Samuel W. Taylor interview with Nettie M. Taylor, 15 Jan. 1936, 6, Taylor Collection). Cowley expressed the same understanding to another of Taylor's sons in 1937: "When we were in council relative to our trouble, brother [Charles W.] Penrose remarked, 'These brethren (Taylor and Cowley) are not on trial nor have they committed any offense, but if they are willing to offer the sacrifice and stand the embarrassment, we will admit them back after the situation clears' " (Raymond W. Taylor to Samuel W. Taylor).

But opposition from apostles F. M. Lyman, Reed Smoot, and Smoot's colleagues in the Senate made it impossible to return the two to the quorum. Carl Badger noted in a 21 February 1907 letter to his wife that Smoot said "if Taylor and Cowley are brought back and placed in the quorum of the apostles nothing will save us from the wrath of the American people." Badger agreed: "To think of it as being possible is to make the Church out a hypocritical fraud" (Badger Collection).

Cowley, less combative than John W. Taylor, did not initially harbor ill feelings towards other church leaders. "I have no fault to find, no opposition, no kicking, no grumbling," he wrote to Jessie N. Smith in 1906. "I love all of my brethren, although there are times when I think some of them do not know my heart, and are laboring under misunderstanding of the causes and motives which have prompted my course." Cowley was particularly gracious toward "our beloved leader, Pres. Joseph F. Smith. He is not responsible for the unhappy conditions that have been forced upon us. I know he is awfully tried. God bless and protect him forever" (Smith 1953, 462). John W. Taylor felt less generous towards his brethren. Visited in Mexico by apostles John Henry Smith, Francis M. Lyman, and Anthony W. Ivins, Taylor accused the church of cowardice in giving up plural marriage in the face of government pressure.

The failure to reinstate Cowley and Taylor into the Quorum of the Twelve Apostles as promised estranged them even more from other church leaders. For their part in taking additional plural wives and encouraging others to do so, they were summoned to appear before the Quorum of the Twelve on 13 October 1910. Neither man responded. Francis M. Lyman issued another summons for Taylor on 15 February 1911. Three days later, Taylor stormed into the office of the First Presidency, ordered President Lund and Patriarch John Smith out and demanded an interview with President Joseph F. Smith and his counselor John Henry Smith. For more than two hours he reportedly shouted threats (George Albert Smith Letterbooks, 18 Feb. 1911). Nevertheless, Taylor's trial before his former quorum members began on 22 February 1911. Throughout the questioning Taylor maintained a non-penitent, arrogant attitude, saying that he wished never again to be associated with his quorum in time or eternity. On 28 March he was excommunicated for "insubordination to the government and discipline of the Church."

Reed Smoot, who had been in Salt Lake for the Taylor trial, was convinced that the upsurge in opposition to new polygamy was a result of the numerous newspaper and magazine articles flooding the country. He reiterated his long-standing position that to lessen outside criticism church action should be taken against all cases of post-1890 polygamy. "The church or church authorities cannot or will not be believed," he argued, "if men violating the rules . . . are sustained as officers of the church" (Smoot Journal, 16 March 1911).

After returning to Washington, Smoot sent a 31 March telegram to Joseph F. Smith repeating his recommendation to remove new polygamists from church positions. The senator expressed disappointment at President Smith's reply. "He does not understand the feeling of the people," Smoot wrote in his diary on 2 April of his church leader; "the country will not accept excuses and they will not consider it humiliating a man to punish him for same. It is evident no action against the persons taking polygamist wives before 1904 will be taken."

Five days later President Smith requested Smoot to make arrangements for releasing a statement through the Associated Press that had been prepared for General Conference. This statement answered charges of new polygamy made by various news articles. To Smoot's disappointment the statement made no mention that new polygamists would be released from their positions. Concerned that President Roosevelt would not be satisfied, Smoot wired for more specific directions. "If the President inquires about new polygamy," Smith wired back on 11 April, "tell him the truth, tell him that Prest. Cannon was the first to conceive the idea that the Church could consistently countenance polygamy beyond confines of the republic where there was no law against it, and consequently he authorized the solemnization of plural marriages in Mexico and Canada after manifesto of 1890." Careful not to expose his own involvement in post-Manifesto marriages, Smith defended post-Manifesto polygamists as individuals who "married in good faith." "Under the circumstances," Smith asked Smoot, "could we consistently be expected to humiliate them by releasing them?"

Those who married plural wives after April 1904 or who encouraged others to do so were a different matter in the minds of church leaders. John W. Taylor and many other new polygamists were excommunicated. But Matthias Cowley, though more of an influence in performing post-Manifesto marriages than Taylor, did not meet the same fate. Appearing before the quorum on 10 May 1911, Cowley was much less defiant than Taylor had been, though his testimony was no less revealing. He laid the blame for his "performing surreptitious plural marriages on his 'file leaders,' " from whom he claimed to have received authority. He also viewed the "announcements of Presidents as 'bluffs' for the world and not as taking away authority already conferred" (Charles A. Penrose Journal, 10 May 1911).

But Cowley, unlike Taylor, wanted to stay in the church. "I want you brethren," he said, according to the official minutes, "to prove John W. Taylor a false prophet when he said that I would be excommunicated from the Church. If there is anything I can do to make good our honor to the nation and to the saints I am willing to do it. I want you to know that I am not rebellious and never have been and if I have erred it has been because of these circumstances and the example of my brethren. I am in harmony with you and I would like you to put me upon my honor to make that good in the future. I would rather die than be cut off from the Church."

Cowley, "deprived of the right and authority to exercise any of the functions of the Priesthood," remained in a state of limbo until he signed a prepared statement for the First Presidency in 1936. "I have been deceived," the statement began, "and . . . wherever and whenever I have given counsel or taken action contrary to the principles, rules, and regulations of the Church, as adopted by the Church and in force, I have been wholly in error in counsel, and my actions have been null and void. This I now plainly see and freely confess, and humbly and with a contrite spirit of true repentance I ask forgiveness" (*Deseret News*, 1 April 1936). Though he was accepted into full fellowship, Cowley apparently had signed the statement for reasons other than confession. He admitted to a son of John W. Taylor that "they held us up, in the eyes of the lay members of the church, and the nation, as the 'ring leaders' when in fact we were no more guilty than those who supposedly took action against us" (Raymond Taylor to Samuel W. Taylor, 3 May 1937).

Cowley and Taylor were not out of harmony with church leaders from 1890 to 1904. Though they may have been "sacrificial lambs" when they resigned their quorum positions for involvement in post-Manifesto polygamy, the action against their church membership was because of post-1904 activities. The two ex-apostles interpreted Joseph F. Smith's 1904 declaration differently than other church leaders. Taylor, in his 22 February 1911 trial, explained his view that "the Lord was anxious to put everybody upon his own responsibility and take the responsibility from the Church."

Cowley and Taylor were only two of many who interpreted the 1904 statement this way. Several prominent Salt Lake and Davis County patriarchs were also excommunicated for holding these views and for performing plural marriages. When he received word of the patriarchs' involvement, President Smith issued another church-wide directive to stake presidents. "Having reason to believe that some members of the Church are secretly engaged in advising and encouraging others to enter into unauthorized and unlawful marriages," he warned, "we direct your special attention to them, with a request that any information received by you from time to time relating to cases of this character be followed up and investigated with a view to having this class of offenders placed on trial for their fellowship in the Church, as we regard them equally culpable with actual offenders" (Clark 1965-75, 4:301).

Mormon polygamists who today rationalize plural marriage on the grounds that polygamy can be rightly maintained by a special dispensation of priesthood authority independent from the church organization usually refer to themselves as Fundamentalists. Most Fundamentalists trace their authority to President John Taylor, who, on the underground at the John W. Woolley home in Centerville, Utah, in September 1886, allegedly "asked the Lord if it would not be right under the circumstances to discontinue plural marriages." Taylor's son, John W., claimed he found among his father's papers after his death the response to this question—"a revelation given him of the Lord, and which is now in my possession, in which the Lord told him that the principle of plural marriage would never be overcome" (Abraham H. Cannon Journal, 29 March 1892). In his 22 February 1911 trial before the Quorum of the Twelve, young Taylor explained that several individuals, including Joseph Fielding Smith (later to become church president), took the document and made a copy of it.[3]

Fundamentalists insist that President Taylor secretly commissioned several priesthood holders to continue the practice of plural marriage as individuals rather than as church representatives. John W. Woolley's son, Lorin C. Woolley, in a 1912 account of the events at the Woolley home related a visionary experience of President Taylor wherein he supposedly told Woolley and others one morning that "I had a very pleasant conversation all night with the Prophet Joseph." Regarding a proposed document which would surrender plural marriage, Woolley has Taylor saying, "Brethren, I will suffer my right hand to be cut off before I will sign such a document."

In 1922, Fundamentalist Joseph W. Musser recorded several oral accounts of the 1886 revelation from Lorin Woolley and Daniel Bateman, another individual reported to be in attendance at the 1886 meeting. Musser's consolidated these accounts and arranged for their publication in 1929 in what has become the standardized version of the event accepted by the majority of Fundamentalists. Whereas the 1912 account referred only to the month of September 1886, the 1929 account specifically dates the incident as 26-27 September 1886. This expanded account details a visit to Taylor not only from Joseph Smith but from Jesus Christ as well. An eight-hour meeting is said to have been held on 27 September. Those present—John Taylor, George Q. Cannon, L. John Nuttall, John W. Woolley, Samuel Bateman, Charles H. Wilkins, Charles Birrell, Daniel R. Bateman, Samuel Seden, George Earl, Julia E. Woolley, Amy Woolley, and Lorin C. Woolley—were reportedly put "under covenant that he or she would defend the principle of Celestial or Plural Marriage, and that they would consecrate their lives, liberty and property to this end" (Joseph Musser Journal, 12 March, 9 April, 14 June, 5 July, and 6, 7, 10, 13 Aug. 1922).

Musser records that President Taylor called together Samuel Bateman, Charles H. Wilkins, George Q. Cannon, John W. Woolley, and Lorin C. Woolley and gave them authority both to perform plural marriage ceremonies and to ordain others with authority to perform polygamous marriages, thus insuring that children would be born to polygamous parents each year thereafter to the Millennium. The account relates one of the most important prophetic statements in Fundamentalist history. "In the time of the seventh president of this Church," Taylor reportedly said, "the Church would go into bondage both temporally and spiritually and in that day . . . the One Mighty and Strong spoken of in the 85th Section of the Doctrine and Covenants would come."[4]

Numerous Fundamentalists since have declared themselves the One Mighty and Strong. Such claims became a serious enough concern during President Joseph F. Smith's administration that the First Presidency published a lengthy discussion of the matter in the 13 November 1905 *Deseret News*. Those proclaiming themselves the "One Mighty and Strong" were declared "vain and foolish men" who make the claim to "bolster up their vagaries of speculation, and in some cases their pretensions to great power and high positions they were to attain in the Church." During a special priesthood meeting on 8 April 1912, President Smith announced that the "One Mighty and Strong to deliver as referred to in the D and C Sec. 85 has no application to the Church at present" (A. W. Ivins Journal, 8 April 1912).[5]

President Smith made a total of nine public statements denouncing new polygamy during his administration (Clark 1965-75, 5:194). His successor, Heber J. Grant, seventh president of the church, experienced no fewer difficulties. Though a polygamist himself, Grant was pragmatic and moved in wealthy and powerful circles where plural marriage was the chief stumbling block preventing Mormon entrance into mainstream America. During the April 1931 General Conference, Grant added a new dimension to his campaign to eradicate Mormon polygamy. In addition to excommunication—

"the limit of Church jurisdiction"—he further announced that "we have been . . . [and] are entirely willing to give such legal assistance as we legitimately can in the criminal prosecution of such cases." Explaining the need to distance orthodox Mormons from polygamists, he added: "We are willing to go to such limits . . . because we wish to do everything humanly possible to make our attitude toward this matter so clear, definite, and unequivocal as to leave no possible doubt of it in the mind of any person" (ibid., 292).

During a 25 July 1937 interview conducted in London, Grant expanded his view that the demands of the law superseded any commandment to live polygamy. "We never believed polygamy was wrong," the church president said, "and never will." Despite the fact that Grant had violated his 1891 amnesty agreement with the government, had attempted unsuccessfully to take Fanny Woolley as a post-Manifesto plural wife, and had been found guilty of "unlawful cohabitation" in 1899, he declared in his newspaper interview that "one of the cardinal rules of the Church is to obey the law. So long as polygamy is illegal we ourselves will strictly enforce the law" (*Salt Lake Tribune*, 26 July 1937).

President Grant had a well-qualified counselor to assist him in suppressing polygamy. J. Reuben Clark, Jr., a respected legal scholar, had extensive experience with the federal government as an adviser to the State Department and as ambassador to Mexico. Clark, like many young Mormons of his generation, had assumed that Wilford Woodruff's 1890 Manifesto ended the polygamy issue once and for all. But investigations into new polygamy revealed that Apostle John W. Taylor, husband of one of Clark's cousins, had married several post-Manifesto plural wives. Another cousin had become the post-Manifesto plural wife of a Salt Lake City patriarch. Clark's aunt, Fanny Woolley, who had been courted after the Manifesto by Heber J. Grant, later became the plural wife of stake president George C. Parkinson in a 1902 Colorado ceremony performed by Apostle Matthias Cowley. The bishop of Clark's ward in Grantsville, Utah, had also married a plural wife in 1900 and as late as 1909 was advocating that "if [people] could find a way to get in, it would be all right to take a plural wife." The most bitter polygamous pill for Clark to swallow was the disclosure that his venerated uncle, Patriarch John W. Woolley, had been excommunicated in 1914 for performing plural marriages.[6]

These discoveries of polygamy so close to home, especially those tarnishing his mother's maiden name, caused Clark acute embarrassment. Though relatively unfamiliar with the arguments for new polygamy due to his near-constant absence from Utah, Clark, as a rank-and-file church member, drafted a 1923 anti-polygamy statement he hoped the First Presidency would adopt in fall General Conference. Although President Grant did not adopt Clark's brief, he was already waging a campaign against Fundamentalists, particularly Clark's cousin, Lorin C. Woolley. Grant dismissed Woolley's claims to special authority, insisting that the man was a "pathological liar," and saw to it that he was excommunicated for "pernicious falsehood" in January 1924 (Anderson 1979, 146).

After Clark's April 1933 appointment to the First Presidency, Lorin C. Woolley tried to link his cousin in various ways to his Fundamentalist claims. President Clark ultimately put the rumors to rest, after Woolley's death, by asserting that "whether [Lorin] knew he was falsifying I did not know, but he did not tell the truth" (Quinn 1983, 183).

One of Clark's initial assignments upon joining the First Presidency was to write a lengthy document outlining the church's opposition to polygamy. This position paper was approved by the other members of the First Presidency and issued as an "Official Statement." "As to this pretended revelation," the statement, as published in the 18 June 1933 *Church Section* of the *Deseret News*, read, "the archives of the Church contain no such revelation; nor any evidence justifying a belief that any such revelation was ever given. From the personal knowledge of some of us, from the uniform and common recollection of the presiding quorums of the Church, from the absence in the Church Archives of any evidence whatsoever justifying any belief that such a revelation was given, we are justified in affirming that no such revelation exists." Whether unintentionally so or not, Clark's statement proved to be incorrect on virtually every point. Though church leaders did not have the original revelation, they owned the copy which John W. Taylor had given Wilford Woodruff in 1887. Furthermore, Heber J. Grant was in attendance at the 22 February 1911 Quorum of the Twelve meeting when the 1886 revelation was discussed and entered into the minutes.

One month after the First Presidency issued the statement, Frank Y. Taylor donated the original handwritten 1886 revelation to the Church. A year later President Grant's counselor and cousin, Anthony W. Ivins, noted in a 1934 letter to the wife of Fundamentalist leader Rulon C. Allred: "The . . . purported revelation of John Taylor has no standing in the Church. I have searched carefully, and all that can be found is a piece of paper found among President Taylor's effects after his death. It was written in pencil and only a few paragraphs [and] had no signature at all. It was unknown to the Church until members of his own family claimed to have found it among his papers. It was never presented or discussed as a revelation by the presiding authorities of the Church" (Anthony W. Ivins Papers, 10 Feb. 1934, LDS Church Archives).[7]

Though the Mormon position is that the authenticity of the 1886 revelation has not been verified, the First Presidency has never released the paper for critical scrutiny. Even if tests proved the document to be in John Taylor's hand, the official Mormon position would still be that the revelation was not submitted to a General Conference of the Saints for approval and was therefore not binding. Fundamentalists would argue that when God has spoken, he does not need the confirming vote of the church. They would also point out that the church has systematically suppressed critical documents related to the 1886 revelation. Not only the original handwritten copy, but the journals of George Q. Cannon, John Taylor, and Francis M. Lyman, as well as portions of the L. John Nuttall journals have been tightly controlled by the First Presidency. Even serious Mormon scholars are denied access to these documents.

"The suppression of Church records in the past," Fundamentalist writer Fred Collier argued in 1981, "especially in a selective way by denying those who believe in the old ways access even to the General Archives has created a great suspicion for the Church in the minds of thousands of Fundamentalist believing people, who feel that the problem is not in a genuine lack of extant evidence but in its inaccessibility in the hands of those whose purposes the truth would not serve. . . . The real problem is not so much the lack of evidence to demonstrate its veracity [e.g., the 1886 revelation of John Taylor] as it is with the problems which it creates for the Church if accepted as authentic" (pp. 2, 12).

NOTES

1. During this period considerable attention was given to the authorship of the Woodruff Manifesto. George Reynolds, secretary to the First Presidency, testified at the Smoot Hearings that he, Charles Penrose, and John R. Winder edited the work for publication (*Proceedings* 2:52-53).

Thomas J. Rosser, in a sworn statement, described a 24 May 1908 meeting in Bristol, England, where a variety of questions were asked of Penrose. When asked if the Manifesto was a revelation he answered, "Brethren, I will answer that question, if you will keep it under your hats. I, Charles W. Penrose, wrote the Manifesto with the assistance of Frank J. Cannon and John White. It's no revelation from God, for I wrote it. Wilford Woodruff signed it to beat the Devil at his own game" (Newson 1956, 6-8).

Penrose's involvement with the writing of the Manifesto is supported by a statement of Matthias F. Cowley, who declared during a Quorum of the Twelve meeting 10 May 1911: "Brother Penrose told me once in the city of Mexico, that he had written the manifesto, and it was gotten up so that it did not mean anything and President [Joseph F.] Smith had told me the same." D. Michael Quinn has documented the editing steps in which Woodruff's handwritten manifesto of 510 words was cut to 356 words on 24 September 1890. That morning the First Presidency was busy with other matters and asked George Reynolds, Charles W. Penrose, and John R. Winder to "take the document and arrange it for publication." After this group worked on it for a time, George Q. Cannon "suggested several emendations, which were adopted." At 2:30 p.m. the revised work was read to the meeting of the First Presidency and three apostles, and "one or two slight alterations were made in it." Afterwards George Reynolds incorporated the document into a telegram—the published version of the Wilford Woodruff Manifesto (Quinn 1985, 44-45).

2. George F. Richards later became a member of this committee and served as its secretary. See Richards Journal, 14, 15, 22 July, 22 Sept. 1909.

3. The John Taylor Papers in LDS Church Archives contain a typewritten copy of the revelation with the notation: "Revelation given to John Taylor, September 27, 1886, copied from the original manuscript by Joseph F. Smith, Jr., August 3, 1909."

Quinn has noted that in 1887 John W. Taylor gave President Wilford Woodruff a collection of John Taylor articles, including the 1886 revelation, which was eventually deposited in the Joseph F. Smith Collection in LDS Church Archives. Quinn points out that John W. Taylor was correct in 1911 when he said he had the original 1886 revelation in his possession. Taylor's brother, Frank Y. Taylor, donated it to the First Presidency on 18 July 1933 (1985, 28-29).

4. For a discussion of this 1886 event from a mainstream Mormon perspective, see M. Anderson 1979. A comparable study from the Fundamentalist point of view is Collier 1981.

5. For a thorough discussion of the "One Mighty and Strong" issue, see Wright 1963, 27-50.

6. For details on these situations, see Quinn 1983, 180-81; Parkinson 1967, 251; Minutes of the Quorum of the Twelve, 10 May 1911; and A. W. Ivins Journal, 20 Sept. 1909.

7. The most significant mainstream Mormon work on the background of the 1886 revelation is M. Anderson 1979; see also Jessee 1959.

CRUSADES AGAINST THE PRINCIPLE

In conversation with a non-Mormon shortly after the release of the 1933 statement from the First Presidency, J. Reuben Clark, Jr., explained that they had issued the public release because "some carnally-minded old birds are saying the Church is not in earnest about the matter, and were winking at the situation" (Quinn 1983, 184). The official 1933 pronouncement pacified mainstream Mormons and others who had long opposed polygamy. But it also unintentionally served as a catalyst for unifying the various factions of the Fundamentalist movement.

J. Reuben Clark's assignment as chief enforcer of the church's anti-polygamy efforts had previously been the assignment of Apostle James Talmage and before him Francis M. Lyman. Clark carried out his assignment vigorously, his previous experience in supervising the U.S. Justice Department's World War I activities against suspected subversives serving him well in dealing with new polygamists. He favored a church-wide loyalty oath which he felt would smoke out Fundamentalists from within Mormon ranks. Scores of Mormons were consequently excommunicated because of their refusal to sign such statements.[1]

To strengthen the legal battery in the war against new polygamy, Utah lawmakers on 14 March 1935 passed an act "Making Unlawful Cohabitation a Felony, and Providing That All Persons Except the Defendant Must Testify in Proceedings Thereof."[2] Responding to this and other anti-polygamy actions of the day, Fundamentalist leader Joseph W. Musser, who had been planning an underground publication for years, initiated a monthly periodical in June 1935. *Truth*, devoted to fervent defense of plural marriage, contained numerous statements of prominent Mormons of the past advocating polygamy as essential to exaltation, an eternal law that would never be done away with.

To counteract the growing strength of Fundamentalists, Clark, in the late 1930s, began authorizing loyal Mormons to conduct surveillance on persons attending meetings in the Salt Lake City homes of known Fundamentalists. He urged the Salt Lake City library to exclude Fundamentalist literature and in 1940 asked the Salt Lake City postmaster to prohibit the mailing of Fundamentalist tracts. In March of 1940, during a meeting with

Salt Lake County stake presidents, the prosecution of polygamists was discussed. One stake president noted that the district attorney "was a good Latter-day Saint and would prosecute the 'new polyg's' criminally if it were deemed wise." Clark ordered that such prosecution begin immediately (ibid., 185).

Church leaders also sought to suppress the rise of Fundamentalism through other avenues. During a 5 June 1939 meeting of Salt Lake City's Pioneer Stake, stake president Paul C. Child reportedly instructed his bishops that all polygamists "are in very humble circumstances, being practically destitute, and if we help them we are helping to support plural families." He instructed bishops to withold church relief from such families (Truth 5 [Aug. 1939]: 59). A short time later the Presiding Bishopric's office sent out a church-wide circular (Church Bulletin, No. 223) to all stake presidencies and ward bishoprics advising that children of polygamous parentage be denied baptismal rites until old enough to "repudiate the principle that gave them birth."

Despite the opposition of church and law enforcement officials, or perhaps because of it, the Fundamentalist movement continued to spread. Much of this growth can be attributed to Joseph W. Musser's editorial work on Truth. Son of a former assistant church historian, Musser had access to sensitive documents in the church archives. He charged that the Wilford Woodruff Manifesto was issued for political expediency only and filled the columns of Truth with incident after incident of authorized post-Manifesto plural marriage. Claiming that the church had been led astray in abandoning "God's order of marriage," he alleged that Fundamentalists held the authority for continuing plural marriage.

Truth was such an irritant to Mormon leaders that in 1944 efforts were undertaken to silence the publication and to jail major Fundamentalist leaders, including Musser. About 6:00 a.m., 7 March 1944, a Salt Lake City raid, coordinated by FBI agents, U.S. marshals, deputy sheriffs, and Salt Lake City policemen, netted forty-six suspected Fundamentalists. Without search warrants, law enforcement officials confiscated issues of Truth and additional documents they felt could be used as evidence against the individuals.

Fifteen of the defendants were booked for "unlawful cohabitation" and/or "conspiracy" to promote the practice of "unlawful cohabitation." Thirty-four were indicted solely on the latter charge, which referred to sending Truth through the mail. The indictment alleged that the periodical was "obscene, lewd, lascivious, indecent and immoral in that sexual offenses against society, to-wit, plural marriages, were to be and were advocated and urged, thereby tending to deprave and corrupt the morals of those whose minds were and are open to such influences, and into whose hands said Truth might fall" (Salt Lake Tribune, 8 March 1944).

The First Presidency, consisting of Heber J. Grant, J. Reuben Clark, and David O. McKay, applauded the arrests. "Since the Manifesto by President Woodruff was adopted by the Church," the three men noted in an official release appearing in the *Salt Lake Tribune*, 8 March, "the first presidency and other general authorities have repeatedly issued warnings against an apostate group that persisted in the practice of polygamous marriages." "We commend and uphold the federal government," the statement concluded, "in its efforts through the office of the United States district attorney and assisting agencies to bring before the bar of justice those who have violated the law."[3]

Church leaders did not wish to be implicated directly in the "Boyden Crusade," as the 1944 raid was called. But during the court hearing one witness testified that he had been given an ecclesiastical calling by David O. McKay to spy on suspected Fundamentalists and gather information for the prosecution. The church was unwillingly drawn farther into the case by a letter from fledgling apostle Mark E. Petersen to Murray Moler, the local United Press bureau manager, which was read into the court record. Petersen, former editor of the *Deseret News*, requested that Moler print "another statement or two setting forth the Church's position" on polygamy, so that the recent arrests not be connected in the public mind with the Mormon Church. Petersen wanted it known that "1. All the cultists are not former members of the Church. Some have been recruited from various protestant faiths. 2. All cultists who have held membership in the L.D.S. Church have been excommunicated by the Church, some of them, as Joseph Musser, the ring-leader, having been excommunicated many years ago. 3. The Church has actively assisted federal and state authorities in obtaining evidence against the cultists and helping to prosecute them, under the law. 4. Among witnesses for the prosecution are men who have been appointed by the Church to search out the cultists, turning over such information as they gather to the prosecution for their use; these men have also been appointed by the Church to do all they can to fight the spread of polygamy. 5. The Church has opposed the practice and teaching of plural marriage since the adoption of a Manifesto in an official conference of the Church held in Salt Lake City, October 6, 1890, and has excommunicated members since that date who have either taught or practiced it. 6. The cultists use the name fundamentalists which is regarded by the Church as a misnomer. They are not fundamentalists in the sense of holding to the fundamental doctrines of the Church, for the fundamental doctrines of the Church are now opposed to polygamy. Use of this name has caused confusion in the public mind and has tended to give the impression (which is what the cultists sought) that they are old line Mormons, which they are not."

The conspiracy charges brought against the individual Fundamentalists were quickly quashed, but violations of the Mann Act (husbands crossed

191

state borders with plural wives) and charges of kidnapping (three individuals had transported a pregnant plural wife across state lines to give the baby benefit of legitimate birth) were upheld, resulting in the imprisonment of fifteen men.

Over the protest of Brigham E. Roberts, who had led the prosecuting efforts against the Fundamentalists, the state board of pardons decided to parole the fifteen men, each of whom had served a term of seven months, so that they could be home for Christmas. But there were stiff conditions to be met before and during parole. The pardoned polygamists were expected to live "only with their legal wives, in homes separate from those occupied by their plural spouses and the children." They had to "make a sincere effort to support the other women and the scores of minor children." The official pardon also stipulated that the former polygamists attend no "meetings espousing polygamy."

Joseph W. Musser, Rulon C. Allred, Albert E. Barlow, Edmund F. Barlow, Ianthus W. Barlow, John Y. Barlow, Oswald Brainich, Heber K. Cleveland, David B. Darger, Joseph Lyman Jessop, and Alma A. Timpson were freed 15 December 1944. Arnold Boss, Morris Q. Kunz, Louis Alma Kelsch, and Charles F. Zitting were not paroled until later because they refused to sign the pledge, an action which made them heroes among independent Fundamentalists.

District Attorney Roberts questioned the wisdom of releasing the men before they had served the full five years of their sentences. In a letter to the board of pardons he called attention to recent articles in *Truth* which "eulogized the prisoners as martyrs and commended the inmates for 'upholding the practice of plural marriage.' " He charged that the "cultists" still advocated polygamy in their meetings and insisted the only way the practice could be "rubbed out" was to keep the ringleaders in prison. "I question the good faith of their pledges," he added. "These people have practiced polygamy for years knowing it was against the law. However, now for their own convenience and advantage, they are willing to make this promise. No security is given that the promise will be kept." Roberts pointed out that "these people will return to their families and cult, and it will again be necessary for the law enforcement agencies to build a case against them. That will take a great deal of time and money" (*Salt Lake Tribune*, 27 Nov. 1945).

Although Roberts's prediction proved to be prophetic, the effort and expense of building another case against polygamists was the burden not of Utah but of Arizona. Short Creek, Arizona, was founded in 1913 by non-polygamist J. M. Lauritzen on the Arizona-Utah border. The first polygamists in the area, Price W. Johnson, Edner Allred, and Carling Spencer, recognized the strategic location of the townsite for polygamists on the run. Situated in the part of Mohave County known as the "Arizona strip," a geographical area cut off from the rest of the state by the Grand Canyon, this community twenty-eight miles south of Hurricane, Utah, was situated four hundred miles from the Mohave County seat of Kingman, Arizona.

In 1935 Short Creek was a small town of twenty houses plus a combination store and gas station, with a post office serving patrons on alternate days. Several polygamist Mormon families had moved into the area and joined with other plural families in a cooperative organization designed to build up the community as "the first city of the Millennium." This concerned some of the old, non-polygamist Mormon settlers, who reported the action to church officials. Ex-senator Reed Smoot, a member of the Quorum of the Twelve, was sent to Hurricane at the request of Zion Park stake president Claude Hirschi. Twenty-one members of the Short Creek Branch were excommunicated for refusal to sign the following pledge: "I, the undersigned member of Short Creek Branch of the Rockville Ward of the Church of Jesus Christ of Latter-day Saints, declare and affirm that I[,] without any mental reservation whatsoever, support the presidency of the church, and that I repudiate any intimation that any of the Presidency or Apostles of the Church are living a double life, and that I repudiate those who are falsely accusing them, and that I denounce the practice and advocacy of plural marriage as being out of harmony with the declared principles of the Church at the present time."

Excommunication was as far as Mormon church leaders could go in curtailing polygamy in Short Creek, but they also encouraged legal action against the offenders. Mohave County officials noticed that county welfare records often showed several Short Creek women married to the same man. In September 1935, County Attorney Elmo Bollinger and the county sheriff visited Short Creek to investigate the situation. They arrested Price W. Johnson and his cousin Carling Spencer. Brought before Short Creek justice of the peace J. M. Lauritzen, the two were released for lack of evidence. Later in the day, after obtaining more conclusive information, the officers sought to arrest the two again. But they, along with Spencer's plural wife Sylvia, had taken refuge in a nearby cave where they remained for seven days. On 28 September they surrendered in Kingman on "open and notorious cohabitation" charges. Commenting on the arrests, Bollinger reported that "officials of the regular (Mormon) Church were assisting to bring about the arrest and conviction of polygamists" (*Truth*, 1 [1 Oct. 1935]: 50).[4]

Short Creekers could not understand why they were not left alone. "Why come up four hundred miles to that desert 'Arizona strip' to pounce upon a peaceful, hard-working, struggling, christian community, suspected only of having more married women than men?" Joseph Musser editorialized in the 1 October 1935 *Truth*. "Surely the great State of Arizona—great in its western atmosphere and broad tolerance—is not so free from moral delinquencies as to justify its officials leaving the more populous sections of the State to train their legal artillery on this little community" to "break up homes and fasten unreasonable hardships upon men and women—with their children—whose only offense, if offense it be, is to make sexual virtue a crowning point in their lives."

Mohave County officials did not see the situation that way. The three defendants were found guilty of the charges in December 1935 and given an eighteen-to-twenty-four-month prison sentence. Sylvia Spencer's sentence was suspended because of her advanced pregnancy, but her husband and Price Johnson, after spending one month in the county jail at Kingman, were sent to the Arizona State Penitentiary at Florence. Model prisoners, they were made trustees after their third day of imprisonment and spent the duration of their eleven months' incarceration working in the prison garden, tannery, and dairy. Returning home to Short Creek after their 8 November 1936 release, Spencer and Johnson, like the more than 1,300 Mormon men and women who had been "prisoners for conscience sake" during the 1880s, were hailed as folk heroes.

Short Creek's population continued to grow. By the early 1950s the community numbered close to four hundred citizens, nearly all of whom were polygamists. Polygamy-related trouble in the area surfaced again when Utah cattlemen with grazing rights in the Short Creek area began to grumble that their grazing fees were used to support the education of polygamous children. The Arizona state legislature secretly appropriated $10,000 to employ the Burns Detective Agency of Los Angeles to probe Short Creek polygamy. Rumor had it that church leaders in Salt Lake City had made a standing offer of $100,000 to Arizona officials if the state would eradicate the Short Creek colony. Mormon bishops in Phoenix and Mesa began quiet surveys of their congregations to determine which homes could accommodate additional children.

Short Creekers were forewarned of the impending raid. Advance notice of the action published in Salt Lake City newspapers was telephoned to Short Creek. At 4:00 a.m., Sunday morning, 26 July 1953, with the moon in full eclipse, more than one hundred heavily armed law enforcement officers arrived at the Short Creek community square, car sirens wailing, red lights flashing, spotlights glaring. The posse was accompanied by national guardsmen, the Arizona attorney general, superior and juvenile court judges, policewomen, nurses, doctors, twenty-five carloads of newspapermen, and twelve liquor control agents. They expected to find the community sleeping. Instead they found most members of the colony grouped around the city flagpole singing "America" while the American flag was being hoisted.

By dawn the entire town was under martial law. Each home was carefully searched. Literature and personal effects were confiscated by the officers. Women and children were rounded up while the national guard set up road blocks, field kitchens, a radio station, and a medical unit. Witnesses familiar with community members began the process of identifying the leaders of the communal "United Effort Plan." Governor J. Howard Pyle climaxed the more than two years of planning that had gone into the raid by issuing a radio report that Short Creek was "dedicated to the wicked theory that every maturing girl child should be forced into the bondage of a multiple wifehood with men of all ages for the sole purpose of producing more children to be reared to become more chattels of this lawless enterprise." He defended the police action as necessary to quell an "insurrection against the state of Arizona," and wipe out "a community dedicated to the production of white slaves." He charged the community with "conspiracy to commit statutory rape, adultery, bigamy, open and notorious cohabitation, marrying the spouse of another, and various other crimes" (*Salt Lake Tribune*, 27 July 1953).

Though Arizona officials had expected violence from the community, the raid was, in the words of a *Salt Lake Tribune* reporter, "like a lawn party at a country church." Younger prisoners joked about their plight, eagerly posed for pictures, and spoke readily with newsmen and officers. But leaders of the Short Creek community did not view the police action as a "lawn party." LeRoy Johnson, leader of the group, said the raid was the "most cowardly act ever perpetrated in the United States." Jeremiah C. Jessop objected that "this raid is one of the most flagrant, profane and dramatic acts ever performed. If Gov. Pyle had wanted us to be at a certain place at a certain time we would have been there. . . . There was no need to spend the taxpayers money on this. Was it for us, or a show for the public?" (ibid.).

Regardless of the motivations behind the raid, officials quickly began the legal processing of Short Creekers. The community Sunday school room became a temporary court chamber. Upon completion of the necessary legal work, the male prisoners were led to private cars and taken to jail in Kingman. Mothers refused to leave their children, all of whom had been declared wards of the state, and it was nearly a week before the confusing array of children and wives could be straightened out by the officials. The women and 263 children were then loaded on five large buses for the 400-mile trip to Kingman.

The buses had scarcely unloaded their human cargo before criticisms of "Operation Short Creek" were launched in the Arizona press. Blatant civil rights violations were pointed out and probing questions asked. "By what stretch of the imagination could the actions of the Short Creek children be classified as insurrection?" the 28 July 1953 *Arizona Republic* asked. "Were those teenagers playing volleyball in a school yard inspiring a rebellion?" wondered the paper. "Insurrection? Well, if so, an insurrection with diapers and volleyballs!" the editor concluded. "Odious and Un-American" and "circuslike" were typical criticisms published elsewhere.

Difficult questions about the cost of the entire operation followed. The initial funding for the raid was secretly appropriated by the state legislature from a special fund set up to handle such emergencies as "flying hay to cattle in distress" or "in case Elk Hunters became lost." But costs quickly escalated. The state welfare department incurred expenses of more than $500 per day in caring for the women and children who were confined in Phoenix area homes. In addition, editors of the *Arizona Free Press* pointed out that attorneys for the 107 Short Creek defendants were demanding separate trials for each defendant. Legal expenses for the 107 trials would be prohibitively high for Maricopa County, where a change of venue had located the trials.

Reaction in Utah was more favorable. The 27 July *Deseret News* issued an editorial entitled, "Police Action At Short Creek." "Law-abiding citizens of Utah and Arizona," the paper began, "owe a debt of gratitude to Arizona's Governor Howard Pyle and to his police officers who, Sunday, raided the polygamous settlement at Short Creek and rounded up its leaders for trial. The existence of this community on our border had been an embarrassment to our people and a smudge on the reputations of our two great states." The *Deseret News* expressed the hope that "Governor Pyle will make good his pledge to eradicate the illegal practices conducted there "before they become a cancer of a sort that is beyond hope of human repair." Announcing that the Short Creekers were "in no way connected with the Church," the editorial pointed out that the polygamists were living in violation of both church and civil laws. "As one of its fundamental tenets," the paper pronounced, "the Church teaches that its members believe 'in obeying, honoring, and sustaining the law.' "

The $600,000 "Operation Short Creek" failed to eradicate polygamy from the community. In less than two years the children, many of whom had been placed in foster homes, returned with their mothers to Short Creek. Men returned from their jail sentences to their wives and children with increased resolve to "live the principle" of polygamy. Typical of the determination displayed by the jailed men was Price W. Johnson's speech before the parole board. One month after his arrest one of his wives petitioned for his release. The board was willing to grant the request provided that Johnson "sign a statement agreeing to straighten out [his] family affairs" and to "conform with the law in the future." He stood before the group and proclaimed that "having more than one wife . . . is an essential part of my religious belief, and I firmly believe that if I keep the covenants I made with these women and with my god, I will have them in the eternal worlds after this life is ended; and before I would break these covenants, I would remain in this prison the remainder of my life; yes, before I would break these covenants, I would go to that gas chamber over there" (Baird and Baird 2:27).

The 1953 Short Creek raid was the last large-scale operation against polygamists in America. But one year later Utah district judge David F.

Anderson presided over court proceedings which eventually removed eight children from the household of Utah Short Creeker Vera Black, the plural wife of Leonard O. Black, husband of three wives and father to twenty-six children. The Black case was based on the premise that the example of polygamous parents would contribute to the delinquency of their children. Therefore it was charged that the children should be removed from that "immoral environment" and placed in foster homes. When the Blacks refused to sign a sworn statement promising to "refrain from teaching polygamy to their children, obey the laws of Utah regarding polygamy, and teach their children to obey the same," the court removed the children from the home on 4 June 1954 and placed them in a foster home in Utah County. Defense attorneys immediately filed a writ of habeas corpus and Provo judge William S. Dunford ruled that the children should be returned to the custody of their parents pending an appeal by the couple to the Supreme Court. But the Blacks lost that appeal. On 3 December 1956 Vera Black was ordered to prepare to turn her children over to the State Bureau of Services for Children.

The church-owned *Deseret News* editorialized that though "separating children from their parents is a heart-breaking and difficult thing to do," in this case it was warranted: "The continued teaching of children to break the law is an extreme provocation. This practice on the part of parents, as much as abandonment or neglect, justifies the state's intervention both for the welfare of the children and of society." The *News* thought the removal of the children worth the disruption of the home if "the practice of polygamy can be entirely ended among those who still practice it."

Many Utahns were stunned that a church which for more than fifty years had opposed anti-polygamy statutes could support removing children from a polygamous home. Juanita Brooks, a prominent St. George Mormon historian, was the foremost voice in opposing the court's ruling and the church's position. Maintaining that "it is a subject upon which I cannot be silent and maintain my self-respect," Brooks first wrote the "Justices of the Utah Supreme Court" on 29 January 1956. Arguing that it was difficult to see how polygamy during Joseph Smith's or Brigham Young's day was any different than in the present, Brooks agreed that "it has been made illegal now. Certainly people should no longer live it. But when a few, driven by the same convictions that our grandparents had, will continue in defiance of the law, shall we commit a greater crime than theirs in attempting to force conformity?" (*Truth*, 21 [Feb. 1956]: 311).

In a 1 February 1956 letter to the editors of the *Deseret News* Brooks expressed dismay at the paper's 28 January editorial. "I was shocked and saddened," she wrote, "that the official organ of the Church of Jesus Christ of Latter-day Saints should approve of such a basically cruel and wicked thing as the taking of little children from their mother." Brooks thought the injustice was of historic proportions: "Since the days of negro slavery children have not been torn from parents who loved them and wanted them and provided for them. . . . In trying to stamp out one evil, let us not commit another so black that it will shame us for ages to come." Leonard and Vera Black eventually signed an anti-polygamy pledge and the children were returned to their custody.

Public opposition to the handling of the Black case and the 1953 Short Creek raid, plus the unacceptable financial burden on taxpayers, evidently altered the way many Americans, particularly Mormons, viewed prosecution of polygamy. In 1955 and 1956, extensive law enforcement efforts in Utah's Davis and Salt Lake counties netted only four polygamists. The 21 November 1955 *Newsweek* attributed the poor showing to "little cooperation from sympathetic Utahans." The magazine added that "citizens were irked by the fact that the drive against the Fundamentalist sect was being financed by a $20,000 appropriation made by the 1954 legislature – a secret appropriation never revealed to press and public." The periodical found the Mormon pulse when it observed that "many a Utah Mormon takes quiet pride in his polygamous forebears and is inclined to be lenient toward the Fundamentalists."

The last concerted attempt in Utah to prosecute polygamy occurred in 1960. After six months of questioning witnesses, a grand jury indicted fifteen people on various charges. A single individual was cited for illegal cohabitation, but he evaded arrest.[5]

NOTES

1. Copies of such statements can be seen in the Stanley S. Ivins Collection and *Truth*, 1 (March 1936): 128.

2. This act was reportedly drafted by Hugh B. Brown, a prominent attorney who later become a member of the First Presidency.

3. Hugh B. Brown, European mission president, writing to explain church action against polygamists, said: "Much publicity has been given to the prosecution recently of certain members of a group of apostates who are alleged to be practicing polygamy, but most of the papers have been fair enough to point out that this group is in no way connected with the Church. The Church has in fact assisted in obtaining the information leading to the indictments, and a 'Mormon Elder' is the prosecuting attorney" (MS, 106 [July 1944]: 795).

4. Apostle Melvin J. Ballard, who had been John Y. Barlow's mission president in the Northwestern States Mission, commented on the actions of the leader of the Short Creek Fundamentalists in an 11 November 1935 interview in the *Kansas City Times*: "[John Y. Barlow] was following his occupation as a farmer last spring, when the church authorities urged Arizona officials to act against him and his followers."

5. In the decade following the Short Creek raid, thirteen polygamy-related arrests in Utah resulted in nine convictions (Hilton 1965, 73-74). This small number is noteworthy when one considers the number of polygamists in Utah during this period.

In 1956 the Utah State Welfare Commission estimated two thousand persons to be living in polygamous homes (*Deseret News*, 29 Feb. 1956). The Utah Attorney General's office in 1961, however, reported the number as closer to 20,000 (Cahn 1961). The discrepancy may be related to the welfare's inclusion of only those polygamists on the relief roles.

Nineteen

POLYGAMISTS IN THE NEWS

During the decades since the Short Creek Raid, many changes have occurred within Mormonism. Today the church basks in the respect and admiration it so strongly desired at the beginning of the twentieth century. Its international expansion has been phenomenal. The racial tensions of the late 1960s and early 1970s caused by the church's refusal to allow blacks the priesthood quickly dissipated after church president Spencer W. Kimball's 1978 announcement that all worthy males, regardless of race, could henceforth be ordained into the Mormon priesthood.

Despite dramatic shifts in social programs and a new world-wide emphasis, including proselytizing in areas where polygamy is an accepted tradition, the church still officially opposes the practice. A 1974 pronouncement of Kimball warned against "the so-called polygamy cults which would lead you astray. Remember the Lord brought an end to this program many decades ago through a prophet who proclaimed the revelation to the world. People are abroad who will deceive you and bring you much sorrow and remorse. Have nothing to do with those who would lead you astray. It is wrong and sinful to ignore the Lord when he speaks. He has spoken—strongly and conclusively" (*Conference Reports*, Oct. 1974, 5).[1]

Though some Mormons would take issue with President Kimball's historical interpretation of the Manifesto, few could successfully untangle the complicated maze of individuals and doctrines supporting the "polygamy cults." But such a study is, in fact, essential to gain an understanding of modern polygamy. The first successful Fundamentalist group was organized in 1929 when Lorin C. Woolley, claiming direct authority from President John Taylor, ordained J. Leslie Broadbent, John Y. Barlow, Joseph W. Musser, and Charles F. Zitting "high priest-apostles" to comprise the "Council of Friends." When Woolley died on 19 September 1934, Broadbent became the presiding official. Following his death the next year, John Y. Barlow, the senior member of the council, assumed the leadership position. Joseph W. Musser took over after Barlow's death on 29 December 1949.

During Musser's administration a few small independent groups broke away, but in 1951 a major schism occurred in the Fundamentalist organization, a division that resulted in the two major groups that have survived to the present. In early 1949 Musser suffered the first of a series of strokes which eventually resulted in his death on 29 March 1954. These health problems compromised his leadership. The council reached a crisis on 18 September 1951 when Musser ordained Rulon C. Allred as a high priest-apostle and appointed him his "second Elder." Objections were raised to Allred's ordination as well as to the ordination of a Mexican Indian, Margarito Bautista. When the council refused to accept Musser's actions, declaring him mentally incompetent, he dissolved the council and organized a new one with Allred second in seniority.

Most lay members continued to support the original council, though the group had difficulty retaining a leader. Charles F. Zitting, the senior member of the council, died only four months after Musser's passing. The next two men in line of seniority, LeGrand Woolley and Louis A. Kelsch, had not had their "high priest-apostleship" confirmed and therefore declined the leadership position. LeRoy Johnson of Short Creek finally agreed to assume the office, which he held until his 1987 death when he was succeeded by Rulon T. Jeffs, a Sandy, Utah, accountant. Rulon C. Allred maintained leadership in the second group, known as the Apostolic United Brethren, until his 1977 murder, after which his brother Owen assumed the position.

Prior to the formation of the Fundamentalist movement by Lorin C. Woolley, there were several small, loosely-knit polygamous groups in Utah. The first of these, organized in the early 1900s by Josiah Hickman, met with little success.[2] Another was begun by John Tanner Clark, excommunicated in Provo, Utah, on 18 May 1905 for circulating letters declaring the Woodruff Manifesto to be a "covenant with death and an agreement with hell." Clark claimed to receive revelations and on one occasion reported that a "voice from heaven [told] him that he was the most literal descendant of Jesus Christ living on the earth." In addition, members of his organization put Clark forth as the "one mighty and strong" mentioned in section 85 of the Doctrine and Covenants. Joseph Musser, a member of the short-lived group, assisted Clark in publishing a booklet entitled, "The One Mighty and Strong."

A third relatively obscure group was led by Nathaniel Baldwin, an inventor who claimed during World War I to have received a revelation directing him to build a radio set superior to anything on the market. He eventually constructed a factory in Salt Lake City and advocated polygamy among his employees. The company rapidly expanded until Baldwin encountered difficulties with the law, after which the group gradually disbanded.

Moses Gudmundsen, a violin teacher at Brigham Young University, joined a polygamist group of approximately 120 faithful in the 1920s. Eventually assuming the leadership of the group, Gudmundsen convinced sixty members, including a body of "Springville Separatists," to establish headquarters on a dry farm in western Utah, near Eureka. The group, claiming to be the chosen people of God, established a cooperative order. Gudmundsen grew a long white beard and wore a white robe to minister to his people.

One morning Gudmundsen was observed leaving the residence of May Holtz, who was married to another man. When confronted, Gudmundsen announced a revelation regarding "true wives" or "spiritual wives." According to Gudmundsen's revelation, which bore remarkable similarities to the spiritual wifery practices of Joseph Smith's early New York contemporaries, a married person often found in another mate his or her social, intellectual, and spiritual equal. If such a spiritual mate were married to another, as May Holtz was, Gudmundsen encouraged the practice of "wife sacrifice." Mr. Holtz went along with the action. Mormon church leaders, discovering the group's activities, were less generous. In 1921 five members of the colony were excommunicated and seven more disfellowshipped. Shortly thereafter civil authorities made an investigation of the community. Though no charges were filed, the group disbanded and Gudmundsen drifted to California.

A more prominent Fundamentalist group—one still in existence—is the Davis County Cooperative Society. In 1935 Elden Kingston, who claimed to have been Leslie Broadbent's "second elder," organized the co-op after his claims to leadership in the primary Fundamentalist group were not recognized. Kingston's group, with more than five hundred members, has steadily evolved financially until its assets are estimated at more than $50 million (Bradlee and Van Atta 1981, 167). Ironically, the members of this group eschew wealth. Initially male adherents wore only blue coveralls with a string tied around the waist. Women, to show their renunciation of the world and its emphasis on acquiring wealth, wore plain blue dresses with no pockets in which to put possessions. This attire was later abandoned for more modern clothing.

Today the Kingston community, described by a Salt Lake County sheriff's lieutenant as "a very close-knit, impregnable polygamist group," has expanded its commercial interests beyond Davis County (ibid.). The co-op presently owns over thirty businesses in Utah, as well as several farms, a 300-acre dairy farm in Woods Cross, a thousand-acre farm in Tetonia, Idaho, and a large cattle ranch in Emery County in central Utah. Their largest operation is a coal mine in Huntington Canyon, Utah. Though group leaders claim today that they no longer practice polygamy, numerous co-op members living around the Huntington Canyon mine were excommunicated during the early 1960s on grounds of polygamous cohabitation (Hilton 1965, 40-41).

Recently the Church of the Firstborn of the Fulness of Times has received more notoriety than any other Fundamentalist group. This organization was incorporated in Salt Lake City on 21 September 1955 by three brothers: Joel, Ross, and Floren LeBaron. Unlike most other Fundamentalist factions, the Church of the Firstborn claims no authority from Lorin C. Woolley.

Rather, they make the claim that Joseph Smith secretly passed on the presidency of the High Priesthood, or the Right of the Firstborn Sceptre in Israel, to his close friend Benjamin F. Johnson in Nauvoo, Illinois. Johnson in turn supposedly conferred this authority on his grandson, Alma Dayer LeBaron. As soon as his boys "could understand things," the elder LeBaron began to tell his sons about Benjamin F. Johnson. He told them that in Salt Lake City in the 1920s the angelic form of Johnson appeared to him and told him of the mission he was to perform. LeBaron promised one day to pass the "authority" or "mantle of Joseph Smith" on to the most worthy of his sons.

Despite LeBaron's 1924 excommunication for polygamy, his seven sons remained Mormons while growing up in Colonia Juarez, Mexico. But their father's teachings had taken hold. Benjamin, the oldest, claimed in 1933 that his father had given him the "mantle." Within two years he began proclaiming that he was the "One Mighty and Strong" who would "set the house of god in order" and reconcile the Mormon church with the Fundamentalists. Ben's strongest supporters were his brothers Ervil and Alma. But those close to the oldest LeBaron son noticed episodes of irrational behavior. At inappropriate times he would let out a loud roar to prove he was the "Lion of Israel." On one occasion he stretched out in the busy Salt Lake City intersection of 33rd South and State street where he held up traffic for half an hour doing two hundred pushups. "See," he said to the bewildered police officer who came to untangle the traffic, "nobody else can do that many. That proves I'm the One Mighty and Strong" (Van Atta 1977).

When Ben was eventually committed to the Utah State Mental Hospital in 1953, even his brothers, who had been excommunicated in 1944, no longer believed his claims. The younger LeBaron boys had by this time established a communal society on their ranch under the direction of Margarito Bautista, the Mexican leader of Rulon Allred's group. But friction developed between the two groups. On a trip to Salt Lake City in 1955, Joel and Floren affirmed their continued support of Allred's group. Afterwards, however, they, along with their brother Ross, filed incorporation papers for their own organization. Bickering broke out at once among the LeBarons. Ross claimed it was his idea to incorporate and that Joel had agreed that he would lead the organization "until the coming of the One Mighty and Strong." When Joel announced that he was the "One Mighty and Strong," Ross broke away and formed his own Church of the Firstborn.

When Joel and Floren returned to Mexico they were able to convert Ervil and Alma as well as their mother. Following years of missionary work under Ervil's direction, the group claimed a membership of more than five hundred people. The most important influx to the organization outside the LeBaron family was the 1958 conversion of a number of Mormon missionaries in France. William Tucker, a counselor to the French mission president, was the ringleader of the group. Having read Fundamentalist literature prior to his mission, he apparently became converted to some of their views, particularly those on priesthood, and began secretly spreading the teachings to other missionaries.

When Tucker's former missionary companion David T. Shore finished his mission and returned to Utah in January 1958, he obtained a copy of Ervil LeBaron's "Priesthood Expounded" and sent it to Tucker. With his influence among other missionaries, Tucker gathered about him a small core of sympathizers, including J. Bruce Wakeham, Stephen M. Silver, Daniel Jordan, Ronald M. Jarvis, and Marilyn Lamborn. Mission president Milton Christensen discovered the activities of his charges and arranged to have Tucker, Silver, and Wakeham interviewed by Mormon apostles in Europe for the dedication of the London Temple on 8 September 1958. All other missionaries in France were closely questioned about their beliefs. Ultimately nine French missionaries were excommunicated and sent home: Tucker, Wakeham, Silver, Jordan, Lamborn, Neil Poulsen, Loftin N. Harvey, June Abbott, and Nancy Fulk. In addition, missionaries Ron Jarvis, Harvey Harper, and Marlene Wessel returned on their own without being excommunicated.

Seven of the former missionaries, four elders and three sisters, joined the LeBaron movement in Mexico and never returned to the LDS church. Tucker (who died in 1967), Silver, Jordan (who was murdered 1987), and Wakeham served as apostles in the Church of the Firstborn of the Fulness of Times. Marilyn Lamborn and Nancy Fulk married Tucker, and June Abbott married Wakeham. Shore also joined his former missionary friends in Mexico but later became disillusioned and rediscovered his faith in the LDS church, as did Harvey, Poulsen, Jarvis, Harper, and Wessel (Mehr 1988, 27-45).

Members of the "French Group," while dynamic proselyters for the LeBaron-dominated Church of the Firstborn, eventually left the movement. The LeBarons continued to attract believers, however. Much of the success of the Church of the Firstborn can be attributed to Joel LeBaron. Followers and family members described him as "Christ-like." But Ervil was the unofficial church spokesman and authored most of the church's literature, which stressed such principles as the concept of two grand heads of the priesthood, priesthood authority, the Adam-God doctrine, and the theory that Joseph Smith was the Holy Ghost. The group also claimed supremacy over other Fundamentalist organizations, which merely prepared one for membership in the higher organization. Joel eventually came to view the unstable Ervil as a threat to the organization and cast him out of the church. Ervil, in return, said that Joel's action stripped Firstborn leaders of their authority. The dispute escalated to bloodshed. In August 1972, on Ervil's instruction, Joel was shot to death. Ross reported from Salt Lake that the action boiled "down to a fight over the birthright, just like in the Bible" (Van Atta 1977).

Ervil pursued that birthright with a passion. In the first half of 1975 five persons associated with LeBaron and his ragtag band of followers were killed. Several others narrowly escaped death. The first known act of violence during this period occurred at Los Molinos, Mexico, a small hamlet founded by Joel LeBaron some years earlier. Ervil's "Lambs of God," as they liked to be called, led a commando-like night raid on the community, fire-bombing homes and gunning down residents. Fifteen people were wounded; two men died. When witnesses appeared to testify about Ervil's involvement in the raid, they were fired at with a shotgun while waiting outside the courtroom in Ensenada.

A few days after the Los Molinos incident, Neomi Zarate, wife of one of Ervil's followers, disappeared and was presumed to have been killed on Ervil's orders. Robert Simons, an eccentric polygamist in Grantsville, Utah, was reported missing after last being seen with some of Ervil's henchmen.[3] Seven-foot-tall "Lamb of God" defector Dean Vest was shot to death in National City, California, by Vonda White, one of Ervil's plural wives.[4]

Ervil, convicted of complicity in Joel's 1972 murder, served only eight months of his twelve-year sentence before being released by a Mexicali court for "lack of evidence." The frenzy of killings in early 1975 put him again on the wanted list of Mexican and American authorities. A Mexican policeman finally arrested him on 2 March 1976. While he was in jail in Ensenada, members of a front organization called The Society of American Patriots distributed his literature from a post office box in South Pasadena, California. With rabid rhetoric the society denounced rival polygamists, government taxes, the press, welfare programs, and gun control. They threatened an invasion of Mexico and decried the U.S. presidential candidacy of Jimmy Carter, announcing, "We would rather have the death penalty placed upon Jimmy Carter, than to see him proceed further" (LeBaron 1981, 271).

Ervil's chief antagonist in the Fundamentalist movement was Rulon C. Allred. LeBaron had accused Allred in the fall of 1975 of "engaging in psychological warfare against one of the foremost champions of liberty of all time [LeBaron]." His letter closed with a warning: "We have very *impressive* methods of causing the rights of honorable men to be recognized, respected and upheld" (Bradlee and Van Atta 1981, 215). Having Ervil tucked away in a Mexican jail provided a small measure of security to those who knew and feared him. But their peace was shattered when he was released in early November 1976 for "lack of evidence." Bribery was suspected. Ervil and one of his plural wives relocated to Yuma, Arizona.

By early spring he had ordered the murder of a wayward daughter, Rebecca LeBaron. During a 20 April 1977 meeting of followers in Dallas, Texas, he announced that the Lord wanted members of the group to prepare for a mission to Utah. He decreed that on 3 May there was to be a funeral in Salt Lake City at which his brother Verlan LeBaron should be killed. Furthermore, Ervil announced, the funeral would be Rulon Allred's. The self-proclaimed prophet of God announced that Allred's murder should be

done by the group's two prettiest women. The floor was opened to nomina-
tions and two young women were chosen (ibid., 232-36).

Rulon C. Allred was a naturopath by profession, treating health dis-
orders by prescribing special diets, sunshine, massage, and exercise. Born to
a prominent polygamous family in the Mexican state of Chihuahua in 1906,
the seventy-one-year-old husband of at least eleven women was the spiritual
leader of thousands of Fundamentalists by 1977. At 4:45 on the afternoon of
10 May 1977 Allred was finishing the day at his Murray, Utah, office when
two young women later identified as Rena Chynoweth and Ramona Marston
entered the building where Allred, his wife and assistant Melba, and several
patients remained. "Oh my God! My God!" witnesses heard Allred scream
as Chynoweth allegedly pumped several bullets into his body.

Initial suspicion for the murder centered on Alex Joseph. Journalists
loved Joseph's quotable humor and candor and his willingness to be photo-
graphed with his attractive wives. He had received wide media coverage in
national as well as local publications. The highly visible polygamist had fallen
from Allred's favor in 1970 over financial disagreements. But Joseph denied
killing Rulon Allred. His best guess, he informed police officers, was that
Ervil LeBaron had orchestrated the murder.

Funeral services for Allred were held on 14 May 1977 at the Bingham
High School auditorium—the only facility in the area large enough to accommodate the anticipated thousands of mourners. Television cameras and news
reporters were everywhere. Verlan LeBaron, sitting in the back of the room,
did not find out until much later that the mass presence of the news media
and tight police security had saved his life. A hit squad, sent by Ervil to
assassinate Verlan, dared not attempt the deed after surveying the situation.

After four months of painstaking investigation, prosecutor David
Yocum and investigating officers Dick and Paul Forbes met with a Salt Lake
City judge and presented their evidence. The judge signed complaints against
eleven persons for murder, conspiracy to commit murder, and attempted
murder. On 23 September 1977 more than a hundred law enforcement officers simultaneously raided ten different locations in Denver and Dallas. The
operation netted only four of the principles; Ervil LeBaron was not among
them. It was 6 March 1979 before the long-awaited murder trial got under-
way, with only four of the accused present: Rena, Mark, and Victor Chynoweth
and Eddie Marston. After two weeks of testimony the jury found all four
defendents innocent.

Ervil LeBaron was not apprehended by Mexican officials until 25
May 1979. He came to trial in a U.S. courtroom for the first time in his life on
Monday, 12 May 1980. After listening to more than two weeks of testimony,
the jury retired to deliberate. Foreman Andrew Smith shortly called for a
vote on the most serious charge that "on or about the 10th day of May

1977 . . . [Ervil LeBaron] did solicit, request, command, encourage or intentionally aid others to intentionally or knowingly cause the death of Rulon Clark Allred"—murder in the first degree. The vote was eleven to one for conviction. The decision required unanimity. After three more hours, the jury returned to the court. The group found LeBaron guilty of the murder of Rulon Allred and guilty of conspiring to murder his own brother, Verlan LeBaron.

Many Utahns were surprised to hear news reports on 16 August 1981 that Ervil LeBaron had been found dead at 5:30 a.m. in his maximum security cell at the Utah State Prison. Cause of death: a massive heart attack. Two days later Verlan LeBaron, whom Ervil had ordered murdered on at least two occasions, met his death in a grinding head-on collision near Mexico City. The final scenes in the Ervil LeBaron saga seemed to come to a close on 21 August when the *Salt Lake Tribune* reported that Anna Marston, one of the fourteen wives of the self-proclaimed "One Mighty and Strong," claimed her husband's body and had him interred in Resthaven Cemetery in Bellaire, Texas.

But LeBaron's influence would soon extend beyond the grave. Prior to his death he compiled a "hit list" of people he felt had betrayed him during his imprisonment. Recorded in a "Book of New Covenants," these individuals were singled out for execution, apparently by some of LeBaron's children. The first target of LeBaron's divine justice was Leo Evoniuk, who in a power struggle had earlier killed LeBaron's son Arturo. In May 1987, Watsonville, California, authorities found Evoniuk's dentures in a pool of blood with several casings from a 9-mm handgun strewn about. The man was presumed dead though his body was not recovered. The case remains unresolved.

Daniel Jordan, one of the "French Missionaries," met his death five months later, on 16 October 1987, while deer hunting with nine of his wives and twenty-one of his children in Sanpete County, Utah. An unknown assailant gunned him down. Aaron LeBaron, the twenty-year-old son of Ervil, was hunting with the group. Hours after Jordan's funeral in Bennett, Colorado, young LeBaron declared himself new patriarch of the clan with the "keys to civil power"—essentially the power of life and death—over family members. Terrified, Jordan family members had LeBaron arrested on charges of making threats. The charges were later dismissed, and he left the state, taking with him eight other of Ervil LeBaron's children who had been placed in Colorado foster homes.

On 27 June 1988, near 4:00 p.m., the 144th anniversary of Joseph Smith's death, the "Lambs of God" struck again. In a coordinated operation, former LeBaron henchman Duane Chynoweth and his young daughter Jennifer were shot to death in a pickup truck parked outside a vacant house in Houston, Texas. Chynoweth's brother Mark, a son-in-law of Ervil LeBaron, was simultaneously murdered near his business about ten miles away, while three hundred miles away, Eddie Marston, one of LeBaron's stepsons, was also killed.

Investigators in these murders suspected that three of LeBaron's sons—Andrew, 28; Heber, 27; and Aaron, 20—were leading a small band of teenage brothers and sisters, the next generation of followers of LeBaron's "Church of the Lamb of God." Heber LeBaron and four other members of the elusive clan were arrested in a stolen vehicle in Arizona on 1 July 1988. A recovered truck matched the suspect vehicle in the Chynoweth and Marston slayings. But despite additional evidence and extensive police investigation, none of those arrested were charged with any of the murders, all six of which remain unresolved.

Ervil LeBaron's body was scarcely cold in his Texas grave before other tales of blood atonement, conspiracy, and polygamy again hit the newsstands. On the evening of 24 July 1984, a young American Fork husband and father, Allen Lafferty, returned home from work to discover the slashed bodies of his wife Brenda and fifteen-month-old daughter Erica. Investigative efforts of law enforcement officials resulted in the arrest of two of Allen's brothers, Ronald W. and Daniel C., and two alleged accomplices. Polygamy was rumored to be at the bottom of the slayings.

Ron and Dan Lafferty grew up in a strong Mormon household in Payson, Utah. After serving as LDS missionaries (Ron in Florida and Dan in Scotland), both returned to Utah and married in LDS temples. Their lives, however, were anything but normal Mormon. They became heavily involved in the study of Fundamentalist teachings and writings, and both were excommunicated from the LDS church, for, among other reasons, their belief in the practice of polygamy.

The brothers found a kindred spirit in Bob Crossfield, a self-proclaimed prophet who had recently moved with his plural wives from Canada to Genola, Utah. Crossfield had been receiving revelations for twenty years, many of which he had forwarded to Mormon church officials in Salt Lake City. In 1979 he was commanded by God to move his families to Utah, where he wanted to re-establish the "School of Prophets" originally instituted by Joseph Smith. Crossfield's millennialistic views were quickly accepted by the Lafferty brothers.

Members of the "School of Prophets" believed that a "city of refuge" would be established in Salem, Utah, near the entrance of a controversial mine, established in 1894 when its founder reported that he had been directed to the spot by an angel.[5] According to Dan Lafferty, part of the visionary plans of the "School of Prophets" included the re-establishment of the United Order and the Council of Fifty. Plural marriage was a prominent part of these plans. Members of the "School of Prophets," according to Dan Lafferty, believed that "in an early premortal existence everyone was created with a soul-mate of the opposite sex—an eternal companion. For every man there was a woman, and for every woman a man. But there was a war in heaven in which one-third of the souls, all men, rebelled against God and were cast out, leaving most of the women without companions. To solve the problem, the extra women were assigned as plural mates to the remaining men." Lafferty elaborated that "while the duty of every man in this world is to live as good a life as possible, to become sanctified, the primary goal of every woman is to find the man to whom she was assigned in the pre-existence" (Nelson 1984, 8).

The difficulties for Ron Lafferty, according to one source, began when he had trouble convincing his wife that he should take plural wives. Apparently when she was warming to the concept, his sister-in-law, Brenda Lafferty, persuaded her against it. The articulate Brenda, who had worked as a hostess for a newsmagazine program at KBYU-TV, was the most formidable anti-polygamy force in the Lafferty family.

Ron and other members of Crossfield's "School of Prophets" had been instructed in how to obtain revelations. In March 1984 Ron received a revelation in which the Lord purportedly told him to "remove" four individuals who were "obstacles in my path." Brenda and Erica were on that list. While refusing to divulge details of the 24 July murders, Dan Lafferty admitted in the 23 September 1984 *Central Utah Journal* that the revelation his brother had received required that a "show" be made of the killings "as a warning to others on 'the Lord's hit list' who need to repent."

Chip Carnes, one of two drifters accompanying Ron and Dan Lafferty to Brenda Lafferty's home on 24 July 1984, agreed to testify against the Laffertys in order to have capital homicide charges against him dropped. On that fateful summer day, Carnes said, the brothers forced themselves into Brenda's home and began to beat her. Ron Lafferty later related "he didn't know what got into him, whether it was the Lord or what, but he went and cut a piece of cord off the vacuum cleaner and while Dan held her down, he tied the cord around her throat until she went limp. Then he grabbed her chin, pulled her head back, and cut her throat from ear to ear." Walking into the bedroom where the crying baby was, Dan killed her as well, later saying "no problem, it was easy" (*Salt Lake Tribune*, 2 May 1985).

A few weeks following the double killing the brothers were captured in Nevada and returned to Utah where both were eventually found guilty. Dan was sentenced to life imprisonment because of a hung jury in the penalty phase of his trial. Ron, whose trial was delayed because of a suicide attempt, was sentenced to death despite defense attorneys' strategy to convince jurists that he was suffering from "paranoid delusions and believed he was granted a God-given 'moral imperative' to murder."

A less dramatic, contemporary case was the 1982 firing of a Murray, Utah, policeman, Royston Potter, for having two wives. The Jehovah's Witness-turned-Catholic-turned-Mormon was trying to "save" a neighbor from Mormon Fundamentalism in 1979 when the polygamist instead swayed Potter's perspective. "It was like being hit right between the eyes," Potter recalled in the 26 February 1983 *Salt Lake Tribune*. The discovery that Fundamentalism was more compelling than mainstream Mormonism "devasted me, yet I couldn't soak up enough knowledge." Though they found polygamy "threatening," Potter and his temple-married wife Denise became convinced that plural marriage was necessary "in order to obtain the highest level of existence in the next life" (Strack 1983, 7). On 26 April 1980 Potter took a second wife, Vera Lee Delancey. Fully aware that his Fundamentalist views could get him into legal trouble, he wanted to be a policeman nevertheless, "to help people." After his polygamous lifestyle was exposed, Potter was interviewed by a Murray internal affairs officer on 15 November 1982. Two weeks later he was terminated from his job, according to Mayor LaRell D. Muir, for "failure to comply with his oath of office and rules and regulations of the police department." He was also excommunicated from the LDS church.

Like most polygamists with roots grounded in Mormonism, Potter viewed the Utah anti-polygamy laws as unconstitutional, an interference with his First Amendment rights. After his firing, he protested publicly that he was being denied his legal rights. He argued that his marital status had not affected his work performance and objected to unequal enforcement of the law. Other police officers, he argued, were guilty of fornication and adultery, both misdemeanors under Utah law, but were still working for Murray City. When the Murray Civil Service Commission upheld his dismissal, Potter filed a civil suit in U.S. district court. Requesting reinstatement and retroactive pay, Potter insisted that the right "to practice plural marriage is protected under the freedom of religion clause in the First Amendment," and that "the U.S. Constitution takes precedence over the State Constitution" (*Salt Lake Tribune*, 19 Feb. 1983).

Though there has never been a federal or state court ruling that has held polygamous marriage to be constitutional, neither has the issue of polygamy been tested in the U.S. Supreme Court since *Reynolds*. Potter claimed that he did not want to become a "battering ram of the Lord," but he was prepared to take his grievance far enough to effect reversal of the 1879 *Reynolds v. the United States* decision, which had stood for more than a century as the landmark case respecting religious freedoms in the United States.

Potter lost his first round of appeals when U.S. district court judge Sherman Christensen ruled on 27 April 1984 that Potter's assertion of First Amendment protection was without merit. "The practice of polygamy," the judge ruled, "is not a fundamental right constitutionally protected by the Free Exercise clause of the First Amendment or any right of privacy or liberty under the Fourteenth Amendment" (*Salt Lake Tribune*, 28 April 1984). In Potter's second appeal, before the U.S. Tenth Circuit Court of Appeals, justices ruled that, because monogamy is the "bedrock upon which our culture is built," the State of Utah is justified in upholding and enforcing its ban on plural marriage (*Salt Lake Tribune*, 13 May 1985). Potter subsequently petitioned the U.S. Supreme Court in hopes that it would consider his appeal, but the high court declined, without comment, in early October 1985 to review the case, leaving intact the ruling of the Tenth Circuit Court. For the meantime, *Reynolds v. the United States* stands unmarred: polygamy is not protected by the First Amendment to the U.S. Constitution.

Many historians and legal scholars believe that *Reynolds* will eventually be modified. Social attitudes influence judicial decisions. Popular opinion and legislative action since 1879 have demonstrated significant change in the way variant lifestyles are viewed by many Americans. Legal scholar Robert G. Dyer pointed out in a 1977 *Utah Bar Journal* article that "more tolerant social attitudes toward homosexuality, adultery, obscenity, prostitution, and unusual marriage styles would make it difficult to attack polygamy as being violative of the peace and good order of society. Judicial attitudes towards obscenity, privacy, and the protection of individual freedoms, even if manifested by socially deviant behavior, have made necessary a clear showing of danger or detriment to other members of society in order for the conduct to be validly regulated." As Dyer indicates, "while there was much nineteenth century rhetoric concerning the evils of polygamy, there is no solid scientific data indicating that the practice is detrimental to society. In fact, the success with which many nations have long lived with polygamy is indicative that it is an alternate family style, no better and no worse, perhaps, than monogamy" (p. 45).

Additionally, Edwin Firmage, prominent University of Utah law professor, feels that "the basic underpinnings of *Reynolds v. the United States* have been shredded" (Strack 1983, 8). His view finds support in several cases. In *Cantwell v. Connecticut* (1940), a Jehovah's Witness suit claimed unjust police interference with missionary efforts. The U.S. Supreme Court, though not unaware of "abrasive" techniques used by the group, nevertheless ruled in favor of their religious rights. The court also upheld in *Sherbert v. Werner* (1965) the right of a Seventh-Day Adventist woman to refuse to work on her Sabbath day.

Perhaps the most significant blow to *Reynolds* was *Wisconsin v. Yoder* (1972). A group of Amish parents refused to send their children to secondary schools, claiming that allowing them to mix with non-Amish children endangered the salvation of their children by exposing them to the very worldliness their religion taught them to shun. When the court's decision went to the Amish, Justice William O. Douglas noted that the decision was a departure from *Reynolds* and suggested that "in time *Reynolds* will be overruled" (Dyer 1977, 44).

Royston Potter's legal claim centered on First Amendment rights, but his case raised other legal and social questions. Why were anti-polygamy laws passed in the first place? Why have countless violations of anti-bigamy and anti-polygamy laws gone unprosecuted for nearly twenty-five years in Utah and elsewhere? Although these and other questions will undoubtedly be resolved some day before the highest court of appeals, countless nagging theological issues will remain. To the historian, relevant questions might center on how the course of Mormon history would have been altered had the federal government not opposed polygamy or had Joseph Smith not introduced plural marriage in the first place. Much of the development of Mormonism can be linked to the introduction, promotion, and eventual abnegation of polygamy. To those who accept Joseph Smith as a prophet of God, plural marriage can be evidence of his divine calling; to those who question or reject his prophetic claims, polygamy is more readily explained as evidence of his downfall.

While Independent Fundamentalist Roy Potter's confrontation with the federal government ended on a peaceful note, such was not the case in early 1988 at the Singer/Swapp family compound in Marion, Utah. Fifteen years earlier John and Vickie Singer had removed their children from the public school system to educate them at home instead. Later the effectiveness of this home-schooling came into question. Officials contended with Singer in numerous court settings in which he was usually uncooperative. The matter was further complicated when Singer took a second wife, Shirley Black, who was legally married to another man. As her children joined her at the Singer house, a custody battle ensued. Singer illegally supported Black's efforts to keep her children from being turned over to their father.

After considerable friction local authorities attempted to serve Singer with an arrest warrant as he walked out to his mail box on 18 January 1979. He reportedly threatened them with a gun and then tried to flee. He was shot in the back and killed during the confrontation. While many felt the officers were justified in their actions, John Singer's family view the act as cold-blooded murder.

The Singer scenerio was being closely watched at the time by nineteen-year-old Addam Swapp, a budding Fundamentalist from Fairview, Utah, who held John Singer in awe. Swapp visited the Singer home in early 1980 and vowed to marry sixteen-year-old Heidi Singer. Three years after marrying her, he also married her younger sister Charlotte.

Moving into the Singer compound Swapp assumed the patriarchal role left vacant by John Singer and began his own dynasty by fathering six children by his two wives. He was also being steeped in the family's views of John Singer's death. His anger seemed to grow like a cancer. In a 22 June

1988 letter to *Utah Holiday* writer Jean Bucher, Swapp wrote: "The Government of the State of Utah, combined with the powers of the Mormon Church, tried to make a publick example out of [Vickie and John] when they took their children out of the school system. They wanted to show the rest of the free and independent thinkers in Utah, whom I call Free Men, that they are the Supreme Power. They did not want anyone to oppose their will, for they felt that if one man could stand against them, he might start a chain reaction causing others also to stand against their corrupt system. . . . Because he would not bend his knee to the wicked rule of the State, Church combination, [John Singer] was murdered in cold blood, by hired Government assassins" (p. 38).

During the early morning hours of 16 January 1988 Swapp and other family members, following what they believed to be a divine edict, broke into the Kamas, Utah, LDS Stake Center, near their house, and left a bomb consisting of eighty-seven sticks of dynamite and an alarm clock timing device. They left behind an Indian-like spear, with an attached noted bearing the date "Jan. 18, 1979," stuck into a baseball diamond near the church. At 3:00 a.m. a powerful explosion severely damaged the vacant $1.5 million building.

The Singer/Swapp clan was immediately suspected in the blast. Law enforcement officials surrounded the family farm and ordered Addam Swapp and Vickie Singer to surrender. They refused, promising a fight if lawmen came on their property. One of Swapp's cousins, Roger Bates, told police that Swapp sought an armed confrontation because he had received a "revelation from God that John Singer will rise from the dead to protect them at the moment police launch their attack." Furthermore, Bates explained that family members believed "John Singer's resurrection will trigger the downfall of corrupt government and religious institutions and clear the way for the second coming of Jesus Christ" (*Salt Lake Tribune*, 29 Jan. 1988).

Warrants for the arrest of Addam Swapp and Vickie Singer were signed by Fifth Circuit judge Maurice D. Jones, charging the them with aggravated arson, criminal mischief, and possession of an infernal device in connection with the bombing. But they were not about to surrender. For thirteen days the compound was under seige by scores of law enforcement personnel. Early on 28 January, officers with dogs hid in a nearby building and waited for Addam Swapp to start his morning chores. Emerging at about 8:30 a.m., Swapp and his brother Jonathan were surprised by the hidden lawmen. During the gun battle, Addam Swapp was wounded and police officer Fred House was killed. The remaining family members in the Singer home surrendered. Charges were brought against four of them.

Nine months later, on 2 September, and after a thirteen-day trial in U.S. District Court, Judge Bruce Jenkins awarded all four convicted Singer/Swapp members minimum sentences. Seige leader Addam Swapp was ordered to prison for fifteen years, Vickie Singer received five years, and co-defendants Jonathan Swapp and John Timothy Singer were each given ten years. Five days later John Timothy Singer, the trigger-man in Officer House's death, and the two Swapp brothers were charged by the state with second-degree murder. After deliberating for three days in late December, a jury found Addam Swapp and Singer guilty of manslaughter, a second-degree felony, and Jonathan Swapp guilty of misdemeanor negligent homicide (*Salt Lake Tribune*, 23 Dec. 1988).

Third district court judge Michael R. Murphy ruled on 26 January 1989 that "these defendants acted as anarchists and this court has been presented with no credible information that, if given the opportunity, they would not again engage in anarchism and armed conflict." He then imposed the maximum sentence possible on the trio: one-to-fifteen years in the Utah state prison for Addam Swapp and John Timothy Singer and one year in prison for Jonathan Swapp. These sentences will not be served until the men have completed their lengthy federal prison terms (*Salt Lake Tribune*, 27 Jan. 1989).

Aside from their practice of polygamy, most Fundamentalists are law-abiding citizens. High-profile polygamists such as the Singers, Swapps, Laffertys, and LeBarons are throwbacks to late-nineteenth-century Mormonism when opposition to the federal government was a badge of courage and honor. The leaders of smaller—although sometimes no less bizarre—splinter groups, such as John W. Bryant, usually maintain lower profiles.

Like many other Independent Fundamentalists, Bryant first converted to mainstream Mormonism. Obsessed with early Mormon teachings on polygamy, he later joined the Apostolic United Brethren (the Rulon Allred group) and soon took a second wife, Dawn Samuels (not her real name), now totally disaffected from Mormonism and Mormon Fundamentalism. Dawn's experiences with modern polygamy shed light onto the psychology of conversion to Fundamentalism, as well as on the practices of her ex-husband, who has attracted followers in Utah, Oregon, and California.

Also a convert, Dawn joined the LDS church because of its emphasis on families and eternal marriage. "Most of the guys I'd dated before seemed too immature or superficial to fit into that dream. I wanted a man of greater spiritual substance who would somehow make my life more meaningful and secure." She had known Bryant years before in Connecticut, and they renewed their acquaintance in Utah after he married her former roommate. Though initially opposed to polygamy, Dawn, who believed her life had "become an emotional and financial struggle leading nowhere," felt pressured to join the Allred group and to become Bryant's second wife. Though not in love with Bryant at the time, she remembers that "part of the appeal of conversion is that they make you feel that you are something special and also that you really 'belong' in that group."

Other members of the Allred group pushed her to join them as well, but Bryant was the deciding factor. "People like John," Dawn says today, "are either sure they have all the answers or they're in the process of getting them. Part of his charisma was that he wasn't just some con man selling a bill of goods to gullible people. He was so single-minded in his own search for God that his enthusiasm created a sense of certainty. He believed that he was being led by God and his sincerity and intelligence convinced others. People trapped in nine-to-five routines without an overriding purpose can be easily motivated by someone who seems to have some answers."

For a time Bryant and his wives remained with the Allreds, even moving to Pinesdale, Montana, where some of the group attempted to live communally. But after staying in that depressed area through one "bitter cold winter," the Bryants returned to Salt Lake City. Within three years, Bryant was claiming a "visionary experience" in which he was told "he was the right person to fulfill a certain position in the priesthood." Dawn relates that he claimed "Joseph Smith, Brigham Young and Jesus had appeared to him" after which "he was transported to the City of Enoch where the Melchizedek and Patriarchal Priesthoods were bestowed on him." He was then "put through certain ordinances and then spent the next three days writing [them] down."

With Dawn set apart as "The High Priestess of the Last Dispensation," Bryant began bestowing his newly revealed ordinances on others. Collecting a small group of followers, which he called The Church of Christ Patriarchal, Bryant wrote prolifically while operating a Salt Lake City bookstore. Dawn joined him in highly secretive "sacred ordinances" which soon evolved into sexual rites.

Bryant would conduct a special "marriage ceremony before each time we had intercourse with someone we weren't married to." Dawn adds that there were various levels to this procedure: "one level was that you would have a marriage ceremony before each time you'd sleep together. The next level was that you'd be 'sealed' [joined or united] for a certain period of time, like a month or two. Then you were allowed to have sex with that person any time you wanted, provided John gave permission at the specific time. The third level was to be sealed into a family unit. For instance, if a single person were sealed into mine and John's family, then all the sexual rights of marriage existed within that unit as long as John approved." This applied to heterosexual and homosexual couplings.

Though the "sacred ordinances" were secret, they were not private. "John was always there whenever I was with someone else," Dawn continues, "there were usually three together and John didn't just observe. He would take part or guide us. . . . There were strong, caring feeings involved. I had a total of seven husbands over the years and had children by three of them. John considered these 'holy children' and claimed that having sex with more than one man at a time allowed the child-spirit to have a choice of more

215

than one sperm. So the spirit could choose who would be the father. It probably sounds shocking, but it seemed like we were helping each other through this intimate sharing of ourselves. After all, John made it seem like God approved and considered it a necessary part of our spiritual development."

Eventually Bryant's group included a millionaire and funds were sufficient to purchase a 360-acre ranch near Mesquite, Nevada. Initially such isolation seemed desirable, but at "The Ranch," the group soon attracted notoriety because of Bryant's expansion of the third level of ordinances— family sealings. He was sealed within many families, and "soon it was opened up so that sex, even incest, could be with almost anyone, anytime." The situation became impossible for Dawn. She became angry at what was happening and refused to take part when "things had deteriorated to a level that wasn't good or Christlike." Gradually Dawn began to feel that Bryant had lied and manipulated them to have power over them—often sexually. She described Bryant as being attracted to a polygamous lifestyle since it accommodated both his sexual and religious urges.

Once she decided to leave, Dawn feared that she would not be allowed to take her children with her. "I knew the only way I'd be able to take my children would be through a show of force." She enlisted the aid of the local police. When the officers arrived and confronted Bryant, he argued that without birth certificates Dawn could not prove the children were hers. One officer replied that "he couldn't image any woman in her right mind wanting a whole bunch of kids that weren't hers." Dawn left with the children.[6]

Moving back to Salt Lake City, Dawn began a new life. Despite economic hardships and raising six children alone, she finished her degree at the University of Utah. She then obtained a good job and is today "determined to not fall into the trap of thinking that someone else has better answers for me than I do."

When asked why she initially believed in Bryant's teachings, she responds today: "He was very charismatic, very convincing. He'd show certain scriptures and then quote something out of the journals or writings of [nineteenth-century] Mormon prophets. . . . It didn't seem like he was manipulating the situation because he appeared to believe in what he was saying. I didn't realize the mind control he was using until years later. We were so conditioned to believe in biblical and Book of Mormon-era prophets that it didn't seem unreasonable that God could work through Joseph Smith or John [Bryant]. . . . It's hard for me to look back and realize that I could make these 'leaps-of-faith' so easily. But I cared deeply about what I believed to be spiritual living that would one day lead us to heaven. And conversely I was terrified of apostasy and ending up consigned to outer darkness if I showed a lack of faith. There was an implicit view that individual doubts, skepticism, and criticisms were invalid, or possibly evil, if they differed with accepted ideas of the group. It wasn't a giant step to take from Mormon prohibitions about 'evil speaking of the Lord's anointed' to accepting John's visionary claims to priesthood leadership." Finally, Dawn remembers achieving a spiritual awareness that "we find God from within. Religion [can] help that process or hinder it, but it [isn't] necessary. All those things I'd been told were necessary to find God really weren't. That was when I felt really free of John and that whole mindset, and could leave without guilt or regret."

Certainly, the final chapter on Mormon polygamy has yet to be written. Its roots have spread far and deep, and plural marriage will probably be practiced for generations to come by Mormon splinter groups. The subject, long the focus of heated debate in the past, will continue to be a controversial one for many Mormons. Yet if Mormons and non-Mormons alike are ever to understand the heritage of one of America's most successful native religions it seems important for them to begin asking why.

NOTES

1. LDS president Spencer W. Kimball was aware that it was in 1904 and not in 1890 that the church officially intended to stop polygamy. Interviewed by Gary L. Shumway in 1972 as part of the James M. Moyle Oral History Program, LDS Archives, Kimball, in explaining Fannie Woolley's post-Manifesto marriage to George C. Parkinson, said: "It was about 1902. I don't know just when the Manifesto was made operative in all the world, including Canada and Mexico, but Aunt Fannie was married before the late President Joseph F. Smith 'locked the gate.' "

2. For discussions of these various groups, see Hilton 1965; Shields 1982; Wright 1963; Jessee 1959; and Rich 1967.

3. Simons was last seen alive on 23 April 1975 in the company of Lloyd Sullivan. According to Sullivan's later testimony, Simons was killed that evening near Price, Utah, by Eddie Marston and Mark Chynoweth. Simons's body was exhumed from its makeshift grave on 31 March 1978. Marston, the only individual brought to trial on this case, was later found innocent (Bradlee and Van Atta 1981, 181-91, 288-92).

4. This shooting occurred on 16 June 1975. White was found guilty of the murder on 14 May 1979 and given a life sentence (Bradlee and Van Atta 1981, 192-202, 328-29).

5. John Koyle's Relief Mine is on a mountainside northeast of Salem, Utah, in Utah Valley. In 1894, Mormon bishop Koyle claimed a vision in which a heavenly messenger appeared to him on three separate nights, showing him vast stores of gold coins and rich ore deep in the mountain which, it was said, would be for the purpose of "saving the Church." Hundreds of thousands of dollars were contributed by Mormons to the mining venture. Thousands of feet of shaft were sunk, and eventually Koyle was excommunicated for seeking financial support despite the advice of church leaders to abandon the efforts.

6. For a public account of the raid on Bryant's settlement, see "Metro Raids Polygamy Cult," Las Vegas Sun, 27 March 1981, 1.

BIBLIOGRAPHY

Aaron, Richard I. "Mormon Divorce and the Statute of 1852: Questions for Divorce in the 1880's." *Journal of Contemporary Law* 8 (1982): 5–45.

Alexander, Thomas G. "The Utah Federal Courts and the Areas of Conflict, 1850–1896." M.A. thesis, Utah State University, 1961.

_____. "The Church and the Law." *Dialogue: A Journal of Mormon Thought* 1 (Summer 1966): 123–28.

_____. "Charles S. Zane, Apostle of the New Era." *Utah Historical Quarterly* 34 (Fall 1966): 290–314.

_____. "Federal Authority Versus Polygamic Theocracy: James B. McKean and the Mormons, 1870–1875," *Dialogue: A Journal of Mormon Thought* 1 (Autumn 1966): 85–100.

_____. "Wilford Woodruff and the Changing Nature of Mormon Religious Experience." *Church History* 45 (March 1976): 56–69.

_____. *The Mormon People: Their Character and Traditions.* Provo, UT: Brigham Young University Press, 1980.

_____. " 'To Maintain Harmony': Adjusting to External and Internal Stress, 1890–1930." *Dialogue: A Journal of Mormon Thought* 15 (Winter 1982): 44–58.

Allen, James B. "One Man's Nauvoo: William Clayton's Experience in Mormon Illinois." *Journal of Mormon History* 6 (1979): 37–59.

_____. " 'Good Guys' vs. 'Good Guys': Rudger Clawson, John Sharp, and Civil Disobedience in Nineteenth-Century Utah." *Utah Historical Quarterly* 48 (Spring 1980): 148–174.

_____, and Glen M. Leonard. *The Story of the Latter-day Saints.* Salt Lake City: Deseret Book, 1976.

Allred, Harvey B. *A Leaf in Review.* Draper, UT: Review and Preview Publishers, 1968.

Allred, William B. Journal. Archives, Historical Department, Church of Jesus Christ of Latter-day Saints, Salt Lake City; hereafter LDS Archives.

Anderson, Jack N. "Polygamy." *Parade* section of the *Salt Lake Tribune*, 25 June 1961, 6–7.

_____. "My Boyhood Search For the Polygamists." *Parade* section of the *Salt Lake Tribune*, 19 Oct. 1980, 11–12.

Anderson, Jerry. "Polygamy in Utah." *Utah Law Review* 5 (Spring 1957): 381–89.

Anderson, Mary Audentia Smith, ed., condensed by Bertha Audentia Anderson Hulmes. *Joseph Smith III and the Restoration.* Independence, MO: Herald House, 1952.

Anderson, Max. *The Polygamy Story: Fiction and Fact.* Salt Lake City: Publishers Press, 1979.

Anderson, Nels. *Deseret Saints: The Mormon Frontier in Utah*. Chicago: University of Chicago Press, 1942.

"Annual Report of the Utah Commission, 22 August 1890." *Messages and Documents*. Washington, D.C.: Department of the Interior, 1890–91.

Anti-Polygamy Standard. Salt Lake City.

Archer, Jules. "We're Headed for Polygamy." *Stag*, Dec. 1949, 10–11.

"Arizona, the Great Love-nest Raid." *Time*, 3 Aug. 1953, 16.

Arrington, Leonard J. "The Economic Role of Pioneer Mormon Women." *Western Humanities Review* 9 (Spring 1955): 145–64.

_____. *Great Basin Kingdom: An Economic History of the Latter-day Saints, 1830–1900*. Cambridge, MA: Harvard University Press, 1958.

_____, ed. "Crusade Against Theocracy: The Reminiscences of Judge Jacob Smith Boreman of Utah, 1872–1877." *Huntington Library Quarterly* 24 (Nov. 1960): 1–45.

_____. "Women as a Force in the History of Utah." *Utah Historical Quarterly* 38 (Winter 1970): 3–6.

_____. "Blessed Damozels: Women in Mormon History." *Dialogue: A Journal of Mormon Thought* 6 (Summer 1971): 22–31.

_____. *Charles C. Rich—Mormon General and Western Frontiersman*. Provo, UT: Brigham Young University Press, 1974.

_____. *From Quaker to Latter-day Saints: Bishop Edwin D. Woolley*. Salt Lake City: Deseret Book, 1976.

_____, and Jon Haupt. "Intolerable Zion: The Image of Mormonism in Nineteenth-Century American Literature." *Western Humanities Review* 22 (Summer 1968): 243–60.

_____, Feramorz Fox, and Dean L. May. *Building the City of God: Community and Cooperation Among the Mormons*. Salt Lake City: Deseret Book, 1976.

_____, and Davis Bitton. *The Mormon Experience: A History of the Latter-day Saints*. New York: Alfred A. Knopf, 1979.

_____. *Brigham Young: American Moses*. New York: Alfred A. Knopf, 1985.

Arthur, Christopher Jones. Diary. LDS Archives.

Avery, Valeen Tippets, and Linda King Newell. "The Elect Lady: Emma Hale Smith." *The Ensign* 9 (Sept. 1979): 64–67.

_____, et al. "The Lion and The Lady: Brigham Young and Emma Smith." *Utah Historical Quarterly* 48 (Winter 1980): 81–97.

Bachman, Danel W. "A Study of the Mormon Practice of Plural Marriage Before the Death of Joseph Smith." M.A. thesis, Purdue University, 1975.

_____. "New Light on an Old Hypothesis: The Ohio Origins of the Revelation on Eternal Marriage." *Journal of Mormon History* 5 (1978): 19–32.

Badger, Carl A. Collection. Archives and Manuscripts, Special Collections, Harold B. Lee Library, Brigham Young University, Provo, UT; hereafter BYU Library.

Bailey, Paul. *Polygamy Was Better than Monotony*. Los Angeles: Western-lore Press, 1972.

Bailey, Raymond T. "Emma Hale: Wife of the Prophet Joseph Smith." M.A. thesis, Brigham Young University, 1952.

Bair, JoAnn W., and Richard L. Jensen. "Prosecution of the Mormons in Arizona Territory in the 1880's." *Arizona and the West* 19 (Spring 1977): 25–46.

Baird, Mark J., and Rhea A. [Kunz]. *Reminiscences of John W. and Lorin C. Woolley*. 4 vols. N.p.: n.d.

Ball, Larry Durwood. *The United States Marshals of New Mexico and Arizona Territories, 1846–1912*. Albuquerque: University of New Mexico Press, 1978.

Balser, Roy P., ed. *The Collected Works of Abraham Lincoln*. New Brunswick, NJ: Rutgers University Press, 1953.

Banes, Sally, Sheldon Frank, and Tem Horlwitz, eds. *Our National Pastime: 200 Years of Sex in America*. Chicago: Follett Publishing Co., 1976.

Barnes, Sisley. "The Short Creek Incident." *Liberty*, July/Aug. 1979, 7–9.

Barnwall, Myrtle C. "Polygamy Among the Mormons up to 1896." B.A. thesis, Duke University, 1933.

Barry, Richard. "The Mormon Evasion of Anti-Polygamy Laws." *Pearson's Magazine*, Oct. 1910, 443–51.

Bartch, George W. "Is Polygamy Doomed in the United States?" *Bohemia* 1 (1904): 107–16.

Barton, Helyn. "The Mormons and Polygamy." *The American Mercury* 30 (Nov. 1933): 373.

Bashore, Melvin. "Life Behind Bars: Mormon Cohabs of the 1880's." *Utah Historical Quarterly* 47 (Winter 1979): 22–41.

Baskin, Robert N. *Reminiscences of Early Utah*. Salt Lake City: Tribune Reporter Printing Co., 1914

Bates, Irene M. "William Smith, 1811–93: Problematic Patriarch." *Dialogue: A Journal of Mormon Thought* 16 (Summer 1983): 11–23.

Bates, Nephi J. Diary. LDS Archives.

Beadle, John H. "Social Experiments in Utah." *Popular Science Monthly* 9 (Aug. 1876): 479–90.

Bean, Lee L., Geraldine Mineau, and Douglas Anderson. "Residence and Religious Effects on Declining Family Size: An Historical Analysis of the Utah Population." *Review of Religious Research* 35 (Dec. 1983): 91–101.

Beck, James. Notebooks, 1859–65. LDS Archives.

[Beecher], Maureen Ursenbach, ed. "Eliza R. Snow's Nauvoo Journal." *Brigham Young University Studies* 15 (Summer 1975): 391–415.

Bennet, Dana. "Mormon Polygamy in Early Southeastern Idaho." *Idaho Yesterdays* 28 (Spring 1984): 24–30.

Bennett, Fred. *A Detective's Experience Among the Mormons*. Chicago: Laird & Lee, 1887.

Bennett, John C. *The History of the Saints; Or an Expose of Joe Smith and Mormonism*. Boston: Leland and Whiting, 1842.

Bennett, Richard E. *Mormons at the Missouri, 1846–1852*. Norman: University of Oklahoma Press, 1987.

"Bennettiana: or the Microscope with Double Diamond Lenses." *The Wasp* (Extra), 27 July 1842.

Bennion, Lowell, Jr. "The Geography of Polygamy Among the Mormons in 1880." Paper presented at 1984 Mormon History Association Meeting, Provo, UT.

_____. "The Incidence of Mormon Polygamy in 1880: 'Dixie' versus Davis Stake." *Journal of Mormon History* 11 (1984): 27–42.

Bergera, Gary J. "Men and Women of Mormondom: Lorena Eugenia Washburn Larsen." Unpublished paper, 1977.

_____. "The Church and Plural Marriage." *7th East Press*, 12 Oct. 1982.

_____. "Secretary to the Senator: Carl A. Badger and the Smoot Hearings." *Sunstone* 8 (Jan.-April 1983): 36–41.

Bernhisel, John M., to Brigham Young, 14 Aug. 1852. Andrew Love Neff Collection. Special Collections, Western Americana, J. Willard Marriott Library, University of Utah, Salt Lake City; hereafter University of Utah Library.

Bishop, Lynn L., and Steven L. Bishop. *The Truth About John W. Woolley and Lorin C. Woolley and the Council of Friends*. Draper, UT: N.p., 1972.

Bishop, Michael G. "The Celestial Family: Early Mormon Thought on Life and Death, 1830–1846." Ph.D. diss., Southern Illinois University, 1981.

Bitton, Davis. "Mormon Polygamy: A Review Article." *Journal of Mormon History* 4 (1977): 106–11.

_____. *Guide to Mormon Diaries and Autobiographies*. Provo, UT: Brigham Young University Press, 1977.

Black, Joseph Smith. Diary. LDS Archives.

Blair, Alma R. "The Reorganized Church of Jesus Christ of Latter Day Saints: Moderate Mormonism." In F. Mark McKiernan, Alma R. Blair, Paul M. Edwards, eds., *The Restoration Movement: Essays in Mormon History*. Lawrence, KS: Coronado Press, 1983.

_____. "RLDS Views of Polygamy: Some Historiographical Notes." *John Whitmer Historical Association Journal* 5 (1985): 16–28.

Blair, W. W. "The Ministry of Joseph's Sons." In *One Wife Or Many*. Lamoni, IO: Reorganized Church of Jesus Christ of Latter Day Saints, n.d.

The Braden and Kelley Debate. Saint Louis, MO: Christian Publishing, c. 1884.

Bradlee, Ben Jr., and Dale Van Atta. *Prophet of Blood—The Untold Story of Ervil LeBaron and the Lambs of God*. New York: G. P. Putnam's Sons, 1981.

_____. "The Mormon Manson." *New Times*, 6 March 1978, 38–43.

Bradley, Martha Sonntag. " 'Hide and Seek': Children on the Underground." *Utah Historical Quarterly* 51 (Spring 1983): 133–53.

Briggs, Jason W. *The Basis of Brighamite Polygamy: A Criticism upon the (so called) Revelation of July 12th, 1843*. True Latter Day Saints Tract No. 28. Lamoni, IO: Reorganized Church of Jesus Christ of Latter Day Saints, 1875.

Brigham Young Manuscript History. LDS Archives.

Brigham Young's Office Journal. LDS Archives.

Brodie, Fawn. *No Man Knows My History: The Life of Joseph Smith, the Mormon Prophet*. 2nd ed. New York: Alfred A. Knopf, 1975.

Brooks, Juanita. "A Close-up of Polygamy." *Harper's Magazine*, Feb. 1934, 299–307.

Brown, James S. *Life of a Pioneer*. Salt Lake City: George Q. Cannon & Sons, 1900.

Brown, Orson Pratt. Journal. Utah Historical Society Library.

Bucher, Jean. "Inside Addam Swapp." *Utah Holiday*, Oct. 1988, 31–47.

"Buckeye's Lamentation For Want of More Wives." *Warsaw Message*, 7 Feb. 1844.

Buerger, David John. " 'The Fullness of the Priesthood': The Second Anointing in Latter-day Theology and Practice." *Dialogue: A Journal of Mormon History* 16 (Spring 1983): 10–44.

_____. "Politics and Inspiration: An Historical Analysis of the Woodruff Manifesto." Unpublished paper, 1978.

Bullough, Vern L. "Polygamy: An Issue in the Election of 1860." *Utah Historical Quarterly* 29 (April 1961): 118-26.

Burgess-Olson, Vicky. "Family Structure and Dynamics in Early Utah Mormon Families—1847-1885." Ph.D. diss., Northwestern University, 1975.

_____. "A Feminist Studies Mormon Polygamy." *People*, 10 July 1978, 55-56, 58.

_____., ed. *Sister Saints*. Provo, UT: Brigham Young University Press, 1978.

Burton, Richard F. *The City of the Saints and Across the Rocky Mountains to California*. Fawn M. Brodie, ed. New York: Alfred A. Knopf, 1963.

Bushman, Claudia, ed. *Mormon Sisters*. Cambridge, MA: Emmeline Press, Ltd., 1976.

Bywater, James. Diary. LDS Archives.

Cahn, Robert. "The New Utah: Change Comes to Zion." *Saturday Evening Post*, 1 April 1961, 46.

Cairncross, John. *After Polygamy Was Made a Sin*. London: Routledge & Kegan Paul, 1974.

Caldwell, Gaylon Loray. "Mormon Conceptions of Individual Rights and Political Obligation." Ph.D. diss., Stanford University, 1952.

Callear, Clark E. *The Falling Away of the Latter-day Saints*. West Jordan, UT: Clark E. Callear, 1979.

Callister, E. H., to Reed Smoot, 27 March 1904. Smoot Collection. BYU Library.

Campbell, Eugene E., and Bruce L. Campbell. "Divorce Among Mormon Polygamists: Extent and Explanations." *Utah Historical Quarterly* 46 (Winter 1978): 4-23.

Cannon, Abraham H. Journal. BYU Library.

Cannon, Angus Munn. Collection. LDS Archives.

_____. "Statement of an Interview With Joseph Smith, President of the 'Reorganites,' by Elder Angus M. Cannon. Oct 12th 1905." LDS Archives.

Cannon, Charles A. "The Awesome Power of Sex: The Polemical Campaign Against Mormon Polygamy." *Pacific Historical Review* 43 (Feb. 1974): 61-82.

Cannon, Donald Q., and Lyndon W. Cook. *Far West Record—Minutes of The Church of Jesus Christ of Latter-day Saints, 1830-1844*. Salt Lake City: Deseret Book, 1983.

Cannon, Frank J., and Harvey J. Higgins. *Under the Prophet in Utah*. Boston: G. M. Clark Publishing Co., 1911.

Cannon, George Q. *A Review of the Decision of the Supreme Court in the Case of George Reynolds v. the United States*. Salt Lake City: Deseret News Printing Establishment, 1879.

_____. Letterbooks. LDS Archives.

Cannon, Kenneth II. "Beyond the Manifesto: Polygamous Cohabitation Among LDS General Authorities after 1890." *Utah Historical Quarterly* 46 (Winter 1978): 24-36.

_____. "After the Manifesto: Mormon Polygamy, 1890-1906." *Sunstone* 8 (Jan.-April 1983): 27-41.

Cannon, M. Hamlin, ed. "The Prison Diary of a Mormon Apostle." *Pacific Historical Review* 16 (Nov. 1947): 393-409.

Cannon, Mark Wilcox. "The Mormon Issue in Congress, 1872-1882, Drawing on the Experience of Territorial Delegate George Q. Cannon." Ph.D. diss., Harvard University, 1960.

Cannon, Martha Hughes. Collection. LDS Archives.

Cannon, Oa J. "History of Henry Bailey Jacobs." LDS Archives.

_____. "Short Sketch of the Life of Henry B. Jacobs, Prepared for 1977 Reunion." LDS Archives.

Carter, Kate B., comp. *Heart Throbs of the West.* 12 vols. Salt Lake City: Daughters of the Utah Pioneers, 1939-51.

_____, comp. *Treasures of Pioneer History.* 6 vols. Salt Lake City: Daughters of the Utah Pioneers, 1953.

_____, ed. *Our Pioneer Heritage.* 18 vols. Salt Lake City: Daughters of the Utah Pioneers, 1958-75.

_____. *Denominations That Base Their Beliefs on the Teachings of Joseph Smith.* 2nd ed. Salt Lake City: Daughters of the Utah Pioneers, 1969.

Casterline, Gail Farr. " 'In the Toils' or 'Onward for Zion': Images of the Mormon Woman, 1852-1890." M.A. thesis, Utah State University, 1974.

Chamberlin, Ralph. Collection. Utah State Historical Society Library, Salt Lake City.

Chandless, William. *A Visit to Salt Lake and Mormon Settlements in Utah.* London: Smith Elder, 1857.

Chase, Daryl. "Sidney Rigdon–Early Mormon." M.A. thesis, University of Chicago, 1931.

Christiansen, John P. "Contemporary Mormons' Attitudes Towards Polygymous Practices." *Marriage and Family Living* 25 (May 1963): 167-70.

Christiansen, Steven J. "The Joseph West Smith Family: Polygamy, Politics, and Persecution in Northern Arizona." *Thetean,* April 1980, 1-24.

Clark, James R., ed. *Messages of the First Presidency of the Church of Jesus Christ of Latter-day Saints.* 6 vols. Salt Lake City: Bookcraft, 1965-75.

Clayton, James L. "The Supreme Court, Polygamy and the Enforcement of Morals in Nineteenth Century America: An Analysis of Reynolds v. United States." *Dialogue: A Journal of Mormon Thought* 12 (Winter 1979): 46-61.

Clawson, Rudger. "Penitentiary Experiences." LDS Archives.

_____. Diary. University of Utah Library.

Cluff, Harvey Harris. Diary. LDS Archives.

Cohen, Yehudi. "Social Boundary Systems." *Current Anthropology* 10 (Feb. 1959): 110-121.

Cocheron, Augusta Joyce. *Representative Women of Deseret: A Book of Biographical Sketches.* Salt Lake City: J. C. Graham & Co., 1884.

Codman, John. *The Round Trip.* New York: G. P. Putnam's Sons, 1879.

Collier, Fred C. *The Church of the Firstborn: Part 1.* West Jordan, UT: Mormon Underground Press, 1977.

_____. *Unpublished Revelations of the Prophets and Presidents of the Church of Jesus Christ of Latter-day Saints.* Salt Lake City: Collier's Publishing Co., 1979.

_____. "Re-Examining the Lorin Woolley Story." *Doctrine of the Priesthood* 1 (Feb. 1981): 1-17.

Complainants Abstract of Pleading and Evidence In the Circuit Court of the United States, Western District of Missouri, Western Division at Kansas City. The Reorganized Church of Jesus Christ of Latter Day Saints, Complainant, vs. The Church of Christ at Independence, Missouri. Lamoni, IO: Herald Publishing House and Bindery, 1893.

Comstock, Sarah. "The Mormon Woman, Polygamy as it Works Out." *Collier's* 44 (6 Nov. 1909): 16–17.

Conference Reports of the Church of Jesus Christ of Latter-day Saints. Salt Lake City, Deseret Press, 1890.

Congressional Globe, 36th Cong., 1st sess., 1860.

_____, 37th Cong., 2nd sess., 1862.

_____, 41st Cong., 2nd sess., 17 Feb. 1870.

_____, 43rd Cong., 1st sess., 2 June 1874.

Congressional Record, 49th Cong., 2nd sess., 1886–87, pp. 25–26, 580–96.

Cook, Lyndon W. *The Revelations of the Prophet Joseph Smith.* Provo, UT: Seventy's Mission Bookstore, 1981.

_____. "William Law, Nauvoo Dissenter." *Brigham Young University Studies* 22 (Winter 1982): 47–72.

Cooks, Mrs. S. A. *Theatrical and Social Affairs in Utah.* Salt Lake City: N.p., 1884.

Coulter, Forrest Benjamin. "Elimination of Polygamy Among the Mormons." M.A. thesis, University of Colorado, 1939.

Cowdery, Oliver, to Warren Cowdery, 21 Jan. 1838. Huntington Library, San Marino, CA; copy in LDS Archives.

_____. "To Daniel and Phebe Jackson." 24 July 1846. Library/Archives, Reorganized Church of Jesus Christ of Latter Day Saints, Independence, MO; hereafter RLDS Archives.

_____. Sketchbook. LDS Archives.

Cowley, Matthias F. *Wilford Woodruff.* Salt Lake City: G. Q. Cannon and Sons, 1909.

Curtis, George T., to Franklin S. Richards, 23 Jan. 1887. Curtis Collection. LDS Archives.

D&C. Doctrine and Covenants of the Church of Jesus Christ of Latter-day Saints. Salt Lake City: Church of Jesus Christ of Latter-day Saints, 1982.

Davis, David Brion. "Some Themes of Counter-Subversion: An Analysis of Anti-Masonic, Anti-Catholic, and Anti-Mormon Literature." *Mississippi Valley Historical Review* 47 (Sept. 1960): 205–24.

Davis, Ray Jay. "The Polygamous Prelude." *American Journal of Legal History* 6 (Jan. 1962): 1–27.

_____. "Plural Marriage and Religious Freedom: The Impact of Reynolds v. United States." *Arizona Law Review* 15 (1973): 287–306.

Day, Robert B. "Eli Azariah Day: Pioneer School Teacher and 'Prisoner for Conscience Sake.' " *Utah Historical Quarterly* 35 (Fall 1967): 322–41.

DePillis, Mario S. "The Development of Mormon Communitarianism 1826–1846." Ph.D. diss., Yale University, 1961.

Derr, Jill Mulvay. "Women's Place in Brigham Young's World." *Brigham Young University Studies* 18 (Spring 1978): 377–95.

"The Diary of Reddick N. Allred." In Carter 1953, 5:297–372.

Dix, Fae Decker. "Unwilling Martyr: The Death of Young Ed Dalton." *Utah Historical Quarterly* 41 (Spring 1973): 162–77.

Dixon, William Hepworth. *Spiritual Wives.* 2 vols. London: Hurst and Blackett, 1868.

"Doings of Deputies, A Raid on the Little Town of Parowan, Several Ladies Arrested." *Salt Lake Herald*, 19 Dec. 1885.

Doty, Madeleine Zabriskie. "Mormon Women and What They Think of Polygamy." *The American Magazine* 66 (May-Oct. 1908): 41-47.

Draper, Maurice L. *Marriage in the Restoration: A Brief Historical Doctrinal Review*. Independence, MO: Herald Publishing House, 1968.

Driggs, Ken. "The Prosecutions Begin: Defining Cohabitation in 1885." *Dialogue: A Journal of Mormon Thought* 21 (Spring 1988): 109-25.

Dyer, Robert G. "The Evolution of Serial and Judicial Attitudes Towards Polygamy." *The Utah Bar Journal* 5 (Spring 1977): 35-45.

Eckersley, Joseph. Journal. LDS Archives.

Edmunds, George F. "Political Aspects of Mormonism." *Harper's Magazine* 64 (Jan. 1882): 285-86.

Edwards, Paul M. "William B. Smith: The Persistent Pretender." *Dialogue: A Journal of Mormon Thought* 18 (Summer 1985): 128-39.

Ehat, Andrew F. "Joseph Smith's Introduction of Temple Ordinances and The Mormon Succession Question." M.A. thesis, Brigham Young University, 1982.

_____, and Lyndon Cook. *The Words of Joseph Smith*. Provo, UT: Religious Studies Center, Brigham Young University, 1980.

Elder's Journal of the Church of Jesus Christ of Latter Day Saints. Far West, MO: N.p., July 1838.

"Elizabeth Ashby Snow Ivins Statement." Anthony W. Ivins Collection. Utah State Historical Society Library.

Ellis, John B. *Free Love and its Votaries*. N.p., 1870. Cited in Stanley S. Ivins Collection, Notebook 2:22.

Ellsworth, S. George. "Utah's Struggle for Statehood." *Utah Historical Quarterly* 31 (Winter 1963): 60-69.

_____. *Dear Ellen—Two Mormon Women and Their Letters*. Salt Lake City: Tanner Trust Fund/University of Utah Library, 1974.

Embry, Jesse. "Effects of Polygamy on Mormon Women." *Frontier—A Journal of Women Studies* 7 (1984): 56-61.

_____. "Exiles for the Principle: LDS Polygamy in Canada." *Dialogue: A Journal of Mormon Thought* 18 (Fall 1985): 108-16.

_____. "Master or Slave: The Economic Role of Mormon Polygamous Wives." Undated working paper published by the Southwest Institute for Research on Women.

_____. "Charles Edmund Richardson Families: A Case Study of Mormon Polygamy." Unpublished paper.

_____. "The Role of Women in LDS Polygamous Families—Blanding: A Case Study." Unpublished paper.

_____. "Sisters or Competitors: The Role of Women in a Polygamous Family—A Case Study." Unpublished paper.

_____. *Mormon Polygamous Families: Life in the Principle*. Salt Lake City: University of Utah Press, 1987.

_____, and Martha S. Bradley. "Mothers and Daughters in Polygamy." *Dialogue: A Journal of Mormon Thought* 18 (Fall 1985): 99-107.

"The End of Polygamy." *California Illustrated Magazine* 3 (April 1893): 662.

Ericksen, Ephraim Edward. *The Psychological and Ethical Aspects of Mormon Group Life*. Chicago: University of Chicago Press, 1922.

Evans, Richard C. *Was Joseph Smith a Polygamist?* Toronto: R. C. Evans, 1919.

"Far West Record." LDS Archives.

Faulring, Scott H., ed. *An American Prophet's Record: The Diaries and Journals of Joseph Smith.* Salt Lake City: Signature Books in association with Smith Research Associates, 1987.

Faux, Steven. "Genetic Self-Interest & Mormon Polygyny: A Sociobiological Perspective of the Doctrinal Development of Polygyny." *Sunstone* 8 (July/Aug. 1983): 37–40.

Ferris, Benjamin G. *Utah and the Mormons.* 1856. New York: A.M.S. Press, 1971.

Fife, Austin, and Alta Fife. *Saints of Sage and Saddle: Folklore Among the Mormons.* Bloomington: Indiana University, 1956.

Firmage, Mary. "Recollections of Zina D. H. Young." LDS Archives.

First Presidency (Smith, Winder, Lund) to George Teasdale, 2 Nov. 1905. Joseph F. Smith Collection. LDS Archives.

Fisher, Josephine L., to Andrew Jenson, 24 Feb. 1915. Jenson Collection. LDS Archives.

Fitzpatrick, Doyle. *The King Strang Story.* Lansing, MI: National Heritage, 1970.

Flanders, Robert Bruce. "The Mormons Who Did Not Go West: A Study of the Emergence of the Reorganized Church of Jesus Christ of Latter Day Saints." M.A. thesis, University of Wisconsin, 1954.

_____. *Nauvoo: Kingdom on the Mississippi.* Urbana: University of Illinois Press, 1965.

Ford, Thomas. *History of Illinois, From its Commencement as a State in 1818 to 1847.* Chicago: S. G. Griggs, 1854.

Forman, William. Journal. Utah State Historical Society Library.

Foster, Lawrence. "A Little-known Defense of Polygamy from the Mormon Press in 1842." *Dialogue: A Journal of Mormon Thought* 9 (Winter 1974): 21–34.

_____. *Religion and Sexuality: Three American Communal Experiments of the Nineteenth Century.* New York/Oxford: Oxford University Press, 1981.

_____. "Polygamy and the Frontier: Mormon Women in Early Utah." *Utah Historical Quarterly* 50 (Summer 1982): 268–89.

Foulger, Herbert J. Diary. LDS Archives.

Froiseth, Jennie Anderson, ed. *The Women of Mormonism.* Detroit: C. G. G. Paine, 1884.

Fulton, Gilbert A., comp. *The Most Holy Principle.* 4 vols. Murray, UT: Gems Publishing Co., 1970–75.

Furniss, Norman F. *The Mormon Conflict, 1859–1859.* New Haven: Yale University, 1960.

Gallichan, Walter Matthew. *Women Under Polygamy.* New York: Dodd, Mead and Co., 1915.

Gates, Susa Young, and Leah D. Widtsoe. *Women of the "Mormon" Church.* Salt Lake City: Deseret News Press, 1926.

Gaylor, George R. "The 'Expositor' Affair, Prelude to the Downfall of Joseph Smith." *Northwest Missouri State College Studies* 25 (Feb. 1961): 3–15.

Gibbs, George F., to Reed Smoot, 21 April 1911. Smoot Collection. LDS Archives.

_____, to George Teasdale, 20 Aug. and 6 Jan. 1904. LDS Archives.

Giles, Alfred E. *Marriage, Monogamy, and Polygamy on the Basis of Divine Law, of Natural Law, and of Constitutional Law.* Boston: James Campbell, 1882.

Godbe, William S. *Polygamy: Its Solution in Utah—A Question of the Hour*. Salt Lake City: Salt Lake Tribune, 1871.

Godfrey, G. L. "Political History of Polygamy and Utah." *Our Day* 1 (1888): 192-216.

Godfrey, Kenneth W. "Causes of Mormon Non-Mormon Conflict in Hancock County, Illinois, 1839-1846." Ph.D. diss., Brigham Young University, 1967.

_____. "Joseph Smith and the Masons." *Journal of the Illinois State Historical Society* 64 (Spring 1971): 66-78.

_____. "The Coming of the Manifesto." *Dialogue: A Journal of Mormon Thought* 5 (Autumn 1975): 11-25.

_____, Audrey M. Godfrey, and Jill Mulvay Derr. *Women's Voices—An Untold History of the Latter-day Saints, 1830-1900*. Salt Lake City: Deseret Book, 1982.

Goldberg, B. Z. *The Sacred Fire: A History of Sex in Ritual, Religion and Human Behavior*. Secaucus, NJ: Citadel Press, 1974.

Graff, Leo William. "The Senatorial Career of Fred T. Dubois of Idaho, 1890-1907." Ph.D. diss., University of Idaho, 1968.

Grant, Heber J., to Katherine H. Allred, 15 Nov. 1935. Grant Letterbooks. LDS Archives.

Grant, Jedediah M., to Brigham Young, 7 Sept. 1844. Young Collection. LDS Archives.

Gregory, Thomas J. "Sidney Rigdon: Post Nauvoo." *Brigham Young University Studies* 21 (Winter 1981): 51-67.

Groves, Ernest Rutherford. *The American Family*. Chicago: J. B. Lippincott Co., 1934.

Grow, Stewart L. "A Study of the Utah Commission, 1882-1896." Ph.D. diss., University of Utah, 1954.

Gunnison, John W. *The Mormons, or Latter-Day Saints, in the Valley of the Great Salt Lake*. Philadelphia: Lippincott, Grambo, 1852.

HC. Smith, Joseph, et al. *History of the Church of Jesus Christ of Latter-day Saints*. 6 vols. Introduction and Notes by B. H. Roberts. Salt Lake City: Deseret Book, 1978.

Haldeman, John R. *Origin of Polygamy Among Latter-Day Saints*. Independence, MO: Church of Christ Publishing House, 1904.

Hall, William. *The Abominations of Mormonism Exposed*. Cincinnati: I. Hart & Co., 1852.

Hansen, Klaus J. "The Making of King Strang: A Re-Examination." *Michigan History* 46 (Sept. 1962): 201-19.

Hardin, J. G., to W. B. Warren. Cited in Ellen Hardin Walworth. "The Mormon Theocracy in Illinois, 1840-45." *Journal of Illinois State Historical Society* 1 (1907): 10-20.

Hardy, B. Carmon. "The Mormon Colonies of Northern Mexico: A History 1885-1912." Ph.D. diss., Wayne State University, 1963.

_____. "The American Siberia: Mormon Prisoners in Detroit in the 1880's." *Michigan History* 50 (Sept. 1966): 197-210.

Hardy, John. *History of the Trial of Elder John Hardy, Before the Church of Latter Day Saints in Boston, for Slander, in Saying that G. J. Adams, S. Brannan and William Smith Were Licentious Characters*. Boston: Conway, 1844.

Hardy, Mary P. *Through Cities and Prairie Lands: Sketches of an American Tour*. New York: R. Worthington, 1881.

Hartwig, Chester Wendall. "Mormon Polygamy: A Study of Change in a Group's Value System." M.A. thesis, University of Wisconsin, 1950.

Hatch, Nelle S. *Colonia Juarez: An Intimate Account of a Mormon Village*. Salt Lake City: Deseret Book, 1954.

Hatch, Robert Duane. "The Pratt-Newman Debate." M.A. thesis, Brigham Young University, 1960.

Hatfield, Joseph T. "Congress, Polygamy, and the Mormons." M.A. thesis, Ohio University, 1954.

Haynes, Alan Elmo. "Brigham Henry Roberts and Reed Smoot: Significant Events in the Development of American Pluralism." M.A. thesis, Catholic University, 1966.

Hayward, Barbara. "Utah's Anti-Polygamy Society, 1878-1884." M.A. thesis, Brigham Young University, 1980.

Heckel, Willard C. "Mormonism and the Federal Government in Utah 1850-1896." M.A. thesis, Columbia University, 1936.

Hendrick, Burton J. "The Mormon Revival of Polygamy." *McClure's Magazine* 36 (Feb. 1911): 449-64.

Hill, Donna. *Joseph Smith: The First Mormon.* Garden City, New York: Doubleday, 1977.

Hill, James B. "History of the Utah State Prison, 1850-1952." M.A. thesis, Brigham Young University, 1952.

Hill, Marvin S. "The Role of Christian Primitivism in the Origin and Development of the Mormon Kingdom, 1830-1844." Ph.D. diss., University of Chicago, 1968.

_____. "Secular or Sectarian History? A Critique of *No Man Knows My History.*" *Church History* 43 (March 1974): 79-96.

_____. "Quest for Refuge: An Hypothesis as to the Social Origins and Nature of the Mormon Political Kingdom." *Journal of Mormon History* 2 (1975): 3-20.

Hillman, Eugene. *Polygamy Reconsidered; African Plural Marriage and the Christian Churches.* New York: Orbis, 1975.

Hilton, Jerald A. "Polygamy in Utah and Surrounding Area Since the Manifesto of 1890." M.A. thesis, Brigham Young University, 1965.

Hickman, Josiah. "A Critical Study of the Monogamic and Polygamic Offspring of the Mormon People." M.A. thesis, Columbia University, 1907.

Hinsdale, B. "The State of Utah and Polygamy." *The Independent* 46 (1899): 1368-69.

Hollister, Col. O. H. Interview with John Taylor, 13 June 1879. Taylor Collection. LDS Archives.

Holm, Francis W., Sr. *The Mormon Churches—A Comparison From Within.* Kansas City: Midwest Press, 1970.

Holsinger, M. Paul. "J. C. Burrows and the Fight Against Mormonism, 1903-1907." *Michigan History* 52 (Fall 1968): 181-95.

_____. "Philander C. Knox and the Crusade Against Mormonism, 1904-1907." *Western Pennsylvania History Magazine* 57 (Jan. 1969): 47-56.

_____. "For God and the American Home: The Attempt to Unseat Senator Reed Smoot, 1903-1907." *Pacific Northwest Quarterly* 60 (July 1969): 154-60.

_____. "Senator George Graham Vest and the 'Menace' of Mormonism, 1882-1887." *Missouri Historical Review* 65 (Oct. 1970): 23-36.

Homer, Michael W. "The Judiciary and the Common Law in Utah Territory, 1850-61." *Dialogue: A Journal of Mormon Thought* 21 (Spring 1988): 97-108.

Homespun (pseud.). "Lydia Knight's History." *The First Book of Noble Women's Stories.* Salt Lake City: Juvenile Instructor's Office, 1893.

House Reports, 39th Cong. 2nd sess. 1867.

Howard, Richard P. "The Reorganized Church in Illinois, 1852–1882: Search for Identity." *Dialogue: A Journal of Mormon Thought* 5 (Spring 1970): 63–75.

_____. "Themes in Latter Day Saint History." *John Whitmer Historical Assocation Journal* 2 (1982): 22–29.

_____. "The Changing RLDS Response to Mormon Polygamy: A Preliminary Analysis." *John Whitmer Historical Association Journal* 3 (1983): 14–29.

_____. "Filtered Facts (concluded)." *Saints' Herald* 131 (1 June 1984): 24.

Hughes, A. "Cohab Canyon." *Deseret Magazine*, June 1963, 27–29.

Hulett, James Edward, Jr. "The Sociological and Social Psychological Aspects of the Mormon Polygamous Family." Ph.D. diss., University of Wisconsin, 1939.

_____. "Social Role and Personal Security in Polygamy." *American Journal of Sociology* 5 (Jan. 1940): 538–49.

Huntington, Oliver. "History of the Life of Oliver Huntington Also His Travels and Troubles—Written by Himself." Unpublished manuscript. Utah State Historical Society Library.

_____, to Zina D. H. Jacobs Young, 27 Aug. 1847. Ora J. Cannon Collection. LDS Archives.

Hutchins, Robert D. "Joseph Smith III: Moderate Mormon." M.A. thesis, Brigham Young University, 1977.

Hyde, Orson. Journal. Utah Historical Society Library.

_____. *Speech of Elder Orson Hyde, Delivered Before the High Priest's Quorum, in Nauvoo, April 27th, 1845, Upon the Course and Conduct of Mr. Sidney Rigdon, and Upon the Merits of His Claims to the Presidency of the Church of Jesus Christ of Latter-day Saints*. Liverpool: James and Woodburn, 1845.

Illinois. Laws and Statutes of the State of Illinois. *Revised Laws*. Vandalia, IL: Greiner and Sherman, 1833. *Public and General Statute Laws*. Chicago: Scammon, 1839. *Revised Statues*. Springfield: Braymon, 1845.

Illinois Statutes, 1844–45, Division XI, Section 121.

Ingram, Fern Cluff. Oral History. Interview by Leonard R. Grover, 1980. LDS Polygamy Oral History Project, Charles Redd Center for Western Studies, BYU Library.

"The Inner Facts of Social Life in Utah." Interview of Mrs. Hubert Howe Bancroft with Mrs. F. D. Richards. Hubert Howe Bancroft Collection, Bancroft Library, University of California, Berkeley.

Ivins, Anthony W. Collection. Utah State Historical Society Library.

_____, to H. Grant Ivins, 7 March 1911. Anthony W. Ivins Collection.

Ivins, H. Grant. "Polygamy in Mexico as Practiced by the Mormon Church, 1895–1905." Anthony W. Ivins Collection.

Ivins, Stanley S. Collection. Utah State Historical Society Library.

_____. "Notes on Mormon Polygamy." *Western Humanities Review* 10 (Summer 1956): 229–39.

JD. *Journal of Discourses*. 26 vols. London: Latter-day Saint's Book Depot, 1854–86.

JH. Journal History. A multi-volume daily history of the Mormon church compiled by official church historians. LDS Archives.

Jackson, Joseph H. *A Narrative of the Adventures and Experiences of Joseph H. Jackson in Nauvoo: Disclosing the Depths of Mormon Villany Practiced in Nauvoo*. Warsaw, IL: N.p., 1844.

Jacob, Udney Hay. *An Extract, From a Manuscript Entitled The Peace Maker, or the Doctrines of the Millennium: Being a Treatise on Religion and Jurisprudence. Or a New System of Religion and Politicks.* Nauvoo, IL: J. Smith, 1842.

_____, to Oliver Granger, 3 March 1840. LDS Archives.

_____, to Martin Van Buren, 21 March 1840. Illinois State Historical Society.

Jacobs, Henry B. Collection. LDS Archives.

Jecks, E. N. *The History and Philosophy of Marriage: or Polygamy and Monogamy Compared.* Boston: James Campbell, 1869.

Jensen, Kimberly James. "Between Two Fires: Women on the 'Underground' of Mormon Polygamy." M.A. thesis, Brigham Young University, 1981.

Jenson, Andrew, comp. *The Historical Record: A Monthly Periodical Devoted Exclusively to Historical, Biographical, Chronological, and Statistical Matters.* 9 vols. Salt Lake City: Andrew Jenson, 1887.

_____. *LDS Biographical Encyclopedia.* 4 vols. Salt Lake City: Andrew Jenson Historical Co., 1901-36.

Jessee, Dean C. "A Comparative Study and Evaluation of Latter-day Saint and 'Fundamentalist' Views Pertaining to the Practice of Plural Marriage." M.A. thesis, Brigham Young University, 1959.

_____. "Brigham Young's Family: The Wilderness Years." *Brigham Young University Studies* 19 (Summer 1979): 474-500.

_____, comp. and ed. *The Personal Writings of Joseph Smith.* Salt Lake City: Deseret Book, 1984.

John, David. Journal. BYU Library.

Johnson, Annie Richardson. *Heartbeats of Colonia Diaz.* Mesa, AZ: N.p., 1972.

Jones, John Lee. Diary. LDS Archives.

Jorgensen, Victor W., and B. Carmon Hardy. "The Taylor-Cowley Affair and the Watershed of Mormon History." *Utah Historical Quarterly* 48 (Winter 1980): 4-36.

Kassel, Victor. "Polygyny After 60." *Geriatrics* 21 (April 1966): 214-18.

Keller, Karl, ed. " 'I Never Knew A Time When I Did Not Know Joseph Smith.' " *Dialogue: A Journal of Mormon Thought* 1 (Winter 1966): 14-42.

Kelly, William. *Across the Rocky Mountains.* London: Simms and McIntyre, 1852.

Kempe, Christopher I. *A Voice From Prison.* Salt Lake City: Deseret News, 1895.

Kephart, William M. *The Family, Society and the Individual.* Boston: Houghton Mifflin, 1961.

_____. *Extraordinary Groups: The Sociology of Unconventional Lifestyles.* New York: St. Martin's Press, 1976.

Kenney, Scott G., ed. *Wilford Woodruff's Journal, Typescript.* 9 vols. Midvale, UT: Signature Books, 1983-85.

Kimball, Abraham Alonzo. Diary. LDS Archives.

Kimball, Lucy Walker. "Recollections." LDS Archives.

Kimball, Stanley B. "Heber C. Kimball and Family: The Nauvoo Years." *Brigham Young University Studies* 15 (Summer 1975): 447-79.

_____. *Heber C. Kimball, Mormon Patriarch and Pioneer.* Urbana: University of Illinois Press, 1981.

_____, ed. *On the Potter's Wheel: The Diaries of Heber C. Kimball.* Salt Lake City: Signature Books in association with Smith Research Associates, 1987.

Kingsbury, Joseph. "History of Joseph Kingsbury Written by His Own Hand." Utah State Historical Society Library.

Kingston, Charles W. *An Interesting Letter to Judge Roberts*. Idaho Falls, ID: N.p., 1932.

Kirby, Thomas Wright. Diary. LDS Archives.

Kirkham, Francis W. Diary. University Archives, BYU Library.

Kirkham, James. Diary. LDS Archives.

Knapp, George L. "The Crusade Against Mormonism." *The Christian Statesman* 52 (March 1918): 123–35.

Kraut, Ogden. *Polygamy in the Bible*. Salt Lake City: Kraut's Pioneer Press, 1983.

Kunz, Rhea Allred. *Voices of Women Approbating Celestial or Plural Marriage*. Draper, UT: Review and Preview Publishers, n.d.

Lamar, Howard R. "Political Patterns in New Mexico and Utah Territories, 1850–1900." *Utah Historical Quarterly* 28 (Oct. 1960): 363–87.

_____. "Statehood for Utah: A Different Path." *Utah Historical Quarterly* 39 (Fall 1971): 307–27.

Larsen, Herbert R. " 'Familism' in Mormon Social Structure." Ph.D. diss., University of Utah, 1954.

Larson, Andrew Karl. *Erastus Snow: The Life of a Missionary and Pioneer for the Early Mormon Church*. Salt Lake City: University of Utah Press, 1971.

_____, and Katharine Miles Larson, eds. *Diary of Charles Lowell Walker*. 2 vols. Logan, UT: Utah State University Press, 1980.

Larson, Gustive O. "An Industrial Home for Polygamous Wives." *Utah Historical Quarterly* 38 (Summer 1970): 263–75.

_____. *The "Americanization" of Utah for Statehood*. San Marino, CA: The Huntington Library, 1971.

_____. "The Mormon Reformation." *Utah Historical Quarterly* 26 (Jan. 1958): 46–63.

"Last Testimony of Sister Emma." *Saints' Herald* 26 (1 Oct. 1879): 289–90.

Launius, Roger D. "Methods and Motives: Joseph Smith III's Opposition to Polygamy, 1860–90." *Dialogue: A Journal of Mormon Thought* 20 (Winter 1987): 105–20.

Law, Richard. "An Interesting Testimony." *The Improvement Era*, May 1903, 507–10.

Law, William, to Isaac Hill, 20 July 1844. William Law Collection. LDS Archives.

LeBaron, Verlan M. *The LeBaron Story*. Lubbock, TX: Keele, 1981.

Lee, John D. *Mormonism Unveiled, or, The Life and Confessions of the Late Mormon Bishop, John D. Lee*. Ed. W. W. Bishop. St. Louis: Byron, Brand, 1877.

Lee, Lawrence B. "The Mormons Come to Canada, 1887–1902." *Pacific Northwest Quarterly* 59 (Jan. 1968): 11–22.

Lee, Mark S. "Legislating Morality: Reynolds vs. United States." *Sunstone* 10 (April 1985): 8–12.

Lewis, Alfred Henry. "The Great Mormon Conspiracy." *Collier's*, 26 March 1904, 11–12.

Lewis, Catherine. *Narrative of Some of the Proceedings of the Mormons*. Lynn, MA: N.p., 1848.

Lightner, Mary E. Collection. LDS Archives.

_____, to Emmeline B. Wells, 21 Nov. 1880. LDS Archives.

_____, to John R. Young, 25 Jan. 1892. George A. Smith Collection. University of Utah Library.

_____. 8 Feb. 1902 Statement. Lightner Collection.

Lieber, Constance L. " 'The Goose Hangs High': Excerpts from the Letters of Martha Hughes Cannon." *Utah Historical Quarterly* 48 (Winter 1980): 37–48.

Linford, Orma. "The Mormons and the Law: The Polygamy Cases." Ph.D. diss., University of Wisconsin, 1964.

_____. "The Mormons and the Law: The Polygamy Cases." *Utah Law Review* 9 (Winter 1964/Summer 1965): 308–70, 543–91.

Logue, Larry. "Time of Marriage: Monogamy and Polygamy in a Utah Town." *Journal of Mormon History* 11 (1984): 3–26.

"The Lonely Men of Shortcreek." *Life*, 14 Sept. 1953, 35–39.

Lowe, Richard J. "Fred T. Dubois, Foe of the Mormons: A Story of the Role of Fred T. Dubois in the Senate Investigation of the Hon. Reed Smoot and the Mormon Church, 1903–1907." M.A. thesis, Brigham Young University, 1960.

Lund, Anthon H. Journal. LDS Archives.

Lyman, Albert R. *Francis Marion Lyman: Apostle*. Delta, UT: Melvin A. Lyman, 1958.

Lyman, Leo Edward. "Isaac Trumbo and the Politics of Utah Statehood." *Utah Historical Quarterly* 41 (Spring 1973): 128–49.

_____. "A Mormon Transition in Idaho Politics." *Idaho Yesterdays* 20 (Winter 1977): 2–11.

_____. "The Mormon Quest for Utah Statehood." Ph.D. diss., University of California at Riverside, 1981.

_____. "The Alienation of an Apostle From His Quorum: The Moses Thatcher Case." *Dialogue: A Journal of Mormon Thought* 18 (Summer 1985): 67–91.

Lyman, Francis M. Letterbooks. LDS Archives.

Lyon, T. Edgar. "Orson Pratt: Early Mormon Leader." M.A. thesis, University of Chicago, 1932.

_____. "Religious Activities and Development in Utah, 1847–1910." *Utah Historical Quarterly* 35 (Fall 1967): 292–306.

Lythgoe, Dennis L. "The Changing Image of Mormonism in Periodical Literature." Ph.D. diss., University of Utah, 1969.

MS. *Latter-day Saints' Millennial Star*. Liverpool, 1841–.

Ms History. Manuscript History of the Church. LDS Archives.

Madsen, Carol Cornwall. "Remember the Women of Zion: A Study of the Editorial Content of the Woman's Exponent, A Woman's Journal." M.A. thesis, University of Utah, 1977.

_____. "Emmeline B. Wells: A Voice for Mormon Women." *John Whitmer Historical Association Journal* 2 (1982): 11–21.

Madsen, Truman. *Defender of the Faith: The B. H. Roberts Story*. Salt Lake City: Bookcraft, 1980.

Magrath, C. Peter. "Chief Justice Waite and the 'Twin Relic': Reynolds v. United States." *Vanderbilt Law Review* 18 (1965): 507–43.

"Manners and Morals—the More the Merrier." *Time*, 14 Jan. 1952, 22.

Marquardt, H. Michael. *The Strange Marriages of Sarah Ann Whitney to Joseph Smith the Mormon Prophet, Joseph C. Kingsbury, and Heber C. Kimball*. Salt Lake City: Modern Microfilm, 1973; rev. ed., Salt Lake City: Utah Lighthouse Ministry, 1982.

Marquis, Kathleen. "Diamond Cut Diamond: Mormon Women and the Cult of Domesticity in the Nineteenth Century." *University of Michigan Papers in Women's Studies* 2 (1974): 105–23.

Marsden, William. Collection. LDS Archives.

Marsh, Eudocia Baldwin. "Mormons in Hancock County: A Reminiscence." Douglas L. Wilson and Rodney D. Davis, eds. *Journal of the Illinois State Historical Society* 64 (Spring 1971): 22–65.

McGee, I[ncrease], and Maria Van Deusen McGee. *A Dialogue Between Adam and Eve, the Lord and the Devil, Called The Endowment.* Albany, NY: C. Killmer, 1847.

McKiernan, F. Mark. *The Voice of One Crying in the Wilderness: Sidney Rigdon, Religious Reformer, 1793–1876.* Lawrence, KS: Coronado Press, 1971.

McLellin, William, to Joseph Smith III, 10 Jan. 1861 and 8 July-Sept. 1872. RLDS Archives.

Mehr, Kahlile. "Women's Response to Plural Marriage." *Dialogue: A Journal of Mormon Thought* 18 (Fall 1985): 84–97.

_____. "The Trial of the French Mission." *Dialogue: A Journal of Mormon Thought* 21 (Summer 1988): 27–45.

"Memoir of Romania B. Pratt, M.D." LDS Archives.

"Memoirs of Matthias the Prophet Prepared for the *New York Sun.*" Stanley S. Ivins Collection.

"Memorial Adopted by Citizens of Salt Lake City, Utah Territory." Present to 41st Congress, Second session (Senate), Misc. document No. 112.

Merrill, Melissa (pseud.). *Polygamist's Wife.* Salt Lake City: Olympus Publishing Co., 1975.

Merrill, Milton R. "Reed Smoot: Apostle in Politics." Ph.D. diss., Columbia University, 1951.

Merson, Ben. "Husbands With More than One Wife." *Ladies Home Journal* 84 (June 1967): 78–111.

Meservy, Joseph R. "A History of Federal Legislation Against Mormon Polygamy and Certain United States Supreme Court Decisions Supporting Such Legislation." M.A. thesis, Brigham Young University, 1947.

Metcalf, A. *Ten Years Before the Mast.* [Malad City, ID: N.p., 1888.]

Miller, Reuben. *James J. Strang, Weighed in the Balance and Found Wanting.* Burlington, WI: N.p., 1849.

Mindel, Charles H., and Robert W. Habenstein, eds. *Ethic Families in America: Patterns and Variations.* New York: Elsevier, 1976.

Minutes of the High Council of the Church of Jesus Christ of Latter-day Saints, Nauvoo Illinois. LDS Archives.

Minutes of the Quorum of the Twelve, 20 Jan. 1843. Brigham Young Collection.

Minutes of the Quorum of the Twelve, 22 Feb. and 10 May 1911. LDS Archives.

Morgan, Dale L. "A Bibliography of the Church of Jesus Christ of Latter Day Saints [Strangite]." *Western Humanities Review* 5 (Winter 1950–51): 42–114.

_____, to Stanley S. Ivins, 27 May 1951. Ivins Collection.

_____. *Saturday Review*, 31 Aug. 1954, 14.

"Mormonism and Polygamy." *The Literary Digest*, 12 March 1904, 359–60.

"Mormonism on the Rack." *The American Monthly*, April 1904, 388–400.

"Mormons and Polygamy." *Time*, 29 April 1940, 20.

"The Mormons in Nauvoo—Three Letters from William Law on Mormonism," *Salt Lake Tribune*, 3 July 1887.

Morris, J. H. C. "The Recognition of Polygamous Marriages in English Law." *Harvard Law Review* 66 (April 1953): 961–1012.

Mouritsen, Glen. "The Office of Associate President of the Church of Jesus Christ of Latter-day Saints." M.A. thesis, Brigham Young University, 1972.

Mulder, William. "Prisoners for Conscience Sake." In Thomas E. Cheney, ed. *Lore of Faith and Folly*. Salt Lake City: University of Utah Press, 1971.

_____, and A. Russell Mortensen, eds. *Among the Mormons—Historic Accounts by Contemporary Observers*. New York: Alfred A. Knopf, 1958.

"Multiple Wives: Arizona Prisoner Defends His Conduct on Religious Grounds." *Literary Digest*, 1 Aug. 1936, 9–10.

Muney, Robert Lee, ed. *Sex and Marriage in Utopian Communities*. Bloomington: Indiana University Press, 1973.

Musser, Joseph W. Journal. LDS Archives.

_____, ed. *The New and Everlasting Covenant of Marriage an Interpretation of Celestial Marriage, Plural Marriage, Polygamy*. Salt Lake City: Truth Publishing Co., 1934.

_____, ed. *Truth*. 21 vols. Salt Lake City: Truth Publishing Co., 1935–56.

_____. *An Open Letter to Heber J. Grant, April 15, 1935*. Salt Lake City: Truth Publishing Co., 1935.

_____. *Celestial or Plural Marriage: A Digest of the Mormon Marriage System as Established by God Through the Prophet Joseph Smith*. Salt Lake City: Truth Publishing Co., 1944.

_____, ed. *The Star of Truth: In Memory of Our God, Religion, Our Freedom, and Peace*. 4 vols. Murray, UT: N.p., 1953–56.

Nauvoo City Council Minutes. LDS Archives.

Nebelsick, Alvin Louis. "The Admission of Utah." M.A. thesis, University of Nebraska, 1924.

Neibaur, Alexander. Journal. LDS Archives.

Nedrow, G. Keith. "Polygamy and the Right to Marry: New Life for an Old Lifestyle." *Memphis State University Law Review* 2 (Spring 1981): 203–49.

Nelson, Christa Marie Sophie Ranglade. "Mormon Polygamy in Mexico." M.A. thesis, University of Utah, 1983.

Nelson, Lee. "A 20th Century School of the Prophets." *Central Utah Journal*, 23 Sept. 1984.

"The New Anti-Polygamy Legislation." *The Nation* 34 (23 Feb. 1882): 161.

Newell, Linda King, and Valeen Tippetts Avery. *Mormon Enigma: Emma Hale Smith*. Garden City, NY: Doubleday, 1984.

Newson, Robert C. *Is the Manifesto a Revelation?* N.p.: n.p., 1956.

Nibley, Preston. *Brigham Young, the Man and His Work*. 7th ed. Salt Lake City: Deseret Book, 1974.

Nichols, Thomas L. *Marriage in all Ages and Nations As It Has Been—as It Is—As It Might Be: Its History, Physiology, Morals, and Laws*. London: W. Foulsham, 1886.

Nicholson, John. *The Martyrdom of Joseph Standing*. Salt Lake City: Deseret News, 1886.

Nuttall, L. John. Collection. BYU Library.

Oaks, Dallin H. "The Suppression of the Nauvoo Expositor." *Utah Law Review* 9 (Winter 1965): 861–903.

Olney, Oliver H. *The Absurdities of Mormonism Portrayed.* Hancock County, IL: N.p., 1843.

_____. Journal. William Robertson Coe Collection. Beinecke Library, Yale University.

Orr, John William. "Federal Anti-Polygamy Legislation." M.A. thesis, Ohio University, 1954.

"Orson Pratt's Harem." *New York Herald*, 18 May 1879.

Palmer, Michael Dalton. "A Welded Link: Family Imagery in Mormonism and American Culture." Ph.D. diss., University of California, Santa Barbara, 1982.

Parkin, Max H. "The Nature and Causes of Internal and External Conflict of the Mormons in Ohio Between 1830 and 1838." M.A. thesis, Brigham Young University, 1966.

Parkinson, Preston Woolley. *The Utah Woolley Family.* Salt Lake City: Preston W. Parkinson, 1967.

Parrinder, E. G. *The Bible and Polygamy; A Study of Hebrew and Christian Teaching.* London, S.P.C.K., 1958.

Paxton, James Mills. *The Cotter and the Prisoner, or Whisperings from the "Pen."* Salt Lake City: N.p., 1889.

Penrose, Charles W. Journal. Utah State Historical Society Library.

_____. "The Plural Marriage Problem." *Arena Magazine*, June 1902, 604–610.

_____. *Utah and Statehood. Objections Considered. Simple Facts Plainly Told.* New York: Hart & Von Arx, 1908.

"The Persecution of the Plural-Marriage Mormons." *The Independent* 55 (June 1956): 1–10.

Phelps, W. W., to Brigham Young, 12 Aug. 1861. Young Collection.

_____, to Sally Phelps, 9 and 16 Sept. 1835. Phelps Collection. LDS Archives.

Pitcher, Joe. "Ex-Cop Royston Runs Afoul of Utah Law But Not His Three Wives." *People*, 28 Nov. 1983, 83, 86–87.

"Plural Marriage." MS 16 (22 July 1854): 454.

Poll, Richard D. "The Twin Relic: A Study of Mormon Polygamy and the Campaign by the Government of the United States for Its Abolition, 1852–1890." M.A. thesis, Texas Christian University, 1939.

_____. "The Mormon Question, 1850–1865: A Study in Politics and Public Opinion." Ph.D. diss., University of California at Berkeley, 1948.

_____. "The Mormon Question Enters National Politics, 1850–1856." *Utah Historical Quarterly* 25 (1957): 117–31.

_____. "The Political Reconstruction of Utah Territory, 1866–1890." *Pacific Historical Review* 27 (May 1958): 111–26.

_____. "The Americanization of Utah." *Utah Historical Quarterly* 44 (Winter 1976): 76–93.

"A Polygamist Congressman." *Literary Digest*, 10 Dec. 1898, 682–83.

"Polygamist Alex Joseph Finds That 13 of a Kind Make for a Mighty Full House." *People*, 12 May 1975.

"Polygamy Battle." *Time*, 23 Jan. 1956, 70.

"Polygamy: Court Says Religious Freedom Includes But One Wife." *Newsweek*, 21 Dec. 1935, 12.

"Polygamy in Utah: How to Suppress it." *Current Literature*, April 1904, 369–70.

Post, Stephen, to J. M. Adams, 16 May 1866. RLDS Archives.

Potter, Royston. *An Offender for a Word*. Salt Lake City: Pioneer Press, 1986.

Pratt, Belinda Marden. *Defense of Polygamy, by a Lady in Utah. In a Letter to Her Sister in New Hampshire*. Salt Lake City: N.p., 1854.

_____. Diary. Utah State Historical Society Library.

Pratt, Orson. *The Seer*. Washington, D.C., Jan. 1853–Aug. 1854.

_____. *The Bible and Polygamy*. 2nd ed. Salt Lake City: Deseret News Steam Printing Establishment, 1877.

_____, to Sarah Pratt, 18 September 1878. Orson Pratt Collection. LDS Archives.

Pratt, Parley P. *Autobiography of Parley Parker Pratt: One of the Twelve Apostles of the Church of Jesus Christ of Latter-day Saints, Embracing His Life, Ministry and Travels, with Extracts, in Prose and Verse, from His Miscellaneous Writings*. Parley P. Pratt, Jr., ed. 1874. 3rd ed. Salt Lake City: Deseret Book, 1938.

Pratt, Steven. "Eleanor McLean and the Murder of Parley P. Pratt." *Brigham Young University Studies* 15 (Winter 1975): 225–56.

Pratt, Teancum. Diary. LDS Archives.

"The Present Status of Polygamy in the United States." *McClures*, Dec. 1910, 242.

"President Woodruff on the Admission of Utah." *The Independent* 16 (Feb. 1893): 11.

A Priesthood Issue and the Law of Plural Marriage. Salt Lake City: Truth Publishing Co., n.d.

Proceedings Before the Committee on Privileges and Elections of the United States Senate in the Matter of the Protests Against the Right of Hon. Reed Smoot A Senator from the State of Utah, to Hold his Seat. 4 vols. Washington, D.C.: Government Printing Office, 1907.

Pusey, Merlo J. *Builders of the Kingdom—George A. Smith, John Henry Smith, George Albert Smith*. Provo, UT: Brigham Young University Press, 1982.

Quaife, Milo. "Polygamy at Beaver Island." *Michigan History Magazine* 5 (July/Oct. 1921): 333–55.

_____. *The Kingdom of Saint James: A Narrative of the Mormons*. New Haven: Yale University Press, 1930.

Quinn, D. Michael. "Organizational Development and Social Origins of the Mormon Hierarchy, 1832–1932: A Prosopographical Study." M.A. thesis, University of Utah, 1973.

_____. "The Mormon Hierarchy, 1832–1932: An American Elite." Ph.D. diss., Yale University, 1976.

_____. "The Mormon Succession Crisis of 1844." *Brigham Young University Studies* 16 (Winter 1976): 187–233.

_____. "Echoes and Foreshadowings: The Distinctiveness of the Mormon Community." *Sunstone* 3 (March/April 1978): 12–17.

_____. "Latter-day Prayer Circles." *Brigham Young University Studies* 19 (Fall 1978): 79–105.

_____. "The Council of Fifty and Its Members, 1844–1945." *Brigham Young University Studies* 21 (Winter 1980): 163–96.

_____. "On Being A Mormon Historian." A Lecture Before the BYU Student History Association. Fall 1981.

_____. *J. Reuben Clark—The Church Years*. Provo, UT: Brigham Young University Press, 1983.

_____. "LDS Church Authority and New Plural Marriages, 1890-1904." *Dialogue: A Journal of Mormon Thought* 18 (Spring 1985): 9-105.

"A Record of the Organization and Proceedings of the Female Relief Society of Nauvoo." Joseph Smith Collection.

Reinman, Paul E. *Plural Marriage Limited*. Salt Lake City: Utah Printing, 1974.

"Report of Messrs. Brandebury, Brocchus, and Harris to the President of the United States, Washington, Dec. 19, 1851." *House Exec. Doc. No. 25* (1852): 8-9.

Report of the Utah Commission, 22 Aug. 1888. Washington, D.C.: Government Printing Office, 1888.

Revised Laws of Illinois. Vandalia: Greiner & Sherman, 1833.

Reynolds v. United States, 98 U.S. 145 (1879).

Reynolds, George. Diary. LDS Archives.

Rich, Russell. *Those Who Would Be Leaders*. 2nd ed. Provo, UT: Brigham Young University Extension Publications, 1967.

Richards, George F. Journal. LDS Archives.

Richards, Levi. Journal. LDS Archives.

Richards, Willard. Diary. LDS Archives.

Richardson, James Daniel. *A Compilation of the Messages and Papers of the Presidents, 1789-1897*. 10 vols. Washington: Government Printing Office, 1896-99.

Rigdon, John W. "Affidavit 28 July 1905." Rigdon Collection. LDS Archives.

_____. "Life Story of Sidney Rigdon." LDS Archives.

Riegel, O. W. *Crown of Glory: The Life of James J. Strang, Moses of the Mormons*. New Haven: Yale University Press, 1935.

Roberts, Brigham H. *A Comprehensive History of the Church of Jesus Christ of Latter-day Saints*. 6 vols. Salt Lake City: The Church of Jesus Christ of Latter-day Saints, 1930.

_____. *Life of John Taylor*. Salt Lake City: Bookcraft, 1965.

Robinson, Ebenezer, to Jason W. Biggs, 28 Jan. 1880. LDS Archives.

Robinson, Joseph Lee. Journal. BYU Library.

Robinson, Philip S. *Sinners and Saints: A Tour Across the States and Round Them*. Boston: Roberts Brothers, 1883.

Romney, Thomas C. *The Mormon Colonies in Mexico*. Salt Lake City: Deseret Book, 1938.

Roosevelt, Theodore. "Mr. Roosevelt to the Mormons." *Collier's*, 15 April 1911, 28.

St. George Stake General Meeting Minutes, 23 Dec. 1880. LDS Archives.

St. George Historical Record, 26 Nov. 1882. LDS Archives.

Samuels, Dawn (pseud.). Interview, 20 June 1988. Typescript in author's possession.

Seifrit, William B., ed. " 'To Get U[tah] in U[nion]': Diary of A Failed Mission." *Utah Historical Quarterly* 51 (Fall 1983): 358-81.

"Senator Smoot's Defence." *The Literary Digest*, 23 Jan. 1904, 104-105.

Searle, Howard C. "The Mormon Reformation of 1856-57." M.A. thesis, Brigham Young University, 1956.

Shields, Steven L. *Divergent Paths of the Restoration*. 3rd ed. Bountiful, UT: Restoration Research, 1982.

Shipps, Jan. "Utah Comes of Age Politically: A Study of the State's Policies in the Early Years of the Twentieth Century." *Utah Historical Quarterly* 35 (Spring 1967): 91-111.

_____. "The Principle Revoked: A Closer Look at the Demise of Plural Marriage." *Journal of Mormon History* 11 (1984): 65-77.

_____. *Mormonism—The Story of a New Religious Tradition*. Urbana: University of Illinois Press, 1985.

Shook Charles A. *The True Origins of Mormon Polygamy*. Cincinnati: Standard Publishing, 1914.

Short, Dennis R. *Questions on Plural Marriage*. Draper, UT: Dennis R. Short, 1974.

Smith, Alexander A. *Polygamy: Was It an Original Tenet of the Church of Jesus Christ of Latter Day Saints?* Lamoni, IO: Reorganized Church of Jesus Christ of Latter Day Saints, n.d.

Smith, Elbert A. *Differences That Persist Between the Reorganized Church of Jesus Christ of Latter Day Saints and the Utah Mormon Church*. Independence, MO: Herald House, 1943.

Smith, Gary E. "The Patriarchal Crisis of 1845." *Dialogue: A Journal of Mormon Thought* 16 (Summer 1983): 24-36.

Smith, George A. Letterbooks. LDS Archives.

_____, to Joseph Smith III, 9 Oct. 1868. RLDS Archives.

Smith, James E., and Philip R. Kunz. "Polygyny and Fertility in Nineteenth-Century America." *Population Studies* 30 (1976): 565-80.

Smith, John Henry. Journal. University of Utah Library.

_____, to Joseph F. Smith, 3 April 1888. Joseph F. Smith Collection. LDS Archives.

Smith, Joseph. Collection. LDS Archives.

_____, Oliver Cowdery, Sidney Rigdon, Frederick G. Williams, comps. *Doctrine and Covenants of the Church of Jesus Christ of Latter-Day Saints: Carefully Selected from the Revelations of God*. Kirtland, OH: Frederick G. Williams & Co., 1835.

_____. "To The Church of Jesus Christ of Latter Day Saints, and to All The Honorable Part of the Community." *Times and Seasons*, 1 July 1842.

_____. "To Dear and Beloved, Brother and Sister, Whitney, and &c.," 18 Aug. 1842. Smith Collection.

Smith, Joseph III. *A Reply to Orson Pratt, By Joseph Smith, President of the Reorganized Church of Jesus Christ of Latter Day Saints*. Lamoni, IO: N.p., 1870.

_____. "Memorial to Congress From a Committee of the Reorganized Church of Jesus Christ of Latter Day Saints on the Claims and Faith of the Church." *True Latter Day Saints' Herald* 17 (1 June 1870): 321-27.

_____. *One Wife, or Many?* Lamoni, IO: Reorganized Church of Jesus Christ of Latter Day Saints, n.d.

_____, to E. L. Kelley, 10 June 1883. Kelley Collection. RLDS Archives.

_____, to John Henry Smith, 20 Jan. 1886. George A. Smith Collection. University of Utah Library.

_____. "Ways That are Doubtful." *Saints' Herald* 36 (5 Oct. 1889): 654-57.

_____. "Mormons Who are not Polygamists." *Everybody's* 25 (Sept. 1911): 427-28.

_____, to John W. Rigdon, 29 April 1905. Rigdon Collection.

_____, and Herman C. Smith. *The History of the Reorganized Church of Jesus Christ of Latter Day Saints*. 4 vols. Lamoni, IO: Herald House, 1896–1903.

_____. "The Memoirs of President Joseph Smith (1832–1914)." Serialized in *Saints' Herald*, 1934–37.

Smith, Joseph F. "Polygamy in the United States—Has it Political Significance?" *North American Review*, March 1903, 450–58.

_____, to Anthony W. Ivins, 6 Feb. 1900. Ivins Collection.

_____, to Reed Smoot, 9 April 1904 and 11 April 1911. Smoot Collection.

_____. "The Mormons To-day." *Collier's*, 12 Aug. 1911, 26–29.

Smith, Joseph Fielding. *Blood Atonement and the Origin of Plural Marriage: A Discussion*. Salt Lake City: Deseret News Press, 1905.

_____. *Essentials in Church History*. 26th ed. Salt Lake City: Deseret Book, 1973.

Smith, Mary Audentia, ed., and Vertha Audentia Anderson Hulmes, cond. *Joseph Smith III and the Restoration*. Independence, MO: Herald House, 1952.

Smith, Oliver, ed. *Six Decades in the Early West: The Journal of Jesse Nathaniel Smith; Diaries and Papers of a Mormon Pioneer, 1834–1906*. 3rd ed. Oliver R. Smith, ed. Provo, UT: Jesse N. Smith Family Association, 1970.

Smith, Prescindia L. Kimball. "Prescindia L. Kimball Smith, to her eldest grand-daughter living in 1880." LDS Archives.

Smith, Ralph. Diary. LDS Archives.

Smith, William. *Defense of Elder William Smith, Against the Slanders of Abraham Curtis, and Others*. Philadelphia: Brown and Guilbert, 1844.

"The Smoot Case." *The Outlook*, 2 March 1907, 494–96.

Smoot, Reed. Collection. BYU Library.

_____, to E. H. Callister, 22 March 1904. Smoot Collection.

_____, to Jesse M. Smith, 22 March 1904. Smoot Collection.

_____, to George F. Gibbs, 6 Dec. 1905.

_____, to First Presidency, 8 Dec. 1905.

_____, to Joseph F. Smith, 10 May 1906. Smoot Collection.

Snow, Eliza Roxcy. Diary. LDS Archives.

_____. *Decision of the Supreme Court of the United States in the Reynolds Case*. Salt Lake City: N.p., 1879.

Snow, Edwina Jo. "Singular Saints: The Images of the Mormons in Book Length Travel Accounts, 1847–1857." M.A. thesis, George Washington University, 1972.

Snow, Reuben Joseph. "The American Party in Utah: A Study of Political Party Struggles During the Early Years of Statehood." M.A. thesis, University of Utah, 1964.

Solomon, Dorothy. "A Very Different Kind of Family." *Good Housekeeping*, April 1979, 141, 246–250.

_____. *In My Father's House*. New York: Franklin Watts, 1984.

Stead, D. *Doctrines and Dogmas of Brighamism Exposed*. Independence, MO: Reorganized Church of Latter-Day Saints, 1911.

Stenhouse, Fanny. *Expose of Polygamy in Utah: A Lady's Life Among the Mormons*. New York: American News Company, 1872.

_____. *Tell It All: The Story of A Life's Experience in Mormonism*. Hartford: A. D. Worthington, 1874.

_____. *An Englishwoman in Utah: The Story of A Life's Experience in Mormonism.* London: Sampson, Low, Marston, Searle, & Rivington, 1880.

Stenhouse, T. B. H. *Rocky Mountain Saints.* New York: D. Appleton, 1873.

Strack, Linda Ostler. "Plight of the Polygamist." *Sunstone Review* 3 (June 1983): 7-9.

Strang, James J. Papers. William Robertson Coe Collection, Beinecke Library, Yale University.

_____. *The Diamond: Being the Law of Prophetic Succession, and a Defense of the Calling of James J. Strang as Successor to Joseph Smith.* Voree, WI: Gospel Herald, 1848.

_____. *Book of the Law of the Lord.* St. James, MI: Royal Press, 1856.

Strang, Mark A., ed. *The Diary of James J. Strang: Deciphered, Transcribed, Introduced and Annotated.* Ann Arbor: Michigan State University, 1961.

The Supreme Court Decision in the Reynolds Case: Interview between President John Taylor and O. J. Hollister Reported by G. F. Gibbs. Salt Lake City: Deseret News, 1879.

Tagg, Melvin S. *A History of the Mormon Church in Canada.* Lethbridge, Alberta: Lethbridge Herald, 1968.

Tannahill, Reay. *Sex in History.* New York: Stein and Day, 1981.

Tanner, Jerald, and Sandra Tanner. *Joseph Smith and Polygamy.* Salt Lake City: Modern Microfilm, n.d.

_____. *Clayton's Secret Writings Uncovered: Extracts from the Diaries of Joseph Smith's Secretary William Clayton.* Salt Lake City: Modern Microfilm, 1982.

Tanner, Obert C., ed. *A Mormon Mother: An Autobiography by Annie Clark Tanner.* Salt Lake City: Tanner Trust Fund/University of Utah, 1976.

Tappan, Paul Wilbur. "Mormon-Gentile Conflict: A Study of the Influence of Public Opinion on In-group versus Out-group Interaction with Special Reference to Polygamy." Ph.D. diss., University of Wisconsin, 1939.

Taylor, John W., to Joseph F. Smith, 16 March 1904. Smith Collection. LDS Archives.

Taylor, Raymond W., to Samuel W. Taylor, 3 May 1937. Raymond Taylor Collection. BYU Library.

Taylor, Samuel W. Collection. LDS Archives and U of U Library.

_____. *Family Kingdom.* New York: McGraw Hill, 1951.

_____. *I Have Six Wives.* New York: Greenberg, 1956.

_____. *The Kingdom or Nothing: The Life of John Taylor, Militant Mormon.* New York: MacMillan, 1976.

TS. *Times and Seasons.* Nauvoo, IL, 1839-46.

"Thomas Ford to Mayor and Council of the City of Nauvoo, 22 June 1844." Joseph Smith Collection.

Thomasson, Gordon C. "The Manifesto Was a Victory." *Dialogue: A Journal of Mormon Thought* 6 (Spring 1971): 37-45.

Tinney, Thomas Milton. *The Royal Family of the Prophet Joseph Smith, Jr.* Salt Lake City: Tinney-Green Family Organization, 1973.

"Too Many Wives." *Newsweek,* 21 Nov. 1955, 98-99.

Tullidge, Edward W. The *Women of Mormondom.* 1877. Salt Lake City: N.p., 1966.

_____. *Life of Joseph the Prophet.* Plano, IL: Reorganized Church of Jesus Christ of Latter Day Saints, 1880.

Truth. 21 Vols. Salt Lake City: Truth Publishing Co., 1935-56. Turley, Louis O. "The Affect of Plural Marriage Upon the Present Membership of the Church." M.A. thesis, Brigham Young University, 1950.

Turner, Charles W. "Joseph Smith III and the Mormons of Utah." Ph.D. diss., Graduate Theological Union, 1985.

United States Reports, Supreme Court, 98, reported by William T. Otto.

Van Atta, Dale. "LeBaron Chronicle Echoes Biblical Stories." *Salt Lake Tribune,* 17 June 1977.

Van Wagoner, Richard S. "Mormon Polyandry in Nauvoo." *Dialogue: A Journal of Mormon Thought* 18 (Fall 1985): 67-83.

_____. "Sarah Pratt: The Shaping of an Apostate." *Dialogue: A Journal of Mormon Thought* 19 (Summer 1986): 69-99.

_____, and Steven C. Walker. *A Book of Mormons.* Salt Lake City: Signature Books, 1982.

_____, and Mary C. Van Wagoner. "Arthur Pratt, Utah Lawman." *Utah Historical Quarterly* 55 (Winter 1987): 22-35.

_____. "Orson Pratt, Jr.: Gifted Son of an Apostle and an Apostate." *Dialogue: A Journal of Mormon Thought* 21 (Spring 1988): 84-94.

Walgren, Kent L. "James Adams: Early Springfield Mormon and Freemason." *Journal of the Illinois State Historical Society* 75 (Summer 1952): 121-36.

Walker, Ronald W. "A Mormon Widow in Colorado: The Exile of Emily Wells Grant." *Arizona and the West* 25 (Spring 1983): 5-22.

Waters, William E. *Life Among the Mormons and a March to Their Zion.* New York: Moorehead, Simpson & Bond, 1868.

Watkins, Ethel. Interview, 4 July 1979. Copy in possession of the author.

Watson, Elden Jay, ed. *Manuscript History of Brigham Young, 1801-1844.* Salt Lake City: Elden Jay Waston, 1968.

Wells, Emmeline B. Diary. LDS Archives.

Wells, Merle W. "The Idaho Anti-Mormon Movement, 1872-1908." Ph.D. diss., University of California at Berkeley, 1950.

_____. "The Idaho Anti-Mormon Test Oath, 1884-1892." *Pacific Historical Review* 24 (Aug. 1955): 235-52.

_____. "Origins of Anti-Mormonism in Idaho, 1872-1880." *Pacific Northwest Quarterly* 47 (Nov. 1956): 109-16.

_____. "Fred T. Dubois and the Idaho Progressives, 1900-1914." *Idaho Yesterdays* 3 (Summer 1960): 24-31.

_____. *Anti-Mormonism in Idaho, 1872-92.* Provo, UT: Brigham Young University Press, 1978.

Whitaker, John Mills. Journal. U of U Library.

Whittaker, David J. "Early Mormon Polygamy Defenses." *Journal of Mormon History* 11 (1984): 43-63.

Whitney, Helen Mar Kimball. "Scenes and Incidents in Nauvoo." *Woman's Exponent* 10 (1 Dec. 1881): 98-99, 106, 114, 122, 130, 138, 159, 162, 178, 184-86; and 11 (1 June 1882): 1, 26, 39, 47-50.

_____. *Plural Marriage as Taught by the Prophet Joseph; a Reply to Joseph Smith, Editor of the Lamoni (Iowa) Herald.* Salt Lake City: Juvenile Instructor Office, 1882.

_____. *Why We Practice Plural Marriage*. Salt Lake City: Juvenile Instructor Office, 1884.

_____. "Helen Mar Kimball's Retrospection About Her Introduction to the Doctrine and Practices of Plural Marriage in Nauvoo at Age 15." A sealed letter to be opened after her death. LDS Archives.

Whitney, Orson F. *A History of Utah*. 4 vols. Salt Lake City: George Q. Cannon & Sons, 1892.

Whittaker, David J. "Mormons and Native Americans: A Historical and Bibliographical Introduction." *Dialogue: A Journal of Mormon Thought* 18 (Winter 1985), 4: 33–64.

Widtsoe, John A. "Did Joseph Smith Introduce Plural Marriage?" *Improvement Era* 49 (Nov. 1949): 721, 766–67.

_____. *Evidences and Reconciliations*. 3 vols. Salt Lake City: Bookcraft, 1951.

Wilcox, Archie G. "Founding of the Mormon Community in Alberta." M.A. thesis, University of Alberta, 1950.

Williams, J. D. "Separation of Church and State in Mormon Theory and Practice." *Dialogue: A Journal of Mormon Thought* 1 (Summer 1966): 30–54.

Winchester, Benjamin F. "Primitive Mormonism–Personal Narrative of It." *Salt Lake Tribune*, 22 Sept. 1889.

Wolfinger, Henry J. "An Irrespressible Conflict." *Dialogue: A Journal of Mormon Thought* (Autumn-Winter 1971): 124–32.

_____. "A Reexamination of the Woodruff Manifesto in the Light of Utah Constitutional History." *Utah Historical Quarterly* 39 (Fall 1971): 328–49.

Wood, George Cotton. Diary. LDS Archives.

Wood, Marriner. Journal. LDS Archives.

Woodruff, Wilford. Collection. LDS Archives.

_____, to Andrew Jenson, 6 Aug. 1887. Woodruff Letterbooks.

_____, to Franklin S. Richards/Charles W. Penrose, 12 April 1888. Woodruff Letterbooks.

_____, to James O. Broadhead, 26 Feb. 1889. Woodruff Letterbooks.

_____, to William Atkin, 18 March 1889. Woodruff Letterbooks.

_____, to Ammon M. Tenney, 2 June 1889. Woodruff Letterbooks.

_____. "Wilford Woodruff Testimony before Master of Chauncery, Judge Loofbourow, 19 October 1891." Utah State Archives. Salt Lake City.

Woolley, Lorin C. "Statement of Facts, 6 October 1912." LDS Archives.

Wright, Lyle O. "Origins and Development of the Church of the Firstborn of the Fulness of Times." M.A. thesis, Brigham Young University, 1963.

Wyl, Wilhelm. *Mormon Portraits, or the Truth About the Mormon Leaders, 1830-1886*. Salt Lake City: Tribune Printing and Publishing, 1886.

Young, Ann Eliza. *Wife Number 19; or, The Story of a Life in Bondage, Being a Complete Expose of Mormonism, and Revealing the Sorrows, Sacrifices and Sufferings of Women in Polygamy*. Hartford: Dustin, Gilman, 1876.

Young, Brigham. Collection. LDS Archives.

_____, to Parley P. Pratt, 17 July 1842. Young Collection.

_____, to President James K. Polk, Summer 1846. Young Collection.

_____, to Samuel Brannan, 6 June 1847. Young Collection.

_____, to John Taylor, 25 March 1857. Young Collection.

_____. Unpublished Address, 8 Oct. 1866. Young Collection.

Young, Brigham, Jr. Diary. LDS Archives.

Young, E[mily]. D. P. "Autobiographical Sketch." LDS Archives.

_____. "Incidents in the Life of a Mormon Girl." LDS Archives.

_____. "Autobiography." *Woman's Exponent* 14 (1 Aug. 1885): 37–38.

Young, John W. Collection. LDS Archives.

_____, to Brigham Young, Jr., and Moses Thatcher, 21 May 1885. Young Collection.

Young, Kimball. *Studies in Personality Contributed in Honor of Lewis M. Terman.* New York: McGraw-Hill, 1942.

_____. *Isn't One Wife Enough?: The Story of Mormon Polygamy.* New York: Henry Holt, 1954.

Zimmerman, Dean R. *I Knew the Prophets, An Analysis of the Letter of Benjamin F. Johnson to George F. Gibbs, Reporting Doctrinal Views of Joseph Smith and Brigham Young.* Bountiful, UT: Horizon, 1976.

Zion's Harbinger and Baneemy's Organ, 7 July 1853, 50–55.

INDEX

C